# Foundations of Binocular Vision

## A Clinical Perspective

# Notice

# Foundations of Binocular Vision

## A Clinical Perspective

Scott B. Steinman, OD, PhD, FAAO
Director of Research
Chair, Department of Biomedical Sciences
Southern College of Optometry
Chair, Vision Science Section American Academy of Optometry
Memphis, Tennessee

Barbara A. Steinman, OD, PhD
President
Software in Motion

Ralph Philip Garzia, OD
Associate Professor of Optometry
Director of Optometric Services
Center for Eye Care
University of Missouri—St. Louis
St. Louis, Missouri

*Illustrations created by*
Dr. Barbara Steinman and Dr. Scott Steinman

**The McGraw-Hill Companies**

New York  St. Louis  San Francisco  Auckland  Bogotá  Caracas  Lisbon  London  Madrid
Mexico City  Milan  Montreal  New Delhi  San Juan  Singapore  Sydney  Tokyo  Toronto

# McGraw-Hill

*A Division of The McGraw·Hill Companies*

**Foundations of Binocular Vision**

Copyright ©2000 by The **McGraw-Hill Companies**, Inc. All rights reserved. Printed in the United States of America. Except as permitted under the United States Copyright Act of 1976, no part of this publication may be reproduced or distributed in any form or by any means, or stored in a data base or retrieval system, without the prior written permission of the publisher.

9 10 11   IBT/IBT   1 9 8 7 6 5 4 3 2 1

**ISBN-13:** 978-0-83-852670-5

**ISBN-10:** 0-83-852670-5

This book was set in Garamond by Progressive Information Technologies.
The editors were Sally J. Barhydt and Karen Edmonson.
The production supervisor was Rohnda Barnes.
The cover designer was Bob Freese.
The index was prepared by Kathy Unger.

This book is printed on acid-free paper.

Library of Congress Cataloging-in-Publication Data

Steinman, Scott B., 1956-
    Foundations of binocular vision: a clinical perspective/Scott B. Steinman, Barbara A.
Steinman, Ralph Philip Garzia; illustrations created by Barbara Steinman and Scott Steinman.
        p.; cm.
    Includes bibliographical references and index.
    ISBN 0-8385-2670-5
    1. Binocular vision. I. Steinman, Barbara A.  II. Garzia, Ralph P.  III. Title.
    [DNLM: 1. Vision, Binocular. WW 440 S823f 2000]
    QP487 .S74 2000
    617.7'5—dc2l

                                                                                    99-088757

*Dedicated to the memory of*
*Robert and Martin Nielsen*

# Contents

# Preface

## INTENDED AUDIENCE

This book is the first introductory textbook on binocular vision in nearly twenty years. While excellent advanced books on binocular vision for researchers are available, only this book takes a clinically-relevant approach to the basic scientific foundations of binocular visual perception, and is therefore is targeted at the student clinician.

This book will be useful as a textbbok for courses dealing with the basis for binocular vision during optometric training, or residencies in pediatric ophthalmology prior to the student's clinical exposure to binocular vision testing and therapy. It also will be of use to practicing clinicians who would like to refresh their knowledge of sensory binocular vision, or to students of sensory psychology.

## SPECIAL FEATURES OF THIS BOOK

Rather than discussing only theoretical research aspects of binocular vision, as previous textbooks on this topic have done, this textbook stresses material that will specifically build a solid framework for practical clinical skills and the diagnosis of clinical binocular vision disorders. In every chapter, clinical applications of the basic scientific background and research are discussed, including clinical examples, testing procedures, diagnostic issues and treatment modalities. This approach will not only prepare students better for their later clinical experiences by bridging the "gap" between the basic sciences and clinical sciences, but will also stimulate a high level of interest on the part of the student.

The authors of this textbook have over forty years of combined experience in basic science, vision research including studies of amblyopia and strabismus, clinical education, and clinical vision care. This unique combination of expertise brings to this book a broad perspective—a solid basis in vision science, with keen awareness of what clinicians need to know for the "real world"—all presented by writers with experience in classroom instruction. The numerous publications of the authors, including research papers, textbooks, and book chapters, as well as the numerous courses taught by the authors, have allowed them to develop a book that will be easily read and understood by students. Two authors have additional skills as illustrators, which they have used to produce clear, striking figures that help bring life to the subject material.

The emphasis of this textbook is on making the subject material easily accessible to the reader. Each chapter contains key terms printed in boldface type to stress their importance. In addition, some sections are marked with special symbols to direct the readers' attention to key points or to information that is of special relevance to clinical application, including clinical tests, "pearls" for differential diagnosis, and clinical treatment issues. Each chapter ends with a summary of the key points to facilitate preparation for course examinations and for National Board of Examiners in Optometry examinations. The material is extensively cross-linked to ensure that students understand the interrelationships among topics.

## ASSUMPTIONS ABOUT THE AUDIENCE

The book assumes a basic knowledge of the sensory basis for vision and of eye movements, as courses on these topics typically precede courses on binocular vision. In addition, several excellent textbooks are in print on these topics, and therefore this material is not duplicated here. For example, the authors recommend the following for background material:

Steven Schwartz's *Visual Perception*, 2nd edition, also available from McGraw-Hill.

## CONTACTING THE AUTHORS

Your comments and suggestions for improvement are important to us. Most importantly, we recognize that it is possible that errors may have eluded our detection. We welcome all discoveries of errata so that instructors may be notified and future editions of this book will be as accurate as possible.
Please send all correspondence to:

Scott B. Steinman, OD, PhD, FAAO
Barbara A. Steinman, OD, PhD
1245 Madison Avenue
Memphis, TN 38104-2222
Email: steinman@sco.edu

Ralph P. Garzia, OD
School of Optometry
University of Missouri-St. Louis
8001 Natural Bridge Road
St. Louis, MO 63301
Email: garzia@umsl. edu

# Acknowledgments

Dr. Scott Steinman would like to thank the people who have guided his career and have made writing this book possible. He thanks his parents, Paul and Flora Steinman, for inspiring him to enter optometry, teaching, and the sciences, and to develop his interest in art. Other important influences include: Dennis Levi, OD, PhD, of the University of Houston, the Chair of his dissertation committee and a friend of almost 20 years; Suzanne McKee, PhD, of the SmithKettlewell Eye Research Institute; Clifton Schor, OD, PhD, of the University of California, who supervised his postdoctoral studies; and Gary Trick, PhD, of the Henry Ford Hospital, who first exposed him to vision science before his doctoral studies. He would also like to express his gratitude to President William Cochran and Vice President Charles Haine of the Southern College of Optometry for their encouragement and support during the writing of this book and to Dr. Barbara Steinman simply for putting up with him.

Dr. Barbara Steinman would like to thank Dr. Scott Steinman for marrying her and acting as a slavedriver during the preparation of this book. She also thanks her father, Melvin Nielsen, DDS, and her husband Scott Steinman, for supporting her education. She thanks her mother, June Nielsen, for stimulating her creativity and providing a background in art and design. Dr. Steinman also thanks Stephen Lehmkuhle, PhD, of the University of Missouri, the Chair of her dissertation committee; John Brabyn, PhD, of the Smith-Kettlewell Eye Research Institute; and Gunilla Haegerstrom-Portnoy, OD, PhD, of the University of California, for encouraging her to become a researcher.

Dr. Ralph Garzia would like to thank Scott and Barbara Steinman for the opportunity to contribute to this book.

# Foundations of Binocular Vision

## A Clinical Perspective

# 1

# Introduction to Binocular Vision: Why Do We Have Two Eyes?

*Binocular vision* literally means vision with two eyes, that is, the special attributes of vision when we have both eyes open as opposed to one eye. Our perception under binocular conditions is markedly different from and richer than vision with one eye alone. What is it that makes having two eyes advantageous, and why do humans have only two eyes? In lower species such as spiders and insects it is common to possess several eyes, but this does not imply that insects see better than humans. More evolved animals like primates always have two eyes.

The addition of a second eye is not without its problems. Having to coordinate the use of two eyes to work as a team can lead to a variety of visual disorders. Aiming the two eyes incorrectly can produce **strabismus** with its associated sensory problems **amblyopia** and **suppression**, or **diplopia**. Even when the two eyes are aimed correctly, the strain of keeping them aligned can cause binocular accommodative and convergence problems that can hamper everyday activities such as reading or sports (Sheedy et al., 1988). Asthenopia secondary to binocular disorders can lead the patient to avoid performing many visual tasks that may be required in their schooling, occupation, or hobby.

Despite the possibility of binocular visual disorders, there must be some advantage to the evolution of two-eyed species. One simple answer is the observation that we simply perform better on many everyday visual tasks when we use two eyes rather than one eye (Jones and Lee, 1981; Sheedy, 1986). However, this simple answer still begs for an explanation.

Two eyes provide us with an "extra" eye that can be used as a spare in case one is damaged or diseased; for example, if one eye has a macular degeneration, and the fovea is destroyed, the fellow eye can provide usable foveal vision and good visual acuity. However, if this were the only advantage to having an extra eye, it would be advantageous to have more than two. After all, the more eyes, the better our insurance against loss of vision. Yet, again, we do not have multiple eyes.

We must also ask if the presence of the second eye makes our vision sharper, clearer, or more sensitive. The answer is yes. Many of our visual thresholds are lower with two eyes than with one, a phenomenon known as **binocular summation**. For example, binocular visual acuity is typically better than monocular visual acuity. Likewise, contrast detection thresholds are better with two eyes than with one eye alone. However, in many cases, this binocular advantage is small, no more than what you would predict statistically by having more than one chance to detect the stimulus. The extra eye does not really give that much of an extra "boost" to our visual capabilities.

The use of two eyes gives us a larger field of view, allowing us to see more of the world around us at a time. In lower species such as frogs, the two eyes nearly double the area over which they can see (Fig. 1-1). This is because their two eyes are on either side of their head and point in different directions. There is little or no overlap between the fields of the two eyes, and frogs can see almost 360°

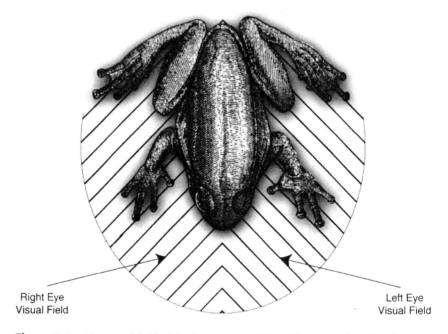

Right Eye
Visual Field

Left Eye
Visual Field

**Figure 1-1**    The visual field of the frog, an amphibian. The eyes of the frog face laterally on either side of the head, resulting in no overlap between the visual fields of each eye.

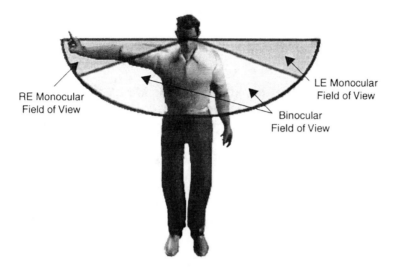

**Figure 1-2**   The visual field of the human, an omnivorous hunting primate. The eyes of the human face frontward, resulting in a large overlap between the visual fields of each eye. The binocular visual field is 120° across. The temporal crescents, each seen by only one eye because of interference by the nose, are about 30° in extent.

around them, a phenomenon called **panoramic vision**. The frog therefore has two eyes and, by definition, binocular vision, but does it derive all of the benefits of binocular vision?

In more highly evolved species such as humans, the eyes face forward, and their combined visual field is much smaller (Fig. 1-2). When our two eyes are used together, their visual fields overlap by about 120°. This overlapping part of the visual field is seen by *both* eyes at the same time and is called the **binocular visual field**. Lateral to the binocular field are crescent-shaped monocular portions of the visual field seen by *each eye alone,* called the **temporal crescents**. Because the uniocular visual field of almost all vertebrates is 170° in extent, the total width of the visual field using both eyes and the width of the overlapped binocular visual field are determined by the position of the eyes in the head.

We can demonstrate and measure monocular and binocular visual fields with a simple experiment. With both eyes open, fixate precisely on a distant object. Now hold a pencil beside your head vertically and even with your left ear. Bring it around toward the front of your head until you can first see it in your peripheral field. Close your left eye. Can you still see the pencil? Why not? The pencil is now located in the portion of the visual field that is monocular and is seen only by your *left* eye, that is, the left eye's temporal crescent. Keeping your left eye closed, keep moving the pencil forward until your right eye first sees it. You have just hit the inner border of the temporal crescent. If you were to repeat this procedure starting with the pencil lateral to your right ear, you would map out the temporal crescent of the right eye. Between the two temporal crescents lies the extent of your *binocular* visual field. Under real-world viewing conditions, with both eyes open at once, you cannot distinguish whether the object falls in the monocular or binocular portions of your visual field, as both regions blend together continuously.

Now let us try a second demonstration. Look at the tip of a pencil located about 40 cm in front of your eyes and notice what you see behind it. Close one eye, then the other. The objects behind the pencil should appear to move. This tells you that the images on the retinas of the two eyes are not *precisely* identical. Even though both of your eyes are looking at the same scene, they are looking at it from two slightly different vantage points because the two eyes are separated by an **interocular distance** of roughly 60 to 65 mm, depending on the population

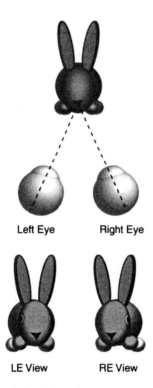

Left Eye        Right Eye

LE View        RE View

**Figure 1-3**  When the two eyes view an object, their respective retinal images are of the object as seen from two distinct vantage points because the two eyes are in different locations in the head separated by the interocular distance. It is the differences between the monocular views that lead to the perception of stereopsis.

(see the example in Fig. 1-3). Also, the nose acts as a **septum** or divider and cuts off the extreme nasal part of each eye's visual field. Despite the differences in the images in each eye, we still see the world as *single* when both eyes are open.

It is the subtle differences between the images in each eye that produce the real advantage of binocular vision, namely **stereopsis**, the binocular form of depth perception. Although we can judge distances somewhat using monocular cues to depth such as perspective, occlusion, elevation, texture gradients, and motion parallax, we see depth much better and more vividly with two eyes together. We can demonstrate this as follows: hold the index finger of your left hand in front of you. Now close one eye and bring the index finger of the right hand so that it is at the same distance from you. Now open both eyes. Are the fingers precisely at the same distance? Probably not. Using *both eyes together* lets you judge relative distance or depth more precisely.

This was probably more of an issue for our evolutionary ancestors. Depth perception first developed in predators and primates by necessity. In a jungle or savannah environment, surrounded by dense leaves or grass, the world around you appears to be flat if viewed with one eye. With two eyes, however, you easily see the three-dimensional structure of grass or the leaves and their branches. This would be quite important to a monkey swinging through the trees or a tiger hunting prey; if their environment looked flat, they could not effectively navigate through the trees or grass and food could be camouflaged. Stereopsis aids in distinguishing objects from their backgrounds (Schneider and Moraglia, 1994). In addition, we are able to navigate through our world more quickly when using two eyes (Eyeson-Annan and Brown, 1992). More importantly, stereopsis allows for more precise hand-eye coordination, and so the development of stereopsis may also be related to the development of manual capabilities in primates.

Yet even in the modern world, binocular vision has important consequences. What we perceive about the world around us may not match precisely what is physically there, since the retinal image does not perfectly represent all of a viewed object's physical attributes. Our visual systems must *interpret* the retinal image to deduce the likely objects that could have produced that particular image. One of the ways in which this is accomplished is by making assumptions about the organization and predictability of the environment around us. Stereopsis gives us one more tool to do so accurately. Stereopsis is an accurate means of determining the position of objects around us in relationship to our own position, and to determine our position relative to our environment. People with abnormal binocular vision may not interpret the visual world exactly the way people with normal binocular vision do. They may judge distances differently, see objects in the wrong location, or see the world as distorted. In a driving task, elderly drivers with compromised binocular vision, yet nearly normal visual acuity, exhibit higher than average accident rates (Gresset and Meyer, 1994).

In addition, the extra precision in depth perception that stereopsis gives us can make a big difference in performing daily activities. Fine near-point tasks such as a dentist drilling a cavity or an eye doctor extracting a foreign body from the cornea require very precise depth judgments. These tasks would be more difficult or impossible to perform if stereopsis were not available and the doctor were restricted to using monocular cues only. Grasping for near objects is more accurate and faster under binocular conditions (Servos et al., 1992).

---

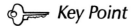 *Key Point*

*Although the use of two eyes offers advantages such as lower detection thresholds, increased visual field, and a spare eye as insurance against loss of an eye by disease or injury, the true advantage of binocular vision is* **stereopsis**.

---

Why then do we not have more than two eyes? Theoretically, three eyes would actually give us better stereopsis than two eyes, as demonstrated by computer scientists working with artificial robotic "trinocular" imaging systems for use in industry. Such systems perform quite well. However, video capture systems can be perfectly aligned. Biological systems are not as precise. Misalignment of two eyes produces **diplopia** via improper registration of the two retinal images; additional strabismic eyes would further increase the number of misaligned images. In addition, the more eyes you have, the more neural circuitry you need to process the information from the extra eyes and to keep the extra eyes' gaze aligned. Obviously, there are diminishing returns with additional eyes. Although additional eyes help us with better acuity and contrast perception, the advantage is not that great, considering the extra neuronal circuitry that is needed. Besides, having just two eyes already provides us with enough depth information. The existence of two eyes is therefore a good compromise; just enough eyes to allow for depth perception, yet not so many that the costs exceed the benefits.

## THE SCOPE OF THE TEXTBOOK

The majority of this book deals with our ability to use two eyes together to see singly and to see depth. Topics explored include the *neurophysiology* of the binocular visual pathways, how we integrate the images of objects viewed by the two eyes into a single image (**sensory fusion**), and the limits of depth perception (**stereoacuity** for the smallest depth and **Panum's ranges** for the largest depth without loss of fusion). We will also explain what happens when we do not have the proper stimulus conditions to see singly (**diplopia** or double vision, **binocular rivalry** in which each eye's image does not combine fully but instead "fights" to win out over the other eye's image, or **binocular suppression,** in which one eye's input is "shut off"). Nevertheless, we do not limit our discussion to theory. Throughout the book, we discuss each of these phenomena in relation to real-life *visual performance* and *clinical disorders* that disrupt or distort our depth perception, such as **amblyopia** ("lazy eye"), **strabismus** (eye turns), and **aniseikonia** (unequal retinal image sizes). We also touch on more common, and subtler, **binocular fusion** disorders in which binocular vision is fairly normal but more difficult or stressful to maintain.

Do we really need an entire book on the topic of binocular vision? Although eye care tends to focus on ocular disease, patients with *vision* problems, many of them attributable one degree or another to binocular dysfunctions, represent a much larger proportion of the patients who consult an eye care professional. A thorough understanding of binocular vision and its clinical ramifications is crucial for the diagnosis and treatment of a wider range of patients with vision problems. Binocular vision problems have also increased in prevalence in modern society because of the amount of nearpoint work in many occupations and hobbies. With the increasing use of computers and the proposed use of three-dimensional stereoscopic graphic user interfaces on computers, the number of patients complaining of binocular vision-related symptoms will probably increase even more in the future.

We hope that, by the time you have finished reading this book, you will appreciate that, despite all of the factors that can go wrong, our binocular visual pathways really do work very well most of the time. You will also understand the basic scientific basis of binocular vision testing and treatment. Our ultimate goal is to blend basic scientific research and clinical expertise to provide a solid background that makes clinical binocular vision more intuitive.

We are now ready to begin our exploration of binocular vision, beginning with an understanding of how each eye *alone* determines the lateral location of objects. This will lay the foundation for understanding how objects are localized three-dimensionally in depth using binocular vision. The next chapter therefore deals with *visual direction*.

## SUMMARY AND KEY POINTS

- **Binocular vision**, the use of two eyes, must be advantageous because humans have two eyes even though there are risks associated with the coordination of two eyes. Aiming the two eyes incorrectly can produce **strabismus** (eye turn), **amblyopia** (reduced spatial vision in one eye), **suppression** ("shutting off" of one eye's information), or **diplopia** (double vision).

- Binocular vision provides us with a usable "spare" eye in case one is damaged or diseased.

- Vision is sharper with two eyes, exhibiting lower thresholds than with one eye alone, a phenomenon known as **binocular summation**. However, the degree of improvement with two eyes is variable with different visual tasks.

- Having two eyes enlarges the field of view, but this is less pronounced in predatory species such as humans, in which the eyes face forward and the combined **binocular visual field** is smaller. Lateral to the binocular field are crescent-shaped monocular portions of the visual field seen by *each eye alone,* called the **temporal crescents**.

- The two eyes view objects from two slightly different vantage points because the two eyes are separated from each other by an **interocular distance** of roughly 60 to 65 mm, depending on the population. The subtle differences in the images in each eye produce **stereopsis**, the binocular form of depth perception.

- Although we can judge distances somewhat using **monocular cues to depth** such as perspective, occlusion, elevation, and texture gradients, we see depth much better with two eyes together.

- The visual system must *interpret* the retinal image by making assumptions about the predictability of the environment around us. Stereopsis is an accurate means of determining the position of objects around us in relation to our own position and to determine our position relative to our environment.

- Stereopsis provides extra precision in depth judgments in daily activities, including grasping near objects and driving a motor vehicle.

- People with abnormal binocular vision may judge distances differently, see objects in the wrong location, or see the world as distorted. Patients with binocular vision problems represent a large proportion of the patients who consult eye doctors.

## BIBLIOGRAPHY

EYESON-ANNAN M *and* BROWN B (1992). *Mobility of normal observers under conditions of reduced visual input.* Perception 21:813–823.

GRESSET JA *and* MEYER FM (1994). *Risk of accidents among elderly car drivers with visual acuity equal to 6/12 or 6/15 and lack of binocular vision.* Ophthalmic Physiol. Opt. 14:33–37.

JONES RK *and* LEE DN (1981). *Why two eyes are better than one: the two views of binocular vision.* J. Exp. Psych. 7:30–40.

SCHNEIDER B *and* MORAGLIA G (1994). *Binocular vision enhances target detection by filtering the background.* Perception 23:1267–1286.

SERVOS P, GOODALE MA *and* JAKOBSON LS (1992). *The role of binocular vision in prehension: a kinematic analysis.* Vis. Res. 32:1513–1521.

SHEEDY JE, BAILEY IL, BURI M *and* BASS E (1986). *Binocular versus monocular task performance.* Am. J. Optom. Physiol. Opt. 63:839–846.

SHEEDY JE *et al.* (1988). *Task performance with base-in and base-out prisms.* Am. J. Optom. Physiol. Opt. 65:65–69.

# 2

# Visual Direction

## *LOCAL SIGN*

In order to move about in the world safely, we must be able to *localize* and *orient* ourselves relative to other objects around us. Information concerning our location is provided by several of our senses. For example, we have proprioceptive and vestibular (balancing) reflexes that help us keep our correct posture as we move within our world or as the world moves relative to us. Our tactile sense (touch) lets us know if we are directly abutting another object. Audition or hearing can tell us if an object is in front of us, behind us, or off to one side or the other. Stereophonic sound systems and recordings take advantage of this to simulate the position of musicians during a performance so that a recording sounds more realistic.

Of all our senses, vision gives us the most detailed and accurate information about our position and the position of other objects in our environment. This is interesting because the visual system, like audition, has no actual contact with the physical world around it, as contrasted with the sense of touch. Instead, the visual system must rely on information acquired about **physical space** (the three-dimensional world around us) through *indirect* means. Our retinas can directly signal that we are or are not *receiving light stimulation*. There is no way of knowing if the light it received originated from a direct light source such as the sun or was reflected off an object. The task of the visual system is to convert the two-dimensional image on the retina into a complex three-dimensional interpretation of the world around us.

The location of an object in space is determined by two values: its direction and its distance relative to ourselves. **Visual direction** is a *two-dimensional* localization of an object, taking into account only the lateral and vertical position of the object, regardless of its distance. **Distance**, on the other hand, is a measure solely of how far the object is from ourselves—the third dimension. As we will see shortly, the perception of distance is dependent on the processing of visual direction. In addition, the perception of distance and the perception of object size are interrelated.

The first step in orienting ourselves relative to any object is to ascertain from *what direction* the light of its image is coming; that is, we must be able to determine the light's **directionality.** The visual system uses directionality, along with other visual cues discussed later in this book, to build its *interpretation* of the physical three-dimensional world, that is, **visual space**. The capacity of visual neurons to process direction is called **local sign** (Hering, 1864). That is, each visual neuron encodes a *unique two-dimensional direction* associated with it. When a given neuron is activated, our percept is of a stimulus located in visual space in a *fixed direction* (Fig. 2-1A). Local sign is made possible by the **retinotopic mapping** of neurons in the visual system and by **labeled lines**, the ability to distinguish the activity of an individual detector from that of its neighboring detectors. An image formed on a given retinal location will stimulate a neuron with a corresponding particular location within the retina, lateral geniculate nucleus, and striate cortex (Fig. 2-1B). In other words, the position of a particular active neuron within the LGN or visual cortex tells you which location of the retina was stimulated, providing a unique measure of the *direction* in space where the stimulus originated. Experiments with direct electrical stimulation of cortical neurons show that subjects perceive flashes of light in a particular direction in space that is dependent on the location of the stimulated neurons (Brindley and Lewin, 1968).

The concept of local sign is not unique to vision; for example, if somatosensory neurons in the cortex are artificially stimulated, we sense a particular place on our bodies being touched according to the location of the neurons stimulated. The visual system uses local sign to determine directionality, which, along with other visual cues to be discussed in Chapter 7, are used to build its *interpretation* of the physical three-dimensional world, which we call visual space.

---

### ⚷ *Key Point*

*Visual space is not always exactly the same as real space. Even so, the visual system invariably assumes that its interpretation of the world is correct. Occasionally, the visual system will misinterpret information.* **Optical illusions** *are the result of mismatches between visual space and physical space.*

---

Visual direction can be represented by a straight line called a **visual line** or **line of sight** that projects from a given point on the retina passing through the *entrance pupil* of the eye and out into physical space (Alpern, 1969). All points in space falling along this visual line, at *any* distance from the eye, appear to lie in

A
B

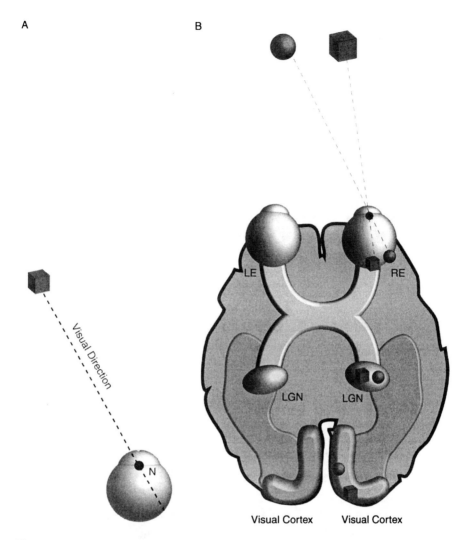

**Figure 2-1** **A:** Every retinal locus has a local sign or unique visual direction in space that it signals. **B:** The local sign is determined by the retinotopic mapping of the retinal locus in the lateral geniculate nucleus and striate cortex.

the same direction in the visual field. The **visual axis** is the visual line that passes specifically from the fovea to an object of regard.

Determining the exact location of an object would be just as simple as determining which point of the retina is being stimulated if the eyes did not move. For example, an object directly in front of us would be imaged on the fovea if we were looking directly at it, but on lateral left retina and nasal right retina if our eyes look toward the right. Even though our eyes have moved to the right, the object is still in the same location (in front of us), and that is where the visual system

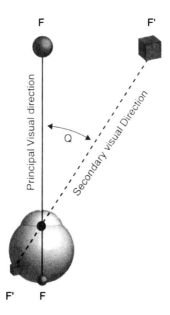

**Figure 2-2**    Under monocular conditions, visual direction is determined relative to the principal visual direction, denoted by the fovea. Objects whose images are formed on the fovea are perceived as being straight ahead. All visual directions other than the fovea, that is, secondary visual directions, are seen as displaced off to the side.

should interpret it to be. Visual direction is not an absolute judgment but instead is a *relative* judgment. We make judgments of the relationships in position between objects and between an object and ourselves. However, this raises an important question: what do we use as the reference point for these judgments? Are these judgments made relative to our eyes, relative to our heads, or relative to our entire bodies?

Let us first consider the mechanisms available for judging direction relative to the eye. If each visual neuron signals a particular direction in space, there must be a reference direction against which all other directions are judged. The reference against which we compare all directions is called the **principal visual direction** (Fig. 2-2). All other directions, such as to the left, right, above, or below the fixation point, are called **secondary visual directions**. The principal visual direction of each eye, the "zero direction" of each eye, so to speak, is the direction signaled by its *fovea*. Visual direction is determined relative to the direction in which the fovea is pointing; that is, relative to where that eye is fixating, as well as how far removed from the fovea the stimulated retinal point lies. As the eye moves, the fovea moves, and so does the principal visual direction; all secondary visual direc-

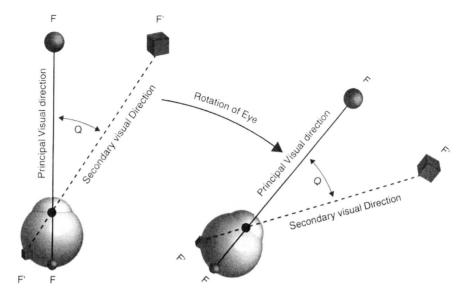

**Figure 2-3**    When the eye and fovea move, the oculocentric visual direction moves accordingly so that the new principal visual direction is of the new foveal position.

tions signaled by retinal points eccentric to the fovea also move to remain in the same positions relative to the primary visual direction (Fig. 2-3). Therefore, local sign provides **oculocentric**, or "eye-centered," visual direction; as the eye shifts position, so does oculocentric direction.

---

### 🔑 Key Point

*The fovea is the "zero reference" for oculocentric visual direction, or principal visual direction. Eccentric retinal points signal secondary visual directions. Oculocentric visual direction is determined by the line of sight from an object through the entrance pupil of the eye to the retina.*

---

Objects with the same secondary visual direction to an eye, on the same line of sight, stimulate the same retinal point. Another way of stating this is that superimposed retinal images will be seen in the same oculocentric visual direction (objects $O_1$ and $O_2$ both stimulate retinal point O'), although they may be perceived at different distances in that direction. This is called the **law of oculocentric visual direction** (Fig. 2-4). Stimulation of a given retinal point by a single stimulus induces the visual system to interpret the location of that stimulus as being out in

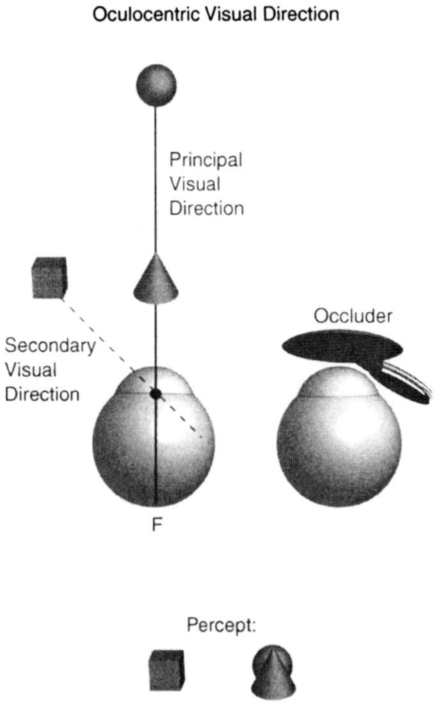

Oculocentric Visual Direction

Principal
Visual
Direction

Occluder

Secondary
Visual
Direction

F

Percept:

**Figure 2-4**    Because every retinal locus
signals a unique visual direction, two images
formed on the same retinal locus will be
seen as superimposed and coming from the
same visual direction, according to the law
of oculocentric visual direction.

visual space in a particular direction; stimulation of a single retinal point by multiple stimuli with the same directional value induces the visual system to interpret
the location of the stimuli as superimposed and with the same direction.

**CLINICAL
APPLICATION**

Clinicians conceptualize this is as monocular visual direction being **"projected" outward into visual space** from the eye by the visual system; that is,
the visual system builds each eye's view of the world from the eye "outward."
This concept can be demonstrated by means of an afterimage. Afterimages are
produced by bleaching retinal photopigment within a given area of the retina,
for example, by viewing the light of a small camera flashbulb. The afterimage,
which affects a fixed region of the retina, is perceived by the viewer as arising
in visual space in a particular direction depending on the particular area
of retina on which the flash was imaged; in other words, the afterimage is
"projected" into space in that direction.

 *Key Point*

*Visual direction and visual projection link the point of regard in visual space with a particular locus on the retina.*

**Figure 2-5**   The accuracy of visual direction is in direct proportion to the size of the receptive fields that determine position. Therefore, visual direction is localized more accurately for images formed on the fovea than for images formed on the peripheral retina.

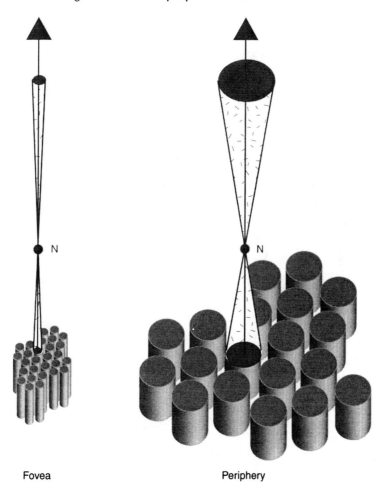

Fovea                    Periphery

As you might infer from these facts, the percept of motion can be thought of simply as a change in the visual direction of an object as a function of time when one, then another, retinal locus is stimulated by its image.

We make our finest judgments of visual direction in *central* visual space near the fixation point (Fig. 2-5) because of the magnified portion of cortical structure devoted to central vision. With smaller receptive fields at the fovea, we can see finer displacements when a neighboring receptive field is stimulated. Judgments of visual direction fall off in accuracy with more peripheral retinal loci because receptive fields are larger there; it takes a larger displacement for an object to be seen in a different direction. Therefore, we are more sensitive to small displacements or slow velocities of motion at the fovea and larger displacements or faster velocities of motion in the periphery.

**CLINICAL PROCEDURE** | The sense of directionality can be disrupted by retinal disorders that dislocate the photoreceptors. For example, in central serous maculopathy, fluid beneath the retina dislodges the photoreceptors. The result is a localized **metamorphopsia**, or spatial distortion of vision, that can be revealed with an Amsler grid target. The regular square array of the Amsler grid appears to such patients to be wavy (Fig. 2-6).

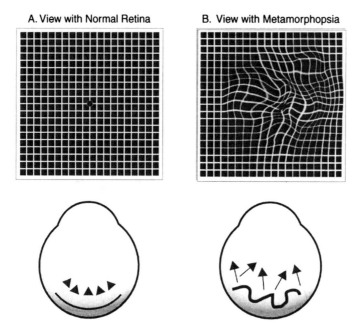

A. View with Normal Retina    B. View with Metamorphopsia

**Figure 2-6**  Disruption of the orderliness of photoreceptors by forces on the retina will displace the visual direction signaled by a given retinal locus, producing metamorphopsia.

**CLINICAL**
**RELEVANCE**

In some abnormalities of the visual system, a point other than the fovea may be used to determine the principal visual direction. This may occur in cases of **eccentric fixation**. In eccentric fixation, an extrafoveal point is used to fixate objects and can be used as the zero reference for visual direction (Fig. 2-7). Eccentric fixation is a common consequence of strabismus and contributes to the vision loss in amblyopia. It is possible that eccentric fixation is a consequence of sensory visual distortions that are most pronounced at the fovea of strabismic eyes (Bedell and Flom, 1983). However, a patient who fixates with an extrafoveal retinal locus does not necessarily have eccentric fixation. In

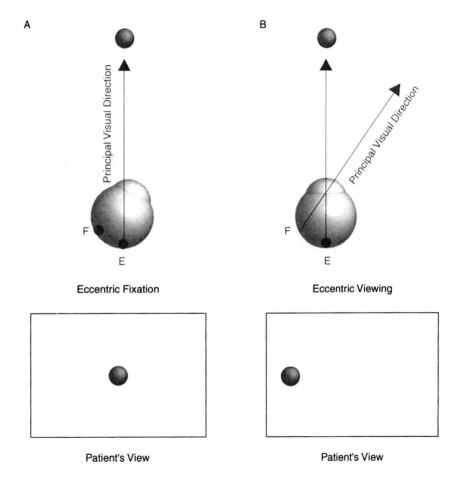

**Figure 2-7** **A:** Eccentric fixation is a neurological remapping of the monocular principal visual direction to a new locus. Images formed on the eccentric point are now perceived as coming from objects that are straight ahead. **B:** Eccentric viewing is a purposeful aiming of a retinal locus other than the fovea toward an object of interest. The fovea is still used as the principal visual direction, and the patient is aware of a need to "look off to the side" of that object to see it.

low-vision patients whose foveal vision is compromised by disease processes, an extrafoveal point may be purposely selected for aiming the eye, identifying objects, and reading. This is called **eccentric viewing**. Essentially, the patient selects a retinal locus with better resolution than the diseased fovea to serve as a replacement fixation point. Eccentric viewing differs from eccentric fixation in that the patient still uses the destroyed fovea as a zero direction reference; the principal visual direction has not changed. These patients are *consciously* "looking off to the side" to see objects clearly. They must *train* themselves not to look directly at an object because even with damaged central vision, the reflex to fixate with the fovea is a strong one.

**CLINICAL PROCEDURE**   The primary visual direction used by a given patient may be determined by means of clinical tests such as **visuoscopy** (Fig. 2-8). The clinician uses an ophthalmoscope to image a small circular fixation target onto the patient's

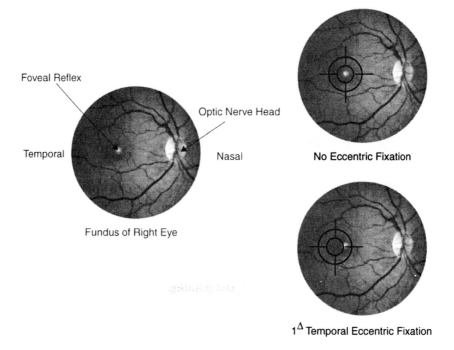

Foveal Reflex

Optic Nerve Head

Temporal

Nasal

No Eccentric Fixation

Fundus of Right Eye

$1^\Delta$ Temporal Eccentric Fixation

**Figure 2-8**   Visuoscopy provides the clinician information about the status of fixation or the primary visual direction. A fixation target is projected by an ophthalmoscope into a patient's eye and imaged on the retina. The patient is asked to look directly at the target. In normal fixation, the fovea is used for fixation, and the clinician sees the ophthalmoscopic target projected onto the fovea. In eccentric fixation, the clinician sees the ophthalmoscopic target projected onto the eccentric point that is now used as the primary visual direction.

retina. While the clinician views the retina, and specifically the foveal reflex, the patient is asked to look directly at the target, which is seen in the center of the ophthalmoscope's light. In normal fixation, the fovea is used for fixation, and the clinician sees the ophthalmoscopic target projected onto the fovea. In eccentric fixation, the clinician sees the ophthalmoscopic target projected onto the eccentric point that is used for the primary visual direction.

---

 *Key Point*

**Eccentric fixation** *and* **eccentric viewing** *must be differentiated. Typically, eccentric fixation develops in childhood in concert with strabismus and amblyopia. The patient is not aware of the problem. Visuoscopy is one technique to diagnose eccentric fixation. If the foveal reflex does not appear in the center of the ophthalmoscopic target when you instruct the patient to fixate there, eccentric fixation is present. Eccentric viewing, on the other hand, requires conscious effort on the part of the patient. It typically occurs after loss of vision from injury or disease and is a normal adaptation to the visual loss rather than an abnormality.*

---

The visual direction associated with stimulation of any particular retinal point is dependent on feedback from other sensory systems and may be altered under certain circumstances. This can be seen by putting on a pair of spectacles with prism lenses that move the entire visual space several degrees to one side. Initially, a person will make errors when attempting to point toward objects in the visual field, a phenomenon known as past pointing, but after a period of trial and error attempting to reach the objects, the visual system will remap itself to associate the stimulation of new retinal locations with particular visual directions. A similar adaptation must then be undergone when the spectacles are removed.

**CLINICAL APPLICATION** The phenomenon of past pointing occurs naturally in patients with a paretic eye muscle. When fixation is attempted into the field of action of the paretic muscle, the patient will reach past an object, apparently perceiving it to be beyond its actual location. The explanation for past pointing is related to a mismatch between the actual eye position and the amount of innervation required to move the eye to its final position. A paretic muscle requires additional innervation from the normal level that is required to move the eye to any particular gaze direction. The additional innervation is interpreted by the patient as meaning that the object must be further beyond the direction of its actual position. The patient reaches for the object where it is misperceived to be.

As precise as oculocentric direction is, it cannot be the only source of information for localizing objects in space. Otherwise we would see objects change position as we move our eyes. Therefore, we must also have some knowledge of the position of the eyes in the head. In other words, we also have **headcentric** directionality. This information could be provided from the efferent motor signal to the extraocular muscles, which would determine the position of the eyes. The **law of headcentric localization** states that for a given position of the eye in the head, objects lying on the same line of sight are seen in the same *headcentric* visual direction.

## BINOCULAR VISUAL DIRECTION AND CORRESPONDING RETINAL POINTS

Usually we are not viewing the world monocularly but instead use both eyes at once. However, because each eye has its *own* frame of reference from which it measures direction, how do we reconcile these two directions when both eyes are open? If the monocular principal visual direction were used as the frame of reference for determining what is straight ahead under binocular conditions, our view of the world would be confusing because the eyes do not necessarily point in the same direction. In this case, we would be receiving two different encodings of "straight ahead," one from each eye. For example, if both eyes converge to fixate on the same near object, each eye *alone* would see that object as being in its principal visual direction, with everything else it sees in a direction relative to the principal visual direction. However, the left eye's view would not match that of the right eye, as we saw in Fig. 1-3, because the left eye is gazing *rightward* and the right eye is gazing *leftward*. Both eyes are actually gazing in different directions *off to the side*. What do we interpret as straight ahead in this situation?

Hering performed an experiment to determine this over 100 years ago (see Fig. 2-9). If a subject fixates on a mark on a window pane, the objects that lie along each eye's principal visual directions when viewed monocularly will then be seen as overlapping in the *same direction—straight ahead, or in the principal visual direction*—when both eyes are open. This is true even though these objects are really separated laterally in space; neither object is physically directly in front of us. The net result is that under binocular viewing conditions, we reference straight ahead in a "compromise" position midway between the two eyes' individual principal visual directions (Fig. 2-10) (Ono et al., 1977; Sheedy and Fry, 1979). Binocular visual direction is determined according to the **law of identical visual directions**. Objects with the same visual direction in each eye will be seen as lying in a single visual direction under binocular viewing conditions. Here, too, the foveas serve as the reference point. The foveas of the two eyes signal the *same* primary visual direction.

Under binocular conditions, we see directions not relative to each eye alone but relative to a *single* reference point within our head that is called the **egocenter**.

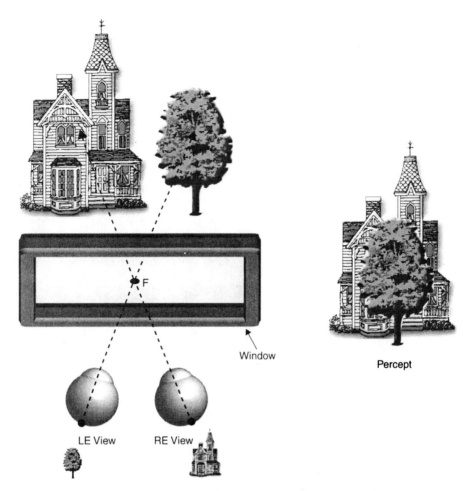

**Figure 2-9** The Hering window experiment demonstrates that even when the eyes are converged and not directed straight ahead of us, objects whose images are formed on the foveas of each eye are seen under binocular conditions as superimposed and arising from a common binocular visual direction straight ahead. That is, the visual direction under binocular viewing conditions does not match the individual monocular visual directions.

This form of directionality is therefore called **egocentric localization**. We see objects whose images are formed on both foveas as if their images instead fell on a single point midway between the two eyes, like an imaginary single eyeball in the middle of our two real eyes. This single **"cyclopean eye"** (Fig. 2-11), albeit imaginary, helps explain how we see under binocular conditions. Strangely, young children who sight a distant object through a tube do so with the *cyclopean* eye rather than either individual eye; that is, they place the tube precisely midway between their eyes (Barbeito, 1983).

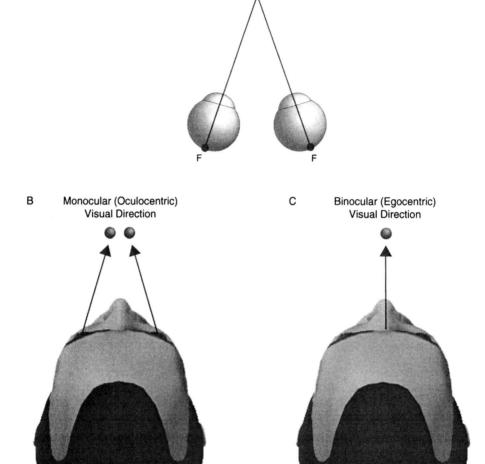

**Figure 2-10**    **A:** The two eyes converge to bifoveally fixate a nearby object. **B:** The monocular visual directions are each directed sideways towards the object of regard. **C:** The binocular visual direction is a compromise between the individual monocular visual directions. The common subjective principal visual direction is that direction seen as straight ahead under binocular conditions.

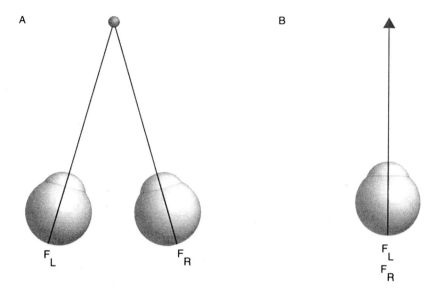

**Figure 2-11** Binocular visual direction is perceived as if we had only a single eye in the center of our foreheads, midway between our left and right eyes. The cyclopean eye is a theoretical construct that explains this percept. **A:** Monocular visual directions. **B:** Binocular visual direction as seen by a single cyclopean eye.

Let us demonstrate egocentric visual direction (Fig. 2-12). Roll a piece of paper into a tube. Close one eye and look through the tube with your open eye at an object across the room. Now move your other hand next to the tube. Open both eyes. What do you see? You should see a "hole" though your hand. In that hole is the scene viewed through the tube. Both your hand and the view in the tube are being fixated, one by each eye. You are combining both monocular visual directions into a single view with a single binocular visual direction.

**CLINICAL PROCEDURE** The existence of a single common binocular visual direction can also be demonstrated with afterimages. Using a camera flash to produce a horizontal linear afterimage at one fovea and a vertical afterimage at the other produces a binocular percept of a single cross in one direction. This **afterimage test** is used as a clinical technique to test for abnormalities of visual direction that we discuss later.

Although oculocentric localization can be explained with either eye in isolation, and egocentric localization is the primary form of directionality under binocular conditions, the reader should not assume that all monocular localization is oculocentric and all binocular localization is egocentric. The visual system can access some egocentric information under monocular conditions as long as sym-

A. Method

B. Target

C. Percept

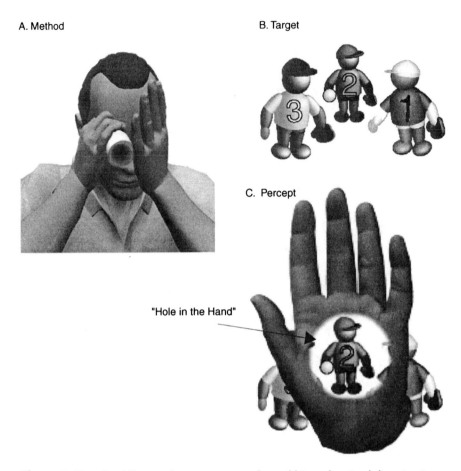

"Hole in the Hand"

**Figure 2-12**   The difference between monocular and binocular visual direction is exemplified by the "hole in the hand" experiment. **A:** The left eye's fovea views an object **(B)** across a room through a tube, while the right eye views the hand directly before it. **C:** The binocular percept is of a hand with a hole in it through which the distant object may be seen.

metrical convergence of the eyes is maintained. Similarly, as we will see when we discuss fusion and fixation disparity in Chapter 3, all oculocentric information is not totally lost under binocular conditions.

It should be noted that although the cyclopean eye is situated midway between our actual left and right eyes, it may not be located *precisely* midway. While the oculocentric positions of an image in the two eyes are averaged to form a binocular egocentric direction (Ono et al., 1977), the two eyes may not exert equal influences on the direction-averaging process. One eye may be favored, a phenomenon called **eye dominance**. Most people tend to have one

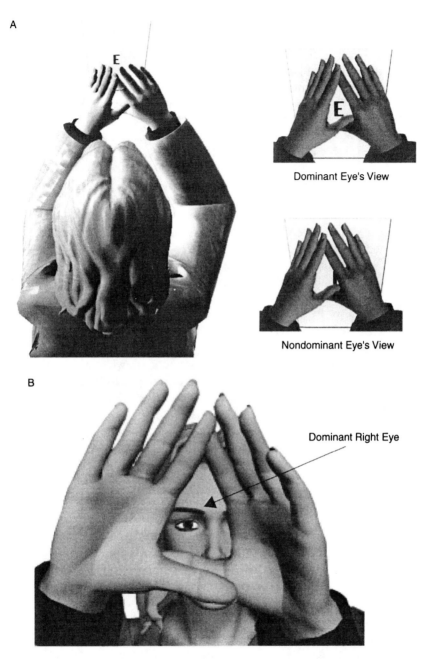

A

E

Dominant Eye's View

Nondominant Eye's View

B

Dominant Right Eye

**Figure 2-13** Eye dominance, the relative contribution of each eye's individual percept to the binocular percept, applies to the phenomenon of visual direction. **A:** The influence of each eye's visual direction on the combined binocular visual direction may be determined by which eye is used to sight a target through a small aperture during binocular viewing. **B:** The clinician can determine which eye is dominant by noting in front of which eye the subject places his or her hands while sighting.

dominant eye. A simple way to determine which eye is dominant is to fixate a distant target binocularly through an opening about the size of a quarter between the thumbs and forefingers of your two hands held together at arm's length, as in Fig. 2-13. Close the left eye alone, then the right eye alone. Does the object seem to move out of the view of that opening? The eye that is open when you can see the object in the opening is your **dominant eye,** in this case, the eye you favor for sighting or aligning objects under binocular conditions. The directionality of the dominant eye is weighted more in determining the binocular common subjective visual direction (Ono and Barbeito, 1982; Porac and Coren, 1986). In strabismus, the egocentric direction can be shifted toward the nondeviating eye (Mann et al., 1979). The loss of one eye at an early age can shift the egocentric direction toward that of the single remaining eye (Moidell et al., 1988).

Eye dominance has several consequences. We will see later that eye dominance can affect other ways in which we combine binocular information, such as *binocular summation*. In addition, eye dominance is important in abnormal binocular visual conditions such as strabismus and amblyopia. It is usually the *nondominant* eye that is strabismic and/or amblyopic.

**CLINICAL RELEVANCE**

Eye dominance is probably most important when it comes to *prescribing lenses*. In normal patients, if you cannot precisely balance the corrected acuity in the two eyes during subjective refraction, you should prescribe the better correction to the *dominant* eye. If a dominant eye is slightly blurred, the patient will be more likely to notice the blur; conversely, a slight blur in the nondominant eye is not likely to be noticed when both eyes are open.

One type of contact lens correction commonly prescribed for presbyopes is the use of a distance correction in one contact lens and a near correction in the other. This allows presbyopic patients to have clear vision at both far and near fixation distances without using bifocals or reading spectacles over their contact lenses. This is called **monovision**. A patient wearing monovision lenses will always have one eye's view blurred (Fig. 2-14). When he or she fixates on a near object, the view of the near-corrected eye will be clear, but that of the distance-corrected eye will be blurred. When monovision lenses are prescribed, the patient's sensitivity to blurring of the *dominant eye* should be taken into account at both distance and near. As a rule, the dominant eye should be given the distance correction, as clear vision of distant objects such as road signs and television screens is important for most patients. However, some patients who spend most of their time doing near-distance work may have the opposite preference. A person who does not have strong eye dominance may adapt to monovision correction more easily. Unfortunately, as we will see later, wearing monovision contact lenses can have a devastating effect on *stereopsis*.

A. Distance Viewing

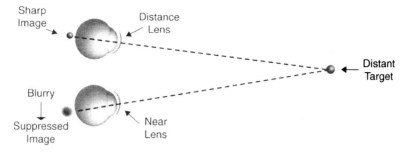

B. Near Viewing

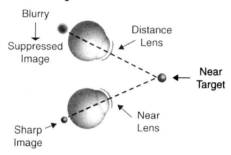

**Figure 2-14**   Monovision contact lens fitting is the prescription of a near correction for one eye and a distance correction for the other eye, removing the need to wear bifocal spectacles. The result is (**A**) a blurred image in the eye with the near correction when viewing a distance target, and (**B**) a blurred image in the eye with the distance correction when viewing a near target. Eye dominance should be determined before prescribing monovision to avoid blurring the dominant eye at the distance needed for critical visual tasks by that patient.

## ⚷ Key Point

*Eye dominance reflects the relative weighting of each eye's input into the binocular percept. It should be taken into account in prescribing spectacle or contact lens corrections to avoid symptoms of binocular vision disruption.*

**CLINICAL RELEVANCE** | In addition to eye dominance, another factor that affects the location of the egocenter is the position of the two eyes. This is why a **heterophoria** can cause a subjective apparent movement of an object when an eye is occluded during the clinical **cover test**. In heterophoria, as the subject attempts to bifoveally fixate a target, one eye will turn to the side when it is occluded. Simultaneously, the patient perceives a displacement of the target in the same direction as the eye rotation. An opposite motion will be seen when the eye is uncovered (Ono et al., 1972). The subjective localization of the target shifts, although the uncovered eye, which is still viewing the target, does not move at all. Therefore, the position of the covered eye must still be exerting an influence on the perceived egocentric direction.

We now know that under binocular viewing conditions, direction is judged relative to a single common visual direction. The visual directions of each eye must somehow be "matched up" to form a single unified visual direction. **Corresponding retinal points** are pairs of points, one in each eye, that, when stimulated simultaneously or rapidly in succession, are perceived to lie in a single common visual direction. Another way of stating this is that corresponding points have corresponding lines of sight; any object lying anywhere on either of these lines of sight will be seen as lying in a single visual direction. When the eyes fixate binocularly, an image formed on both foveas will be seen in a single straight-ahead visual direction called the **common subjective principal visual direction** (Fig. 2-15). Similarly, an image formed of matching secondary points in each retina

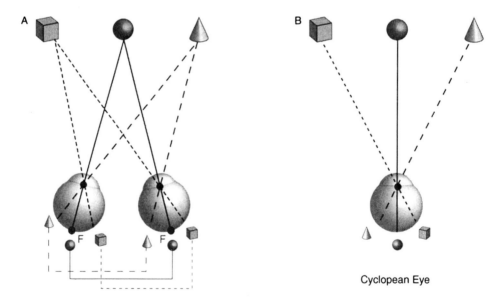

Cyclopean Eye

**Figure 2-15**   **A:** For every point in one eye's visual field, there is a point in the other eye's retina whose visual direction is identical. **B:** The two foveas, which are corresponding points, are seen in a common subjective principal visual direction, that is, straight ahead.

will be seen as lying in a secondary common subjective visual direction. The consequence of this is that for every point in one eye's visual field, there is a point in the other eye's retina whose visual direction is identical. These corresponding retinal points share a common visual direction relative to the common subjective principle visual direction and are said to be *in correspondence* with each other.

---

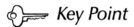 *Key Point*

**Corresponding retinal points** *are pairs of points, one in each eye that, when stimulated simultaneously or rapidly in succession, are perceived to lie in identical visual directions. The zero reference for binocular direction, called the* **common subjective principal visual direction**, *originates from a point midway between the two eyes, called the* **cyclopean eye**. *Binocular directionality is therefore "head-centered" or* **egocentric.**

---

Corresponding points can also be demonstrated for the *tactile* sense, as shown in Fig. 2-16. With the eyes closed to eliminate the influence of visual cues, touching the inside surfaces of two fingers, where corresponding points on the skin of each finger lie, with a pen will lead to a percept of a single pen contacting both fingers from a single direction. If the fingers are then crossed, the corresponding points on each finger will no longer be in proximity to each other. Touching the skin between the crossed fingers with the pen will now stimulate noncorresponding points. The result is a percept of two pens contacting the fingers from different directions.

We now know that each eye's principal visual directions are combined into a single common subjective principle visual direction under binocular conditions. In other words, the foveas of each eye are corresponding points. However, what about other loci in the visual field? Clearly, there must be a *set* of corresponding lines of sight across the visual field, so that when we have both eyes open, we see each location in space in a particular, unique direction. Let us assume that corresponding points in each eye are displaced symmetrically and evenly at the same angular eccentricity from their respective foveas. That is, a retinal locus at eccentricity $\alpha_L$ from the fovea in the left eye will have a corresponding point at an identical angle $\alpha_R$ from the fovea in the right eye (these angles are positive in a clockwise direction from the fovea, negative if counterclockwise). Corresponding points would have the same horizontal displacement from the fovea in each eye as well as the same vertical displacement. If we repeat this for several equal values

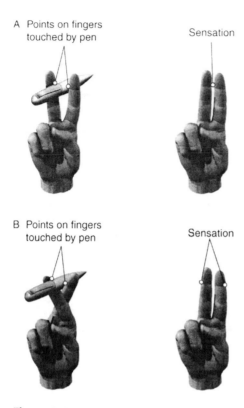

A Points on fingers touched by pen

Sensation

B Points on fingers touched by pen

Sensation

**Figure 2-16** Corresponding points can also be demonstrated for touch. **A:** With the eyes closed, touching the inside surfaces of two fingers with a pen will yield a percept of a single pen contacting both fingers. **B:** If the fingers are crossed, touching the skin between the crossed fingers with a pen will stimulate noncorresponding points, resulting in a percept of pens contacting the fingers from different directions.

of $\alpha_L$ and $\alpha_R$, we obtain a plot of points in visual space, each imaged on corresponding retinal points in the two eyes. This plot forms a *circle* called the **Vieth-Müller circle** that intersects the fixation point and the entrance pupils of each eye (Fig. 2-17). As the eyes are converged to aim at the fixation point, each point along the circle should be imaged on corresponding points along the horizontal retinal meridian in the two eyes and will be seen in a single binocularly derived direction.

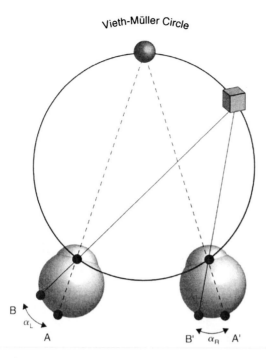

Vieth-Müller Circle

**Figure 2-17** The Vieth-Müller circle is a theoretical prediction of the location of objects in
space that stimulate corresponding points in the
two eyes. It assumes that a given angular displacement from retinal locus A to locus B in the left eye
will be matched by the same angular displacement in the right eye between the retinal loci A′
and B′ corresponding to locations A and B in the
left eye.

## BINOCULAR DISPARITY

Visual direction and correspondence are basic building blocks of our perception
of distance and depth. Corresponding points can be thought of as the "zero
point" for stereopsis; that is, images on corresponding points are perceived as
arising from targets at the same distance. The percept of depth arises from the
stimulation of noncorresponding retinal points.

Images of a single object that do not stimulate corresponding retinal points in
the two eyes are said to be **disparate**. If viewed monocularly, these images would
be perceived as lying in different visual directions. The difference in position in

relation to corresponding points between images in the two eyes is called a **binocular disparity**. Disparity (denoted by the Greek symbol $\eta$) is defined as a difference in the binocular subtense angles $\alpha_L$ and $\alpha_R$, or $\eta = \alpha_L - \alpha_R$. Vertical differences in the positions of similar images are **vertical disparity,** and horizontal differences in retinal image position are called **horizontal disparity.** Corre-

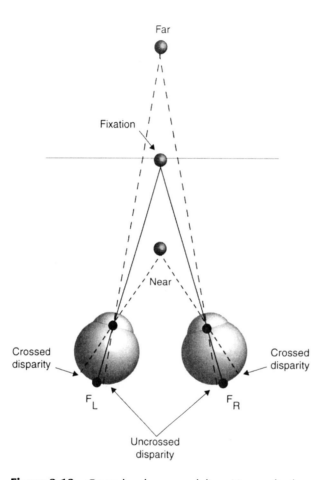

**Figure 2-18**   Crossed and uncrossed disparities result when objects produce images that are formed on closely separated retinal points. With small degrees of binocular disparity, the images may still be fused into a single percept but will be seen at a different distance or three-dimensional depth than the fixation point. Crossed disparity produces a percept of an object closer than the fixation point, whereas uncrossed disparity produces a percept of an object farther away than the fixation point.

sponding retinal points, by definition, have **zero binocular disparity**, that is, $\eta = \alpha_L - \alpha_R = 0$.

It is horizontal binocular disparity that allows the perception of **stereoscopic depth** (to be explored in more detail in Chapter 7). Horizontal binocular disparity can be classified as crossed or uncrossed in relationship to the fixation point, that is, the point at which the two eyes are converged (Fig. 2-18) (Ogle, 1952). Points seen as *nearer* than the fixation point, that is, within the Vieth-Müller circle, have lines of sight that *cross* in front of the fixation point and are said to have **crossed disparity**. Points *farther away* than the fixation point have lines of sight that meet behind the fixation point and are said to have **uncrossed disparity**.

In *crossed* disparity, angle $\eta$ (the difference between the binocular subtense angles $\alpha_L$ and $\alpha_R$) is *positive*, such that $\alpha_L$ is larger than $\alpha_R$. Conversely, in *uncrossed* disparity, angle $\eta$ is *negative*, such that $\alpha_R$ is larger than $\alpha_L$ (see Fig. 2-19). Another way of stating this is that crossed disparity involves a *nasal* shift of the images in one or both eyes, whereas uncrossed disparity involves a *temporalward* shift.

If the binocular disparity is too large, diplopia results. However, with small disparities, the visual system is still able to combine the two images into a single percept. The upper limit of disparities that can still produce single vision is determined by **Panum's area**, which is discussed in Chapter 3.

Small differences in perceived horizontal direction between the two eyes give rise to a percept of three-dimensional depth or **stereopsis**. We noted this in Fig. 1-3, in which an object, a rabbit, is viewed by each eye alone. Each eye receives a slightly different image of the rabbit as seen by two distinct vantage points. The point on the rabbit that is directly fixated is placed on the corresponding foveas of each eye. Other points on the rabbit may be imaged on noncorresponding points in the two eyes. This yields a three-dimensional percept of a rab-

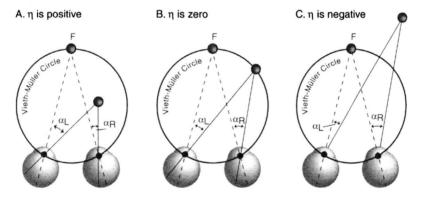

**Figure 2-19** Crossed and uncrossed disparities are defined by $\eta$, the difference between the binocular subtense angles $\alpha_L$ and $\alpha_R$. **A:** In crossed diparity, $\eta$ is positive, that is, $\alpha_L > \alpha_R$. **B:** With zero disparity, $\alpha_L$ and $\alpha_R$ are equal, and $\eta$ is zero. **C:** In uncrossed disparity, $\alpha_L < \alpha_R$ and therefore, $\eta$ is negative.

bit rather than a flat view. You can confirm this by viewing the figure and crossing your eyes until you fuse together one image of the rabbit. You will notice that the rabbit's head appears to be in front of its body; that is, the body is seen as being at a different distance or depth. This principle is used to create **stereograms**, such as the three-dimensional pictures seen in a Viewmaster™.

Vertical disparities do not directly give rise to a percept of depth as do horizontal disparities (Hering, 1864). However, as we shall see in Chapter 7, vertical disparities can still affect our percept of depth indirectly.

## DIPLOPIA AND CONFUSION

Images on widely separated noncorresponding points, that is, points beyond the limits of Panum's area, will not be seen as fused or single. Let us demonstrate this with an experiment (Fig. 2-20). Hold up the index finger of your left hand vertically midway between your eyes about 30 cm in front of you, and the index finger of the right hand directly in front of you at arm's length. Fixate the more distant index finger. How many near index fingers do you see? You should see *two*. Now fixate the near index finger. How many far fingers do you see? Once again, you should see two.

This phenomenon is called **physiological diplopia**, where diplopia means "double vision." It is called *physiological* diplopia because it is normal (we will see later that some abnormalities of binocular vision, i.e., strabismus, can cause pathological diplopia). Although objects whose images are formed on corresponding retinal points are perceived as lying in the same binocular visual direction, images formed on widely separated *noncorresponding* retinal points are perceived as arising from *different* visual directions.

When a *distant* object is fixated bifoveally, a nearer object in front of it will be imaged on the *temporal* retina of each eye on noncorresponding points. If these points are far enough apart, we see the object as double. When this occurs, we get what is called **crossed diplopia** (Fig. 2-21); the right eye sees the image on the left, and the left eye sees the image on the right. You can confirm this by closing one, then the other, eye when performing the physiological diplopia demonstration. When you close the left eye, the right diplopic image will disappear, and vice versa.

The opposite occurs when we fixate a *near* object and a distant object is seen double; this is called **uncrossed diplopia**. In this case, each image is formed on the *nasal* retina of the eye in which it is imaged. Here, the left eye sees the left image and the right eye the right one. When you close the left eye, the left diplopic image will disappear. Closing the right eye will eliminate the right image.

A second, perhaps more amusing, demonstration of diplopia is as follows (see Fig. 2-22): Touch your two index fingers together in front of your eyes at about arm's length. While fixating on a distant target, move your fingers gradually closer to your nose until they are perceived as diplopic. What you should see is a small floating finger that resembles a small "sausage" between your two fingertips.

A. Position for observing physiological diplopia

B. When focused on the distal finger, the near finger is seen as

C. When focused on the near finger, the distal finger appears

**Figure 2-20** **A:** Physiological diplopia is a naturally occurring percept when objects produce images formed on widely separated noncorresponding points. **B:** If a far finger is fixated under binocular conditions, the images of that finger will be formed on each eye's fovea and be seen as single. The near finger's images are formed on noncorresponding points in each eye, and that finger is therefore seen as double. **C:** If the near finger is fixated instead, the near finger will be seen as single, and the far finger will be diplopic.

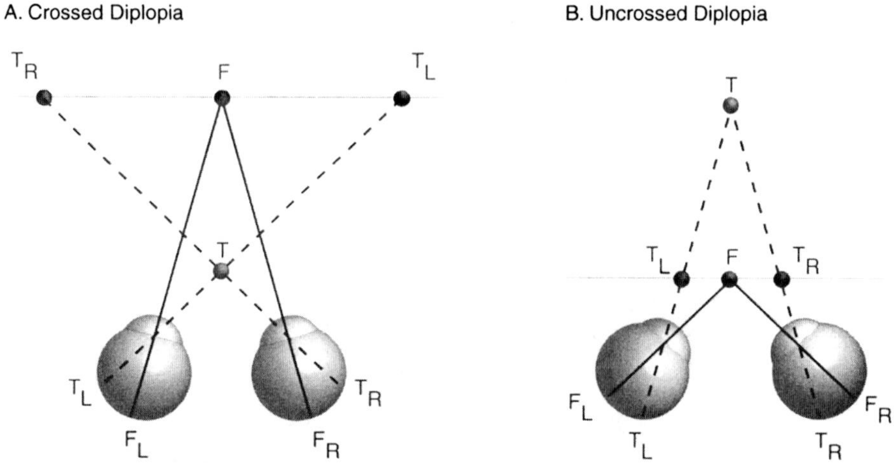

**Figure 2-21**    The nature of diplopia depends on the placement of the noncorresponding images. **A:** Objects nearer than the fixation point produce crossed diplopia because the left eye sees the right double image and the right eye sees the left one. **B:** Objects farther than the fixation point produce uncrossed diplopia, in which the left eye sees the left image and the right eye sees the right image.

The converse of diplopia, that is, two different objects seen in one direction or location, is a phenomenon called **binocular confusion**. This occurs when an image is formed on one locus in one eye but a nonidentical image is formed on its corresponding point in the fellow eye. The result is that two different objects are seen superimposed in the same location. This is predominantly noticed for the foveal area. The distinction between diplopia and confusion is noted in Fig. 2-23.

**CLINICAL APPLICATION** | Diplopia and binocular confusion are major consequences of strabismus. When an eye is turned so that its fovea is no longer aiming at the same object fixated by the fellow eye, the result is diplopia and binocular confusion. Diplopia of the fixation point occurs because the fixation target is not stimulating corresponding points. Confusion results because the two foveas do not point in the same direction; the image at the fovea of the nondeviating eye is that of the fixation target, while the image at the deviating eye's fovea is that of an object other than the intended fixation target. These two dissimilar images are perceived as arising from two different objects at the same locus in space. This can be very devastating to visual function, as it is hard to navigate in a diplopic and/or confused visual world or to reach for an object if another object is also seen at the same location. Many strabismics learn to eliminate the diplopic or confused image by "switching off" the input from the strabismic eye, a process called **suppression**.

A

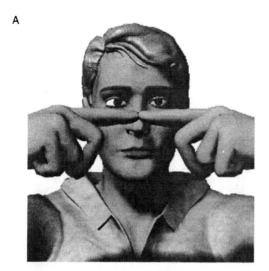

B

**Figure 2-22**   A demonstration of diplopia. **A:** By touching one's fingertips together before one's eyes and fixating at a distant target, diplopia will cause **B:** a small sausage-shaped finger to be seen floating between the fingertips.

**CLINICAL PROCEDURE**

Physiological diplopia can be useful in evaluating binocular vision. Because it is a function of normal binocular vision, its presence or absence can provide the clinician important insight. It not only tells us if a patient has binocular vision or not but also helps us determine where they are fixating binocularly. A commonly used technique called the **Brock string** technique (Fig. 2-24) has a patient view a long string stretched up to his or her nose. The percept of a patient with normal binocular vision fixating a target at the end of the string is of *two* strings, originating from each eye, that converge at the fixation point. The presence of the two strings is actually the physiological diplopia of the single physical string. Knowledge of the location of the string crossing relative to the fixation target helps patients *see for themselves* if they are converging properly, or overconverging or underconverging instead.

A

Stimulus

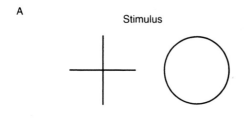

B

Percept

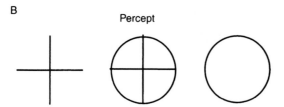

**Figure 2-23**  Diplopia and confusion are both the result of misalignment of the eyes. **A:** The stimulus. **B:** The percept. Diplopia refers to the doubling of both the circle and the cross. Confusion refers to the overlap of the circle and cross such that the two objects are seen in a single direction.

## 🔑 Key Point

*Points lying on the Vieth-Müller circle should be seen as single points lying in a single direction. Points lying off the Vieth-Müller circle should be seen as arising in two distinct directions; in other words, they will be seen diplopically. Nearer points have crossed diplopia, whereas farther ones have uncrossed diplopia.*

As we will see in Chapter 4, although this geometric explanation based on the Vieth-Müller circle is a good model for explaining corresponding points, it is not precisely true. The **horopter** can be used to explain how corresponding points are arranged in the human visual system.

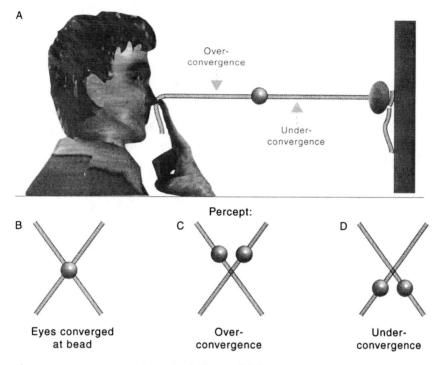

**Figure 2-24**  **A:** The Brock string takes advantage of physiological diplopia to make a patient aware of the binocular percept and degree of convergence. With normal binocular vision, the point along the string at which the eyes aim is seen as single, while all other points along the string are seen as double. **B:** When both eyes are converged on the bead, two strings are seen that cross at the bead; that is, the locus at which the two foveas point (the bead) is seen as single, while all other loci along the string are seen as double. **C:** If the patient overconverges, the two images of the string will be seen as crossing in front of the bead, which is now seen as diplopic. **D:** With underconvergence, the perceived crossing is behind the bead.

## ANOMALOUS RETINAL CORRESPONDENCE

Just as we noted earlier that in abnormal binocular vision, patients might use a point other than the fovea to fixate under monocular conditions (eccentric fixation), a similar condition can occur under binocular viewing as well. With strabismus, the patient may learn to remove the diplopic image not by suppressing it, but by "remapping" the corresponding points. Instead of using the fovea of the strabismic eye as a zero reference, the retinal locus pointing at the same object as the fovea of the fellow eye is now recalibrated to be the zero reference. Now there is no diplopia or confusion when the eye is strabismic because all the points in the field are again corresponding. This is known as **anomalous retinal correspondence** (Fig. 2-25). Note that although the mechanisms underlying anomalous retinal correspondence are cortical, the term connotes the correspondence of the locations of *retinal* points that are assigned the same visual direction

**Figure 2-25**   Anomalous correspondence is an adaptation to strabismus in which an eccentric locus pointing straight ahead in the strabismic eye is remapped to correspond to the fovea of the nonstrabismic eye under binocular conditions. **A:** In normal correspondence, the foveas of each eye receive images of different objects, yielding binocular confusion, a percept of two objects in the same locus in space. In addition, the object whose images are formed on the two foveas will be seen as diplopic. **B:** In anomalous correspondence, both diplopia and binocular confusion are eliminated even in the presence of strabismus.

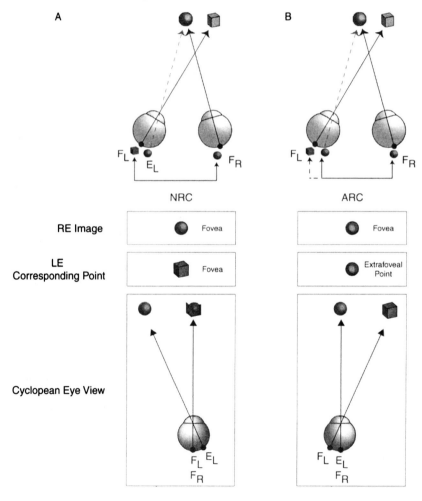

by the visual system. This is a form of binocular vision that, depending on the particular circumstances, can range from crude to surprisingly sophisticated. Because anomalous correspondence associates the fovea of the fixating eye with a peripheral locus of the strabismic eye with less acuity, stereopsis is always affected.

**CLINICAL TIP** | Diplopia and confusion may be eliminated in the strabismic visual system by either *suppressing* the diplopic image in the strabismic eye or by *shifting the zero reference point* for directionality in the strabismic eye (anomalous correspondence). Much of the assessment of strabismics involves the determination of suppression or anomalous correspondence, as the visual therapy techniques to treat the two differ.

Sometimes both of these strategies are employed by the strabismic visual system, with **central suppression** and **peripheral anomalous retinal correspondence** that allows the strabismic some residual stereopsis (Sireteneau and Fronius, 1989).

**CLINICAL APPLICATION** | In vision therapy, one of the first steps taken to realign strabismic eyes is to break down anomalous correspondence and to reestablish normal correspondence. Although the techniques to do so are beyond the scope of this book, one consequence of this therapy should be noted. Sometimes in the course of the therapy, some patients exhibit *both normal and abnormal correspondence* at the same time. The result is transient **binocular triplopia**, or, under monocular conditions, **monocular diplopia**.

## SUMMARY AND KEY POINTS

- **Visual direction** is a two-dimensional localization of objects taking into account only the direction (horizontal and vertical position) of the object. Distance is not a factor in visual direction.

- Each visual neuron has a **local sign**, a unique **line of sight** from a given point on the retina passing through the *nodal point* of the eye and out into visual space. All objects falling along a line of sight appear to be in the same direction. Diseases that affect photoreceptor orientation disrupt local sign, yielding **metamorphopsia**, a spatial distortion of vision.

- Monocular vision is **oculocentric**, with visual direction perceived relative to the **principal visual direction**, the local sign of the fovea. As the eye moves, so does the principal visual direction, as do all **secondary visual directions**. The **law of oculocentric visual direction** states that superimposed retinal images will be interpreted as arising from objects in the same visual direction.

- The most sensitive judgments of visual direction are made in the central retina. In the peripheral retina, larger displacements are needed to evoke a perceptible change in visual direction because of the increase in receptive field size with eccentricity. Motion perception is a change in visual direction of an object over time.

- In **strabismus**, a condition in which one eye is turned so that its fovea no longer is aimed at the same point as the fovea of the fellow eye, the strabismic eye may reflexively use an extrafoveal point as its principal visual direction (**eccentric fixation**) under monocular conditions. Eccentric fixation can be detected by **visuoscopy**. Alternatively, patients with subnormal vision as a result of a disease of the fovea may purposely use an extrafoveal point for fixation (**eccentric viewing**); however, the fovea remains the principal visual direction.

- Binocular vision is **egocentric.** Images formed on both foveas are seen in a single straight-ahead **common subjective principal visual direction**, as if their images actually had formed on a single **cyclopean eye** located midway between the two eyes. However, the binocular common subjective visual direction can be biased toward a **dominant eye**. Eye dominance can also affect other aspects of binocular vision, such as binocular summation (see Chapter 6).

- Whenever the image of an object is formed on **corresponding retinal points** in each retina, the object will be seen as lying in a single **common subjective visual direction**. The **law of identical visual directions** states that objects with the same visual direction in each eye will be perceived as being in a single visual direction under binocular viewing conditions. The **afterimage test** can detect anomalies of binocular visual direction.

- The **Vieth-Müller circle** is a predicted map of each location in space whose images will be formed on corresponding points if corresponding points are defined geometrically.

- The percept of depth arises from the stimulation of noncorresponding retinal points. A difference in visual direction between points in the two eyes is called **binocular disparity**. Large disparities between images result in diplopia, but the visual system can combine images with disparities within **Panum's area** into a percept of a single image. The percept of **stereopsis** occurs with images containing **horizontal disparity**. **Vertical disparity** does not give rise to a percept of depth. Images with **crossed disparity** (angle $\eta$, the difference between the **binocular subtense angles** $\alpha_L$ and $\alpha_R$, is positive; that is, $\alpha_L$ is larger than $\alpha_R$) are perceived as nearer, whereas those with **uncrossed disparity** (angle $\eta$ is negative) appear to be more distant than the fixation point. The fixation point has **zero disparity** (angle $\eta$ is zero).

- Images formed on widely separated noncorresponding points produce **physiological diplopia**. Physiological diplopia can be observed by fixating on a point bifoveally; **crossed diplopia** is perceived for objects much closer than the point fixated, and **uncrossed diplopia** for more distant objects. The **Brock string** makes use of physiological diplopia to provide feedback to a patient about where in space he or she is converging.

- If dissimilar images are formed on corresponding points, **binocular confusion** results, in which two different objects are seen as being in the same visual direction.

- Diplopia and visual confusion often occur in **strabismus**, where one eye is turned so that its fovea no longer is aimed at the same location in space as the fovea of the fellow eye. Many strabismic patients tend to eliminate the diplopic or confused image by **suppression** of the input from the strabismic eye.

- Some strabismic visual systems adapt to binocular confusion by **remapping** corresponding points so that the extrafoveal point in the strabismic eye receiving the same image as the fovea in the nonstrabismic eye now serves as the zero reference; this is known as **anomalous retinal correspondence**. Unfortunately, anomalous correspondence results in a blurred image in the strabismic eye because visual acuity drops with eccentricity from the fovea. This disrupts **stereopsis**, or three-dimensional depth, which requires clear images in both eyes. One goal of vision therapy for strabismics is to break down anomalous correspondence and reestablish normal correspondence.

## QUESTIONS

1. With the fellow eye occluded, a flash of light bleaches an afterimage of a horizontal bar of light on the right fovea. A similar flash bleaches the afterimage of a vertical bar of light on the patient's left fovea. What would you expect a patient with normal correspondence to see under binocular conditions? What would a patient with strabismus see? What would a patient with strabismus and anomalous correspondence see?

2. The visual system is not always accurate in its interpretation of the three-dimensional world around it. Why?

3. A patient who has an identical refractive correction for both eyes is fitted with monovision contact lenses. Would you expect her vision to change in any way if she accidentally switched her lenses between her two eyes? Why?

4. While performing the Brock string test, a patient binocularly fixating on a single bead on a string reports seeing only one string, which seems to extend from the right eye through the bead and beyond it. What does this indicate?

## BIBLIOGRAPHY

ALPERN M (1969). *Specification of the direction of regard. In:* The Eye, *H Davson, ed., vol. 3, Academic Press, New York.*

BARBEITO R (1983). *Sighting from the cyclopean eye: the cyclops effect in preschool children.* Percept. Psychophys. 33:561–564.

BEDELL H *and* FLOM MC (1983). *Monocular spatial distortion in strabismic amblyopia.* Invest. Ophthalmol. Vis. Sci. 20:263–268.

BRINDLEY GS *and* LEWIN WS (1968). *The sensations produced by electrical stimulation of the visual cortex.* J. Physiol. 196:479–493.

HERING (1864). Beitrage zu Physiologie. *W. Engelman, Leipzig.*

MANN VA, HEIN A *and* DIAMOND R (1979). *Localization of targets by strabismic subjects: contrasting patterns in constant and alternating suppressors.* Percept. Psychophys. 25:29–34.

MOIDELL B, STEINBACH MJ *and* ONO H (1988). *Egocenter location in children enucleated at an early age.* Invest. Ophthalmol. Vis. Sci. 29:1348–1351.

OGLE KN (1952). *Disparity limits of stereopsis.* Arch. Ophthalmol. 48:50–60.

ONO H *and* BARBEITO R (1982). *The cyclopean eye vs the sighting-dominant eye as the center of visual direction.* Percept. Psychophys. 32:201–210.

ONO H, ANGUS R *and* GREGOR P (1977). *Binocular single vision achieved by fusion and suppression.* Percept. Psychophys. 21:513–521.

ONO H, WILKINSON A, MUTER P *and* MITSON L (1972). *Apparent movement and change in perceived location of a stimulus produced by a change in accommodative vergence.* Percept. Psychophys. 12:187–192.

PORAC C *and* COREN S (1986). *Sighting dominance and egocentric localization.* Vis. Res. 26:1709–1713.

SHEEDY JE *and* FRY GA (1979). *The perceived direction of the binocular image.* Vis. Res. 19:201–211.

SIRETENEAU R *and* FRONIUS M (1989). *Differences in the pattern of correspondence in the central and peripheral visual field of strabismic observers.* Invest. Ophthalmol. Vis. Sci. 30:2023–2033.

# 3

# Fusion and Correspondence

Over the next few chapters we discuss the different aspects of binocular vision that lead to the percept of three-dimensional depth, or stereopsis. In the present chapter, we begin this discussion by covering **binocular fusion**, the process by which two images, one from each eye, give rise to a unified percept of one single object. Chapters 4 through 6 complete this story, and Chapter 7 discusses how three-dimensional information is inferred from the two-dimensional retinal image.

## *DEGREES OF BINOCULAR FUSION*

One of the first detailed descriptions of binocular fusion was that of Worth (1921), who classified binocular vision as having three levels or grades of fusion: first degree, second degree, and third degree. In Worth's classification, all three degrees of fusion are necessary for deriving the full benefit of binocular vision. First-degree fusion consists of the **simultaneous perception** of each eye's image at once. Second-degree fusion represents the combination of the two images into a single percept and so encompasses the processes of binocular summation (see Chapter 6), binocular correspondence (discussed later in this chapter), and fusion without depth (**flat fusion**). The third degree of binocular vision is **fusion with stereopsis**; that is, deriving binocular three-dimensional depth perception, and was thought of by Worth as representing the highest level of binocular visual function. Worth believed that these three stages formed a *hierarchy* from simple binocular awareness to sophisticated depth analysis. That is, one must have first- and second-degree fusion in order to appreciate third-degree fusion. However, it is now known from scientific studies and clinical cases that although the types of fusion noted by Worth do indeed occur, there are significant exceptions to the concept of a simple fusional hierarchy. For example, as described in Chapter 7, flat fusion is not required to appreciate stereoscopic depth perception. In addition, any of these degrees of fusion may be affected individually or in combination by motor and sensory binocular visual disorders. Even so, the eye care practitioner should be familiar with Worth's classification, as it is still referred to in the clinical literature.

## COMBINING INFORMATION FROM THE TWO EYES

How do we combine the information from our two eyes into a single percept? The most appropriate way for us to do so would be **fusion**, a process of cohesively "merging" the two images together. Here we have to distinguish between two types of fusion (Fig. 3-1). **Motor fusion** is the means by which vergence eye movements are used to position the eyes so that corresponding points (i.e., similar contours in each retinal image) are superimposed. For example, in order to

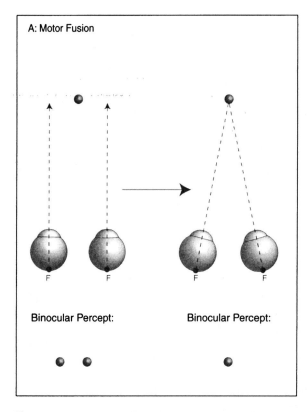
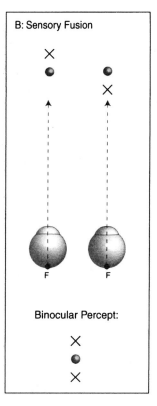

**Figure 3-1**   **A:** Motor fusion involves the use of vergence eye movements to bifoveally fixate a target at a given distance. **B:** Sensory fusion is the combination of the views seen by the individual eyes into a single percept.

fuse the tip of a pencil located a few inches in front of your face, your eyes have to converge toward the pencil until the tip is imaged on the fovea of each eye.

**CLINICAL APPLICATION** | Most patients with strabismus are unable to achieve motor fusion because they cannot simultaneously place the images of an object on the fovea of each eye. In general, impairments of binocular eye movements, whether caused by visual stress, pathology, trauma, drugs, or fatigue will make the task of bringing together similar features in the two retinal images more difficult.

**Sensory fusion** is the neurophysiological and psychological process by which the visual cortex combines the superimposed views obtained independently by the two eyes into one unified percept of visual space. Sensory fusion requires somewhat strict similarity between the two monocular images. Significant dissimilarities between the two retinal images such as size differences induced by anisometropia, visual differences induced by amblyopia, or the absence of motor fusion will disrupt sensory fusion. The visual system must then resort to other methods of combining binocular information to form the percept of a single unified world, such as suppression or anomalous correspondence (discussed in detail in Chapter 5).

**CLINICAL APPLICATION** | Briefly, suppression represents the absence of sensory fusion. So, for example, a strabismic patient who suppresses has inadequate motor and sensory fusion. However, a strabismic patient who compensates by utilizing anomalous correspondence, a somewhat primitive form of binocular vision, has sensory fusion but inadequate motor fusion.

*strabismus = no motor fusion*
*suppression = no sensory fusion*
*ARC = yes sensory fusion*

 *Key Point*

*Motor fusion is the vergence eye movement reflex that brings similar contours into alignment. Sensory fusion is the perceptual phenomenon of combining the superimposed images from the two eyes into a single percept.*

There are essentially two theories of possible mechanisms through which sensory fusion could be accomplished. The first is that we simply *alternate* which one of the two monocular images we allow to reach consciousness; in other words, we never truly have a simultaneous binocular percept, just a rapid succession of alternating left and right monocular views. According to this theory, the two monocular views mutually inhibit each other, preventing us from seeing both at once. This is called the **alternation or suppression theory** of fusion (Fig. 3-2A) (Verhoeff, 1935). We can observe a form of this alternation under artificial viewing

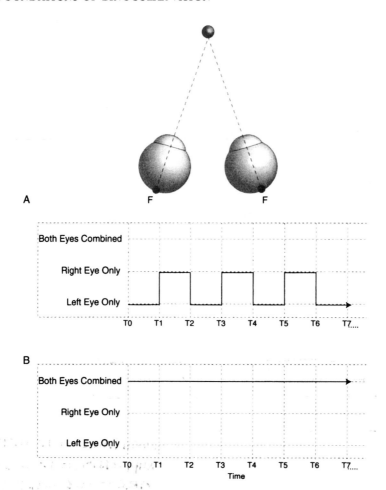

**Figure 3-2**    **A:** The alternation (suppression) theory states that the visual system never simultaneously combines information from the two eyes but instead alternates the percept under binocular viewing conditions from the image received by one eye to that received by the other eye. **B:** The fusion theory states that information from both eyes is perceived simultaneously as a single unified percept incorporating visual information from each eye.

conditions, in a phenomenon known as **binocular rivalry**, where grossly dissimilar images are presented to each eye. However, we do know from experiments on binocular rivalry how long it takes to switch attention from one eye's image to the other. The alternation theory of fusion can be proven to be false under more natural viewing conditions with similar images in both eyes because we can experience stereopsis even with presentations of a binocular stimulus that are too brief to alternate attention from one eye to the other. A reaction time experiment also disproves alternation theory under normal viewing conditions. In this experiment, an observer viewed a sine-wave grating under monocular or binocular conditions. A flash of light was superimposed on only one or the other eye's image of the grating during binocular viewing, and the observer's reaction time to detect the flash of light was measured. It was found that, regardless of the eye stimulated, the reaction time is equally short as it is for detecting the same flash of light during monocular viewing of the grating (Fox and Check, 1966). If one eye's image had been suppressed under binocular viewing conditions, the reaction time would have been longer when that eye was stimulated because the visual system would require additional time to shift attention to that eye. In addition to the above two experiments, Tyler (1983) notes that if the suppression theory held with similar images, we would perceive apparent motion between similar but disparate images as we alternately suppressed one then the other image. In other words if the two images are in slightly different visual directions, when the visual system switches from one eye's input to the other eye's input, the object would seem to move back and forth. This motion would be similar to that seen during the alternate cover test as part of an eye examination of patients with a heterophoria.

The competing theory, called **fusion theory,** states that we really are able to attend to similar images in both eyes at the same time (Fig. 3-2B). The two images are processed simultaneously instead of successively as postulated by the suppression theory. The fusion theory has been proven to be true under normal natural viewing conditions. However, this does not mean that it holds true under all viewing conditions. There are two minor exceptions to the fusion theory: (a) As stated above, binocular rivalry can indeed occur if we present dissimilar images to each eye. Under rivalrous stimulus conditions, not everything in both monocular visual stimuli is seen simultaneously by the two eyes; rather, the visual system will alternatively process information from each eye in sequence. Fusion is the rule with similar monocular images, and rivalry is the rule with dissimilar images. Keep in mind, however, that receiving very dissimilar images in each eye is rare when viewing natural scenes. (b) Even though we combine the two eyes' information, the visual system still has some access to the uncombined monocular information so that it can detect the small differences between the two eyes' images that give us binocular disparity and therefore stereopsis.

---

### ⚷ *Key Point*

*Fusion theory predicts that we see simultaneously from both eyes when the images are similar, even though we may not if they are dissimilar. Suppression theory predicts that we never see both images simultaneously, even if they are similar; we alternate attending to one eye's image, then the other's. The slowness of this alternation, despite the ability to perceive stereopsis rapidly, provides evidence for fusion theory.*

## THE LIMITS OF FUSION

Images formed on corresponding retinal points are seen as single, suggesting a point-to-point correspondence between the two retinas. However, as early as the 1800s, Wheatstone was able to show with stereograms that some images that were not formed on corresponding points could still be fused into single images. However, the single image was now seen at a different depth. This finding was augmented to define **Panum's fusional area** (Panum, 1858), an area on one eye's retina that, when stimulated together with a given single retinal point in the other eye, will produce a single binocular percept (Fig. 3-3). In other words, instead of a point-by-point correspondence between points in the two eyes, there is a point-to-*area* correspondence.

Panum's area shows that visual direction and single vision are not wholly synonymous concepts. Images within Panum's area can be fused and seen as single, yet still have slightly different visual directions in the two eyes. This can be demonstrated by presenting a pair of dichoptic nonius lines within a fused target. While the target itself is presented binocularly, one vertical nonius line is presented to each eye alone, such that if they are seen in the same visual direction, they will be aligned one above the other. Even though the target as a whole is fused, the nonius lines may not be precisely in alignment. The oculocentric directions of each nonius line are preserved even though the target is binocularly fused.

Panum's area is useful to binocular fusion because it allows for some imprecision or drift in eye movements without the introduction of diplopia. For example, the microdrifts and tremors that occur during fixation are uncorrelated between the two eyes, but Panum's area is large enough to allow fusion of the displaced imaged. Similarly, Panum's area reduces the potentially adverse effects of **fixation disparity**, a small binocular misalignment of the eyes in which fusion and single vision are achievable. In fact, Charnwood (1951) notes that the magnitude of a fixation disparity cannot exceed the size of Panum's area.

 *Key Point*

In order for an object to be perceived as single, its retinal images in the two eyes do not have to have identical visual directions. They need only fall within Panum's fusional area. However, differences in visual direction can produce a percept of depth.

The horizontal limits of Panum's fusional area may be measured by taking advantage of **Panum's limiting case** (Fig. 3-4). In Panum's limiting case, three

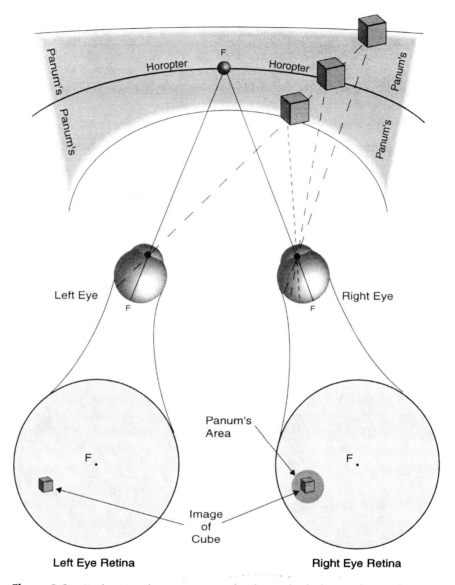

**Figure 3-3**   Single vision does not occur only when individual pairs of precisely corresponding points are stimulated in the two eyes; if this were so, the majority of points in space, imaged on nearby but noncorresponding points, would be seen as diplopic. Each point in one eye's field corresponds with a number of points in the fellow eye; that is, each point in one eye corresponds to a range of points, or an area called Panum's fusional area, in the fellow eye. Fusion of the single point in question with any point within Panum's area yields a percept of a single image; points outside Panum's area produce diplopia.

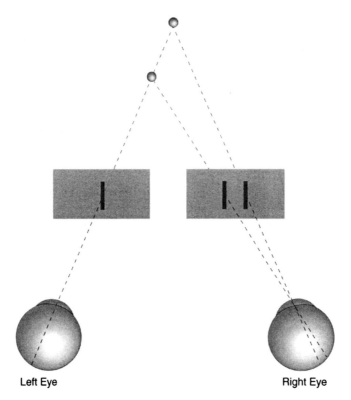

Left Eye                                                    Right Eye

**Figure 3-4**    In Panum's limiting case, three targets are presented, one to one eye and two to the fellow eye. One pair of
targets is foveated and fused, while the third target is placed along
the visual axis of one eye but on a nonfoveal point in the fellow
eye, yielding a binocular disparity. This is called a limiting case
because three targets is the minimum number needed to see
stereopsis in this experiment, as removal of any of the three targets abolishes the percept of depth.

targets are presented, one to one eye and two to the fellow eye. One pair of targets is foveated and fused, while the third target is placed along the visual axis of
one eye but on a nonfoveal point in the fellow eye, yielding a binocular disparity.
This is called a limiting case because three targets is the minimum number needed
to see stereopsis, as removal of any of the three targets abolishes the percept
of depth. To measure the extent of Panum's area (Fig. 3-5), we determine the
leftmost and rightmost positions of the unpaired third target (that is, create the
maximum crossed and uncrossed disparity) at which we still perceive that target
as single (that is, just when the target becomes diplopic 50% of the time). Measurement of the vertical limits of Panum's area requires using Polaroid filters
to separate the images of the two eyes and then moving the two targets apart

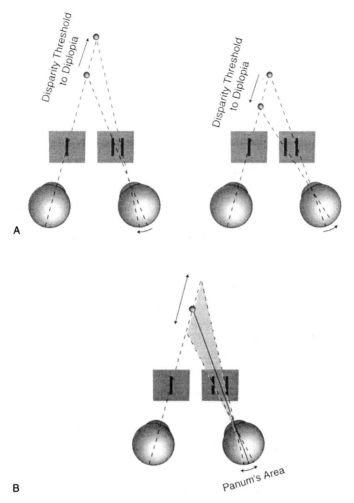

**Figure 3-5** The angular extent of Panum's fusional area may be measured by taking advantage of the target configuration that yields Panum's limiting case. The unpaired third target is moved laterally to yield uncrossed (**A**) and crossed (**B**) disparities until the diplopia limit is reached. The full extent of both of these ranges is the width of Panum's fusional area.

vertically until they are first seen as diplopic. Such measurements have demonstrated that Panum's area is three to six times larger horizontally than it is vertically; that is, it is elliptical. However, there is one flaw to these measurements: we are able to make horizontal fusional eye movements to make up for horizontal displacement of the targets, but vertical vergence eye movements are limited at best. This can be seen clinically; horizontal fusional eye movements, as measured with prism, are much larger than vertical fusional eye movements. These fusional eye movements tend to "stretch" Panum's area by allowing realignment of the retinal images as they are separated; our measurement of Panum's area would simply reflect the limits of our ability to compensate with eye movements. If we remove the influence of fusional eye movements from our measurements of Panum's area by briefly flashing the targets, presenting them too quickly to allow eye movements to occur, Panum's fusional area converts to a more circular shape (Mitchell, 1966). Therefore, our reduced ability to tolerate vertical disparities lies not in a smaller vertical extent of Panum's area but simply in a reduced ability to make vertical fusional eye movements.

The limits of fusion are also influenced by factors other than eye movements. For example, at the fovea, the extent of Panum's fusional area is between 5′ and 20′ of arc, depending on the measurement technique. However, once you move out of the fovea farther and farther into the retinal periphery, the size of the fusional area increases in direct proportion to the eccentricity (see Mitchell, 1966). This is not surprising because we know that receptive fields in the visual system increase in size in the periphery. In general, the size of Panum's area beyond 5° from the fovea is equal to 6% to 7% of the angle of eccentricity (Ogle, 1964).

**CLINICAL APPLICATION** | This central–peripheral difference in the size of Panum's fusional area has important clinical implications. In the periphery a patient can tolerate a 6% to 7% interocular image size difference (**aniseikonia**). However, a similar size difference will result in a loss of binocular fusion if stimuli are small and restricted to the central area. The larger extent of Panum's area in the periphery makes the peripheral visual field more tolerant of larger degrees of disparity and less likely to undergo adaptations to avoid diplopia, such as suppression. As a result, central suppression is much more likely to occur than peripheral suppression with image misalignment such as that caused by strabismus.

The fusion limit is also larger for sine-wave grating targets of low spatial frequency than it is for those of high spatial frequency (Schor et al., 1984). When changes in vergence are controlled for with nonius lines, it was found that as gratings presented to each eye were separated spatially, that is, as a binocular disparity was introduced, the size of Panum's fusional area increased with decreasing spatial frequency content of the target. The rate of change of the size of Panum's area was consistent with predictions of the limitations on Panum's area imposed by grating resolution. When sharp bars were used, however, the size of Panum's area was actually smaller than predicted by grating resolution. This suggests that the size of Panum's fusional area is determined by more than one mechanism that is yet to be uncovered.

Another important spatial effect on Panum's fusional area is the influence of other targets in close proximity. In other words, although a single target with a given binocular disparity may fuse easily, once a second disparate target is introduced nearby, the first target may fail to fuse (Braddick, 1979). This is a binocular analog of the monocular "crowding effect." It may be explained by the larger rate of change in disparity as a function of target separation (**disparity gradient**) for closely spaced targets than for widely separated targets; too pronounced a change in disparity over a short distance may produce a disparity outside the limits of Panum's area.

It is also possible for the size of Panum's fusional area to change, depending on the exposure duration of the target during measurement. The spatial limits of Panum's area increase with longer target exposure durations (Woo, 1974). However, that increase is probably a result of the introduction of fusional eye movements occurring during the longer exposure times. Temporal relationships in Panum's fusional area are best studied with mirror-image pairs of vertical sinusoidal wavy lines, one presented to each eye, whose amplitude of waviness changes over time. The binocular percept is that of a line that starts out flat, then bends sinusoidally toward and away from the observer, then flattens again, and so on. One can measure the largest spatial extent over which the line is seen as single by varying the maximum amplitude of the waviness beyond which the target becomes diplopic. This is repeated for several temporal frequencies of changes in waviness over time. With low-spatial-frequency lines (lines with widely separated waves), the horizontal fusion limit decreases in size as temporal frequency increases. However, temporal frequency has little effect on high-spatial-frequency sinusoidal lines (with closely spaced waves) (Schor and Tyler, 1981). Here, too, we see a distinction between the behavior of low- and high-spatial-frequency channels in binocular vision.

The effects of target orientation on the extent of Panum's area are harder to quantify, as rotations of targets in each eye also introduce confounding horizontal disparities that change in magnitude along the targets. In addition, cyclorotational eye movements tend to cancel out some of the effect of the rotation of the lines.

Changes in luminance within a range of 3 log units above threshold have little effect on the size of Panum's area (Siegel and Duncan, 1960). Similarly, increasing contrast for targets over a wide spatial frequency range has almost no effect on the extent of Panum's area (Schor et al., 1989).

**CLINICAL APPLICATION** | One goal of vision therapy is to improve fusion in patients with binocular problems because such patients typically have difficulty achieving or maintaining fusion. We therefore begin therapy using targets for which Panum's fusional area is largest; that is, large targets (low spatial frequency) moving slowly (low temporal frequency) in the periphery. As the patient's fusional abilities improve, we may then employ small foveal stimuli.

**CLINICAL APPLICATION** | Finally, the size of Panum's fusional area may be affected by the presence of strabismus. In small-angle strabismus, the size of Panum's area may be enlarged (Bagolini and Campobianco, 1965). Similarly, in anomalous retinal correspondence, which is discussed at the end of this chapter, the fusional ranges may also be abnormally large (Pasino and Maraini, 1966).

# MONOCULAR, DICHOPTIC, AND BINOCULAR INFORMATION

As we stated earlier, fusion is the process of combining two independent monocular views into a single percept of the visual world. Once combined, is the monocular information simply lost? Helmholtz argued that it could not be, since the information from each eye alone is what gives rise to binocular disparity and vergence responses. If the visual system totally merged the information together without keeping track of the eye of origin of the information, we would be unable to tell crossed from uncrossed disparities and make appropriate vergence responses to each. However, this does not necessarily mean that this information is available to consciousness; it may be used only internally within the visual system without our being aware of it.

This question has taken decades to be answered. Numerous experiments have been performed on **utrocular discrimination**; that is, the ability to determine which one of the two eyes has been stimulated under binocular conditions. The problem is that it is extremely difficult to totally remove cues that let the subject know which eye has been stimulated; for example, small differences in contrast sensitivity between the eyes, or a perceived shift in target position between the two eyes from a phoria, can provide this cue. However, when such factors are painstakingly controlled, it is found that humans with normal binocular vision are unable to make utrocular discriminations (Barbeito et al., 1985). The monocular information is lost to conscious perception.

The flip side of this is that we can independently present targets to each eye. This is called **dichoptic or bi-ocular stimulation.** Under such conditions we still achieve a single unified percept. This allows the scientist to control each eye's stimulus independently in an effort to study how the two eyes' images are combined and when this combination fails to occur. It also allows the clinician to determine if either of the two eyes is suppressing its information or to manipulate stimulus strengths in each eye to treat amblyopia under conditions of binocular viewing.

Even when individuals with normal binocular vision fuse the images from two eyes, the two eyes may not contribute equally to the binocular combination. One eye may in fact be "favored" over the other. We noted the effects of such ocular dominance on egocentric visual direction in Chapter 2, but ocular dominance may also affect how strong we must make the stimulus to each eye in order to get optimal fusion or binocular summation (see Chapter 6). Functional magnetic resonance imaging (fMRI) of the metabolic activity of the brain shows that the dominant eye activates a larger proportion of striate cortex than does the nondominant eye (Rombouts et al., 1996). However, exactly which eye is dominant may not always be a constant. The dominant eye can differ at distance and near or for different visual tasks.

**CLINICAL APPLICATION**  Do not assume that the dominant eye measured at distance will be the same as that measured at near. It was noted in Chapter 2 that eye dominance can affect the prescription of spectacle lenses or contact lenses. Different dominant eyes at distance and near may result in one eye being left slightly blurred at distance and the other eye at near.

# VERGENCE AND BINOCULAR VISION

Motor fusion is a vital component of binocular vision. If similar contours are not brought into alignment in the two monocular images, sensory fusion will be impaired if not impossible. Stereopsis is dependent on both sensory and motor fusion, especially motor fusion, as the disparities required for stereopsis are relatively small differences in the image position in the two eyes. Errors in motor fusion would greatly distort the depth information obtained from stereopsis or eliminate binocular depth perception. We discuss the process of interocular feature matching and the influence of motor fusion on this process in detail in Chapter 7. However, at this time it is appropriate to examine the effects of vergence errors on fusion.

Motor fusion (or vergence eye movement) is important for the maintenance of binocular vision in the presence of a **heterophoria**. A heterophoria (or phoria) is the position the eyes assume when one eye is covered or when the eyes are **dissociated** so that there are no demands for fusion; this is the *fusion-free position*. Covering one eye eliminates binocular vision, and arranging conditions so that there are dissimilar images in the two eyes suspends the need for vergence eye movements. When there is no need for vergence eye movements, the dissociated eyes assume an "at rest" position. The heterophoria, then, represents the **fusional vergence demand** once fusion is again required, that is, how much *more* the eyes must converge or diverge from their dissociated position to regain binocular vision (motor fusion). In other words, fusional vergence demand describes how much fusional vergence is required to compensate for the phoria.

**CLINICAL APPLICATION**

Patients have **esophoria** if they overconverge under dissociated conditions. Esophoria requires negative fusional vergence eye movements (divergence) to maintain fusion. Conversely, patients have **exophoria** if they underconverge under dissociated conditions. Exophoria requires positive fusional vergence eye movements (convergence) to maintain fusion. In orthophoria, the eyes remain aligned under dissociated conditions and theoretically there is no active demand for fusional vergence. A heterophoria is successfully **compensated** with fusional vergence eye movements such that binocular vision is maintained. An **uncompensated** heterophoria is referred to as a **strabismus**. In strabismus, the eyes are not able to achieve motor fusion, and the patient lacks binocular vision.

**CLINICAL PROCEDURE**

There are several clinical methods to measure a heterophoria. One important one is the **Maddox rod** method. The Maddox rod consists of a series of very high-powered cylindrical lenses that transform a spot source of light to a line segment or streak. When placed before one eye with the lenses oriented horizontally and the patient observing a light source, it produces dissociation by forming dissimilar images; one eye sees a vertical streak of light; the other eye sees the unaltered light source. The eyes will then assume the dissociated or heterophoria position. The patient will see the two images either superimposed (**orthophoria**) or separated (esophoria or exophoria). The magnitude of the separation is a measurement of the heterophoria. Clinicians use prisms to optically move the two images until they superimpose (effectively creating orthophoria). The Maddox rod can be used to measure horizontal as well as vertical ocular deviations.

# FIXATION DISPARITY

When asked to fixate a point using both eyes, some people do not do so precisely bifoveally; their convergence is inaccurate by a few minutes of arc such that one of their visual axes does not intersect the target point. This results in the **vergence angle** of the eyes (in other words, the angle between the visual axes of the two eyes) being slightly inaccurate such that the eyes are actually converged on a point in space in front of or behind the intended fixation target. That is, the **fixation point**, where the primary lines of sight of the eyes intersect, does not coincide with the location of the target they are asked to fixate. The target is still seen binocularly and singly, in that both images are formed within Panum's fusional area. The images of the fixation target simply are not formed on exactly corresponding points because of a small vergence inaccuracy, either a slight over-convergence (*eso fixation disparity*) or underconvergence (*exo fixation disparity*). A **fixation disparity** is a small purposeful error in vergence. Because the level of innervation maintained by the vergence eye movement system is determined by the magnitude and sign of a vergence error signal, this small persistent vergence error (the fixation disparity) serves as a stimulus for the vergence system to maintain its innervational level (Schor, 1983). In other words, in order for a fusional vergence to continue to compensate for a **heterophoria**, a fixation disparity must be maintained. Generally, larger fusional vergence responses require larger amounts of fixation disparity (for example, see Owens and Liebowitz, 1983). Hence, the magnitude of fixation disparity is directly related to the magnitude of the fusional vergence response required for binocular vision (Schor, 1979a). From a clinical perspective, large fixation disparities may signal the presence of binocular vision problems (for example, see Morgan, 1969).

**CLINICAL APPLICATION** | A fixation disparity of more than a few minutes of arc is an indicator of patients with potential binocular vision problems. The larger the fixation disparity, the more likely that a patient will be symptomatic.

As seen in Chapter 4, a fixation disparity will displace the measured horopter off the intended fixation target to where the actual fixation point lies. Because the positions of all of the other points along the horopter depend on the locus where the visual axes truly intersect, the entire horopter curve will be displaced closer or

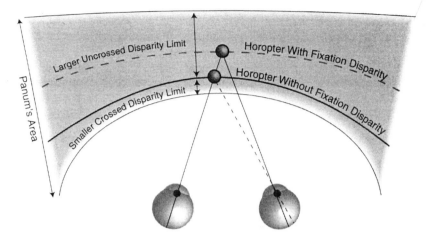

**Figure 3-6** In the presence of a fixation disparity, the horopter is displaced from a position in the middle of Panum's area to one that is closer to one limit of Panum's area.

farther from the intended fixation point. If you measure Panum's fusional area using the horopter in the presence of a fixation disparity, you find that the intended fixation target is not precisely in the middle of Panum's area. The overall size of the fusional area is still the same, and the horopter will still lie in the center of Panum's area, but the *measured* disparity limit on one side of the intended fixation target will be unequal to that on the other side of the fixation target (Fig. 3-6).

**CLINICAL APPLICATION** | This can lead to clinical problems. People with significant fixation disparities will have less tolerance for disparity changes in either the base-in or base-out direction. For example, if the horopter is displaced too far back from the intended fixation plane because of an exo disparity, the person will reach the limit of Panum's area when presented with just a small amount of crossed disparity. Any fixation disparity will also affect stereothreshold by displacing the target off the horopter (Cole and Boisvert, 1974).

Fixation disparity is measured clinically at distance or at nearpoint with simple targets, which generally consist of two parts: (a) some binocularly visible details that serve as a **binocular fusion lock**, and (b) two monocularly seen **nonius lines** (via Polaroid filters). The nonius lines are physically aligned with each other. One line is viewed by the right eye alone, and the other is seen by the left eye. If the patient has a fixation disparity, even though the binocularly viewed targets will be fused and therefore seen singly, one or both of the two nonius lines will be perceived as out of alignment even though they are actually physically aligned with the binocularly viewed target (Fig. 3-7). In other words, while the eyes are converging accurately enough to fuse the binocularly viewed target, the residual

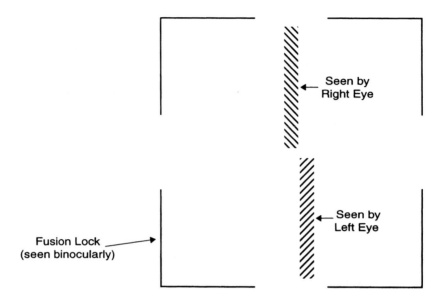

**Figure 3-7**   Clinical measurement of fixation disparity involves the viewing of a pair of nonius lines, one seen by each eye, that may be offset from each other like a vernier acuity target in the presence of a fixation disparity. Fusion is maintained by a fusion lock that is visible to both eyes.

vergence error (the fixation disparity) will create misalignment of the nonius lines because they no longer stimulate corresponding retinal points.

**CLINICAL PROCEDURE**   One of the original clinical instruments to take advantage of fixation disparity was the **Mallett box**. It, too, was a combination of a binocular fusion lock, in this case a set of letters, and monocular nonius lines, placed in a box with a light bulb inside. More modern devices include the **Bernell test lantern**, the **AO vectographic slide**, the **Borish card**, and the **Wesson card**. These devices all have fixed targets with nonius lines. In some, fixation disparity is measurable by noting the degree of nonius line misalignment on an adjacent scale. The Bernell test lantern is very similar to the Mallett box and has panels for both distance and nearpoint fixation disparity testing. The AO vectographic slide is a projector slide designed for the AO projector, so it is only a distance test. The other tests are for nearpoint only and can be either attached to the phoropter's nearpoint rod or held by the patient at his or her habitual working distance.

All of the above clinical tests are useful for crudely quantifying only one aspect of fixation disparity, the **associated phoria** (see below). To make a precise measurement of fixation disparity, we must turn to another instrument, the **disparometer**. The disparometer (Fig. 3-8) is unique because it employs a

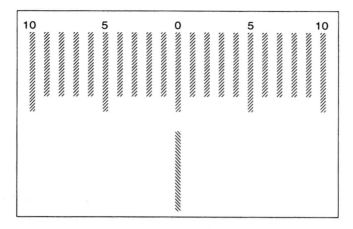

**Figure 3-8** The Wesson disparometer displays a single vernier line to one eye and a scale to the other eye. A fixation disparity displaces the perceived location of the vernier line along the scale. The Sheedy disparometer (not shown) works by a similar mechanism but instead uses a rotating wheel containing vernier targets of different directions and magnitudes of offset. The wheel is rotated until a target comes into view that is perceived as aligned by the patient, and the clinician reads the fixation disparity reading off the wheel.

series of physically offset nonius lines on a rotating wheel (Sheedy, 1980). The examiner turns the wheel, introducing different line offsets in the opposite direction until the subject perceives the lines as aligned. The examiner then reads off the size of the fixation disparity from the back of the rotating wheel.

**CLINICAL APPLICATION**

Fixation disparity and heterophorias are related and usually correlated, more so at near than at distance, in that an esophoria usually will have an eso fixation disparity, and an exophoric patient will more likely have an exo fixation disparity to maintain positive fusional vergence activity. However, this is only a general rule because the two measures do not always yield identical information. For example, some exophoric patients actually overconverge under binocular conditions, resulting in an eso fixation disparity. This clearly suggests that under binocular conditions, these patients are actually esophoric and using negative fusional vergence, not exophoric and using positive fusional vergence as predicted by the dissociated heterophoria test.

**CLINICAL PROCEDURE**

Fixation disparity measurements can be useful to the practitioner. Clinicians use prism in the management of binocular vision disorders. The use of prism can reduce the magnitude of fusional vergence activity required to maintain binocular vision. The concept is that placing a prism in front of the eye can optically move the image closer to the visual axis of the eye in its "at rest" position. This reduces the size of the dissociated heterophoria. Base-in (BI) prisms will move the image temporally, and base-out (BO) prisms will move the image nasally. The strength of the prism will determine the amount the image is moved. Because the prism reduces the need for fusional vergence, the measured fixation disparity should also become smaller.

If a prism neutralizes the heterophoria completely, orthophoria is created. **Orthophoria** can be interpreted as the absence of fusional vergence requirement. Hence, it would be expected that there should be no measurable fixation disparity. Clinicians now more often use direct measurements of fixation disparity to determine prism correction. The amount of prism needed to eliminate the fixation disparity is called the **associated phoria** (because fusion is present, the two eyes are "associated") (Ogle et al., 1967). The horizontal associated phoria is usually smaller than the horizontal dissociated phoria measurement (Tubis, 1954) because of the additional influence of prism adaptation under associated conditions (Schor, 1980). However, this measurement of fusional vergence demand under binocular conditions is felt to be a much more reliable indicator for success of a prism prescription.

Lenses can be used in the same way as prism because of the physiological interactions between the accommodative and vergence systems. It also means that errors in accommodation, through the relationship of accommodation to vergence (AC/A and CA/C ratios) may also produce or contribute to binocular vision anomalies. Plus lenses decrease the amount of accommodative convergence, so the patient will have to make up for it with more fusional convergence. This will decrease the amount of *eso* fixation disparity. Minus lenses have the opposite influence, and so will decrease the amount of *exo* fixation disparity (Hebbard, 1960). What this means is that lenses, instead of prisms, can be used to correct binocular vision anomalies (Schor and Narayan, 1982). Because minus lenses also increase the demand on the accommodative system, clinicians use this option infrequently.

We can probe the robustness of binocular fusion by increasing the vergence demand by introducing prism and then measuring how fixation disparity changes as a function of the power and direction of the prism. The resulting plot of these measurements is called a **forced vergence fixation disparity curve** (Fig. 3-9) (Ogle et al., 1967). Fixation disparity curves tell us how well the vergence system copes with demands on it. In this regard, a fixation disparity curve is a more dynamic measure than a single phoria or vergence measurement and therefore more indicative of how the patient will respond in the real world to visual tasks, particularly at nearpoint. In general, the fixation disparity increases with increasing prism strength (vergence demand), but the precise way in which a particular

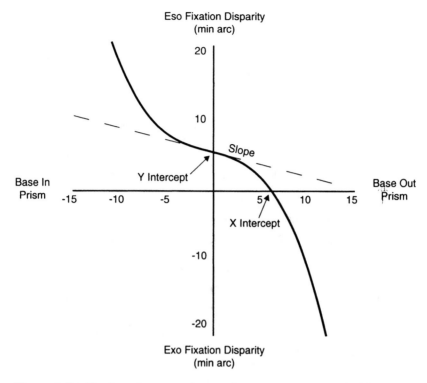

**Figure 3-9**    The forced vergence fixation disparity curve is generated by measuring the patient's fixation disparity in the presence of varying amounts of added prism and plotting the fixation disparity as a function of added prism. The features of note in the curve are the slope, the x-axis intercept (associated phoria), and the y-axis intercept (the magnitude of fixation disparity in the absence of prism).

patient responds to the increasing demand is what determines the shape of their fixation disparity curve.

On the *x*-axis of the forced vergence fixation disparity curve is the amount of prism used to induce negative and positive fusional vergence. The *y*-axis shows the amount and direction of the fixation disparity. Fixation disparity is usually measured in the following sequence: with no prism, 3 diopters BI, 3 diopters BO, 6 diopters BI, and 6 diopters BO. Base-in prism stimulates negative fusional vergence (divergence) and produces eso fixation disparity. Base-out prism stimulates positive fusional vergence (convergence) and induces exo fixation disparity. These points are plotted and connected, yielding the fixation disparity curve. Additional prism can be added, in an alternating BI and BO fashion, until the patient can no longer maintain fusion so that diplopia endpoints are reached to get the entire extent of the curve. The shape of the fixation disparity curve is usually sigmoidal, or S-shaped. The *y*-intercept indicates the amount of fixation disparity *without* added prism. The *x*-intercept, which denotes the amount of prism that produces zero fixation disparity, is the associated phoria.

The response of the vergence system to prism or lenses varies depending on the individual. Many patients will exhibit **vergence adaptation**, in which an applied prism or lens has a full effect initially but has less apparent effectiveness over time, sometimes over the course of only a few minutes or even seconds (Schor, 1979b). To understand vergence adaptation, we must understand the dual nature of the vergence system (Schor and Kotulak, 1986). When a prism is first introduced before a binocularly fixating individual, a fast, immediate response is generated in the **"fast" or disparity vergence system** (Rashbass and Westheimer, 1961). The goal of this fast response is to eliminate the retinal disparity created by the prism and to restore single binocular vision. In an effective system, this takes about 1 second or less to complete. The fixation disparity must remain in order to allow this fast system to continue to function.

But what happens after this? The continued output of the fast disparity vergence system provides the stimulus for activation of the second vergence system component, the **"slow" or vergence adaptation system** (Ogle and Prangen, 1953; Schor, 1979). The "slow" system increases the levels of tonic vergence. With activation of this second system to provide the vergence needed to compensate for the prism, less output of the fast system is required. Therefore, with reduced levels of fast disparity vergence, there should be reduced amounts of fixation disparity observed.

**CLINICAL APPLICATION** | Vergence adaptation is a "good" sign of a healthy vergence system (Carter, 1965). Patients who are poor adapters may run into difficulty (North and Hensen, 1981). It is known that the fast disparity vergence system may become fatigued. Under sustained demands, this could create symptoms of **asthenopia**, or eye strain. The slow vergence system, although slower to initiate its response, can continue to respond for long periods without fatigue. Patients with healthy slow vergence systems will adapt to prism easily (within limits of course), even that prescribed by clinicians. Vergence adaptation has been a troublesome mechanism for unwary clinicians, who will see their prescribed prism adapted to and the heterophoria they were prescribing for return. Patients who adapt well to prescribed prism are most likely indicating that they will not be helped by the permanent prescription of prism. This is why a prudent clinician will test patients for a few minutes with prism in the examination room before prescribing. The effectiveness of vision therapy for patients with binocular vision disorders has been attributed to its enhancement of vergence adaptation mechanisms (Schor, 1979b; North and Hensen, 1992).

It should be noted that the above discussion holds true only for horizontal vergence adaptation. The vertical vergence system is limited to less than 1° amplitude of response (Houtman et al., 1977) and lacks the fast fusional system (Rashbass and Westheimer, 1961). This makes patients more susceptible to the effects of vertical misalignments.

Forced vergence fixation disparity curves may be used to predict how patients will respond to prism and other stresses on the vergence system. The shapes of forced vergence fixation disparity curves can be classified into four basic types, as originally determined by Ogle and coworkers (1967) and shown in Fig. 3-10.

**CLINICAL APPLICATION** | Most patients (60% when tested at near and 70% at distance, according to Sheedy, 1980) show a **type I** curve. The fixation disparity changes relatively gradually with added prism until near the limits of their fusional vergence ranges, when fixation disparity increases more rapidly until diplopia is reached. There is a flatter central region of the curve with a steeper peripheral region.

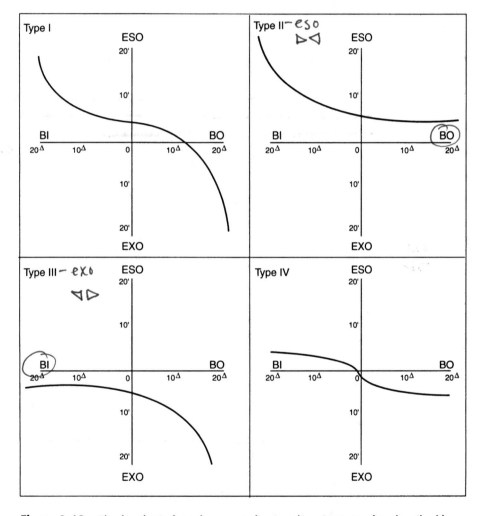

**Figure 3-10** The four basic forced vergence fixation disparity curves first described by Ogle are type I (symmetric), type II (flat on the base-out side), type III (flat on the base-in side), and type IV (little change with added prism) (Modified from Sheedy, 1980).

The central region is flatter because of the operation of vergence adaptation, with a relatively smaller fixation disparity increase with increasing prism power. Because the effective range of vergence adaptation is limited, beyond that range in the peripheral zones of the fixation disparity curve, "tails" emerge with fixation disparity increasing at a faster rate with prism because more is required to maintain fast (disparity) vergence system activity. The tail portion of the fixation disparity curve then is a region beyond the effective range of vergence adaptation. The type I curve is generally symmetrical with similar responses to base-in and base-out prism.

**CLINICAL APPLICATION**  |  The slope and extent of the flatter central portion of the curve give the clinician information about the robustness of binocular visual function. Fixation disparity curves with flatter slopes are usually associated with symptom-free patients because of the effective operation of vergence adaptation. Steeper slopes are often associated with symptomatic patients. They have a narrower range of vergence demands for which effective and comfortable binocular vision is maintained. One of the points of effectiveness of vision therapy is that it increases vergence adaptation capability, which is demonstrable after therapy with a flattening of the fixation disparity curve.

*ℓ SO*  ▷◁

Type II and type III curves are unidirectionally anomalous. The **type II** curve (25% of the population at distance or nearpoint) has a flat region on its *base-out* (convergent) side that may not cross the *x*-axis but is sharply curved on the base-in side. Most patients with type II curves have esophoria and show poor adaptation to base-in prism.

*ℓ X o*
◁▷

The **type III** curve (10% of the population when tested at nearpoint, 0% at distance), on the other hand, is flat on its *base-in* (divergent) side and steep on the base-out side. This is associated with high exophoria. These patients can handle forced divergence well but are intolerant of forced convergence.

**CLINICAL APPLICATION**  |  Type II fixation disparity curves are common in patients with esophoria and poor adaptation to base-in prism, whereas type III curves are typical of exophores, who cannot adapt to base-out prism.

**Type IV** curves (5% of the population at distance or nearpoint) show little change in fixation disparity with increasing vergence demand in any portion of the curve, even near the fusional limits. These curves may show no associated phoria; that is, no prism power that will neutralize the fixation disparity. This curve is rare but has been associated with aniseikonia and other sensory fusion problems.

There have been some attempts to generalize curve type to the effectiveness of therapeutic intervention (e.g., prism or lens prescription vs. vision therapy, etc.). At this time, there has not been conclusive clinical insight to base treatment on curve type alone. Also, there are some clinicians who feel that the classification of fixation disparity curves by type is somewhat artificial and that all curves may in fact be sigmoidal in shape and in fact subtypes of the Ogle type I curve.

CLINICAL
APPLICATION

The **associated phoria**, or the amount of prism that eliminates the fixation disparity, can be used as a prescribing benchmark. One half of the associated phoria prism prescription is considered a reasonable starting point for most patients.

A forced-vergence fixation disparity curve can also be generated to investigate vertical vergence function. Instead of horizontal prism, vertical prisms are used, base up and base down. Of course, because the vertical vergence system is capable of only smaller-amplitude responses than is the horizontal vergence system (Perlmutter and Kertesz, 1978), smaller amounts of prism are used, usually in 0.5 to 1.0 prism diopter increments. Vertical vergence fixation disparity curves are usually steeper than horizontal curves and linear, again pointing out the difference in robustness between the vertical and horizontal vergence systems. From a clinical standpoint, plotting a vertical vergence fixation disparity curve, although helpful, is not necessary for most patients.

CLINICAL
APPLICATION

Sustained nearpoint visual tasks produce stress on the entire binocular vision system, including vergence. Their effects have been shown by increased fixation disparity, increased associated phoria, and increased slope in the forced vergence fixation curve after 20 minutes of reading (Garzia and Dyer, 1986).

Use of open-loop accommodative testing conditions (using a pinhole to eliminate the ability to control accommodation via feedback from blur) has been found to decrease the magnitude of fixation disparity (Semmlow and Hung, 1979). This suggests that both accommodation (by its influence on accommodative vergence) and fusional vergence contribute to fixation disparity.

## *Anomalous Retinal Correspondence*

CLINICAL
APPLICATION

Strabismus can be considered to result from some defect in sensory and/or motor fusion processes. Conditions that make sensory fusion difficult (for example, media opacities such as a cataract, uncorrected anisometropia, or corrected anisometropia that includes aniseikonia) can lead to the development of strabismus. Strabismus is usually manifested as esotropia in children and exotropia when its onset is in adulthood. Disturbances in motor fusion, either through some functional disorder of the vergence system or as a result of damage to oculomotor neurons secondary to brain injury, can also produce strabismus.

When strabismus develops in a patient who has normal binocular vision with normal correspondence, the result will be the perception of visual confusion, where the two foveal images are seen superimposed on one another, and diplopia. Adult visual systems adapt poorly to the onset of strabismus, and these symptoms will persist. However, in a developing visual system with neuroplastic capabilities, such as that found in young children, neurophysiological processes or changes will occur to compensate for and adapt to the new eye position misalignment. The two mechanisms available to the individual are (a) suppression of one eye's image and (b) the creation of a new binocular projection system, a shifting in corresponding points called **anomalous retinal correspondence** (ARC). Note that the use of the word "retinal" in this term recognizes the fact that corresponding points are measured relative to retinal angles and does not connote that correspondence is anything other than a cortical phenomenon. In ARC, the two foveas will no longer correspond to each other. Stimuli presented to each fovea will be perceived in distinctly different locations. This phenomenon is the opposite of what occurs with visual confusion seen with normal correspondence.

In ARC, the fovea of the fixating eye corresponds to a nonfoveal region of the deviating, strabismic eye (von Noorden, 1985), so that under binocular viewing conditions the fovea of the fixating and the nonfoveal area of the deviating eye will both be stimulated by the object of regard. These two points will now correspond, indicating that they have similar projection values. In other words, there has been a precise shift in corresponding points that matches the angle of the strabismic deviation. This is called **harmonious anomalous retinal correspondence (HARC)**. Although there are other forms of anomalous correspondence in which the shifting of corresponding points is less precise (i.e., the overshifting or undershifting of so-called **unharmonious or paradoxical ARC**), HARC is the most common presentation.

**CLINICAL APPLICATION**   HARC is most likely to be observed when viewing objects in a normal environment or under testing conditions that are not grossly unusual, for example, without red–green filters or with optical instruments (stereoscopes).

The patient with strabismus and HARC will generally perceive the world in a normal spatial sense, without diplopia or confusion. Although diplopia and confusion are eliminated, binocular vision is of a rudimentary form, with severely reduced stereopsis resulting from the significant interocular acuity difference. In addition, the vergence eye movements are limited.

**CLINICAL PROCEDURE**   One way of testing retinal correspondence is the **Hering-Bielschowsky afterimage test** (Fig. 3-11). With this test, a vertical line afterimage is placed on the fovea of one eye by a bright strobe light from a camera flash. A horizontal line afterimage is then flashed onto the fovea of the other eye. If a patient has normal correspondence between the foveas, the vertical and horizontal line afterimages will be perceived as superimposed and will be recognized as a cross. In HARC, because the two foveas no longer correspond, the two line afterimages will be seen separated from one another. This separation, if

Left Eye Image          Right Eye Image

Normal Retinal Correspondence (NRC)

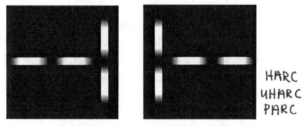

HARC
UHARC
PARC

Abnormal Retinal Correspondence (ARC)

**Figure 3-11**   The Hering-Bielschowski afterimage test is a test for retinal correspondence. A vertical line afterimage is generated in the left eye (the fovea projects to the gap in the line, corresponding to a fixation point on the flash strobe) and a horizontal afterimage in the right eye. In normal retinal correspondence (NRC), a perfect cross is seen, denoting projection of the two foveas to the same locus in space, whereas in anomalous retinal correspondence (ARC) there is a relative displacement of the two afterimages.

measured, will be the exact angular distance from the nonfoveal point in a strabismic eye to the fovea of that eye; in other words, by the angle of the strabismic deviation (Burian, 1947).

## SUBJECTIVE VERSUS OBJECTIVE ANGLE OF STRABISMUS

Because of this shift in correspondence, the patient with strabismus and HARC has no subjective appreciation that the eye is deviated. Two subjective tests to measure the angle of deviation that are used frequently in the evaluation of strabismus are the **Maddox rod** and the **Hess-Lancaster test.** The Maddox rod test has already been described earlier in this chapter. The Hess-Lancaster test is especially useful because it may be used to measure the angle of deviation in the nine cardinal positions of gaze.

**CLINICAL PROCEDURE**

The Hess-Lancaster test is a simple but elegant test of the subjective angle of strabismus. To conduct the test, patients wear anaglyphic (red–green) glasses with the red filter in front of the right eye and face a large white screen in a relatively darkened room. The examiner projects a green circle of light from a hand-held torch onto the screen. The patient then projects a red annulus of light onto the screen. Because of the anaglyphic arrangement, the patient is dissociated, seeing a green circle with the left eye and a red annulus with the right eye. Fusion is suspended because of the dissimilar images seen by each eye. The patient's task is to place the red annulus around or to superimpose it on the examiner's green circle. When this occurs, corresponding points in the two eyes are stimulated. If the patient has normal retinal correspondence, the two test stimuli will be located on the screen in the locations in which the two foveas project. For example, if a patient has orthophoria the examiner's green circle and the patient's red annulus will be located in the same place on the screen. If a patient has a right esotropia, the red annulus will be placed to the left of the green circle. Of course, the patient will perceive the two as superimposed (remember, that's the patient's task, put the annulus around the circle), but the two stimuli will be separated on the screen. The magnitude of the deviation can be determined by measuring the separation of the two stimuli on the screen. The Hess-Lancaster test is used extensively in the diagnosis of paretic eye muscles and the evaluation of **noncomitant strabismus**; that is, strabismus in which the angle of strabismus is not the same in all positions of gaze.

Tests like the Maddox rod (Fig. 3-12) and Hess-Lancaster will yield no demonstrable imbalance and apparent orthophoria (orthotropia in this case) in strabismus patients with HARC. With the Maddox rod, the light and the light streak will each be stimulating corresponding points (the fovea of one eye and a nonfoveal

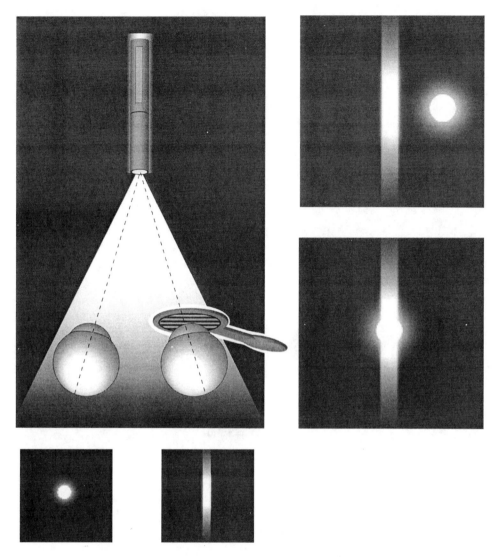

**Figure 3-12** The Maddox rod test can be used as a subjective test of the angle of strabismus or phoria. The patient views a penlight with both eyes, with the right eye covered by a Maddox rod, a red plastic filter with cylindrical surfaces. The left eye sees a point of light, while the right eye sees a linear image; in this case, with the Maddox rod held along the horizontal meridian, a vertical line of light is seen. The relative positions of the point and line of light provide the subjective angle of strabismus or phoria. When the line is to the left of the point, exotropia or exophoria exists; conversely, when the line is to the right, esotropia or esophoria exists. Prisms may be used to move the images to quantify the subjective angle of strabismus. When the line precisely intersects the point, orthotropia or orthophoria is demonstrated.

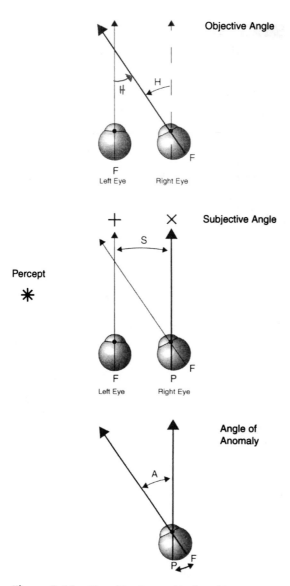

**Figure 3-13**   The objective angle of strabismus is the angle between the foveas' lines of sight as measured by objective cover testing. The subjective angle of strabismus is the separation between the images in the two eyes, as revealed by subjective superimposition of half-views in an amblyoscope. In normal retinal correspondence, these two angles are equal. In anomalous retinal correspondence, these angles differ. The difference is the angle of anomaly.

but corresponding point in the deviating eye). With the Hess-Lancaster, the circle and the annulus will be superimposed by the patient on the screen at the same location. Therefore, you will have a patient with a distinct strabismus on cover testing (the **objective angle of strabismus**, or angle of deviation of the two eyes) but orthophoria (orthotropia) when tested for the **subjective angle of strabismus**, their subjective perceptual alignment of targets presented to the two eyes. In other words, even though you measure an overt strabismus, the patient's percept is that of single vision rather than diplopia.

---

 *Key Point*

*The difference between the subjective and objective strabismus angle measurements is called the **angle of anomaly** (Fig. 3-13). In HARC, the angle of anomaly is equal to the angle of strabismus.*

---

## MECHANISMS OF ARC

There have been several theories advanced to explain the nature of the correspondence shift observed in strabismus. Burian advanced the **sensory theory** (Burian, 1947). He speculated that the correspondence changes related to some unknown but purely sensory processes as a sensory adaptation to the strabismus. This sensory shift takes time to generate and occurs with practice or opportunity for implementation. The patient with a constant angle of strabismus is therefore the most likely to give this sensory mechanism the opportunity to adapt to the strabismus. However, not all strabismic patients have a constant angle of strabismus. The sensory theory cannot adequately explain the presence of anomalous correspondence that occurs in patients with intermittent strabismus, variable-angle strabismus, or the **covariation phenomenon** often seen in these cases. Covariation refers to the phenomenon of the apparent coexistence of both normal and anomalous correspondence in the same individual with strabismus (Sireteneau and Fronius, 1989). Covariation takes several forms. The most common form can be observed in cases of intermittent exotropia of the divergence-excess type: anomalous retinal correspondence is seen when the strabismus is manifest, but normal correspondence is seen when the eyes are fused. In addition, the angle of anomaly can undergo daily variations in proportion to daily fluctuations of the objective angle of strabismus (Hallden, 1952). Also, if multiple tests of correspondence are performed on the same strabismic patient, normal correspondence may be seen on some tests and anomalous correspondence on others.

Another theory dependent on a motor-based mechanism (the **motor theory**) has been articulated by Morgan (1961). In this theory, the change in correspondence is "registered" with the oculomotor system. That is, the pattern of innervation to the oculomotor muscles is registered as altering egocentric direction. The registration process can be thought of as a communication between oculomotor centers and the perceptual system responsible for visual direction. The same innervational signal produces both an eye movement and a change in retinal correspondence.

Another concept of the origins of anomalous correspondence is that it involves **abnormal disparity vergence stimulus detection**. In this way, ARC is thought to be the neurophysiological dysfunction that causes the strabismus (Kerr, 1998). The anomalous disparity vergence system produces eye movements yielding motor fusion between what are clinically observed as anomalous retinal points, producing strabismus. Accommodation and accommodative vergence also produce covariation in the objective angle of strabismus and the angle of anomaly (Daum, 1982).

**CLINICAL APPLICATION** | By whatever mechanism, ARC will develop in visual systems that have the neuroplasticity to do so. An adult who develops strabismus will not have anomalous correspondence or suppression. The ARC is usually associated with strabismus of childhood origin. It is also reversible within this time frame. As the covariation phenomenon suggests, most people with ARC retain the neurophysiology needed to also maintain normal retinal correspondence. This is demonstrated clinically by different outcomes on the many tests of correspondence available to the clinician.

For any strabismus to be effectively treated, that is, to recover normal sensory and motor fusion, ARC must be eliminated. Although it is generally reversible, ARC presents with varying degrees of embeddedness or resistance to alteration. The form of anomalous correspondence associated with esotropia is more resistant than that found in exotropia. Some forms of ARC are so deeply embedded that even after surgical realignment of the eyes, the strabismus recurs, reestablishing the original angle of strabismus and the anomalous retinal correspondence. This **postsurgical drift** seems to support the anomalous disparity vergence theory of ARC. Sometimes with postsurgical reduction of the strabismic angle of deviation, corresponding points change to match the new, smaller angle of deviation. The permanent elimination of ARC, allowing the full recovery from strabismus, usually requires some active form of vision therapy intervention.

## SUMMARY AND KEY POINTS

- **Binocular fusion** is the process by which two images, one from each eye, give rise to a unified percept of one single object.

- The classical model of fusion was composed of three hierarchical degrees. First, **simultaneous perception** of each eye's image; second, the combination or **flat**

**fusion** of the two images into a single percept; and third, **fusion with stereopsis**. Although proven not to be truly hierarchical, **this classification** by Worth is still referred to in the clinical literature.

- **Motor fusion** denotes the use of vergence eye movements to align corresponding contours in the two eyes, whereas **sensory fusion** is the process by which the visual cortex combines the two monocular views into one unified percept. **Suppression** represents the absence of sensory fusion.

- **Sensory fusion** requires similarity between the two monocular images. Disruption of sensory fusion may occur with unequal retinal image quality between the two eyes or the absence of motor fusion to align the monocular images.

- The **alternation or suppression theory** states that fusion is the result of the rapid succession of alternating left and right monocular views, which mutually inhibit each other. Alternation theory does not occur under natural viewing conditions with similar images in both eyes. However, a form of alternation can be observed when grossly dissimilar images are presented to each eye (**binocular rivalry**). The slowness of alternation in binocular rivalry argues against the application of alternation theory to binocular perception with similar images.

- The **fusion theory** states that we simultaneously process similar images in both eyes. This theory holds true under normal natural viewing conditions. The two minor exceptions to fusion theory are (a) binocular rivalry and (b) access to the uncombined monocular information by the visual system under binocular conditions, which is necessary for stereopsis.

- Fusion occurs when a point in one eye and a corresponding region (**Panum's fusional area)** in the other eye are stimulated. Fusion, therefore, is not synonymous with identical visual direction. Images within Panum's area can be fused and seen as single yet still have slightly different visual directions in the two eyes. Panum's area allows for some imprecision or drift in eye movements without the introduction of diplopia.

- The horizontal extent of Panum's area may be measured using **Panum's limiting case,** the minimum target configuration needed to see depth. Measurement of its vertical limits has demonstrated that Panum's area is three to six times larger horizontally than it is vertically. This difference **results from** our reduced ability to make vertical fusional eye movements as horizontal fusional movements "stretch" Panum's area horizontally.

- The limits of fusion increase (a) in direct proportion to the eccentricity of the stimulus, (b) with decreasing spatial frequency content of the target, (c) with longer target exposure, and (d) in the presence of strabismus. The visual system is more tolerant to differences in image size between peripheral stimuli because of the larger extent of Panum's area in the periphery. Therefore, **central suppression** is more common than peripheral suppression.

- Presenting additional targets in close proximity to objects that are normally fused may produce a binocular "crowding effect" as a result of a steep **disparity gradient,** which prevents those objects from being fused.

- With low-spatial-frequency stimuli, the horizontal fusion limit will decrease in size as temporal frequency increases. However, temporal frequency has little effect on high-spatial-frequency stimuli.

- The effects of target orientation on the extent of Panum's area are difficult to quantify because of cyclorotational eye movements and unequal retinal horizontal disparity along the length of the targets.

- Changes in luminance or contrast have little effect on the extent of Panum's area.

- Once combined, monocular information is no longer available to consciousness but is used by the visual system to give rise to binocular disparity and vergence responses. **Utrocular discrimination**, the ability to determine which one of the two eyes has been stimulated under binocular conditions, does not occur in humans with normal binocular vision. This allows for the presentation of **dichoptic or bi-ocular stimulation** to determine if either of the two eyes is suppressing its information or to manipulate stimulus strengths in each eye to treat **amblyopia** under conditions of binocular viewing.

- The dominant eye may differ with different visual tasks, for example, when viewing at near as opposed to distance.

- A **heterophoria** (or **phoria** for short) is the *fusion-free* position the eyes assume when one eye is covered or when the eyes are **dissociated.** It represents the **fusional vergence demand** once fusion is again required.

- **Esophoria** is an overconvergence under dissociated conditions and requires **negative fusional vergence**, whereas **exophoria** is an underconvergence that requires **positive fusional vergence** eye movements (convergence) to maintain fusion. In **orthophoria**, the eyes remain aligned, so there is no active demand for fusional vergence. **Prisms** for superimposition of the monocular views or the **Maddox rod test** can be used to detect heterophoria.

- A heterophoria is successfully **compensated** with fusional vergence eye movements such that binocular vision is maintained. An **uncompensated** heterophoria is referred to as a **strabismus**.

- A **fixation disparity** occurs when the images of the fixation target are not formed on exactly corresponding points as a result of a slight vergence inaccuracy, either overconvergence (*eso fixation disparity*) or underconvergence (*exo fixation disparity*). Fixation disparity is a purposeful error: it is used by the vergence eye movement system to maintain its innervational level and compensate for a heterophoria.

- The degree of fixation disparity is proportional to the fusional demand. Large fixation errors may indicate the presence of binocular vision disorders.

- A fixation disparity will displace the measured horopter closer or farther relative to the intended fixation target. A significant displacement will result in a reduced tolerance for disparity changes in either the base-in or base-out direction.

- Fixation disparity can be measured by tests that generally consist of two parts: (a) binocularly visible details that serve as a **binocular fusion lock** and (b) two monocularly seen **nonius lines**. Although the nonius lines are physically aligned with each other, a patient with a fixation disparity will perceive them as being out of alignment. The misalignment is usually, but not necessarily, in the same direction as the heterophoria.

- The **associated phoria** is the strength of base-in or base-out prisms needed to eliminate the fixation disparity. It is distinguished from the *dissociated* phoria, which occurs in the absence of fusion.

- Lenses, as well as prisms, can be used to correct binocular anomalies. **Plus lenses** decrease the amount of accommodative convergence required, thus decreasing the amount of *eso* fixation disparity. **Minus lenses** have the opposite effect.

- A **forced vergence fixation disparity curve** can be used to probe the robustness of binocular fusion. The **disparometer** is used to measure the fixation disparity evoked by varying strengths of base-in and base-out prisms.

- Many patients exhibit **vergence adaptation**, in which an applied prism or lens has a full effect initially but has less apparent effectiveness over time. The initial effect results from a fast, immediate response generated in the **"fast" or disparity vergence system,** which eliminates the retinal disparity created by the prism and restores single binocular vision. However, there is also a **"slow" or vergence adaptation system,** which increases the levels of tonic vergence, reducing the output of the "fast" system and reducing the amount of fixation disparity. Such adaptation is a sign of a healthy vergence system.

- Forced vergence fixation disparity curves may be used to predict how patients will respond to prism and other stresses on the vergence system. Most patients exhibit a **type I fixation disparity curve** in which the fixation disparity changes little with the addition of prism until near the limits of the fusional vergence ranges. The steeper the central slope of the fixation disparity curve, the more likely the patient will be symptomatic of binocular visual problems. **Type II** and **type III** curves represent intolerance of forced divergence and convergence, respectively. The rare **type IV** curve exhibits little change in fixation disparity even near the limits of vergence but may have no prism power that will neutralize the fixation disparity.

- **Sustained accommodation** during nearpoint tasks such as reading increases fixation disparity, associated phoria, and the slope of the forced vergence fixation curve.

- In strabismus, patients with normally developed binocular vision and normal correspondence will experience diplopia. Developing visual systems can adapt to the misalignment of the eyes by either suppressing one eye's image or creating a new binocular projection system, a shift in corresponding points called **anomalous retinal correspondence** (ARC).

- In **harmonious anomalous retinal correspondence (HARC),** there is a precise shift in corresponding points that matches the angle of the strabismic deviation. HARC is more likely to be observed when viewing under natural conditions. Overshifting or undershifting results in **unharmonious or paradoxical ARC**. Retinal correspondence is tested with the **Hering-Bielschowsky after-image test**.

- The patient with HARC will generally perceive the world in a normal spatial sense, without diplopia or confusion. Although they exhibit a distinct strabismus on cover testing (a measure of the **objective angle of strabismus**), tests for the **subjective angle of strabismus**, such as the **Maddox rod test** or **Hess-Lancaster test**, will result in a finding of orthophoria. The difference between the subjective and objective strabismus angle measurements is called the **angle of anomaly**.

- There are three theories that attempt to explain ARC: (a) **Sensory theory** states that a sensory adaptation compensates for a constant angle of strabismus. (b) **Motor theory** proposes that the change in correspondence is "registered" with the oculomotor system, signaling both an eye movement and a change in retinal correspondence. (c) An **abnormal disparity vergence stimulus detection** system produces eye movements yielding motor fusion between what are clinically observed as noncorresponding points.

- Regardless of the cause, visual systems with sufficient plasticity will develop ARC if given the opportunity. Therefore, any treatment of strabismus must occur after normal retinal correspondence is achieved. This is best accomplished in childhood, when ARC is generally reversible. Treatment of exotropia is generally more successful than treatment of esotropia.

## QUESTIONS

1. Under what conditions might a patient have motor fusion but not sensory fusion? When could a patient have sensory fusion without motor fusion?

2. An infant exhibits exotropia. When this infant reaches adulthood, how do you predict his or her binocular visual system will function? How would this patient's binocular visual system differ from that of a patient who suddenly develops exotropia in adulthood?

3. If a centrally viewed stimulus is located close enough to the observer to be beyond the limits of binocular motor fusion, in what two ways could the patient fuse the stimulus without changing its distance from the eyes?

4. What is the difference between a fixation disparity and a heterophoria?

5. If you were to prescribe a prism correction for a patient with a fixation disparity curve as shown in Fig. 3-9, what type and amount of prism would you prescribe and why?

6. Why is it that a patient with HARC will see a cross in the Maddox rod test but not in the Hering-Bielschowsky test?

# BIBLIOGRAPHY

BAGOLINI B *and* CAMPOBIANCO NM (1965). *Subjective space in comitant squint.* Am. J. Ophthalmol. 59:430–442.

BARBEITO R, LEVI DM, KLEIN SA *and* LOSHIN DS (1985). *Stereo-deficients and stereoblinds cannot make utrocular discriminations.* Vis. Res. 25:1345–1348.

BRADDICK OJ (1979). *Binocular single vision and perceptual processing.* Proc. R. Soc. Lond. B204:503–512.

BURIAN HM (1947). *Sensorial retinal relationship in comitant strabismus.* Arch. Ophthalmol. 64:336–368.

CARTER DB (1965). *Fixation disparity and heterophoria following prolonged wearing of prisms.* Am. J. Optom. 42:141–152.

CHARNWOOD L (1951). *Retinal slip.* Trans. Int. Optics Cong. Br. Opt. Assoc. Cond. 165–172.

COLE RG *and* BOISVERT RP (1974). *Effect of fixation disparity on stereoacuity.* Am. J. Optom. 51:206–213.

DAUM K (1982). *Covariation in anomalous correspondence with accommodative vergence.* Am. J. Optom. 59:146–151.

FOX R *and* CHECK R (1966). *Binocular fusion: a test of the suppression theory.* Percept. Psychophys. 1:331–334.

GARZIA RP *and* DYER G (1986). *Effect of nearpoint stress on the horizontal forced vergence fixation disparity curve.* Am. J. Optom. Physiol. Optics 63:901–907.

HALLDEN U (1952). *Fusional phenomena in anomalous correspondence.* Acta. Ophthalmol. [Suppl.] 37.

HEBBARD FW (1960). *Foveal fixation disparity measurements and their use in determining the relationship between accommodative convergence and accommodation.* Am. J. Optom. 37:3–26.

HOUTMAN WA, ROZE JH *and* SCHEPER W (1977). *Vertical motor fusion.* Doc. Ophthalmol. 44:179–185.

KERR KE (1998). *Anomalous correspondence—the cause or consequence of strabismus?* Optom. Vis. Sci. 75:17–22.

MITCHELL DE (1966). *A review of the concept of "Panum's fusional areas."* Am. J. Optom. 43:387–401.

MORGAN MW (1961). *Anomalous correspondence interpreted as a motor phenomenon.* Am. J. Optom. Arch. Am. Acad. Optom. 38:131–148.

MORGAN MW (1969). *Anomalies of binocular vision. In:* Vision of Children, MJ Hirsch and RE Wick, eds., Chilton, Philadelphia.

NORTH R *and* HENSEN DB (1981). *Adaptation to prism-induced heterophoria in subjects with abnormal binocular vision or asthenopia.* Am. J. Optom. Physiol. Optics 58:746–752.

NORTH R *and* HENSEN DB (1992). *The effect of orthoptic treatment upon the vergence adaptation mechanism.* Optom. Vis. Sci. 69:294–299.

OGLE KN (1964). Researches in Binocular Vision. Hafner, New York.

OGLE KN *and* PRANGEN A (1953). *Observations of vertical divergences and hyperphorias.* Arch. Ophthalmol. 49:313–334.

OGLE KN, MARTENS T *and* DYER J (1967). *Oculomotor Imbalance in Binocular Vision.* Lea & Febiger, Philadelphia.

OWENS DA *and* LIEBOWITZ HW (1983). *Perceptual and motor consequences of tonic vergence. In:* Vergence Eye Movements, MC Schor *and* K Ciuffreda, eds., Butterworths, Boston.

PANUM PL (1858). Physiologische Untersuchungen über das Sehen mit zwei Augen, Schwers, Kiel.

PASINO L *and* MARAINI G (1966). *Area of binocular vision in anomalous retinal correspondence.* Br. J. Ophthalmol. 50:646–650.

PERLMUTTER AL *and* KERTESZ AE (1978). *Measurement of human vertical fusional response.* Vis. Res. 18:219–223.

RASHBASS C *and* WESTHEIMER G (1961). *Disjunctive eye movements.* J. Physiol. 159:339–360.

ROUMBOUTS SARB, BARKHOF F, SPRENGER M, VALK J *and* SCHELTENS P (1996). *The functional basis of ocular dominance: functional MRI (fMRI) findings.* Neurosci. Lett. 221:1–4.

SCHOR CM (1979a). *The relationship between fusional vergence eye movements and fixation disparity.* Vis. Res. 19:1359–1367.

SCHOR CM (1979b). *The influence of rapid prism adaptation upon fixation disparity.* Vis. Res. 19:757–765.

SCHOR CM (1980). *Fixation disparity: a steady state error.* Am. J. Optom. 57:618–631.

SCHOR CM (1983). *Fixation disparity and vergence adaptation. In:* Vergence Eye Movements: Basic and Clinical Aspects, CM Schor and KJ Ciuffreda, eds., Butterworths, London.

SCHOR CM *and* Kotulak JC (1986). *Dynamic interactions between accommodation and convergence are velocity sensitive.* Vis. Res. 26:927–942.

SCHOR CM *and* NARAYAN V (1982). *Graphical analysis of prism adaptation, convergence accommodation and accommodative convergence.* Am. J. Optom. Physiol. Optics 59:774–784.

SCHOR CM *and* TYLER CW (1981). *Spatio-temporal properties of Panum's fusional area.* Vis. Res. 21:683–692.

SCHOR CM, WOOD I *and* OGAWA J (1984). *Binocular sensory fusion is limited by sensory resolution.* Vis. Res.24:661–665.

SCHOR CM, HECKMANN T *and* TYLER CW (1989). *Binocular fusion limits are independent of contrast, luminance gradient and component phases.* Vis. Res. 29:821–835.

SEMMLOW JL *and* HUNG G (1979). *Accommodative and fusional components of fixation disparity.* Invest. Ophthalmol. 18:1082–1086.

SHEEDY JE (1980). *Fixation disparity analysis of oculomotor imbalance.* Am. J Optom. Physiol. Optics 57:632–639.

SIEGEL H *and* DUNCAN CP (1960). *Retinal disparity and diplopia vs. luminance and size of target.* Am. J. Psych. 73:280–284.

SIRETENEAU R *and* FRONIUS M (1989). *Differences in the pattern of correspondence in the central and peripheral visual field of strabismic observers.* Invest. Ophthalmol. Vis. Sci. 30:2023–2033.

TUBIS RA (1954). *An evaluation of vertical vergence tests on the basis of fixation disparity.* Am. J. Optom. Arch. Am. Acad. Optom. 31:624–635.

TYLER CW (1983). *Sensory processing of binocular disparity. In:* Vergence Eye Movements: Basic and Clinical Aspects, CM Schor and KJ Ciuffreda, eds., Butterworths, Boston.

VERHOEFF FH (1935). *A new theory of binocular vision.* Arch. Ophthalmol. 13:151–175.

VON NOORDEN GK (1985). *Burian and von Noorden's Binocular Vision and Ocular Motility:* Theory and Management of Strabismus, 3rd ed., CV Mosby, St. Louis.

WOO GCS (1974). *The effect of exposure time on the foveal size of Panum's area.* Vis. Res. 14:473–480.

WORTH C (1921). Squint—Its Causes, Pathology and Treatment. C Blakiston's Son, Philadelphia.

# 4

# The Horopter

## THE HOROPTER

We know from Chapter 2 that images formed on corresponding points in the two eyes will be perceived as coming from the same visual direction. Our discussion about corresponding points has treated corresponding points in the visual field one pair at a time. However, discussions of individual pairs of corresponding points do not provide the full story of how we perceive the visual world. Our visual neurons must encode all of the corresponding and noncorresponding points for *each* location in the binocular visual field simultaneously in order to fuse the world around us and see depth. Therefore, in order to understand how we perceive visual space as a whole, we must examine how *groups* of corresponding or noncorresponding points are processed. The locus of all points in visual space that are imaged on corresponding points in each eye when the eyes are converged to aim at a particular fixation point is called the **theoretical point horopter**. The horopter is a spatial map of corresponding points across the retina. It just so happens that the set of all points in visual space that are imaged onto corresponding points in each retina also appear to be at the same distance from the observer as the fixation point, having zero disparity, and so may be thought of as an "equidistant horopter." The horopter is therefore a way of representing how we perceive three-dimensional visual space, but it is also useful in explaining other aspects of binocular vision such as fusion and stereopsis. We should note that the entire theoretical point horopter extends both horizontally and vertically from the fixation point. However, the vertical axis of the horopter is less well understood, so we focus our discussion on a slice of the horopter along the horizontal plane, called the **longitudinal or horizontal horopter**. Not only does this make the horopter easier to understand, but this plane alone is most important to our binocular space perception and how we perceive three-dimensional physical space under a variety of conditions. For a full discussion of the theory underlying the horopter, see Tyler (1983).

Where in visual space might you expect each pair of corresponding retinal points to project while a subject fixates on a single location in space? Let us

**81**

consider one possible scenario: that all corresponding points are evenly spaced in each eye at precisely equal angles relative to the oculocentric primary visual direction. The two foveas, each representing the oculocentric primary visual direction, are corresponding points. A displacement by a degree off the fovea in one eye and an equal displacement off the fovea in the same direction in the other eye would therefore locate another pair of corresponding points. If this model is valid, the set of all possible pairs of corresponding points would be stimulated by objects lying anywhere on a circle that intersects the fixation point and the nodal points of the two eyes. This theoretical horopter circle is called the **Vieth-Müller circle** (refer to Fig. 2-17), named after the scientists who proposed this arrangement of corresponding points, or the **geometric horopter** because it predicts the shape of the horopter solely by the geometry, or angular arrangement, of corresponding points in each eye.

To determine if the horopter actually coincides with this theoretical Vieth-Müller circle, we must be able to empirically measure the horopter on human subjects. If the measured horopter does indeed lie on the Vieth-Müller circle, it may be concluded that our corresponding points are precisely evenly spaced relative to the

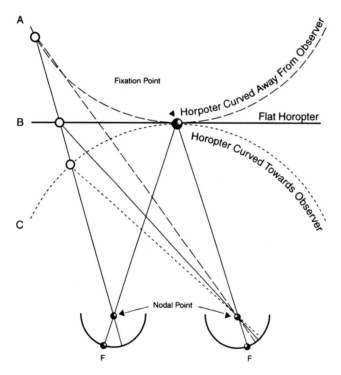

**Figure 4-1**    Different horopter shapes, ranging from concave to convex, would result from different pairings of corresponding points in the two eyes.

fovea. Conversely, if the horopter falls off the Vieth-Müller circle, the corresponding points could not be arranged in such an orderly manner; an angular excursion of a degree from the fovea in one eye would have to be paired with a slightly *different* angle in the other eye to stimulate a pair of corresponding points (Fig. 4-1).

## METHODS OF MEASURING THE HOROPTER

Because we cannot stimulate retinal points directly in human subjects, we must determine the location of corresponding points in each eye by placing objects in physical space so that its images in each eye are formed on corresponding points. With the eyes stationary, that is, with convergence symmetrically fixed on a given fixation target (the target is on the midline between the two eyes), we can then map out the horizontal location of all points in physical space whose images stimulate corresponding retinal points. The horopter represents that set of corresponding points.

The question that remains is how to measure whether or not the images of an object are formed on corresponding points. Luckily, we already know some facts about corresponding points that can help us to solve this problem. First, corresponding points are perceived as having identical visual directions in the two eyes. We can therefore split the image of an object into two independent, segregated images, each presented to one eye, and see where the object must be placed in space to yield a percept of the image in each eye coming from identical visual directions.

We also know that corresponding points have no binocular disparity. The horopter shows us all of the points in space that are perceived as being *at the same distance from the eye as the fixation point*. All of the points on the horopter will therefore have zero disparity and be seen in a flat plane equidistant to the fixation point. We may then record all points in physical space that appear to be at the same distance as the fixation point as lying on the horopter. In addition, all points seen as equidistant will require no fusional eye movements as one, then the other, point is viewed.

Remember that if images are displaced off the corresponding retinal points in one direction, we get *crossed disparity;* in the other direction, we get *uncrossed disparity*. The horopter therefore also represents the locations in visual space of the boundaries between crossed and uncrossed disparities as we fixate a particular point. The horopter will, in addition, be the place in space where we are *most sensitive to changes in depth* because, as the disparity changes sign from crossed to uncrossed, objects will appear to change from being closer than the fixation point to farther away than the fixation point.

If images are formed on noncorresponding points that are sufficiently widely separated, a diplopic perception will be produced. As locations in space deviate more from the horopter, crossed or uncrossed disparity will be introduced, and eventually diplopia will occur as the limits of Panum's area are reached. We can therefore think of the horopter as the *center of the range in which we have single vision*.

These facts all lead to several ways in which the horopter can be measured, called the **horopter criteria**:

- **Identical visual directions.** When two targets, each presented to one eye, are perceived as lying in a single visual direction, the images of those targets must be formed on corresponding retinal points (Tschermak, 1900).
- **Equidistance (or stereoscopic depth matching).** That is, locations perceived as lying at the same distance from the observer as the fixation point define a horopter. This is also called the **apparent frontoparallel plane (AFPP) horopter** because every point on this horopter is perceived as lying in a plane parallel to the subject's head and equidistant from it at the same distance as the fixation point (Meissner, 1854).

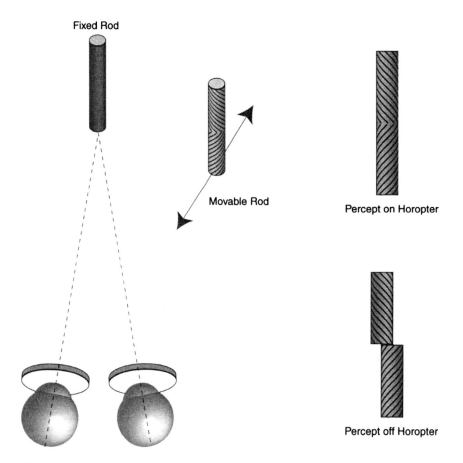

**Figure 4-2**    The nonius horopter is measured by exposing only one-half of the view of a test rod to each eye. As the two eyes fixate a binocularly viewed fixation rod, the test rod is moved closer to or farther from the observer. When the two half-views of the test rod are perceived as aligned, they are seen in identical visual directions and therefore stimulate corresponding points in the two eyes.

- **Singleness (or haplopia).** Objects on or near the horopter will be seen singly; those far removed from the horopter in either direction will be diplopic. Objects on the horopter lie in the middle of the zone of singleness, Panum's fusional limits.
- **Minimum stereoacuity threshold.** The finer the stereoscopic threshold, the closer a point is in space to the horopter (Tschermak, 1900).
- **Zero vergence.** Points in space seen as equidistant will not stimulate a motor fusional response (Ogle, 1964).

---

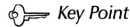 *Key Point*

*Of these horopter criteria, the two most commonly used are the* **identical visual direction** *and* **stereoscopic matching (apparent frontoparallel plane)** *methods.*

---

The **identical visual direction horopter** is measured by comparing two rods (Fig. 4-2). One rod is viewed by both eyes and serves as the fixation point.

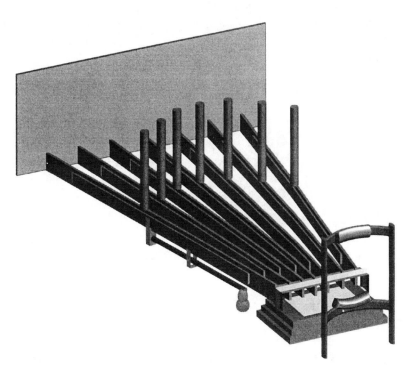

**Figure 4-3** Apparatus for measuring the nonius horopter. The device for isolating the views of each eye (grid or Polaroid filters) is not shown. The central rod is the fixation rod. The remaining rods are movable in tracks and are adjusted by the subject.

The other rod is viewed so that one eye can see only the bottom half of the rod while the other eye can see only the top half of the rod. This can be achieved by the use of oppositely oriented Polaroid filters on the top and bottom halves of the rod and in front of the two eyes to segregate the images of the two eyes. It can also be accomplished by having each eye view the test rod through a grid such that one eye then the other sees alternate parts of the rod, a technique known as the **grid nonius method**. The subject moves the rod forward and backward until both half-images are seen as lying in the same *visual direction*. That is, the top and bottom half-images of the rod appear to line up perfectly, one above the other, and a single continuous rod is seen. This task is akin to removing the break in a vernier acuity target, but in this case each eye sees only one line of the target. The point in space at which the two half-images are seen in an identical visual direction is then marked. If this procedure is repeated for several lateral positions or eccentricities of the measuring rod from the fixation point in a horopter apparatus (Fig. 4-3), a plot of the set of corresponding points, that is, the horopter, is produced. In actuality, this plot is not exactly a perfect narrow line but is instead a thick line because most subjects demonstrate a few seconds of arc of error in their directionalization. This thickness increases as the test rod is moved more peripherally relative to the fovea because of the elevated spatial localization thresholds in the peripheral retina. The identical visual direction horopter is difficult to measure, but it can be argued that this is the only truly correct horopter criterion because it is the only one that directly measures identical visual direction, the true definition of corresponding points.

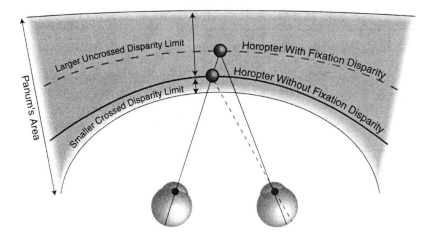

**Figure 4-4**    Fixation disparity displaces the horopter so that it is no longer in the center of Panum's fusional area. This decreases the width of the fusional range on one side of the horopter. Smaller amounts of disparity than normal will then result in diplopia.

The horopter will precisely intersect the fixation rod only when no **fixation disparity** exists. Fixation disparity, which is discussed later in this chapter, is a small inaccuracy in vergence angle. When a fixation disparity exists, the horopter will be displaced inward (for an eso fixation disparity) or outward (for an exo fixation disparity) relative to where the physical fixation rod lies. This displacement occurs because the eyes are not really aiming at the physical fixation rod; rather, they are aimed at a true fixation point slightly in front of (eso fixation disparity, i.e., overconvergence) or behind it (exo fixation disparity, i.e., underconvergence) (Fig. 4-4). The horopter is then simply shifted toward where the visual axes of the two eyes truly are crossing, that is, the actual fixation point.

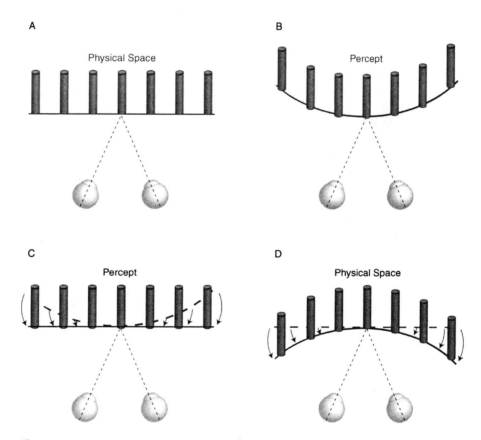

**Figure 4-5** Measuring the apparent frontoparallel plane (AFPP) horopter. When the test rods physically lie in the objective frontoparallel plane (**A**), they may be perceived as curving away from the observer (**B**). The subject then moves the rods inward until they are perceived as being in the frontoparallel plane (**C**), which causes the rod settings to curve inward (**D**). The rod positions follow the shape of the horopter.

---

## 🗝 Key Point

*The horopter can theoretically serve as another method to determine the presence of fixation disparity in a patient as well as its effects on the perception of visual space by that patient. Practically, however, it is unlikely to be used because its measurement is time-consuming.*

---

The **equal-distance or stereoscopic depth-matching horopter** (also known as the **apparent frontoparallel plane method**) is a more precise procedure for measuring the horopter and is easier to do with untrained subjects (Fig. 4-5). This horopter criterion takes advantage of the fact that corresponding retinal points, by definition, have zero retinal disparity. If an object produces monocular images that have zero disparity, the visual directions of their images must also be identical. In the AFPP horopter, the subject views a number of rods while fixating the middle rod. The subject then adjusts the distances of all of the other rods until they all appear to be *at the same distance away as the middle rod* in a plane parallel to the subject's face. The horopter itself will be curved, but the percept of the subject will be that of a flat plane. It is important to note that

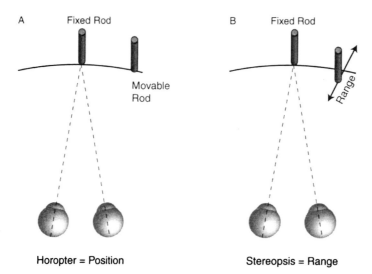

Horopter = Position     Stereopsis = Range

**Figure 4-6    A:** The position at which the rod is placed in the horopter apparatus (the constant error) reflects the location of the horopter. **B:** The variability of the horopter settings provides a measure of stereoacuity.

the shape of the frontoparallel plane as perceived by the subject will be the *mirror image* of the horopter settings. When subjects move a rod closer than fixation, they do so because the ~~horopter~~ ⟨original perceived frontoparallel plane⟩ is farther away from fixation and they are trying to compensate for this by moving the rods inward to make their positions appear in alignment to them. A fortunate side effect of this method is that the examiner can actually see the shape of the horopter directly from the subject's placement of the rods in the apparatus. The disadvantage of the AFPP method is that it fails to reflect the effects of fixation disparity, as does the identical visual directions horopter. – **The AFPP method may, in fact, exhibit effects due to fixation disparity.**

The horopter is related to the absolute placement of the rods in space, that is, the *bias* in the rod settings, and stereoscopic thresholds can be obtained from the *variance* of those settings, or our sensitivity at detecting binocular disparities between the images of the rods (Fig. 4-6). Images on slightly noncorresponding points may be fused into a single percept, so long as they lie within Panum's fusional area. The **singleness or haplopia horopter** in fact measures the extent of Panum's fusional area at the fovea and at eccentric locations (Fig. 4-7). Here,

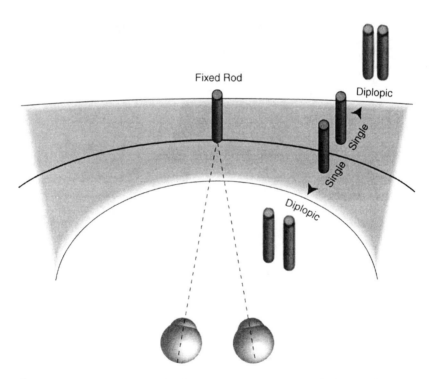

**Figure 4-7**  The singleness (haplopia) horopter is measured by bifoveally fixating the fixation rod, then moving a test rod inward until it is seen double; this process is then repeated for farther distances. The range in which the rod is seen as single represents Panum's fusional area, and the center of this range is taken as being the location of the haplopia horopter.

the arrangement of the rods is similar to that for measuring the AFPP horopter. One rod is always fixated; then a second test rod is moved closer to the subject until diplopia threshold is reached (that is, the rod first appears double). This process is then repeated moving the rod farther away. Between these two limits is a zone of singleness within which the rod appears single or fused even though its images are disparate. Measurements are made with test rods at several eccentricities on either side of the fixated rod. The center of this zone of singleness is taken to be the singleness horopter. The haplopia horopter indicates where corresponding points lie. The width of the zone of singleness reflects Panum's area, the zone of singleness surrounding corresponding points in which noncorresponding points are still seen as single (see Fig. 4-8). Once an object is far removed from the haplopia horopter, in other words, is outside of Panum's area, it will be perceived as diplopic. However, just as in the nonius horopter, the presence of fixation disparity can bias the location of the haplopia horopter.

The **maximum stereoacuity horopter** (or minimum stereoacuity *threshold*) is measured by fixating on a central rod while measuring stereoscopic thresholds for a second, more eccentric rod, that is, determining the smallest stereoscopic disparity or change in depth that can be detected for that rod (Fig. 4-9). This horopter relies on the observation that we are most sensitive to changes in disparity from zero disparity and less so from changes relative to a nonzero, or standing,

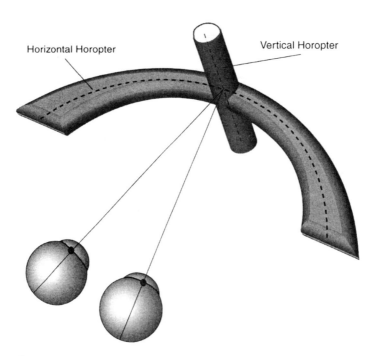

**Figure 4-8**   Fusion horopter for both horizontal and vertical disparities. The thickness of the horopter represents Panum's fusional area.

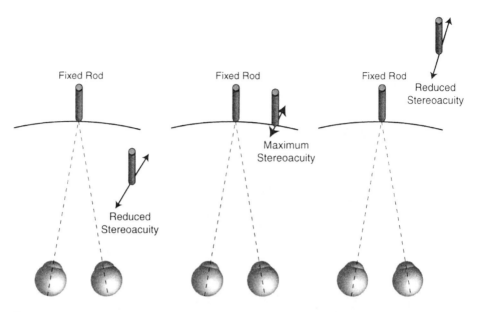

**Figure 4-9**  The maximum stereoacuity horopter is determined by measuring stereo-scopic thresholds (that is, the minimum rod displacement needed to see a change in depth) for various starting rod distances. The distance at which stereoacuity is optimal (the disparity thresholds are lowest) is the location of the horopter.

disparity. Here we start with the test rod at the same perceived distance as the fixation point. We then move it in depth until the subject just perceives it as being at a different distance. We repeat this for different target distances. The measurement is obtained by determining the *variance* of the rod settings that are seen as lying at the same distance. The location in space at which the variance is the smallest corresponds to the location of that eccentric point on the horopter because we will be most sensitive to changes in disparity when we change from zero disparity (on the horopter) to a finite disparity (off the horopter). All other distances will yield larger stereoacuities (variances in distance) because we are less sensitive when comparing two finite disparities to each other (Blakemore, 1970). The problem with this technique is that it is extremely time-consuming and difficult and therefore is not of practical use.

The **zero vergence horopter** criterion is perhaps the most difficult horopter to measure because it requires measurements of extremely small fusional movements of the eyes using sensitive objective eye movement recording equipment. It has never been measured empirically. In this technique, the subject would view the fixation target, and a second target would be flashed momentarily. If the test target fell on noncorresponding points in the two eyes, the exposure of the test target elicits a motor fusional response from the subject (Fig. 4-10). The vergence system attempts to minimize the amount of disparity in the test target,

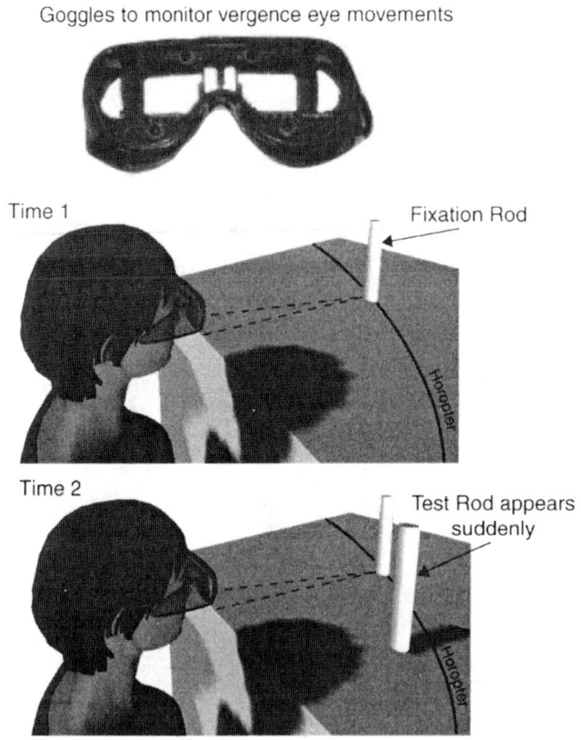

Goggles to monitor vergence eye movements

Time 1                                    Fixation Rod

Time 2                                    Test Rod appears
                                          suddenly

**Figure 4-10**   The zero-vergence horopter requires
highly sensitive eye movement monitoring devices. While
the subject views the fixation rod, a second rod is momentarily exposed. If the second rod is perceived to be
in a different depth plane, that is, at a different distance,
a reflexive vergence eye movement will be made.

even if this means creating a little disparity at the fixation target by changing the
vergence angle of the eyes. In other words, if the test target has a binocular disparity because it lies off the horopter, it would serve as a stimulus to the vergence
eye movement system; if the test target lies on the horopter, no vergence eye
movement will be noted. Therefore, to measure this horopter, one would need to
look for all points in the visual field that did not stimulate fusional eye movements
when the subject bifixated a central fixation target.

It is important to note that for all of the horopter criteria, horopters are
typically measured with the eyes fixating a target at the same vertical height as the
eyes and a fixation rod at a particular distance from the observer along the vertical
midline of the head. This is to ensure **symmetric convergence** (the same angle
of vergence in each eye). With vertical gaze displacements or asymmetric convergence, the shape of the horopter is affected, as we will see shortly.

## THE SHAPE OF THE EMPIRICAL HOROPTER
## AND ITS ANALYSIS

The Vieth-Müller circle is defined by three points: the fixation point and the entrance pupils of the eyes. For any point on the circle, the angle between that point, the entrance pupil, and the fixation point for the left eye (angle $\alpha_1$) is equal to same angle for the right eye (angle $\alpha_2$). For points off the Vieth-Müller circle, angles $\alpha_1$ and $\alpha_2$ are unequal (Fig. 4-11). Angles $\alpha_1$ and $\alpha_2$ are called **external longitudinal angles** to signify that they are external to the eye because we cannot directly measure these angles within the eye. We use them to infer the angles inside the eye as formed by both the layout of corresponding points on the retina and the bending of light onto those points by the optics of the eye. The Vieth-Müller circle is, therefore, the loci of all corresponding retinal points *as influenced by the optics of the eye*. As we will see shortly, optical changes can affect angles $\alpha_1$ and $\alpha_2$.

The value **R** represents the ratio of the tangents of the two external longitudinal angles at any point on the horopter:

$$R = \frac{\tan \alpha_2}{\tan \alpha_1}$$

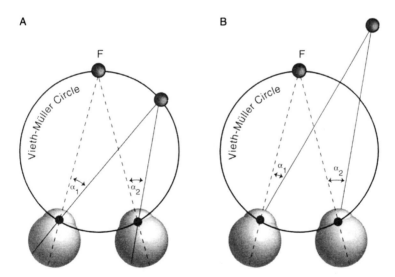

**Figure 4-11**  **A:** The angular separation between two points in space in the left eye's retinal image ($\alpha_1$) and the right eye's image ($\alpha_2$) will be equal when the two points lie on the Vieth-Müller circle. **B:** If the second point does not lie on the Vieth-Müller circle, angles $\alpha_1$ and $\alpha_2$ will not be equal.

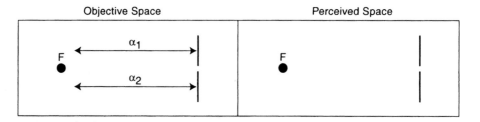

**Figure 4-12**    When $R = 1$, objective space matches perceived space. When an observer aligns two halves of the test rod (each seen by one eye alone) in the ~~AFPP~~ horopter
nonius
apparatus, they will in fact be aligned in objective space.

In other words, $R$ states the **relative magnification** of the retinal images between the two eyes. When $R = 1$, then the left and right eye magnifications are equal in the two eyes. This is true for all points on the Vieth-Müller circle. Another way of stating this is that when targets lie at the same angle relative to the fixation point in *objective* space, they must be on the Vieth-Müller circle, where $R$ is equal to 1, for the targets also to be seen as lying at the same angle relative to the fixation point in *perceived* space (Fig. 4-12).

For all points off the Vieth-Müller circle, $R \neq 1$. Here, the physical targets are not actually lined up in physical space, although they are perceived as being lined up. This is because one eye's image is magnified or minified relative to that of its fellow eye (Fig. 4-13). When $R > 1$, angle $\alpha_2$ exceeds angle $\alpha_1$ in physical space; that is, the right eye's image is magnified relative to that of the left eye. When $R < 1$, $\alpha_1$ is the greater angle, signifying that the left eye's image is relatively magnified.

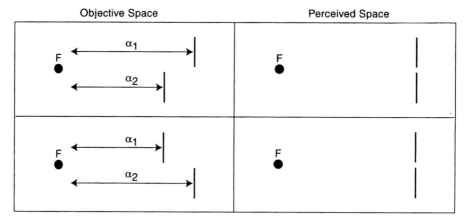

**Figure 4-13**    When $R \neq 1$, objective space and perceived space are not in agreement. When an observer aligns two halves of the test rod (each seen by one eye alone) in the ~~AFPP~~ horopter apparatus, they are in fact not aligned in objective space.
nonius

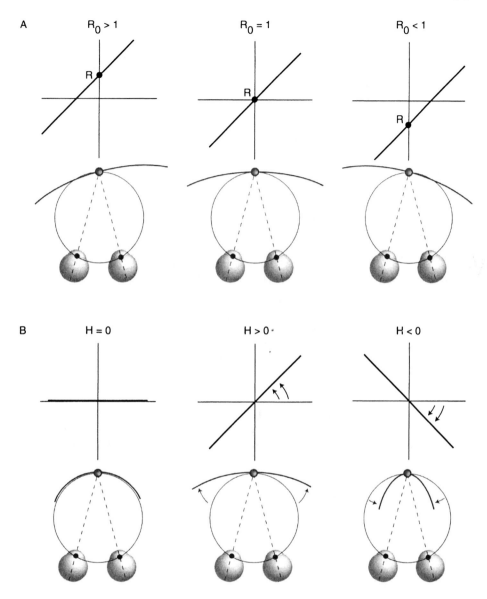

**Figure 4-14**    The analytical plot is a graph of $R$ versus angle $\alpha_2$. **A:** The $y$-intercept of the analytical plot, $R_0$, is determined by the slope of the horopter at the fixation point. **B:** The slope of the analytical plot, $H$, is determined by the degree of curvature of the horopter.

    By plotting the value of $R$ for each data point on the horopter as a function of the magnitude of the angle $\alpha_2$, we obtain what is called the **analytical plot** (Fig. 4-14). Without expounding on the mathematics of this plot, we are interested in two values obtained from it: its slope, $H$, and its $y$-intercept, $R_0$. That is, the analytical plot is simply the graph of the equation:

$$R = H(\tan \alpha_2) + R_0$$

The value $R_0$ tells us the value of the tangent ratio $R$ measured at the fixation point, that is, the ratio of the magnification of the image size in one eye relative to that of the image in the fellow eye. This relative magnification results in a tilting or skewing of the horopter relative to the frontal plane (Fig. 4-14A). If $R_0 = 1$, there is no skewing of the horopter; the horopter has a flat slope at the fixation point. This is usually the case in the normal visual system. When $R_0 \neq 1$, there is a **uniform relative magnification** (equal magnification at every retinal location) of one eye's image across the visual field, tilting the horopter and one's percept of the world. This can occur with optical magnification or minification of one eye's image relative to that of the fellow eye.

**CLINICAL APPLICATION** | One cause of relative magnification is **optical aniseikonia**, which occurs when unequal spectacle lens correction of the two eyes produces image size or shape differences. When $R_0 > 1$, the left eye's image is larger, and the horopter is rotated toward that eye, and when $R_0 < 1$, the right eye's image is larger, and the horopter skews toward the right eye. The magnification difference (in percent) is given by:

$$M = (R_0 - 1) \times 100$$

When we measure the horopter empirically, we find that it does not coincide with the theoretical Vieth-Müller circle. The horopter tends to be less sharply curved than the Vieth-Müller circle (Fig. 4-15) (Ogle, 1932). The difference in

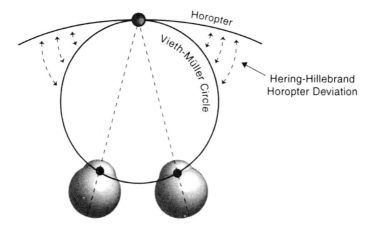

**Figure 4-15**   The Hering-Hillebrand deviation is the displacement of the empirical horopter off the Vieth-Müller circle.

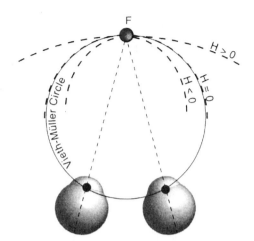

**Figure 4-16**  When the nonuniform magnification factor, $H$, is equal to zero, the horopter lies on the Vieth-Müller circle (that is, the Hering-Hillebrand deviation is zero). When $H$ is less than zero, the horopter falls inside the Vieth-Müller circle. Values of $H$ exceeding zero indicate that the horopter falls outside of the Vieth-Müller circle.

curvature between the horopter and the Vieth-Müller circle, as measured at the fixation point, is called the **Hering-Hillebrand horopter deviation**, and its value, **$H$**, can be calculated from the horopter data. This deviation shows that corresponding points are not laid out in an evenly spaced distribution between the two eyes. It tells us that our perception of space is *warped* a little. The value of $H$ tells us the relative curvature of the horopter (Fig. 4-16; see also Fig. 4-14B). When the measured horopter lies on the Vieth-Müller circle, $H$ is equal to zero. When $H$ is a positive value, the horopter is less curved than the Vieth-Müller circle, and when $H$ is negative, the horopter is more curved than the Vieth-Müller circle. The value of $H$ is typically in the range of +0.1 to +0.2, indicating a horopter flatter than the Vieth-Müller circle. $H$ is a measure of **nonuniform relative magnification** across the visual field, that is, how magnification changes across the visual field because of a deviation of the horopter from an exact geometric (angular) layout. Thus, the horopter cannot be explained fully by optical means; it also reflects *neural* magnification by the arrangement of corresponding points in the retina.

The positive value of $H$ in human subjects can be attributed to a layout of corresponding points that creates a relative magnification of the temporal retina relative to the nasal hemiretina. In monocular partitioning experiments, where subjects are asked to judge the midpoint of a line (that is, bisect the line), it is found that subjects overestimate the length of the line segment on its temporal side and underestimate it on the nasal side. This is because the local signs in the nasal retinal are spaced closer together (**nasal packing**) than those of the temporal retina; that is, the eccentricity of a given point in the nasal retina is less than that of its corresponding point in the temporal retina of the fellow eye. Local signs are not laid out equiangularly, as Vieth and Müller proposed; rather, there is an asymmetry in the spacing of retinal points between the nasal and temporal retinas, which in turn produces an asymmetry or "stretching" between corresponding points. Because of the different angular positions of a temporal retinal point in one eye and its corresponding nasal retinal point in the other eye, corresponding points cannot arise from locations on the Vieth-Müller circle.

The precise shape of the empirical horopter is a function of the *fixation distance* used when measuring it. The horopter is concave toward the observer and less curved than the Vieth-Müller circle for near fixation and slightly convex at far viewing distances. That is, with greater fixation distances, the horopter curves more and more away from the observer, eventually becoming convex (Fig. 4-17). The **abathic distance** is that viewing distance at which the apparent and objective frontal planes coincide; that is, the horopter truly is flat. At the abathic distance,

$$H = \frac{2a}{b}$$

where *2a* is the interpupillary distance and *b* is the fixation distance.

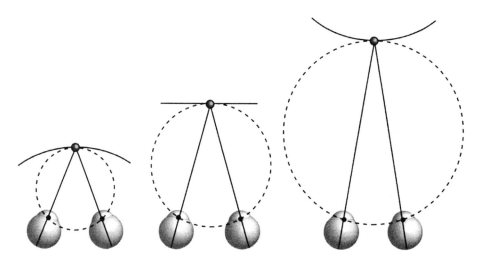

**Figure 4-17**  With increasing fixation distance, the curvature of the horopter changes so that it goes from being convex to flat (at the abathic distance), than concave. However, the changes in curvature of the horopter mirror changes in curvature of the Vieth-Müller circle, yielding no net change in the value of *H*.

The abathic distance is typically about 6 m from the observer (Ames et al., 1932).

It should be noted, however, that the curvature of the Vieth-Müller circle is also changing proportionately with increased fixation distance. The net result is that the Hering-Hillebrand deviation (*H*) remains the same at all fixation distances. That is, although the absolute curvature of the horopter and the Vieth-Müller circle change with viewing distance, the difference in curvature of the horopter relative to the Vieth-Müller circle does not. The constancy of the value of *H* across viewing distances means that the layout of corresponding points in the two retinas remains constant with changes in vergence (Flom and Eskridge, 1968).

So far, we have discussed the horizontal (longitudinal) horopter but have ignored the **vertical horopter**. At nearpoint fixation distances, the theoretical vertical horopter is a straight line parallel to the head and intersecting the Vieth-Müller circle at the fixation point (Fig. 4-18A). When measured empirically, the vertical horopter tilts away from true vertical (Fig. 4-18B) (Nakayama, 1977). The

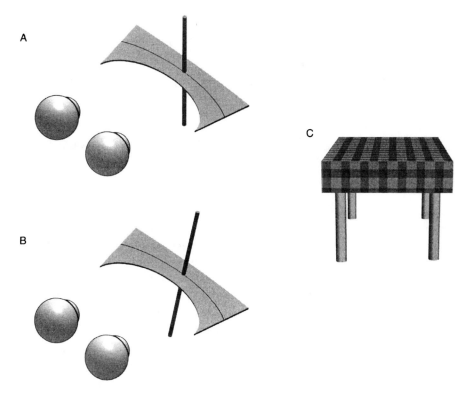

**Figure 4-18** **A:** The vertical horopter should theoretically be parallel to the head.
**B:** When measured empirically, the vertical horopter tilts away from the observer.
**C:** Our percept of horizontal surfaces is as being tilted slightly upward.

vertical horopter actually inclines with its top farther away from the observer than its bottom. However, the amount of tilt changes with viewing distance, with the vertical horopter being less inclined relative to the visual axis with near fixation and more inclined with distance fixation. This inclination increases until, at distance, the empirical vertical horopter tends to lie parallel to the ground below eye level. This probably is a consequence of the fact that most natural horizontal surfaces at distance are below eye level. These surfaces are perceived by us as we look off at the horizon as being tilted slightly upward (Fig. 4-18C). The tilt of the vertical horopter has been explained as arising from a relative excyclotorsion of the vertical meridians of the retinas, that is, a relative shearing effect between corresponding points in the two eyes as one progresses vertically along the visual field (Nakayama, 1977). However, the perceptual system compensates almost completely for the vertical tilt under natural viewing conditions, so that vertical lines in real space do not appear to tilt as much as predicted by the tilt of the vertical horopter (Cogan, 1979).

# THE HOROPTER IN ABNORMAL BINOCULAR VISION

Now that we have discussed how normal individuals perceive visual space, as measured by the horopter, let us look at some conditions in which the binocular perception of the world can be distorted.

**CLINICAL APPLICATION** | Intermittent exotropes may exhibit a horopter that is excessively curved such that, when the patient is fusing, the horopters may actually lie *within* the Vieth-Müller circle (Flom, 1980). It is feasible that their abnormal horopter may be the cause of their strabismus, rather than the strabismus resulting in this horopter abnormality.

**CLINICAL APPLICATION** | In constant strabismic subjects, the horopter will be shifted toward the intersection of their visual axes, just as in fixation disparity. However, additional severe abnormalities may also be present in the horopters of esotropic subjects. The horopters of esotropes do not follow the smooth curve typical of normal subjects. Instead, there is a large "notch" in the horopter near the fixation point (Fig. 4-19), which is called the **Flom notch** (Flom, 1980). The notch lies within the region between the visual axes of the two eyes. The presence of the notch, suggestive of a regional spatial distortion under binocular conditions, may be a result of anomalous correspondence. The Flom notch exhibits changes in the covariation phenomenon in that, as the objective angle of strabismus is reduced to align the eyes, the horopter notch disappears (Boucher, 1967).

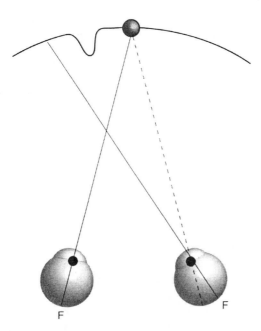

**Figure 4-19**    In some esotropic patients, there is a distortion of the horopter from its normal smoothly arced shape such that it deviates closer to the observer in the region near the crossing of their visual axes. This is called the Flom horopter notch.

**CLINICAL APPLICATION**    Adult patients with a history of early-onset strabismus, particularly esotropia, can demonstrate a condition called **horror fusionis**, a seeming *avoidance* of fusion by the patient. In this condition, the patient may be thought of as having no corresponding points or corresponding points that shift or recalibrate in real time. Under certain testing conditions, as targets are moved together in a stereoscope so that they approach superimposition. Therefore, as they move toward presumably corresponding points, the targets may appear to the patient to jump past the superimposed position without fusion occurring. The subject does not accept the simultaneous stimulation and changes the state of correspondence. Griffin and Grisham (1995) suggest, instead, that this horror fusionis is associated with anomalous correspondence. Indeed, Flom (1980) states that the sudden motion seen near the point of superimposition simply reflects the target of the deviating eye crossing the rapidly changing portion of the horopter notch.

**Aniseikonia**, a condition affecting about 2% to 3% of the population, is a difference in magnification between the two eyes, so that objects viewed by both eyes are perceived to be a different size or shape. Aniseikonia may be of optical or neural origin. **Optical aniseikonia** is caused by a difference in retinal image size between the two eyes and may be caused by axial anisometropia (**axial aniseikonia**) or refractive anisometropia (**refractive aniseikonia**). **Induced aniseikonia** is a form of optical aniseikonia specifically caused by *external* optical factors such as an **afocal magnifier**, also called a **size lens**. **Neural or essential aniseikonia** is a small-magnitude nonoptical aniseikonia that can occur even in emmetropes, in which the two retinal images are physically equal in size yet still perceived to be different in size. Optical and neural aniseikonia are independent phenomena that can either have an additive effect or cancel out one another. Aniseikonia may have a substantial effect on binocular visual perception, distorting our three-dimensional perception, degrading stereopsis, or, if large enough, inducing binocular suppression. Exactly to what degree a given amount of anisometropia degrades stereopsis depends somewhat on the particular test of stereopsis employed.

A **size lens** is a thick lens with parallel front and back surfaces that changes the magnification of an image without having any dioptric power. Size lenses magnify the entire image (**overall magnifier**) if their front and back surfaces are spherical surfaces. If the front and back surfaces are cylindrical, they induce magnification in one meridian, much in the same way a cylinder refracting lens has refractive power in one meridian. A size lens with magnification in only one meridian is called a **meridional size lens**. Magnification in one meridian causes *shape changes* in viewed objects.

Because size lenses are a specialized form of thick lens, their magnification is governed by the same factors as any thick lens. The total magnification of a thick lens is governed by the magnifying effects of both its power factor and shape factor. The **power factor** is the magnification induced by the refractive power of the lens, as given by:

$$M_P = \frac{1}{1 - bF_v}$$

where $b$ is the vertex distance and $F_v$ is the back vertex power of the lens. The **shape factor** is the magnification induced by the thickness and base curve of the lens, independent of its power, as given by:

$$M_s = \frac{1}{1 - \left(\frac{t}{n'}\right)F_1}$$

where $t$ is the lens thickness, $n'$ is the index of refraction, and $F_1$ is the front surface power (inversely proportional to its radius of curvature). In an ophthalmic lens, both of these factors come into play. In an afocal magnifier, because there is

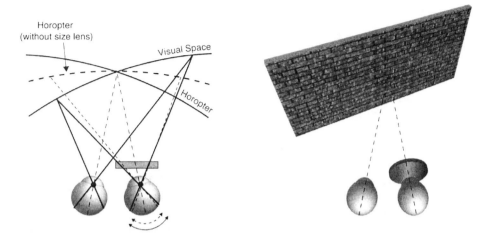

**Figure 4-20** When an axis 90 meridional magnifier is placed in front of the right eye, its image is magnified horizontally, producing retinal disparities that yield a percept of the world tilting away from the right eye. This is called the geometric effect. The horopter measured on this observer slants closer to the right eye.

no refractive power, only the shape factor—dependent on the lens index, thickness, and base curve—influences the total magnification.

Let us discuss meridional magnifiers first, as they are the simpler case. When an afocal meridional magnifier *axis 90* is placed in front of an eye, its magnification occurs along the *horizontal* meridian, and the perceived apparent frontoparallel plane is *rotated* about the fixation point. This is because the difference in horizontal image sizes between the two eyes introduces horizontal binocular disparities that are not present in the unmagnified view, and therefore stereopsis where it should not be present. Remember that the value of *R* is also changed by magnification of one eye's image, and the measured horopter would then be rotated in the *opposite* direction as the apparent frontoparallel plane (Fig. 4-20). This is called the **geometric effect**. The geometric effect was named that because it can be explained easily by the geometry of the horopter and of the magnified image. In the geometric effect, the horopter is rotated *toward the magnified eye*, and the observer perceives the world as *rotated away from the magnified eye*. For example, with a magnifier axis 90 in front of the *right* eye, the horopter rotates *toward* the right eye (*clockwise*) and the apparent frontoparallel plane rotates in the opposite direction, *away* from the right eye (*counterclockwise*). The resultant percept is that the entire visual world appears tilted. The degree of rotation or tilting of the visual space is determined by the following equation:

$$\tan \alpha = \left( \frac{M - 1}{M + 1} \right)\left( \frac{d}{a} \right)$$

where $M$ is the magnification of the size lens, $d$ is the viewing distance, and $a$ is one-half the interpupillary distance. The stronger the magnification, the greater the degree of rotation or tilting. Similarly, the shorter the viewing distance, the greater the tilt. The value $R_0$ of the analytical horopter plot designates the degree of uniform magnification. Therefore, we can also relate $R_0$ to the relative magnification of each eye's image:

$$R_0 = M_{OS}/M_{OD}$$

This condition is quite confusing to the patient because the depth information obtained from the available binocular cues (that is, the introduction of horizontal disparities) conflicts with the depth information obtained from monocular cues such as overlap, texture gradients, and so forth, which are not affected by the aniseikonia.

The tilt and distortion of the visual world induced by uniocular magnification is made more apparent in the **leaf room** (Fig. 4-21A). The leaf room is literally a room in which the walls, floor, and ceiling are covered with leaves to help obscure monocular cues to depth. The *entire room* looks tilted and distorted when a magnifier is placed before one eye (Fig. 4-21B). The percept in the geometric effect is that the walls, floor, and ceiling all appear to slant. With an axis 90 afocal

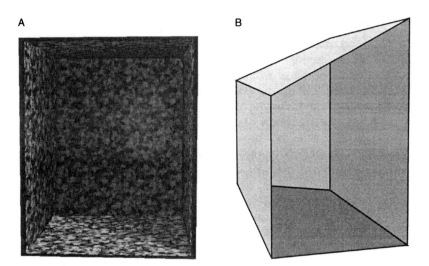

**Figure 4-21** The leaf room is used to determine the effects of lens- or prism-induced magnification on the space perception of a patient. **A:** The densely packed leaves mask many of the available monocular cues, allowing direct observation of changes in binocular perception. **B:** Perception of the leaf room with axis 90 magnification. The geometric effect is accompanied by alterations in perceived size that make the right wall appear to be larger than the left wall, distorting the perceived shape of the leaf room.

magnifier on the right eye, the right wall appears to be farther away than the left wall, as expected from the tilting of the apparent frontoparallel plane in the geometric effect. In addition to the depth changes, the apparent size of the leaves on the wall varies as a function of the perceived distance of the walls, with the leaves on the right-hand wall appearing to be larger than those on the left-hand wall. Surprisingly, the floor appears to slant downward to the right, while the ceiling appears to slant upward to the right. The net result is that the square leaf room no longer appears to be square. The changes in the vertical position of the floor and ceiling cannot be directly explained by the magnification itself because the magnification induces only horizontal binocular disparity. However, the changes in the apparent size and distance of the side walls create a secondary illusion of slant in the floor and ceiling.

What happens when you magnify the image *vertically* with an *axis 180* meridional size lens; that is, what if a vertical magnification is created between the two eyes? Until this point, we have discussed only horizontal disparities. However, vertical binocular disparities are physically possible. However, only *horizontal* disparities produce a percept of depth—*vertical disparities do not*. We do not see depth when a vertical disparity is introduced. In addition, even a small amount of vertical disparity leads to diplopia because humans have limited vertical fusional eye movement capabilities (Kertesz, 1983).

Because vertical disparities by themselves do not yield a stereoscopic percept, one would predict that an *axis 180* meridional size lens would produce no change in the apparent frontoparallel plane or the horopter. However, with an *axis 180* meridional size lens, the world *will* seem tilted. This effect is identical to the effect produced by an axis 90 magnifier placed in front of *the fellow eye*, at least for low-power magnification. Nobody knows why vertical magnification in one eye looks like horizontal magnification in the other, but it does indeed happen. This effect is called the **induced effect** because it cannot be explained in terms of geometry (Fig. 4-22); it is as if the vertical magnification in one eye *induces* an apparent horizontal magnification in the fellow eye.

The changes in perceived depth arising from the induced effect may be measured by a tilting of the apparent frontoparallel plane horopter. However, because there is no physical horizontal binocular disparity created by the induced effect, the identical visual direction (nonius) horopter will not be rotated. The precise cause of the induced effect is still disputed.

When one eye's image is *uniformly* magnified in the horizontal and vertical meridians, both geometric and induced effects will be generated. The strength of these two percepts is roughly equal for small degrees of overall magnification; that is, magnifying horizontally by 2% yields the same amount of tilted percept as a 2% vertical magnification, but in the opposite direction. This means that if you *uniformly* magnify an image in one eye by a small amount, it will have little or no effect on the orientation of the apparent frontoparallel plane; the geometric and induced effects will simply cancel each other out (Fig. 4-23). Although the spatial distortions are not significant, consistent fusion of the two different-sized images may be difficult.

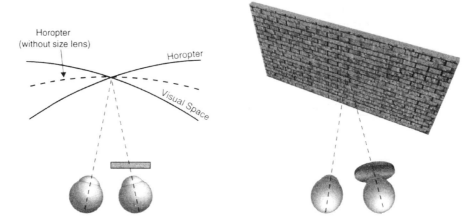

**Figure 4-22**   When an axis 180 meridional magnifier is placed in front of the right eye, its image is magnified vertically. Although no horizontal retinal disparities are created, the observer perceives the world as tilting toward the right eye, a phenomenon called the induced effect. The horopter measured on this observer slants away from the right eye.

An aniseikonic effect can also be produced with asymmetric convergence, that is, converging to bifoveally fixate a nearpoint target that is not on the vertical midline. In this situation, the fixated target is closer to one eye than the other, yielding a difference in retinal image size between the two eyes.

**CLINICAL APPLICATION**   As we have just seen, aniseikonia is not a problem if the relative magnification is not pronounced. In general, for every diopter of refractive difference between the two eyes, there is approximately a 1.4% relative magnification difference between the images of the two eyes. Patients with a small degree of aniseikonia will have unequal image sizes in their two eyes, but with magnification that is equal in all meridians, their worlds will not appear tilted. Unfortunately, the induced effect breaks down with magnification greater than approximately 5% to 7% (Ogle, 1938). With greater degrees of aniseikonia, an *uncorrected geometric effect* and its accompanying rotation of visual space will be perceived.

If the relative magnification difference in aniseikonia is greater than 7%, binocular problems may also be manifested, such as disruption of fusion. The disruption of fusion can result in amblyopia if aniseikonia is present in an infant.

Oblique magnification of one eye's image produces a different kind of tilted percept. Oblique magnification introduces cyclodisparity, in which vertical lines are seen as tilted toward the meridian of magnification. This tilt translates to horizontal binocular disparities that increase in magnitude as you move vertically from the fovea, where the horizontal disparities are opposite in sign for the upper and

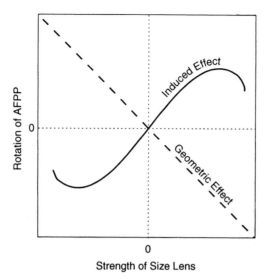

**Figure 4-23** Overall uniform magnification simultaneously creates both a geometric effect and an induced effect. With low degrees of uniform magnification, the geometric and induced effects are equal and opposite in effect and cancel one another. The net result is no perceived tilting of surfaces. However, with large degrees of overall magnification, the magnitude of the induced effect tapers off, leaving an unopposed geometric effect and perceived tilt.

lower visual fields. The result is an **inclination/declination effect**, a percept that the world is tilted about the horizontal meridian, with the visual field skewed so that its top is tilted away from you and the bottom toward you, or vice versa (Ogle, 1964). In the leaf room, the percept is that of the rear wall tilting about a horizontal axis, with the ceiling, floor, and side walls distorted as a result of the apparent size differences imposed by the rear wall. With magnification in *meridian* 45° (axis 135) in the left eye and *meridian* 135° (axis 45) in the right eye, the upper part of the leaf room appears to be larger and farther away, whereas with the meridians of magnification reversed between the two eyes, the opposite effect occurs. Other oblique angles of magnification can be resolved into combinations of horizontal, vertical, and meridian 45° and 135° oblique magnification.

 **Cyclovergence eye movements** can produce a similar effect, such as when an observer looks downward while the eyes are converged. In the case of oblique magnification, cyclorotary eye movements act in a compensatory manner, lessening the perceptual effects of the cyclodisparity, but this compensation is only partial because cyclovergence eye movements are limited in amplitude (Kertesz, 1983). In these cases, patients may complain of the floor appearing to tilt upward or downward. Oblique axis cylindrical lenses may also produce this effect.

**CLINICAL APPLICATION**

The relationship between anisometropia and aniseikonia is dependent on the cause of the anisometropia. Axial anisometropes will experience image magnification (in myopic anisometropia) or minification (in hyperopic anisometropia) when corrected with contact lenses, but refractive anisometropes will not; this is simply the logical prediction of the optical rule of thumb known as **Knapp's law**. Conversely, refractive anisometropes will have an aniseikonia introduced if corrected by spectacle lenses, with refractive myopic anisometropes experiencing image minification from the minus lens correction and hyperopes experiencing magnification. Contact lenses will not produce aniseikonia in refractive anisometropes.

Uncorrected refractive ametropia has little effect on image size relative to that of the emmetropic eye. However, correcting the refractive ametropia with spectacles creates image magnification in hyperopes and minification in myopes. Correction with contact lenses would be the treatment of choice in refractive anisometropia because image sizes would be close to that of emmetropia.

Uncorrected axial ametropia produces an image size much different from that of the emmetropic eye, smaller in hyperopia and larger in myopia. Correction with spectacle lenses placed near the anterior focal plane of the eye will produce an image size that is the same as that of an emmetropic eye (Knapp's law). Even so, contact lenses are the method of choice for correction of significant axial anisometropia, particularly axial myopia. Although the contact lens will produce an image larger than that in an emmetropic eye, measurable aniseikonia may actually be much less than predicted. One plausible explanation is that the eye with axial myopia is stretched, and photoreceptor density is reduced; in other words, the photoreceptors are spaced farther apart than in an emmetropic eye. Therefore, the magnification that is optically induced by the contact lens more closely matches the anatomic "magnification" of the photoreceptor array.

---

## ⌛ *Key Point*

*In general, axial anisometropes should be corrected with spectacle lenses to offset their existing aniseikonia, but refractive anisometropes should be fitted with contact lenses to avoid introducing an aniseikonia.*

These same considerations apply to patients receiving unilateral **intraocular lens implants (IOLs)** following cataract extraction. Many such patients exhibit substantial aniseikonia, especially if the IOL is fit in the anterior chamber. However, even some patients with bilateral IOLs can still experience some aniseikonia if there are subtle differences in IOL placement (Lakshminarayanan et al., 1993). Less common is **unilateral aphakia**, in which one cataractous crystalline lens has been removed, but for medical reasons an IOL could not be implanted. Similarly, patients who have undergone monocular **refractive surgery** are at risk for aniseikonia.

**CLINICAL APPLICATION**

Another significant situation in which the geometric and induced effects are unequal is the correction of high degrees of astigmatism. An astigmatic lens, by having unequal power in different meridians, will also yield *unequal magnification* in these meridians. This explains in part why patients first given an astigmatic correction will feel disoriented, experiencing distortions of depth and possibly vertigo, before they adjust to the lenses.

The skewing of the horopter with spectacle correction of high anisometropia and astigmatism explains in part the complaint that such patients have of distortions of the environment around them.

It should also be noted that aniseikonia and its associated distortions of perceived space have more than just sensory consequences. When the image of one eye is magnified relative to that of the fellow eye, and the patient must make a saccadic eye movement to an eccentric target, each eye's image of that target will be in a different retinal location. This forces the patient to make unequal amplitude saccades in each eye, a clear violation of Hering's law (Schor et al., 1990). Similar unequal pursuits have been demonstrated as well in aniseikonia.

**CLINICAL PROCEDURE**

Magnification differences between the two eyes may be diagnosed using the **Brecher Maddox rod technique** (Brecher, 1951) (Fig. 4-24). The left eye views two penlights, with the right eye viewing them through a Maddox rod. The Maddox rod serves to convert the image of a penlight into a streak of light; in this manner, the percept of each individual eye is identified. In normal (iseikonic) vision, the perceived spacing between the penlights equals that of the perceived spacing between the streaks of light. In aniseikonia, the two spacings are unequal (see also Figs. 4-12 and 4-13).

**CLINICAL PROCEDURE**

Although one can demonstrate tilted percepts caused by magnification effects most effectively with a leaf room, most eye doctors do not own leaf rooms. Fortunately, there is a better alternative that takes up a lot less space. We can directly measure the distortions of stereoscopic vision and, indirectly, the degree of aniseikonia with a device called the **space eikonometer** (Fig. 4-25). It is essentially a form of stereoscope with two vertical lines and an oblique cross (X) as targets. A person with aniseikonia (and intact stereopsis) will see the cross as

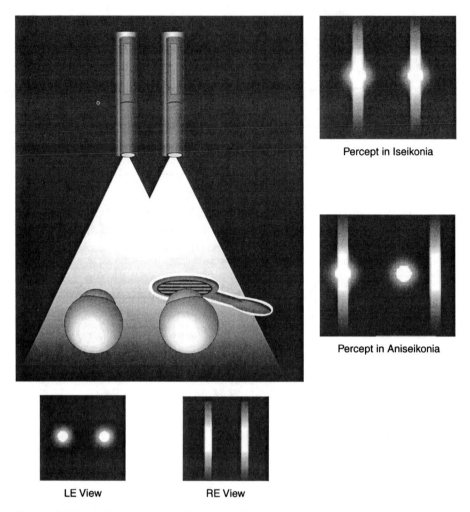

Percept in Iseikonia

Percept in Aniseikonia

LE View                    RE View

**Figure 4-24**   In the Brecher Maddox rod technique for diagnosing aniseikonia, one eye views two lights while the other views the two lights through a Maddox rod. For axis 180 testing, the Maddox rod is oriented vertically, whereas for axis 90 testing it is oriented horizontally. In normal iseikonic vision, the percept is of two streaks of light intersecting each of the penlights' points of light; that is, the spacing of the percepts of the penlights equals that of the spacing between the streaks. In aniseikonia, the spacing between the streaks does not equal that of the points of light.

rotated instead of in a flat plane parallel to the eyes and/or one of the vertical lines closer to the observer. In front of each eye is a set of afocal magnifiers whose magnification can be increased or decreased in order to nullify the amount of apparent rotation of the targets. Once the rotation is neutralized, you can calculate the magnification difference between the two eyes. This can be used to design an **iseikonic lens** to correct the aniseikonia (by modifying the

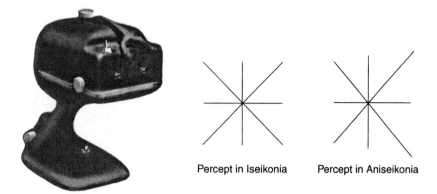

Percept in Iseikonia          Percept in Aniseikonia

**Figure 4-25**   The space eikonometer is a specialized stereoscope whose target allows quantification of the degree of perceived tilting of the frontoparallel plane in aniseikonia. Variable size lenses in the eyepieces allow the clinician to design a corrective lens.

front surface curvature, thickness, and refractive index). Although the space eikonometer is no longer manufactured, the Keystone Optical Company produces telebinocular stereoscopic cards with targets that serve the same purpose.

All of the manipulations of visual space that we have discussed so far— changes in fixation distance, the geometric effect, and the induced effect—distort our percept of space and therefore distort the horopter. However, in each of these cases, it is the value of $R$ (uniform magnification) in the analytical plot that has been altered, not $H$ (the nonuniform magnification). This is an important fact, as it tells us that although the uniform magnification of the horopter is altered, the nonuniform magnification, which reflects the orderly arrangement of corresponding points, does not change. These manipulations all reflect optical changes to the horopter rather than neural changes. The neural organization of corresponding points is quite robust, and the value of $H$ does not change even under a variety of conditions.

There is, however, one apparent exception to this rule. Not only lenses can distort visual space. *Prisms* as well can cause distortions of visual space. However, unlike lenses, there is a **nonuniform magnification** across the prism, with more magnification at the apex than at the base. This causes nonuniform distortions in the perception of visual space and in the horopter (Ogle, 1964). **Base-out prisms** cause visual space to curve concave toward the viewer. The corresponding horopter change is for the horopter to "bow out" away from the observer. **Base-in prisms** cause visual space to curve more away and the horopter to curve convex (Fig. 4-26). However, even in this case, the change in the nonuniform magnification factor ($H$) of the horopter can be explained fully by the *nonuniform* optical effects of the prisms and not by neural changes in the arrangement of corresponding points. It should be noted that only the prism effects along the horizontal meridian are being considered here; vertical distortions also occur in the form of vertical tilting.

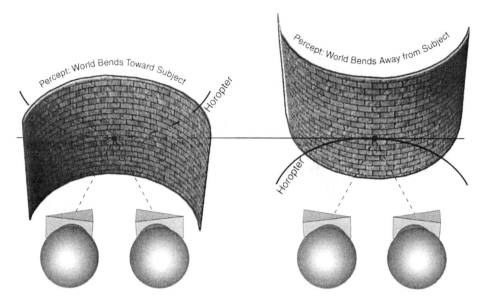

**Figure 4-26**   Prisms induce a nonuniform magnification of the retinal image, manifested as a curved distortion of visual space and the horopter. The effects of horizontal prisms along the horizontal axis are depicted here, with vertical effects disregarded.

---

### ⊶ Key Point

*In the normal binocular visual system, all changes in the horopter caused by changes in fixation distance or the application of lenses or prisms may be explained solely by optical factors. The arrangement of corresponding points remains stable under each of these conditions. However, the arrangement of corresponding points can be altered in abnormal binocular vision. Such anomalous correspondence can produce abnormalities in the horopter.*

---

## ADAPTATION TO LENSES AND PRISMS

We have seen that lenses and prisms can greatly affect the binocular percept of the visual world. Similarly, the prescribing of new lenses or prisms to a patient can cause binocular visual distortions. This must be taken into account when prescribing so that space perception is not sacrificed in the attempt to obtain the best visual acuity. For example, even if a high cylinder would give an astigmatic patient the best possible acuity, the clinician should use caution if that lens induces aniseikonia.

Fortunately, the visual system is capable of adapting to distortions of visual space. The degree of adaptation may vary from complete adaptation to none, but in general the adaptation is only partial, in that there is still some remaining spatial distortion, though less severe than it was before adaptation. The degree of adaptation noted experimentally depends on the horopter criterion used and the length of time over which the subject was allowed to adapt.

In free space and natural viewing conditions, subjects showed greater adaptation, with the geometric effect being neutralized within 3 to 4 days and the induced effect taking 5 to 6 days. However, in artificial settings, such as deprived visual environments or during the use of instruments such as binoculars or microscopes, the perceived distortions reappeared (Remole, 1991). This adaptation could be accounted for by psychological factors such as increased reliance on monocular depth cues, especially perspective, to determine the location of objects in space in the face of inaccurate binocular information. When those cues are removed, the distortions resurface. Furthermore, although some instruments such as the AFPP horopter and the space eikonometer can reveal some adaptation to aniseikonia as well, Burian (1943) showed no change in the more reliable and precise nonius horopter with adaptation, suggesting that there is no physiological recalibration of corresponding retinal points and visual directionality with adaptation or, in other words, that the binocular stereoscopic system (unlike the oculomotor system) does not adapt to the presence of induced aniseikonia.

Some researchers have shown adaptation effects for oblique magnification as well, but the strength of this adaptation is less, with some subjects still experiencing distortions that were severe enough to induce nausea. The adaptation that does occur may be explained by the generation of cyclorotational eye movements that compensate for the introduced horizontal disparities.

Studies of short-term adaptation to aniseikonia reveal that the adaptation process begins quite rapidly, after only about 20 minutes (Lee and Ciuffreda, 1983). Such perceptual adaptation is dependent on motor feedback for orientation in the visual world and on the availability of contours in the visual field (for example, see Ciuffreda et al., 1976).

The binocular visual system can tolerate small amounts of aniseikonia without loss of function. Approximately 40% of emmetropes have **neural aniseikonia** of at least 0.8%. It is generally agreed that clinical symptoms of aniseikonia (that is, headaches or asthenopia) can occur with only 1% to 2% magnification differences. Aniseikonia beyond 5% begins to influence stereoscopic thresholds (although the magnitude of the effect depends on the test used to measure stereopsis). Aniseikonia in the 20% range, commonly found in patients with aphakia corrected with spectacle lenses, is incompatible with binocular vision.

**CLINICAL APPLICATION** | There is considerable variability in the degree of adaptation from subject to subject. Rutstein and Daum (1998) note that no clinical test exists to assess the degree to which a patient will adapt to magnification differences. Therefore, the clinician has no choice but to prescribe refractive correction judiciously and see if the patient's symptoms of spatial distortion improve.

## SUMMARY AND KEY POINTS

- The horopter is the set of all points in visual space that will stimulate pairs of corresponding retinal points. It is a *three-dimensional* structure, but the slice of it along the horizontal plane, the **longitudinal horopter**, is most important to the study of binocular vision.

- The **Vieth-Müller circle** or **geometric horopter** is a theoretical horopter that is based on an equiangular arrangement of corresponding retinal points in each eye. It assumes that all pairs of corresponding retinal points occur at equal angles from the fovea. In this horopter, all objects lying anywhere on a circle that intersects the fixation point and the nodal points of each eye will stimulate pairs of corresponding points.

- Properties of corresponding retinal points provide criteria that can be used to measure the horopter. When both eyes fixate on a given point in space, it is possible to map out all points in space that seem to come from the same visual direction **(identical visual direction or nonius horopter)**. These points will appear to be located in a flat plane equidistant from the observer as the fixation point **[stereoscopic depth matching, or apparent frontoparallel plane (AFPP) horopter]**. Different points along the horopter will not elicit fusional eye movements **(zero vergence horopter)**. The horopter will lie within Panum's fusional area, the basis for the **singleness or haplopia horopter**.

- The horopter represents the boundary between crossed and uncrossed disparities as we fixate a particular point. Objects lying on the horopter have **zero disparity**, whereas objects closer to the observer than the horopter have crossed disparity and those farther away have uncrossed disparity. The horopter is the place in space where we are *most sensitive to changes in depth* because even a slight change will alter the percept of an object from closer to farther away **(minimum stereoacuity threshold horopter)**.

- A **fixation disparity** will cause the horopter to be displaced inward (for an eso fixation disparity) or outward (for an exo fixation disparity) relative to where the *intended* physical fixation point lies, because the visual axes of the two eyes aren't actually crossing at the physical fixation point. The horopter lies where the visual axes cross.

- The apparent frontoparallel plane method is precise and easy to do with untrained subjects. However, it is important to remember that the shape of the frontoparallel plane perceived by the subject will be the *mirror image* of their horopter settings.

- For objects on the Vieth-Müller circle, the **relative magnification** between images formed on corresponding retinal points in the right eye and the left eye ($R$) is equal to 1, where the value $R$ represents the tangents of the **external longitudinal angles** ($\alpha_1$ and $\alpha_2$) for the left and right eyes, respectively. An $R$ value of 1 is necessary for the right eye and left eye targets to be seen as lying at the same angle relative to the fixation point in *perceived* space. $R$ is not equal to 1 for all points off the Vieth-Müller circle.

- Empirical measures have revealed that the horopter tends to be less sharply curved than the Vieth-Müller circle. The difference between the horopter and the Vieth-Müller circle is called the **Hering-Hillebrand horopter deviation** (*H*). The existence of this deviation shows that our perception of space is *warped* a bit; our corresponding points are not laid out in an evenly spaced distribution between the two eyes. The Hering-Hillebrand deviation does not change with fixation distance.

- The **analytical plot** $[R = H(\tan \alpha_2) + R_0]$ tells us the degree of relative magnification via its *y*-intercept, $\boldsymbol{R_0}$. If $R_0 = 1$ there is no skewing of the horopter. If $R_0 \neq 1$, there is a **uniform relative magnification** of one eye's image across the visual field, tilting the horopter and one's percept of the world. This skewing might be caused by aniseikonia or by unequal spectacle lens corrections. The value of the slope of the plot, $\boldsymbol{H}$, is a measure of **nonuniform relative magnification** that tells us the relative curvature of the horopter relative to the Vieth-Müller circle. This value is usually positive, indicating the horopter is less curved than the Vieth-Müller circle. This may be attributed to a layout of corresponding points that creates a relative minification of the nasal retina relative to the temporal hemiretina.

- The shape of the empirical horopter curves more and more away from the observer as the *fixation distance* is increased. However, the curvature of the Vieth-Müller circle changes proportionately, so that the Hering-Hillebrand deviation (*H*) remains the same at all fixation distances. The **abathic distance** is the distance at which the horopter is flat. The abathic distance is calculated by:

$$H = \frac{2a}{b}$$

where *2a* is the interpupillary distance and *b* is the fixation distance, at about six meters from the observer.

- The **vertical horopter** tends to be tilted with its superior portion rotated away from the observer and the inferior portion closer. However, the precise degree of tilt changes with viewing distance.

- In strabismic subjects, the horopter is be shifted toward the intersection of their visual axes, just as in fixation disparity.

- Esotropic subjects have a large "notch" in the horopter near the fixation point (**Flom notch**), which suggests a regional spatial distortion under binocular conditions. **Horror fusionis** may be associated with the Flom notch.

- **Aniseikonia** is a difference in magnification between the two eyes, which may be optical or neural in origin. **Optical aniseikonia** results from a difference in retinal image size caused by internal optical factors such as **axial aniseikonia** or **refractive aniseikonia**. In addition, **unilateral aphakia, intraocular lenses (IOLs)** in one eye alone, or **monocular refractive surgery** may cause aniseikonia. **Induced aniseikonia** is a form of optical aniseikonia caused by external optical factors such as **size lenses** or **high astigmatic corrections**. **Neural**

**(essential) aniseikonia** is a small degree of nonoptical aniseikonia in which the retinal images are of identical size, yet are perceived to be of different sizes.

- A **size lens** is an afocal magnifier that changes the overall magnification of an image without having any dioptric power. The total magnification of a size lens is determined by the same magnifying effects as any thick lens: (a) the **power factor** induced by the refractive power of the lens, and (b) the **shape factor** related to the thickness and base curve of the lens. A **meridional size lens** changes the image magnification in only one meridian.

- Placing an **afocal meridional magnifier *axis 90*** in front of one eye will magnify the *horizontal* meridian, *rotating* the horopter toward the magnified eye and the perceived apparent frontoparallel would then be rotated in the *opposite* direction away from the magnified eye. This is called the **geometric effect**. The stronger the magnification, the greater the degree of perceived rotation or tilting of the visual world. The degree of perceived rotation is determined by:

$$\tan \alpha = \left( \frac{M - 1}{M + 1} \right) \left( \frac{d}{a} \right)$$

where $M$ is the magnification of the size lens, $d$ is the viewing distance, and $a$ is one-half the interpupillary distance.

- In **vertical magnification** with an **axis 180 meridional size lens**, the world will seem tilted in the same way as if an axis 90 magnifier were placed in front of the fellow eye. This is called the **induced effect**.

- Oblique magnification produces disparities that are opposite in sign for the upper and lower visual fields, resulting in an **inclination or declination effect** in which the world seems tilted about the horizontal meridian.

- Uniform magnification less than 4% produces both geometric and induced effects, which will cancel each other out, resulting in little or no effect on the orientation of the apparent frontoparallel plane. However, magnification greater than approximately 5% to 7% breaks down the induced effect leaving an *uncorrected geometric effect* in high anisometropic patients with its accompanying rotation of visual space.

- To correct the geometric effect, axial anisometropes should be corrected with spectacle lenses to offset their existing aniseikonia, and refractive anisometropes should be fitted with contact lenses to avoid introducing an aniseikonia (**Knapp's law**).

- Astigmatic lenses have unequal power in different meridians and can produce geometric and induced effects.

- When the image of one eye is magnified relative to that of the fellow eye, patients will make unequal saccadic and pursuit eye movements.

- We can demonstrate tilted percepts secondary to magnification effects with a **leaf room**, which minimizes monocular cues to depth, a **space eikonometer**, or

**telebinocular stereoscopic cards**. Magnification differences between the two eyes can also be detected with the **Brecher Maddox rod technique**.

- *Prisms* as well can cause **nonuniform magnification** distortions of visual space with more magnification at the apex than at the base. With **base-out prisms**, the horopter "bows out" away from you, whereas **base-in prisms** cause the horopter to curve toward you. As with lenses, visual space appears to move in the opposite direction from the horopter.

- The visual system can adapt to distortions of visual space. **Short-term adaptation** to aniseikonia begins quite rapidly, after only about 20 minutes. The geometric effect is neutralized within 3 to 4 days and the induced effect takes 5 to 6 days. Only minimal adaptation occurs for oblique magnification. Greater adaptation occurs in free space and natural viewing, where factors such as monocular depth cues, contours, and motor feedback have a greater effect. There is no change in the nonius horopter with adaptation, suggesting that there is no physiological recalibration of corresponding retinal points and visual directionality with adaptation.

- Small degrees of aniseikonia (1% to 2%) can still produce clinical symptoms of headache or asthenopia. Aniseikonia beyond 5% will affect stereoscopic thresholds, and aniseikonia above 20% will eliminate binocular vision.

# QUESTIONS

1. If you were sitting in a movie theater in the center of the front row, would you expect all points on the screen to lie on your horopter? Why or why not?

2. A person is holding up a red rod in one hand and a green rod in the other hand. While he is fixating on the red rod, he sees the green rod as double. Are the retinal images of the green rod formed on corresponding retinal points? What about the image of the red rod? Alternately covering each eye while still fixating on the red rod reveals that the right eye's diplopic image appears to be to the right, and the left eye's diplopic image is to the left. Which way would you need to move the green rod in order to position it on the horopter? How would you expect the appearance of the green rod change as you move it? What would happen to the image of the green rod if you moved it too far and overshot the horopter?

3. Under which circumstances might you want to measure the horopter of a patient? Which method would you use and why?

4. Would you recommend using the maximum stereoacuity method to measure the horopter? Why or why not?

5. Under what circumstances might a patient's horopter be skewed? How would you expect a patient with a skewed horopter to perceive the world? What, if anything, can be done by the clinician to correct a skewed horopter?

6.  Would you expect our perception of the world to change if our horopters fell exactly on the Vieth-Müller circle? Why or why not?

7.  A patient has axial anisometropia with a refractive error of +5.00 in the right eye and +1.00 in the left eye. Will this refractive error affect his percept of the apparent frontoparallel plane and horopter? Would this patient's vision be better corrected with spectacles or with contact lenses? Why?

8.  Why do patients with astigmatism have difficulty adjusting to new spectacle lenses? How long should the patient wear the new the lenses to allow the visual system enough time to adjust to them? Can you predict whether a patient's adaptation will be successful?

## *BIBLIOGRAPHY*

AMES A, OGLE KN *and* GLIDDON GH (1932). *Corresponding retinal points, the horopter, and the size and shape of ocular images.* J. Opt. Soc. Am. 22:575–631.

BLAKEMORE C (1970). *The range and scope of binocular depth discrimination in man.* J. Physiol. 211:599–622.

BOUCHER (1967). *Common visual direction horopters in exotropes with anomalous correspondence.* Am. J. Optom. 44:547–572.

BRECHER GA (1951). *A new method for measuring aniseikonia.* Am. J. Ophthalmol. 34:1016–1021.

BURIAN HM (1943). *Influence of prolonged wearing of meridional size lenses on spatial localization.* AMA Arch. Ophthalmol. 30:645–668.

CIUFFREDA KJ, HALSTROM W *and* FLOM MC (1976). *Optically altered horizontal retinal-image disparity: effects of limb activity on short-term adaptation.* Am. J. Optom. Physiol. Optics 53:S532.

COGAN AI (1979). *The relationship between the apparent vertical and the vertical horopter.* Vis. Res. 19:655–665.

FLOM MC (1980). *Corresponding and disparate retinal points in normal and anomalous correspondence.* Am. J. Optom. Physiol. Optics 57:656–665.

FLOM MC *and* ESKRIDGE JB (1968). *Change in retinal correspondence with viewing distance.* J. Am. Optom. Assoc. 39:1094–1097.

GRIFFIN JR *and* GRISHAM JD (1995). *Binocular Anomalies:* Diagnosis and Vision Therapy, 3rd ed. Butterworth-Heinemann, Boston.

KERTESZ AE (1983). *Vertical and cyclofusional disparity vergence. In:* Vergence Eye Movements: *Basic and Clinical Aspects,* CM Schor *and* KJ Ciuffreda, eds., Butterworths, Boston.

LAKSHMINARAYANAN V, ENOCH JM *and* KNOWLES RA (1993). *Residual aniseikonia among patients fitted with one or two intraocular lenses (pseudophakic corrections).* Opt. Vis. Sci. 70:107–110.

LEE DY *and* CIUFFREDA KJ (1983). *Short-term adaptation to the induced effect.* Optom. Physiol. Opt. 3:129–135.

MEISSNER G (1854). Beitrage zur Physiologie des Sehorganes, W. Engleman, Leipzig.

NAKAYAMA K (1977). *Geometrical and physiological aspects of depth perception. In:* Image Processing, S BENTON, ed., Proc. Soc. Photo-Opt. Instr. Eng. 120:1–8.

OGLE KN (1932). *Analytical treatment of the longitudinal horopter.* J. Opt. Soc. Am. 22:665–728.

OGLE KN (1938). *Induced size effect. I. A new phenomenon in binocular space perception associated with the relative sizes of the images of the two eyes.* Arch. Ophthalmol. 20:604–623.

OGLE KN (1964). Researches in Binocular Vision, Hafner, New York.

REMOLE A (1991). *The tilting keyboard.* Clin. Exp. Optom. 74:71–79.

RUTSTEIN RP *and* DAUM KM (1998). *Anomalies of Binocular Vision:* Diagnosis and Management. CV Mosby, St. Louis.

SCHOR CM, GLEASON G *and* HORNER D (1990). *Selective nonconjugate binocular adaptation of vertical saccades and pursuits.* Vis. Res. 30:1827–1844.

TSCHERMAK A (1900). *Beiträge zur Lehre vom Längshoropter.* Pflügers Archiv. 81:328–348.

TYLER CW (1983). *Sensory processing of binocular disparity. In:* Vergence Eye Movements: *Basic and Clinical Aspects,* CM Schor *and* KJ Ciuffreda, eds., Butterworth: Boston.

# Alternatives to Fusion

As seen in Chapter 3, fusion is the process of superimposing and combining similar contours in the images of each eye into a unified binocular percept. The key to combining the two images is the presence of *similar features* in each **dichoptic stimulus (or "half-image")**, that is, the independent stimulus presented to each eye alone (Fig. 5-1). Fusion is difficult, if not impossible, when very different images occur in the two eyes. We have seen one example of this in Chapter 4.

**CLINICAL APPLICATION** With marked anisometropia and aniseikonia, the two monocular images differ greatly in size, disrupting fusion. Similarly, conditions that impair motor fusion, such as drug intake, alcohol use, trauma, fatigue, or oculomotor system pathology, reduce the ability to bring the similar contours in each eye's images into superimposition. If fusional ability is sufficiently affected, similar contours in each image will be formed on widely separated noncorresponding points (that is, outside of Panum's area) and the patient will note **diplopia** (double vision). Patients with intermittent convergence or divergence imbalances can experience diplopia when their eyes are intermittently misaligned, as do strabismics of *recent* and *sudden* onset (such as sudden *muscle palsy or paresis*).

An important consequence of misalignments of the visual axes is that *dissimilar* images can be formed on *corresponding* points. The result is that two different objects are perceived as occupying the same location in visual space, a condition known as **binocular confusion**. How does the visual system handle the conflicting information at these corresponding points? Grossly dissimilar images cannot simply be fused together into a unified percept. The visual system must use other mechanisms to handle the two different monocular images.

**121**

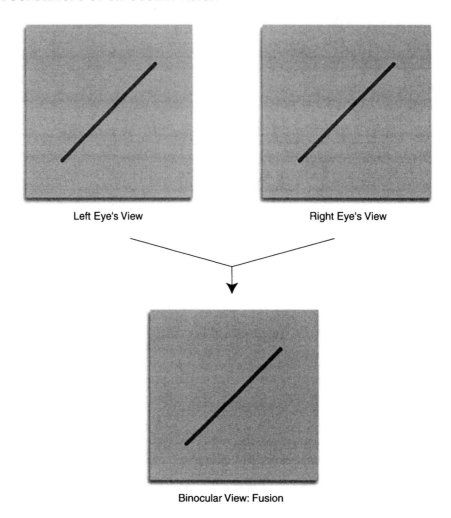

Left Eye's View                    Right Eye's View

Binocular View: Fusion

**Figure 5-1**    Binocular fusion occurs when similar contours or features are presented to each eye.

## BINOCULAR SUPPRESSION

One way the visual system handles conflicting information is to simply "ignore" or "turn off" either all or part of the image to one eye, so that only one of the two different images reaches conscious perception (Fig. 5-2). This process is known as **binocular suppression**. Although the suppression is of one eye, it arises from *binocular* interactions. Suppression is a failure to allow some monocular portion of the binocular field to contribute to the combined binocular percept. The suppressed region undergoes a reduction of sensitivity to visual stimuli with an elevation of light detection thresholds and prolongation of reaction times. The

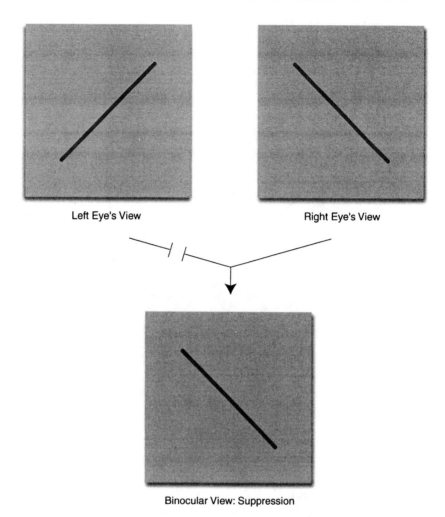

**Figure 5-2**   When dissimilar contours or features are presented to each eye, binocular suppression results.

suppression may not occur instantly once diplopia and confusion are present; it may take up to 75 to 150 ms for suppression to begin (Schor et al., 1976). Figure 5-3 presents a demonstration of suppression. A horizontal line is presented to the left eye and a pair of closely spaced vertical lines to the right eye. One might predict that the binocular percept would be of a horizontal line crossed by two closely spaced vertical lines. However, this does not occur. When these two monocular images are superimposed, part of one eye's view disappears (Kaufman, 1963). In this example, a portion of the left eye's line (between the two vertical lines) disappears in the binocular percept. This corresponds to a *local* suppression of the left eye's information. If we close the right eye, that part of the left eye's image *reap-*

Left Eye's View

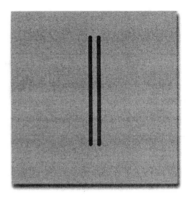

Right Eye's View

Combined Binocular Percept

**Figure 5-3**    Demonstration of binocular suppression. If you fuse the two half-views using the free fusion technique described in Chapter 7, the resulting percept will be as shown in the bottom of the figure. Both eyes' targets will be visible, but the short horizontal line segment between the two vertical lines will be suppressed.

*pears,* as there is no need to suppress the left eye's image when the right eye is closed. The suppression only occurs under *binocular* conditions.

Binocular suppression may seem like an abnormal and detrimental action, but at times, inhibitory binocular processes such as suppression can be both normal and helpful. For example, we have already seen that physiological diplopia results when we fixate a near target while observing a distant target (or vice versa). However, under natural viewing conditions, objects that are closer than or farther away from the object of regard than the limits of Panum's area are not perceived as diplopic. Instead, suppression helps to prevent most of the visual scene from appearing diplopic.

This type of normal binocular suppression is called **physiological suppression**, to distinguish it from binocular suppression that occurs with abnormal binocular vision **(pathological suppression)**. Pathological suppression is usually an adaptation to prolonged diplopia or binocular confusion. Rather than cope with navigating through a doubled visual space, the visual system over a period of time "shuts off" one eye's image to yield single vision. However, the resulting single vision arising from suppression is necessarily deprived of the benefits of having inputs from both eyes at once, that is, binocular summation and stereopsis.

In cases of strabismus, the fixating eye will be the dominant eye, and the nondominant deviating eye will be suppressed. **Alternating strabismics** can switch eye dominance, so that the formerly deviating eye is now the fixating eye and vice versa. When this occurs, the suppression switches to the new deviating eye. Although they are often unaware of the switch in eye dominance, they are able to consciously control it.

In general, if the two eyes are equal in their contribution to the binocular visual system (that is, one eye is not very dominant over the other), the eye presented with a weaker or less salient image will be suppressed. An image that is dimmer, of lower contrast, blurred, stationary, or in the retinal periphery will be more likely suppressed rather than an image that is brighter, high contrast, sharply focused, moving, or at the fovea. It should also be noted that under such conditions of binocular inequality, fusion is less evident.

## BINOCULAR RIVALRY

Suppression may also be triggered by dissimilar binocular inputs, a phenomenon known as **binocular rivalry**. This is an intermittent and alternating suppression of brightness, color, and/or contour of one, then the other, eye. Binocular rivalry usually occurs with *vastly dissimilar* images in each eye, and is strongest when dissimilar *contours* are presented, such as orthogonally oriented gratings (gratings rotated at a 90° angle relative to each other) imaged in each eye. Rivalry is also more likely to occur when the orthogonally oriented gratings are both of medium to high contrast; with both gratings at very low contrast, an unexpected binocular summation may occur between the dissimilar stimuli, producing a percept of a plaid pattern (Liu et al., 1992).

If the dissimilar targets are small in area, each eye's entire image of the target may be alternately suppressed (**exclusive dominance**). However, if larger area stimuli are used, as in Fig. 5-4, the binocular percept is that of a "patchwork" in which the contours continuously change over time (**mosaic dominance**). This alternation occurs *locally* at each location independently, so that at any given location the percept alternates from that of the left eye's image alone to that of the right eye's alone, and so on, with the areas of alternation constantly shifting.

Left Eye's View                    Right Eye's View

Binocular Percept:

Time 1    ⟶    Time 2    ⟶    Time 3

**Figure 5-4**    Demonstration of binocular rivalry. If the two half-views containing orthogonally oriented oblique lines are fused, the percept will be that of a continuously changing "patchwork" of oblique lines as different regions of the figure are suppressed by one, then the other, eye.

These independent areas of alternation have been called **spatial zones of binocular rivalry** (Blake et al., 1992) and have been shown to be similar in size to the portion of the visual field processed by a cortical **hypercolumn** (see Chapter 8). Therefore, the size of a spatial zone of binocular rivalry will increase as more peripheral portions of the visual field are stimulated by rivalrous stimuli.

When a given portion of the visual field is suppressed in one eye's image during rivalry, the sensitivity of that region is inhibited or reduced. Experiments that compared detection thresholds when "probe" stimuli were presented to either the dominant or suppressed eye during rivalry showed that the strength of the inhibition is typically on the order of 0.5 log units; that is, there is a threefold elevation in detection threshold for stimuli presented to the suppressed eye due to the inhibition (Wales and Fox, 1970). It was originally thought that the strength of the inhibition was the same regardless of the type of probe stimulus used (e.g., detection of luminance, detection of contrast or detection of motion); in other words, the strength of rivalry was specific to particular locations in the field at which conflicting stimuli are present, but not specific to the precise characteristics of the stimuli being detected (Blake and Fox, 1974a). However, more recent studies suggest that chromatic stimuli are suppressed to a greater extent than are achromatic stimuli (Smith et al., 1982; Ooi and Loop, 1994). The degree of inhibition remains the same throughout the period of suppression (Fox and Check, 1972).

A visually stronger stimulus is less likely to be suppressed during rivalry, and in fact will be visible a greater proportion of the time than will a weaker stimulus (Fig. 5-5) (Levelt, 1965). For example, two gratings of equal contrast but orthogonal orientations may be perceived alternately, with each eye's view visible for 50% of the time and suppressed for 50% of the time. However, if a high-contrast grating is presented to one eye and a low-contrast grating to the fellow eye, the high-contrast grating will be perceived more than 50% of the time, and the low-contrast grating will be seen less than 50% of the time.

Binocular rivalry shares many of the characteristics of physiological binocular suppression, such as the removal of some portions of the visual field from perception and similar types of dominant visual stimuli, leading some researchers to postulate that rivalry and suppression have common neural mechanisms. However, binocular rivalry does differ in some ways from suppression, so the two phenomena are, in fact, not reflections of the same processes. In both physiological suppression and rivalry, the degree of threshold elevation can vary in strength as a function of stimulus characteristics. Conversely, suppression and rivalry differ in the rate of change of the visibility of targets in each eye. In binocular rivalry, the percept *continually* changes from moment to moment at each local area as a result of alternation of suppression between the two eyes. The rate of rivalrous alternation is not under voluntary control by attentional or cognitive mechanisms (Blake et al., 1971). In addition, although the region of an image that is momentarily suppressed in rivalry is not consciously perceived, it maintains an influence over the visual system. The strength of a suppressed stimulus can still modulate the period of time for which that stimulus is suppressed, that is, the length of its suppression period. Any sudden change made in the suppressed image, for example, a sudden change in orientation, spatial frequency or contrast may terminate the period of suppression and make that image available to perception (Walker and Powell, 1979). Rivalry requires that the images differ in the two eyes, whereas suppression, especially pathological suppression, can still occur when identical stimuli are presented to each eye (Schor, 1977). Finally, the suppression in normal

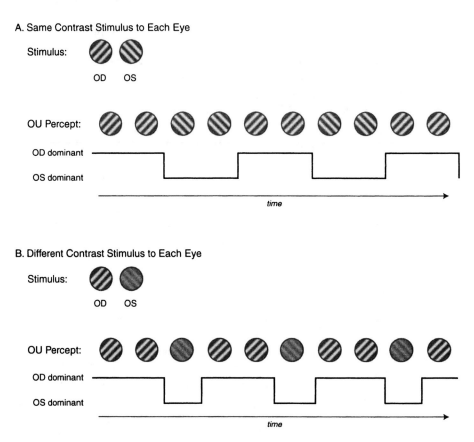

**Figure 5-5**    Influence of stimulus strength on dominance during rivalry. Two stimuli of equal strength or salience will be dominant an equal proportion of the time. When two stimuli are of unequal strength, the stronger stimulus will be dominant a greater proportion of the time.

binocular rivalry tends to be stronger than that of the pathological suppression found in strabismus (Holopigian et al., 1988).

In a direct comparison of binocular rivalry and pathological suppression caused by esotropia (Smith et al., 1985), it was found that normal observers undergoing rivalry exhibited wavelength-specific losses in sensitivity during the suppression phase. This suggests selective inhibition of the chromatic channels to a greater degree than the achromatic channels during binocular rivalry. However, the strabismic observers did not exhibit such wavelength-specific sensitivity losses during suppression. These results suggest that binocular rivalry and strabismic suppression reflect distinct neural processes. In addition, pathological strabismic suppression differs from the binocular suppression that occurs in the normal visual system, with a much slower onset time (as long as 1 to 2 minutes) compared to physiological suppression (under 200 ms) (Jampolsky, 1955; Kaufman, 1963).

One might assume that binocular rivalry occurs only under artificial conditions, such as the intentional presentation of dissimilar images to each eye or under abnormal conditions such as in the presence of binocular confusion. However, binocular rivalry may also be present in normal everyday binocular viewing. Nakayama and Shimojo (1990) describe the beneficial use of binocular rivalry when a near object occludes a farther object. In this situation, called **Da Vinci stereopsis**, one eye may in fact see part of the more distant object that is occluded from the other eye's image. This leads to a rivalrous percept caused by images of the occluding near object and part of the occluded distant object being formed on corresponding points. The rivalrous percept provides the visual system with cues to the relative distances of the two objects. An example of this phenomenon is seen in Fig. 5-6. The left eye's image contains only the flat panel, but the right eye's image includes both a portion of the sphere and the occluding panel. These rivalrous images serve to inform the visual system that the sphere is behind the panel.

The mode of presentation of rivalrous stimuli has been likened to that of **dichoptic masking**, a form of visual masking in which differing stimuli are

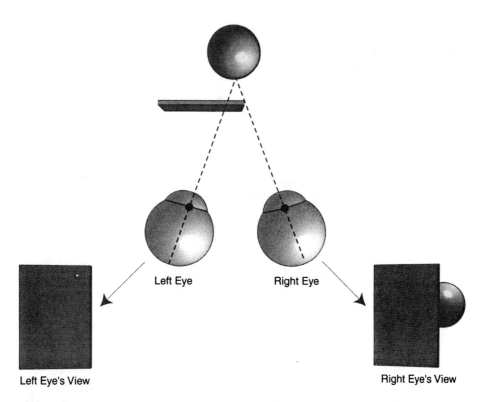

Left Eye                 Right Eye

Left Eye's View                                      Right Eye's View

**Figure 5-6**  Da Vinci stereopsis occurs when a portion of one eye's view is occluded by a nearer object. The lack of matching points in the other eye's half-view provides a cue to the relative depths of the two objects.

presented to each eye as in binocular rivalry. In the case of dichoptic masking, the target to be detected is presented to one eye and a mask that reduces the visibility of the target is presented to the fellow eye (see Chapter 6). However, the behavior of binocular rivalry differs from that of dichoptic masking, and the two effects can be combined, suggesting that they in fact do not represent the same phenomenon. Rivalry is also similar in some respects to monocular forms of inhibition (for example, see Andrews and Purves, 1997), such as the monocular suppression seen in saccadic eye movements, but here, too, the similarities do not prove shared mechanisms. These findings have led scientists to conclude that rivalry is but one of a group of several inhibitory processes in the visual system.

At first, it was thought that rivalry must occur at a relatively high level in the visual system because spatial and motion adaptation can occur in response to a suppressed stimulus during rivalry, even though the suppressed stimulus is not seen (Blake and Fox, 1974b; Lehmkuhle and Fox, 1975). Such adaptation effects are cortical phenomena, and rivalry would therefore need to take place at stages beyond which adaptation occurs; if not, suppressed stimuli could not have an adapting effect. However, more recent studies suggest that suppressed stimuli do not produce adaptation (Lehky and Blake, 1991), leaving the precise locus of binocular rivalry in the visual system still a mystery.

# DETERMINANTS OF FUSION, SUPPRESSION, AND RIVALRY

What determines which particular mechanism of combining information from two eyes is used? That is, under what conditions do we *fuse, suppress,* or undergo *rivalry*? The most important determinant is the **similarity of targets in each eye.** We can demonstrate this principle with a few examples. In Fig. 5-7, we present vastly different images to each eye, in this case, a localized contour (oblique line) to one eye and an empty uniform field to the other. When combined binocularly, the contour suppresses the uniform field of other eye; that is, the more salient contour stimulus suppresses the weaker blank stimulus. Contours can be thought of as dominant over blank fields. The suppression extends over a small area beyond the contour, producing a "halo" or spatial **zone of suppression.** In other words, the suppression is strongest at the contour location and weakens with spatial separation from the contour. It has been suggested that the zone of suppression results from the inhibitory effect of the surround region of center-surround receptive fields excited by the contour. This effect is stronger when the contour is placed at the fovea than when it is placed in the retinal periphery. In addition, the size of the zone of suppression decreases with increasing spatial frequency of the targets (Liu and Schor, 1994), similar to the reduction of the size of Panum's area with increasing spatial frequency noted in Chapter 3.

Suppression may also occur if localized pattern stimuli that differ in some spatial dimension such as orientation are presented to each eye. For example, in Fig. 5-8, single contours (oblique lines) are presented to each eye, but at vastly

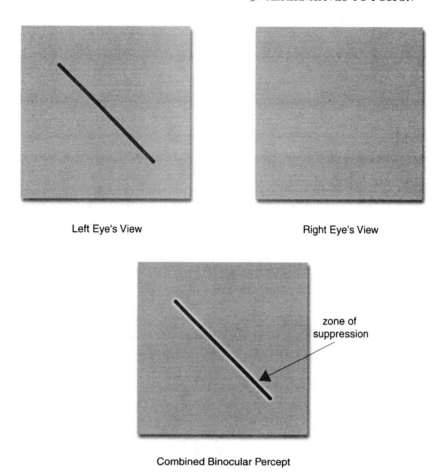

Left Eye's View    Right Eye's View

Combined Binocular Percept

**Figure 5-7**    The presentation of contour in one eye's image and a field without contours in the other's results in a zone of suppression in the uncontoured field's background in the region surrounding the fellow eye's contour.

different orientations to each other. In the binocular percept, the locus where the two lines intersect seems *darker* than the other parts of each line, suggesting that the visual system has combined the information from each line at the location at which the retinal images are similar. However, a halo of **suppression** occurs just outside of the intersection, where the retinal images differ greatly. Once again, large differences in the two eyes' images can lead to suppression.

Binocular suppression does not occur only with contours of different orientations. It can also happen with a focused sharp contour in one eye and a *blurred* contour of the same orientation in the fellow eye. With sufficient blur, the blurred contour may be suppressed. Such suppression is seen in patients with significant degrees of uncorrected anisometropia.

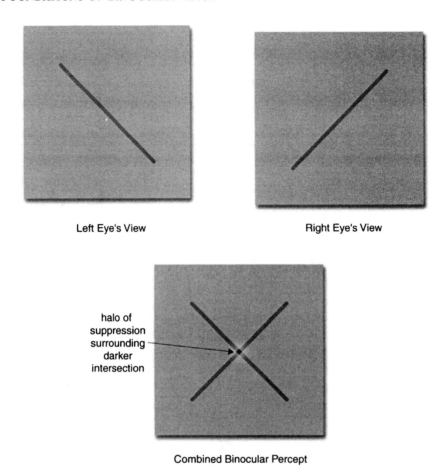

Left Eye's View                                   Right Eye's View

halo of
suppression
surrounding
darker
intersection

Combined Binocular Percept

**Figure 5-8**    Orthogonal single contours viewed binocularly yield an X in which a zone adjacent to the crossing of the X is suppressed. This is caused by the suppression of one contour by the other.

Suppression is more commonly seen with localized stimuli. When large contours are presented to each eye that differ in orientation (see Fig. 5-4), rather than suppression of the entire large image of one eye, **mosaic binocular rivalry** is perceived (Blake et al., 1992). Small rivalrous contours tend to be entirely suppressed. In other words, although *single* or *small* localized dissimilar contours tend to be suppressed, either totally or partially, *groups* of dissimilar contours or large areas of contours tend to undergo rivalry. Rivalry can be thought of as alternating suppression in a number of independent focal *local areas*.

Binocular suppression and rivalry most likely share some underlying cortical mechanisms and share some common features. For example, in suppression, the *stronger* you make the stimulus in one eye (in brightness, contrast, color, motion, or spatial frequency), the more completely it will suppress the other eye's image. Similarly, in rivalry, the stronger you make the target of one eye, the *longer* its view will "win out" in the rivalry. That eye's image in a given area will suppress the other eye's image for a *longer period of time* before the percept switches to that of the other eye. However, the strength of the suppressed image is more influential on the length of the suppression period than the salience of the dominant image. In addition, with rivalrous stimuli, a contour within the dominant image may actually suppress *neighboring* background regions of the other eye's view, replacing them with the background of the dominant image. This is the equivalent of the halo of suppression noted earlier.

In the real world, the contours presented to each eye when one views real objects tend to be similar. Real-world objects provide similar edges or borders to similar locations in each eye's image. In this situation, the visual system can combine the contours in each eye's image together effectively, yielding **binocular fusion**.

## BINOCULAR LUSTER

What if we present contours of similar shape and orientation to each eye, yet they differ greatly in color or luminance or have opposite contrast signs? In Fig. 5-9, we present dark contours on a light background to one eye and light contours on a dark background to the other. The *locations* of the contours are the same in the images of each eye, but the contours are of different *luminances*. The similarity of the spatial properties of corresponding contours in the two images allows fu-

Right Eye's View                                    Left Eye's View

**Figure 5-9** Binocular luster occurs when objects of different contrast polarities are fused. The percept is that of a shimmering silvery surface much like the reflection of light off a chrome surface.

sion to occur. However, the vastly differing luminances of the images are not simply fused. The light and dark regions of each image are not simply averaged out into a uniform gray; we still see the fused shape. However, the background appears "glossy," "silvery," or "shimmering" like polished chrome. This appearance is called **binocular luster** (Panum, 1858) or, in the case of images of differing color, **binocular color mixing** (Walls, 1942). Luster occurs when corresponding retinal points get the same contour information but different luminance or color information; it is simply a specialized form of binocular rivalry. It has been proposed that the shimmering appearance of luster mimics the shiny appearance of chrome because when viewing chrome, one eye tends to receive a bright reflection off the metal surface while the other does not, yielding the same type of luminance-based rivalry.

| | |
|---|---|
| **CLINICAL PROCEDURE** | The phenomenon of luster is useful in vision therapy because many techniques present different stimuli to the two eyes by using a red filter over one eye and a green filter over the other when viewing red and green targets (**anaglyphic** presentations). Under these conditions, luster between the red and green images will be seen if a patient exhibits binocular fusion but fails to be perceived when pathological suppression is present. |

Generally, the smaller the targets, the more likely that color mixing will occur. Large formless displays of differing color (e.g., looking at a blank wall while wearing red/green anaglyphic filters) will more frequently produce color rivalry than luster.

**Figure 5-10** Different forms of binocular combination need not be mutually exclusive. In this figure, a stereoscopic yet lustrous stimulus is displayed.

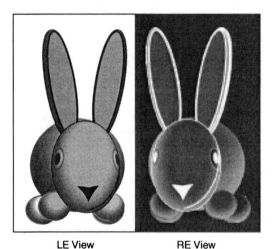

LE View          RE View

Luster does not preclude the existence of concurrent excitatory processing; in other words, the presence of rivalry does not prevent the simultaneous percept of stereopsis. One can present a stereogram in which the disparate elements are of opposite contrasts, yielding luster (Julesz and Tyler, 1976). Figure 5-10 illustrates such a stimulus. The left- and right-eye haploscopic views of a target are shown, but the images are opposite in contrast. If both images are viewed binocularly as a stereogram, the visual system is still capable of fusing the two monocular views into a single stereoscopic percept. This is not to say that the perceived depth is as strong or persistent as it would be in the absence of rivalry (Levy and Lawson, 1978), so rivalry does interfere somewhat with the processing of stereopsis, but stereopsis still can be perceived. This suggests that rivalry and fusion with stereopsis are distinct processes that are mediated by independent mechanisms. Both mechanisms can be activated at the same time at the same spatial location.

## MECHANISMS OF SUPPRESSION AND RIVALRY

Although the precise mechanisms responsible for suppression are not yet fully known, several likely mechanisms have been proposed. One may be inhibitory interactions in which neurons responding to stimulation of the dominant eye actively inhibit the activity of neurons responding to the nondominant eye. As we will see in Chapter 8, such inhibitory interactions may exist between laminae of the lateral geniculate nucleus (LGN). It is also known that there are feedback loops from the cortex back to the LGN. Such feedback, which may form the basis of an attentional gating mechanism, may also serve to shut off information from the suppressed eye. Finally, rich lateral connections exist between cortical cells and between cortical areas, opening the possibility of intracortical pathways for binocular suppression.

Determining which of these proposed mechanisms is truly involved in suppression and rivalry has been an arduous task. Randolph Blake and coworkers have been examining this problem with a technique they call "psychoanatomy," the use of psychophysics to help determine the anatomic locus of a given visual function. By examining what visual functions are and are not interrupted by binocular rivalry, they have determined the order of processing of rivalry relative to the tested functions. For example, if one eye adapts to a tilted grating while the fellow eye is suppressed, and then fixation is alternated, will the fellow eye exhibit a tilt aftereffect when viewing a nontilted grating? It turns out that it will. Aftereffects such as spatial frequency and tilt aftereffects are not adversely affected when the adapted stimulus is suppressed in a rivalrous presentation (Blake and Fox, 1974a). This suggests that the site of binocular rivalry processing must be after the site of processing of spatial frequency and orientation. Because these aftereffects may be generated, the aftereffects must involve some cortical processing. This suggests that binocular rivalry and suppression, too, must be attributed at least in part to cortical mechanisms. Furthermore, Sengpiel and Blakemore (1994) found that binocular cells in cat striate cortex, when stimulated with gratings at their preferred orientation, were inhibited when an orthogonal grating was presented to the receptive field of the fellow eye. Monocular cells in striate cortex did not show this effect, suggesting that rivalry must involve neurons subsequent to the binocular combination of information in striate cortex.

Although the precise neural pathways for suppression are still a mystery, vision research has provided insight into how suppression may work. Much of this research has centered on which stimuli are more or less likely to be suppressed. One way of determining the weighting of a stimulus in the combined binocular percept is by measuring the proportion of time it is seen during a rivalrous presentation. The perceived stimulus is called the **dominant stimulus**, and the stimulus that is not perceived is called the **suppressed stimulus**. The stronger of the two monocular images is more likely to be dominant (Levelt, 1965). It will be seen for longer periods of time during rivalry than will the weaker stimulus, or, stated another way, a stronger stimulus will be suppressed for shorter periods of time than will a weaker stimulus.

We should note that although the duration of suppression during rivalry relates somewhat to the degree to which that same stimulus may be suppressed in nonrivalrous presentations, these two measures are not strictly equivalent. Stimulus conditions that might affect the duration of suppression during rivalry may not affect how deeply the target is suppressed at any given moment. For example, as the contrast or luminance of a monocular image is reduced, that image will be seen for shorter periods of time during rivalry. However, the degree to which its visibility is reduced during its suppressed phase will be independent of its contrast or luminance (Blake and Camisa, 1979). Nonetheless, the interval of suppression during rivalry has still provided useful information. For example, a sharp retinal image will tend to be dominant over a blurred retinal image.

| CLINICAL APPLICATION | The suppression of a blurred image by a sharp image in the fellow eye is why **monovision contact lenses** for the correction of presbyopia work. In monovision, one eye is corrected for far, and the fellow eye is corrected for near, so that at least one eye's vision will be clear at all distances. The eye with the blurrier image during distance or near viewing is more likely to be suppressed, leaving the patient with the percept of the clear image alone. |
|---|---|
| CLINICAL APPLICATION | It is also known that a stimulus presented to the nasal retina of one eye tends to be dominant over a stimulus presented to the temporal retina of the fellow eye (Fahle, 1987) (Fig. 5-11). Fahle suggests that this may explain why esotropes are more likely than exotropes to develop **amblyopia**. In the esotrope, the image formed on the fovea of the nondeviating eye would rival with an image formed on an eccentric point in the nasal retina of the deviating eye. Because the nasal retina is dominant, it would produce a strong binocular confusion when paired with the fellow eye's fovea. To remove the confusion, suppression would be necessary. Conversely, in exotropia, the deviating eye's image is formed on the nondominant temporal retina, making it less likely to interfere with the foveal image of the nondeviating eye and therefore not requiring as deep a suppression. |

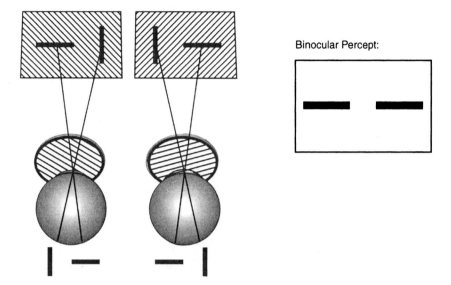

Binocular Percept:

**Figure 5-11**  Stimuli presented to the nasal retina of one eye tend to be dominant over stimuli presented at the corresponding location in the temporal retina of the fellow eye. In this stylized representation, an image of a short horizontal bar is imaged on the nasal retina of each eye, while the temporal retina receives an image of a short vertical bar. The subject's percept is of two horizontal bars.

The likelihood of suppression is also influenced by the temporal frequency of the stimulus. Brief presentations of rivalrous stimuli can prevent a percept of rivalry, resulting instead in the simultaneous perception of the two superimposed monocular images despite their dissimilarity. Blinks can likewise break down rivalry by introducing temporal transients. These observations suggest that rivalry is not an instantaneous percept; rather, it takes time to occur.

**CLINICAL APPLICATION** | Moving stimuli tend to be dominant over stationary ones, allowing motion to be used by the clinician to help break suppression.

If rivalrous stimuli are presented to locations in the peripheral retina, the size of the **spatial zone of suppression** increases with greater eccentricity from the fovea. The extent of the zone is determined by increasing the size of a rivalrous stimulus until its percept changes from the entire stimulus alternating as a whole to piecemeal rivalry in different regions of the stimulus (Blake et al., 1992). The rate of increase in the size of the zone of suppression with increased eccentricity is in agreement with measured values for the cortical magnification factor, suggesting that the spatial zone of suppression may mirror the area of the visual field served by individual cortical hypercolumns. Similarly, the size of the zone of suppression decreases linearly with increasing spatial frequency of orthogonally oriented gratings, reflecting the dependence of the size of the suppression zone on the size of receptive fields.

Finally, suppression requires spatial overlap or close proximity of the dominant and suppressed images. Suppression is less likely to occur when the dominant and suppressed stimuli are spatially separated, and the duration for which the suppression lasts decreases (Kaufman, 1963).

It should be noted that different visual features, such as form, color, and depth, may be suppressed independently of each other. For example, the color of a stimulus but not its form or depth might be suppressed (Treisman, 1962).

Two competing theories have been offered for the phenomenon of rivalry. Helmholtz postulated that the dominant stimulus is perceived because attention is directed to it (see also Lack, 1978). Rivalry therefore would represent an alternation of attention to one, then the other, eye. The competing theory, proposed by Hering, is that the eye with the greater degree of contours present in its image will be dominant. While experiments have shown that the number or density of contours does not by itself account for the dominance of a given eye (see the preceding discussion of stimulus parameters governing rivalry), little conclusive evidence exists to support the attentional model as well (however, see Ooi and He, 1998). It should be noted, however, that stimuli known to break rivalry, such as sudden increases in brightness or apparent motion in one eye's image (Wiesenfeld and Blake, 1991), are also triggers for the activation of transient visual attention (Steinman et al., 1997; Steinman and Steinman, 1998).

More recent models of rivalry incorporate either a reciprocal lateral inhibition between monocular cortical cells just before their convergence on binocular cells or computer neural networks using a comparator neuron that monitors the output of cells and is "switched" alternately to gate (pass or not pass) either the left or the right eye's input. For example, it has been proposed that the visual system maintains independent monocular channels for the processing of left eye and right eye information in addition to a purely binocular channel (Wolfe and Blake, 1985). The binocular channel is activated only when the images presented to each eye are similar and fusible. The monocular channels are mutually inhibitory. This inhibition is what yields rivalry when images are not fusible; one monocular channel will inhibit the other, then fatigue and be inhibited in return, and so on. In other words, the visual system attempts to match similar features in the two monocular images. When this is possible, the binocular channel is activated, and fusion results. When the features of each image are too dissimilar to allow matching, the two monocular channels are each activated, and the features of one image alone are perceived at any given locus, while the fellow eye's image does not reach consciousness. These new models can account for many of the psychophysical and evoked potential data concerning rivalry, but they have not yet been put through rigorous enough testing to determine if they provide a realistic explanation for rivalry and suppression in the human visual system.

Binocular rivalry is thought to occur at a relatively high level in the visual system because adaptation can occur in response to a suppressed stimulus during rivalry, even though the suppressed stimulus is not seen (Blake and Fox, 1974b;

Lehmkuhle and Fox, 1975). Adaptation effects are cortical phenomena, and rivalry must take place at stages beyond those at which adaptation occurs; if not, the suppressed stimuli could not have an adapting effect.

## *MEASURING SUPPRESSION*

**CLINICAL PROCEDURE**

Each of the forms of binocular combination outside of stereopsis can be tested in patients using the **Worth four-dot test** (see Fig. 5-12). The Worth four-dot test uses a flashlight with four small dots of light (one white, one red, and two green lights) viewed by the patient wearing red/green anaglyphic glasses; that is, there is a red filter over the right eye and a green filter over the left eye. The top dot is red, the two side dots are green, and the bottom one is white. The right eye wearing the red filter sees only two dots: the red dot and the white dot (which appears red). The green dots are filtered out by the red filter. Similarly, the left eye sees only three dots: the two green dots and the white dot (which appears green). When tested monocularly, the patient will report seeing two red dots when the left eye is occluded and three green dots when the right eye is occluded.

If the patient has normal binocular vision and is capable of binocular *fusion*, the patient viewing with both eyes will perceive a total of four dots: the red dot seen by the right eye, the green dots seen by the left eye and the white dot seen by both eyes. Remember that the white dot is filtered to be seen as red in one eye and green in the other. The dissimilarity of the colors seen in each eye's image can result in *rivalry*, where the dot keeps changing in color from red to green and so on, or more commonly in *luster*—it will look like a shiny kind of "not quite white." In patients with mild binocular problems, they might even *suppress* only in the spatial region of the bottom white dot and will see four dots, but the white dot will appear to be either red or green all of the time.

Some patients may have difficulty with fusion and may experience *diplopia* on this test. Diplopic patients will see a total of five dots; that is, all of the dots seen by each eye alone separated from each other and not combined into a single unified percept.

A strabismic patient may also exhibit *suppression* on the Worth four-dot test by seeing only the dots detected by one eye alone; that is, only two dots (if the left eye is suppressed) or three dots (if the right eye is suppressed).

**CLINICAL APPLICATION**

In strabismus, the deviation of an eye will lead to diplopia and binocular confusion. Both diplopia and confusion are quite disruptive to the patient because it is difficult to navigate through visual space while seeing double or seeing two different objects in the same location. To avoid confusion, a newly strabismic patient will initially experience rivalry, with only one eye's or the other's image contributing to perception at any given moment. That is, they

A 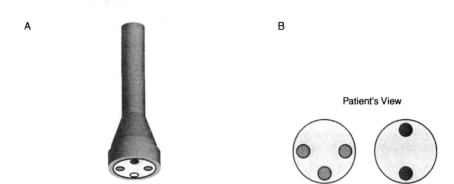 B

Patient's View

Left Eye View    Right Eye View

C    Perceived View

Fusion with Rivalry                Suppression

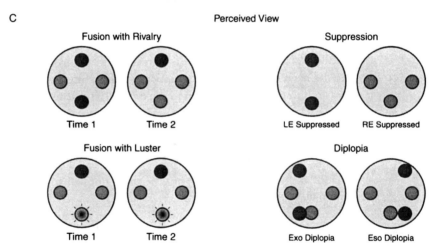

Time 1    Time 2        LE Suppressed    RE Suppressed

Fusion with Luster                 Diplopia

Time 1    Time 2        Exo Diplopia    Eso Diplopia

**Figure 5-12**   **A:** The Worth four-dot test is performed by viewing a flashlight containing four colored lights while wearing red-green glasses. **B:** When viewing monocularly, the left eye sees three green lights, while the right eye sees two red lights. **C:** The perception of the lights differs depending on the degree of binocularity. With fusion, four lights are seen. If the bottom dot, visible to each eye but seen as green by the left eye and red by the right, is fused as well, the patient will see it as having luster; if not, the bottom dot will demonstrate rivalry, an alternating suppression such that it changes color between red and green. If one eye undergoes suppression, only the dots visible through the filter before the other eye will be seen; a left eye suppression will leave two dots visible, whereas a right eye suppression will result in three dots being seen. If a strabismus is present, five dots will be seen, with one eye's dots displaced relative to those of the other eye.

will alternately suppress each eye's view. Over time, some strabismic patients will develop a preference for one eye, leading to longer periods of dominance of the foveating eye during rivalry. With time, a preference for fixation with the dominant eye develops, leading to even longer periods of dominance with the foveating eye. Eventually, they will begin to "shut off" the deviating eye's view continuously rather than intermittently; that is, the strabismic will exhibit **suppression**. This pathological form of suppression involves the same suppression mechanism we discussed earlier for normal vision, but carried out to an extreme degree. Long-term continuous suppression of the deviating eye will lead to **amblyopia** in that eye.

In **esotropia,** one eye is turned inward while the other one fixates normally. In these patients, two images of the same object exist: one on the fovea of the fixating eye and the other on a nonfoveal nasal point of the turned-in eye. The image in the *deviating eye only* can be suppressed from the fovea to the nasal part of the retina, where the deviating eye's image is located. As a result of this suppression, a zone in the patient's visual field is created where binocular vision does not exist. The size of the area of suppression is typically proportional to the size of the angle of deviation of the strabismus. It is common for the region of suppression, the **binocular suppression scotoma**, to encompass images formed on both of these points (Fig. 5-13) (Jampolsky, 1955), producing an area of suppression that can be quite large.

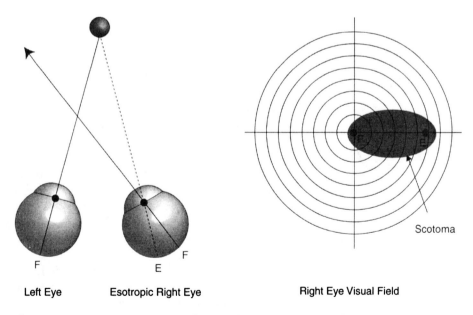

Left Eye    Esotropic Right Eye     Right Eye Visual Field

**Figure 5-13** A binocular suppression scotoma encompasses both the fovea of the deviating eye and the eccentric point now being used for fixation.

CLINICAL | The size of the suppression scotoma is related to the degree of stereopsis.
APPLICATION | These patients will have reduced stereopsis in their central visual fields at the
locus of the suppression zone, yet can retain stereopsis in their peripheral
visual fields outside of this zone. The larger the binocular suppression scotoma, the more peripherally the retinal locus with the best stereoacuity will
lie, and because (as we will see in Chapter 7) stereoacuity is a function of
retinal eccentricity, the worse the stereoacuity.

Suppression in **exotropia** has usually been considered more extensive than
in esotropia, encompassing the entire temporal hemiretina from the fovea to the
retinal periphery. Exotropia is more frequently intermittent than is esotropia, and
suppression will be manifested in intermittent exotropia only during the period in
which the eye is deviated. During the times that there is no strabismus and the
eyes are fused, the suppression will disappear.

Some exotropia is alternating; that is, the patient has no strong preference for
fixating with one eye over the other. Under these conditions, whichever eye is
turned at a given moment is suppressed (alternate suppression). This tells us that
suppression can be a dynamic process. Our brains can turn a given area of one
eye's view on or off from moment to moment.

**Anisometropes** suppress the image of the more blurred eye, that is, the eye
with the larger refractive error. Monocular blur will also allow that eye to be
suppressed during binocular rivalry. After wearing a monovision prescription, a
prescription inducing anisometropia for only 1 day, the depth of the suppression
in the blurred eye will increase (Schor et al., 1987), suggesting that long-term anisometropia may lead to prolonged suppression.

CLINICAL | Regardless of the etiology of the binocular suppression, if the suppression is
APPLICATION | very deep and constant, the patient may develop **amblyopia** (Banks et al.,
1975). In amblyopia, one eye is suppressed to the degree that it remains
abnormal even when the other eye is covered, i.e., under *monocular* conditions (e.g., reduced acuity, which is part of the clinical definition of amblyopia).
Amblyopia typically can result from **strabismus** or **anisometropia**.

Visual acuity in amblyopia may be worse under binocular conditions than
with the amblyopic eye alone (Schor et al., 1976). However, the reduced visual
acuity and stereopsis of amblyopia may persist even after the suppression is reduced or eliminated (Schor et al., 1976), implying that amblyopia does not simply
result from long-standing constant suppression alone; other factors must also
come into play (see also Holopigian et al., 1988). As we will see when we discuss
the neurophysiology of binocular vision, amblyopia is most likely to develop when
strabismus or anisometropia occur in *infancy*, during the development period of
binocular vision. If the images of the two eyes are dissimilar during this **critical
period** of development, because of either a misplaced image or a blurred image,
amblyopia will occur.

**CLINICAL APPLICATION**

Although suppression helps strabismics deal with navigating in the real world by preventing diplopia and confusion, the resultant loss of binocular vision can be a handicap to the patient. The goal of vision therapy is to restore single simultaneous binocular vision with properly aligned eyes. Our clinical treatment of strabismus is difficult because merely providing a clear image to the strabismic eye is not sufficient to produce binocularity. A strabismic who is suppressing has no need to properly align the suppressed eye with the foveating eye. We need to *break down* the suppression with **vision therapy** and make the strabismic use both eyes together *before* we can get him or her to align both eyes properly. Therefore, the first step in the diagnosis and treatment of strabismus is to determine if the patient is suppressing.

**CLINICAL PROCEDURE**

One way to diagnose the presence of suppression, as discussed earlier, is the **Worth four-dot test**. However, the Worth four-dot test also helps us to grade the size of a suppression scotoma. The flashlight that presents the dot targets is simply moved farther away from the patient, reducing the visual angle that its dot targets subtend. If a patient notes suppression (that is, two or three dots seen) at the standard near testing distance of 13 inches, a large suppression scotoma is present. Conversely, if a patient notes no suppression (that is, four dots are seen) at the standard near testing distance of 13 inches but shows suppression at a farther distance, a smaller suppression scotoma must be present. Occasionally, a patient may have a strabismus of sufficiently small angle of deviation that it defies detection with the standard cover test. The detection of a suppression scotoma using the Worth four-dot test at a remote testing distance can confirm the diagnosis.

**CLINICAL PROCEDURE**

Suppression can also be revealed clinically using prisms. A simple test for suppression involves introducing a four-diopter prism, in what is called the **four base-out test**. The patient is asked to fixate a small isolated target, such as a letter on a nearpoint Snellen chart. Prism is then introduced before the eye in question, displacing its image toward the base of the prism. If the eye makes a vergence movement to follow the displacement of the image, the central vision of that eye is not suppressed. If there is no eye movement, the image is presumed to have been displaced within a suppression zone, and hence its displacement remains undetected by the patient. The prism is introduced base-out for detecting suppression in small-angle esotropia.

**CLINICAL PROCEDURE**

Another way a clinician will commonly find suppression is during standard binocular testing in the phoropter. When the images of the two eyes are dissociated with prism during *phoria* **testing**, diplopia should be noted. If diplopia is not perceived, the patient is suppressing (Fig. 5-14). For measuring lateral phorias, the images of the two eyes are separated vertically with prism.

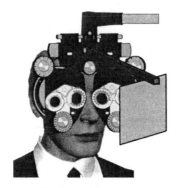

Phoria Testing

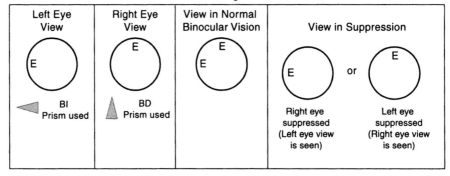

| Left Eye View | Right Eye View | View in Normal Binocular Vision | View in Suppression |
|---|---|---|---|
| E<br>BI<br>Prism used | E<br>BD<br>Prism used | E<br>E | E    or    E<br><br>Right eye suppressed (Left eye view is seen)    Left eye suppressed (Right eye view is seen) |

BO Vergence Testing

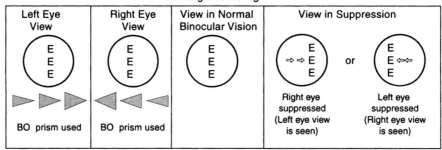

| Left Eye View | Right Eye View | View in Normal Binocular Vision | View in Suppression |
|---|---|---|---|
| E<br>E<br>E<br>BO prism used | E<br>E<br>E<br>BO prism used | E<br>E<br>E | E<br>⇨ ⇨ E<br>E    or    E<br>E ⇦⇦<br>E<br><br>Right eye suppressed (Left eye view is seen)    Left eye suppressed (Right eye view is seen) |

**Figure 5-14** Suppression can be discovered during phoria and vergence testing. During phoria testing, the left eye's view is displaced horizontally by base-in prism, and the right eye's vertically by base-down prism. In normal binocular vision, a diplopic target is seen. With suppression, only one of the two displaced target images will be seen; the fellow eye's target is not seen because it is suppressed. Similarly, in vergence (duction) testing, a set of letters is displaced in opposite directions in each eye, in this case, with base-out prism in each eye, yielding crossed binocular disparity. In normal binocular vision, the two images are fused so long as the prism strength is not enough to create diplopia. With suppression, only one of the two displaced target images will be seen, moving in a direction toward the apex of the prism before the nonsuppressed eye. (Source: Image © www.arttoday.com)

People with normal binocular vision will see two images because the images are formed on widely separated noncorresponding points. If the person is suppressing, however, only one eye's image will be seen. The size of the suppression area can be ascertained by the magnitude of the prism required to produce diplopia.

**CLINICAL PROCEDURE**

**Vergence ranges** (divergence and convergence) are determined by simultaneous application of equal but increasing amounts of base-in or base-out prisms, respectively, to both eyes. A person with normal binocular vision will continue to fuse the target with vergence eye movements. The target will continue to be seen singly and not appear to move laterally. However, a patient with suppression will report seeing a single image that moves in the direction of the prism apex before the nonsuppressing eye. The perceived direction of motion therefore tells you which eye is suppressing.

**CLINICAL PROCEDURE**

Another means of testing for suppression is by using **vectographic visual acuity slides**. The eye chart presents some letters visible only to the right eye and others visible only to the left eye. If the letters presented to one eye are misread or omitted when reading the chart, that eye must be suppressing.

**CLINICAL PROCEDURE**

Finally, you can use **Bagolini lenses** to test for suppression (Fig. 5-15). This test is similar to the Maddox rod test but is less dissociating. Bagolini lenses are lenses with thin striations in them at an angle of 45° for one eye and 135° for the other. A patient views a penlight while wearing these lenses. The monocular percepts are of a dot of light from the penlight with a single oblique line of light spreading out from it orthogonal to the striations. In normal individuals, when the monocular images are combined, they form an "X" meeting at the dot of light. If the entire left eye's image is suppressed, the patient will see only the right eye's oblique line. In some cases, just the foveal region will be suppressed, and the patient sees an "X" where a portion of one line of the "X" is missing, corresponding to the spatial projection of the suppression zone.

By combining Bagolini lenses with **neutral-density filters**, we can *grade* the **degree or "depth" of suppression**. Remember that the depth of suppression is related to the differences in strength between the images of the two eyes. To rate the suppression, the nonsuppressing eye's image is rendered weaker by reducing the luminance of its image by introducing increasingly dense filters. At some point, the patient will start perceiving both images again. The denser the filter required, the deeper the suppression.

**CLINICAL PROCEDURE**

After diagnosing suppression, the clinician must face the challenge of "breaking" the suppression of a strabismic patient, that is, increasing the relative weighting of the image of the suppressed eye until both eyes once again contribute equally to the binocular percept. This may be accomplished to

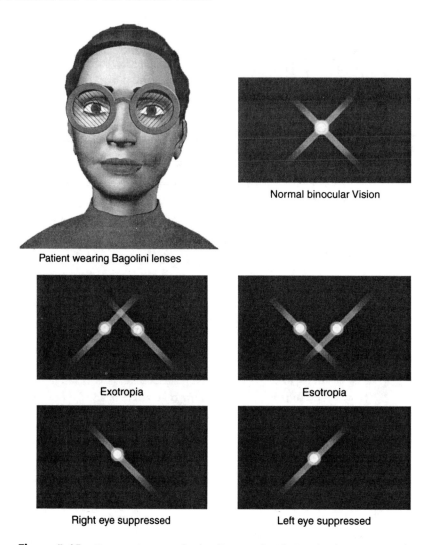

Patient wearing Bagolini lenses

Normal binocular Vision

Exotropia

Esotropia

Right eye suppressed

Left eye suppressed

**Figure 5-15**    Suppression can also be diagnosed with Bagolini lenses, striated plano lenses that produce linear streaks emanating on either side of a point source of light such as that produced by a penlight. With normal binocular vision, the percept is that of a crossed set of lines, where the crossing is exactly at the location of the point of light. In the presence of strabismus, the two streaks do not cross at the points; rather, they are displaced from one another. With suppression, one or the other streak is not seen.

some degree by enhancing the image of the suppressed eye, for example, by properly refracting that eye to remove the deleterious effects of blur, but it is easier to degrade the image of the nonsuppressed eye until the two eyes' images are more equal. This can be done in a variety of ways. A commonly used method is **occluding** the dominant eye with a **patch** for a period of time every day. As noted above, **neutral density filters**, when applied to the non-suppressing eye, can degrade its image quality, reducing the relative weighting of that eye in the binocular percept. Likewise, blur induced by a frosted or blurring lens or chromatic differences between the two eyes introduced by red/green anaglyphic glasses can produce similar results. Finally, if the subject is able to view dichoptic stimuli in a stereoscope, one can use motion or other temporal changes to make the suppressed eye's image more salient. Motion is a strong activator of reflexive attention (Steinman et al., 1997; Steinman and Steinman, 1998); the activation of attention makes that eye's image more difficult to suppress. In addition, the clinician may present visual stimuli to the two eyes alternately with exposure durations shorter than the latency of the onset of suppression.

## SUMMARY AND KEY POINTS

- When very different images are formed simultaneously on corresponding retinal points in the two eyes, **binocular confusion**, an incorrect percept of different objects simultaneously occupying same location, occurs. Because the visual system cannot fuse grossly dissimilar images into a single unified percept, it must use other mechanisms to handle the two differing monocular images.

- **Binocular suppression** occurs when the visual system "ignores" or "turns off" all or part of the image to one eye, so that only one of the two different images is seen. Reduced sensitivity, elevated thresholds, and prolonged reaction times occur in the suppressed zones. Prolonged diplopia may result in **pathological suppression**, in which the visual system "shuts off" the weaker eye's image to yield single vision.

- **Binocular rivalry** is an intermittent and alternating suppression in local areas; focal areas are suppressed in each eye alternately. Small dissimilar targets may result in alternating suppression of each eye's entire image of the target (**exclusive dominance**), but larger dissimilar stimuli are perceived as a "patch-work" in which independent local areas of contour (**spatial zones of binocular rivalry**) alternate over time between the left- and right-eye images (**mosaic dominance**).

- Binocular rivalry and binocular suppression probably share some common neural mechanisms. In both, stronger visual stimuli are more likely to dominate over weaker stimuli. However, this dominance is expressed differently. In binocular suppression, the stronger stimulus will more thoroughly suppress the weaker stimulus, whereas in binocular rivalry the stronger stimulus will be dominant for longer periods.

- Binocular rivalry differs from binocular suppression in several ways. Rivalry is a constantly changing process, is entirely involuntary, can exist concurrently with stereopsis, and always requires competing stimuli in each eye. In binocular rivalry, the suppressed stimulus can influence the visual system, either by modulating the period of time for which it is suppressed based on the strength of the stimulus or by changing its appearance, which will terminate the suppression and make the stimulus dominant. Large areas or groups of contours differing in orientation presented to each eye produce will yield binocular rivalry, but single dissimilar contours tend to be suppressed, either totally or partially.

- Binocular suppression can occur under several conditions. A uniform field in one eye will be suppressed by a contour in the other eye, and a **halo of suppression** will extend slightly beyond the edges of the contour. Localized patterns that differ in spatial aspects such as orientation or blur can produce binocular suppression just outside of the intersection of the two eyes' images, where the retinal images differ greatly. Any large differences in the two eyes' images can lead to binocular suppression.

- A halo of suppression can also occur in binocular rivalry; a contour within the **dominant image** may actually suppress neighboring background regions of the other eye's view, replacing them with the background of the dominant image.

- **Binocular luster** results when contours that differ greatly in color or luminance or have opposite contrast signs are presented to each eye. This may used for testing fusion clinically.

- Pathological binocular suppression can result from strabismus or anisometropia. Esotropes tend to experience **constant strabismus**, whereas exotropes tend to have **intermittent strabismus**. In strabismus both the image from the fovea of the fixating eye and the corresponding nonfoveal point of the deviating eye are enclosed in a **binocular suppression scotoma**. Binocular vision can be experienced only beyond this scotoma.

- Esotropes are more likely to experience **constant unilateral strabismus**, whereas exotropes usually experience **alternating strabismus**. Anisometropes effectively "shut off" the image of the more blurred eye.

- Long-standing monocular suppression can lead to **amblyopia**, in which vision remains abnormal even under monocular conditions, although suppression is not the only mechanism involved in amblyopia.

- Common clinical methods used to measure suppression include the **Worth four-dot test**, **phoria testing**, **vergence ranges**, or **Bagolini lenses**.

- The basic steps in treatment of amblyopia include providing a clear image to the suppressed eye, aligning both eyes properly, and degrading the image to the fellow eye to break the suppression.

- The precise neural mechanisms responsible for suppression are not yet fully known, but some of the proposed mechanisms include **inhibitory interactions** between the dominant eye and the nondominant eye, between laminae of the LGN, between the cortex and the LGN, and between cortical areas.

- Studies have shown that binocular rivalry occurs in the cortex beyond the point where binocular information is combined after the site of processing of spatial frequency and orientation.

- The likelihood of suppression depends on several characteristics of the image. Factors that make an image dominant include location on the nasal retina, high contrast, high luminance, sharpness, motion, and brief image presentation.

- Traditionally there have been two competing theories for the phenomenon of rivalry: Helmholtz's theory is that rivalry is an **alternation of attention** to one, then the other, eye; and Hering's theory is that the eye with the **greater degree of contours** present in its image will be dominant. It is possible that neither of these theories is entirely correct. Recent models of rivalry include **reciprocal lateral inhibition** between monocular cortical cells just before their convergence on binocular cells or the possibility of a **comparator neuron** that monitors the output of a cell whose output is "switched" alternately to gate either the left or right eye's input.

## QUESTIONS

1. Would binocular rivalry occur if two gratings of the same orientation but different spatial frequency were used as stimuli for each eye?

2. Would small focal groups of dissimilar targets in each eye be more likely to produce suppression or rivalry?

3. A patient is reading a vectographic eye chart in which some letters are presented to each eye. He complains that some of the letters seem to disappear and reappear. What is your diagnosis?

4. An amblyopic patient exhibits a deep suppression in the left eye. Degrading the image in the "good" eye does not break the suppression. What are some other methods you might try to break the suppression?

5. Is it possible to have rivalry while viewing the Stereo Fly?

6. On base-out vergence testing, a single column of letters is seen moving to the left as the prism strength is increased. What is the diagnosis?

## BIBLIOGRAPHY

ANDREWS TJ *and* PURVES D (1997). *Similarities in normal and binocularly rivalrous viewing.* Proc. Natl. Acad. Sci. 94:9905–9908.

BANKS MS, ASLIN RN *and* LETSON RD (1975). *Sensitive period for the development of human binocular vision.* Science 190:675–677.

BLAKE R *and* CAMISA JC (1979). *On the inhibitory nature of binocular rivalry suppression.* J. Exp. Psychol. (Hum. Percept.) 5:315–323.

BLAKE R *and* FOX R (1974a). *Binocular rivalry suppression: insensitive to spatial frequency and orientation change.* Vis. Res. 14:687–692.

BLAKE R *and* FOX R (1974b). *Adaptation to invisible gratings and the site of binocular rivalry suppression.* Nature 249:488–490.

BLAKE R, FOX R *and* McINTYRE C (1971). *Stochastic properties of stabilized-image binocular rivalry alternations.* J. Exp. Psychol. 88:327–332.

BLAKE R, O'SHEA RP *and* MUELLER TJ (1992). *Spatial zones of binocular rivalry in central and peripheral vision.* Vis. Neurosci. 8:469–478.

FAHLE M (1987). *Naso-temporal asymmetry of binocular inhibition.* Invest. Ophthalmol. Vis. Sci. 28:1016–1017.

FOX R *and* CHECK R (1972). *Independence between binocular rivalry suppression duration and magnitude of suppression.* J. Exp. Psych. 93:283–289.

HOLOPIGIAN K, BLAKE R *and* GREENWALD MJ (1988). *Clinical suppression and amblyopia.* Invest. Ophthalmol. Vis. Sci. 29:444–451.

JAMPOLSKY A (1955). *Characteristics of suppression in strabismus.* AMA Arch. Ophthalmol. 54:683–696.

JULESZ B *and* TYLER CW (1976). *Neurontropy, an entropy-like measure of neural correlation, in binocular fusion and rivalry.* Biol. Cybernet. 22:107–119.

KAUFMAN L (1963). *On the spread of suppression and binocular rivalry.* Vis. Res. 3:401–415.

LACK LC (1978). *Selective Attention and the Control of Binocular Rivalry.* Mouton, The Hague, Netherlands: Mouton.

LEHMKUHLE S *and* FOX R (1975). *The effect of binocular rivalry suppression on the motion aftereffect.* Vis. Res. 15:855–860.

LEVELT WJM (1965). *On Binocular Rivalry.* National Defense Organization, Soesterberg, The Netherlands.

LEVY MM *and* LAWSON RB (1978). *Stereopsis and binocular rivalry from dichoptic stereograms.* Vis. Res. 18:239–246.

Liu L and Schor CM (1994). The spatial properties of binocular suppression zone. *Vis. Res.* 34:937–947.

LIU L, TYLER CW *and* SCHOR CM (1992). *Failure of rivalry at low contrast: evidence of a suprathreshold binocular summation process.* Vis. Res. 32:1471–1479.

NAKAYAMA K *and* SHIMOJO S (1990). *Da Vinci stereopsis: depth and subjective occluding contours from unpaired image points.* Vis. Res. 30:1811–1825.

OOI TL *and* HE ZJ (1998). *Determining perceptual dominance: beyond local contours.* Invest. Ophthalmol. Vis. Sci. 39:S848.

OOI TL *and* LOOP MS (1994). *Visual suppression and its effect upon color and luminance sensitivity.* Vis. Res. 34:2997–3003.

PANUM PL (1858). *Physiologische Untersuchungen über das Sehen mit zwei Augen.* Schwers, Kiel.

SCHOR CM (1977). *Visual stimuli for strabismic suppression.* Perception 6:583–593.

SCHOR CM, LANDSMAN L *and* ERIKSON P (1987). *Ocular dominance and the interocular suppression of blur in monovision.* Am. J. Optom. Physiol. Optics. 64:723–730.

SCHOR CM, TERRELL M *and* PETERSON D (1976). *Contour interaction and temporal masking in strabismus and amblyopia.* Am. J. Optom. Physiol. Optics. 53:217–223.

SENGPIEL F *and* BLAKEMORE C (1994). *Interocular control of neuronal responsiveness in cat visual cortex.* Nature 368:847–850.

SMITH EL III, LEVI DM, MANNY RE, HARWERTH RS *and* WHITE JM (1982). *Color vision is altered during the suppression phase of binocular rivalry.* J. Psych. 218:802–804.

SMITH EL III, LEVI DM, MANNY RE, HARWERTH RS *and* WHITE JM (1985). *The relationship between binocular rivalry and strabismic suppression.* Invest. Ophthalmol. Vis. Sci. 26:80–87.

STEINMAN SB *and* STEINMAN BA (1998). *Vision and attention I: Current models of visual attention*. Optom. Vis. Sci. **75**:146–155.

STEINMAN BA, STEINMAN SB *and* LEHMKUHLE S (1997). *Transient visual attention is dominated by the magnocellular stream*. Vis. Res. 37:17–23.

TREISMAN A (1962). *Binocular rivalry and stereoscopic depth perception*. Q. J. Exp. Psych. 14:23–37.

WALES R *and* FOX R (1970). *Increment detection thresholds during binocular rivalry suppression*. Percept. Psychophys. 8:90–94.

WALKER P *and* POWELL DJ (1979). *The sensitivity of binocular rivalry to changes in the nondominant stimulus*. Vis. Res. 19:247–249.

WALLS GL (1942). *The Vertebrate Eye*. Cranbrook, Bloomfield Hills, MI.

WIESENFELD H *and* BLAKE R (1991). *Apparent motion can survive binocular rivalry suppression*. Vis. Res. 31:1589–1600.

WOLFE J *and* BLAKE R (1985). *Monocular and binocular processes in human vision. In:* Models of Visual Cortex, D ROSE *and* V DOBSON, EDS., Wiley, New York.

# 6

# Binocular Summation

In Chapter 3, we compared two competing theories for binocular combination of images from each eye, the suppression theory and the fusion theory. We now know that because of the relatively slow rate at which rivalry builds up, it is more likely that the fusion theory, which states that we actually can combine information from the two eyes at any given moment, is correct. Additional evidence for fusion theory would exist if we could prove that light or contrast incident on the two eyes were *added together* in the binocular percept; that is, if thresholds obtained when two eyes are used together were lower than those obtained for either eye alone. The question we must therefore ask is whether we see better with two eyes than with one eye.

## *BINOCULAR SUMMATION*

**Binocular summation** is defined as an additivity of the information from each eye to yield binocular visual performance that exceeds monocular performance. Our performance on many visual tasks, including reading, improves under binocular conditions, whether or not depth information is provided (Sheedy et al., 1986).

One way to determine exactly how the eyes add information together is to compare performance for several tasks [for example, luminance detection, brightness matching, reaction times, critical flicker fusion frequency (CFF), visual acuity] under *binocular* viewing conditions to the performance on the same tasks under *monocular* conditions. For example, if visual acuity is measured under binocular viewing conditions, will the resolution thresholds be lower than when it is measured with one eye alone? If so, by what factor would the binocular thresholds improve? There are several possibilities of what could happen (Fig. 6-1). We could see **complete (or linear) binocular summation** in which the performance of the two eyes together equals the sum of the performance of both individual eyes;

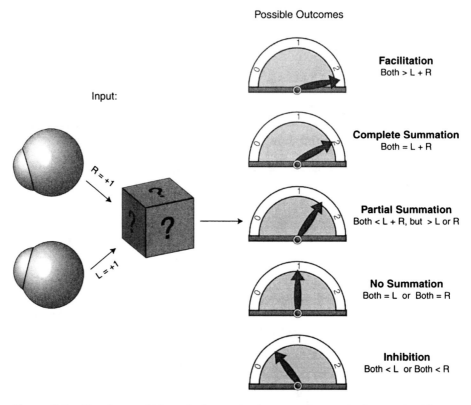

**Figure 6-1** The degree of binocular interaction between the eyes is characterized by whether binocular performance on a task, for example, sensitivity for detecting contrast or an acuity target, is greater than, equal to, or less than the performance of either eye alone.

in other words, two eyes are truly twice as good as one. It is also possible that **binocular facilitation** could occur, in which the performance of both eyes when used together is even greater than the sum of their monocular performances. Conversely, we could find **no binocular summation**, that is, two eyes are no better than one. Yet another possibility is an intermediate between these extremes, that is, **partial binocular summation**, in which two eyes are slightly better than one eye alone, but not twice as good. Finally, we could find that two eyes together perform worse than either eye alone, in other words, **binocular inhibition**. Here, the use of the second eye would degrade the sensitivity of the fellow eye relative to its monocular sensitivity.

The first investigations of binocular summation were carried out at the turn of the century by Sherrington (1909). Sherrington simultaneously stimulated each of the two eyes with square-wave flicker. However, the flicker in the fellow eye could be either in phase or 180° out of phase with the flicker in the first eye (Fig. 6-2). If information from the two eyes did indeed summate, the in-phase

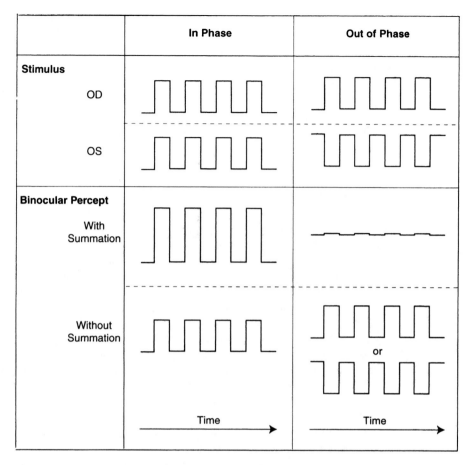

**Figure 6-2** Binocular summation was first demonstrated in an experiment using square-wave flicker. When identical flicker is presented to each eye, that is, to both eyes in phase, binocular summation would predict greater sensitivity to the flicker when viewed binocularly than when viewed monocularly. Conversely, flicker that is 180° out of phase between the two eyes would yield a cancellation of the flicker under binocular conditions if summation occurred, reducing sensitivity. Although flicker modulation detection thresholds could not be measured, the changes in sensitivity predicted by binocular summation were demonstrated via changes in the critical flicker fusion frequency in the in-phase and out-of-phase flicker conditions.

flicker would yield a binocular flicker that is greater in amplitude than either of the two monocular flickers. Furthermore, the out-of-phase flicker would yield little or no response because one eye's flicker would cancel out the other's. If no binocular summation occurred, there would be no difference between in-phase and out-of-phase conditions because the amplitude of flicker would be the same in either eye, no matter what the phase relationship. Sherrington could measure only the CFF. If binocular summation did occur, the higher perceived amplitude of flicker with binocular viewing in the in-phase condition would yield a higher CFF, whereas the lower perceived amplitude in the out-of-phase condition would yield a lower CFF. This is precisely what Sherrington found. With binocular viewing, the CFF for the in-phase condition was 51 Hz, while that of the out-of-phase condition was 49.8 Hz, a small yet statistically significant difference. Sherrington's study provided the first evidence supporting the existence of binocular summation.

Cavonius (1979) repeated Sherrington's flicker experiments but measured temporal contrast sensitivity for several temporal frequencies using sine-wave flicker rather than the CFF alone. The results of this study are plotted in Fig. 6-3A. Here, it can be seen that the binocular in-phase sensitivity is higher than the monocular flicker sensitivity, which is in turn higher than the binocular out-of-phase sensitivity. When the binocular in-phase and out-of-phase flicker sensitivities are compared directly (Fig. 6-3B), we see why Sherrington found such a small difference in the CFF. At high temporal frequencies, there is less difference in the subject's response to binocular flicker. This is also evident when the binocular (in-phase) sensitivity is compared to the monocular sensitivity (Fig. 6-3C). The benefits of binocular summation are seen mostly at the low to medium temporal frequencies. The ratio of binocular to monocular thresholds is 1.4 to 1.6 at low temporal frequencies but drops to only 1.15 at high temporal frequencies. To summarize, this study supports binocular summation by showing that we are much more sensitive to flicker binocularly than monocularly. The degree of binocular summation depends on the temporal frequency of the stimulus. At low temporal frequencies, facilitation occurs; at middle temporal frequencies, complete summation is seen; and at high temporal frequencies, only partial summation occurs. There is never a case in which summation does not occur or where inhibition occurs.

Flicker, however, is not the only visual function. How is information from the two eyes combined for other visual functions? For example, in light detection experiments, we also find that binocular absolute detection thresholds are slightly lower than monocular thresholds; that is, partial binocular summation occurs. Such summation occurs under both photopic and scotopic conditions.

If visual acuity is measured under binocular viewing conditions, acuity thresholds are only slightly better than when measured with one eye alone. These binocular thresholds are not *twice* as good. For example, a patient may have a visual acuity of OD 20/20, OS 20/20, and OU 20/15. In terms of a minimum angle of resolution, this equates to a threshold of 1.00' of arc for each eye alone and a threshold of 0.75' of arc for both eyes together. Clearly, although the binocular resolution exceeds the monocular resolution, the binocular threshold is not *half* the monocular threshold (or, stated another way, binocular sensitivity is not *twice* the monocular sensitivity). This corresponds to *partial binocular summation*.

One problem with using visual acuity as a measurement of binocular summation is that acuity represents only one point on the spatial contrast-sensitivity curve. It is the upper cutoff of the spatial contrast-sensitivity curve, just as the CFF is

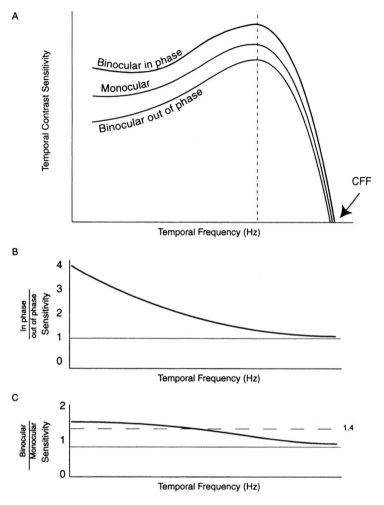

**Figure 6-3** By repeating the experiment of Fig. 6-2 with sine-wave flicker, flicker modulation detection thresholds could be measured. The CFF is altered to a small degree in accordance with binocular summation, and flicker modulation detection thresholds are affected to an even greater degree by binocular summation.

the cut-off of the temporal sensitivity curve. We might also expect that there is greater summation for middle- and low-spatial-frequency targets. Figure 6-4 shows *spatial contrast sensitivity* measured using one eye alone and with both eyes together. It should be noted that the shape of the contrast-sensitivity plot in this figure differs from that of a typical contrast-sensitivity plot because it is plotted on a linear x-axis scale rather than a logarithmic scale. The binocular sensitivity or performance exceeds the monocular sensitivity. For spatial contrast sensitivity, binocular

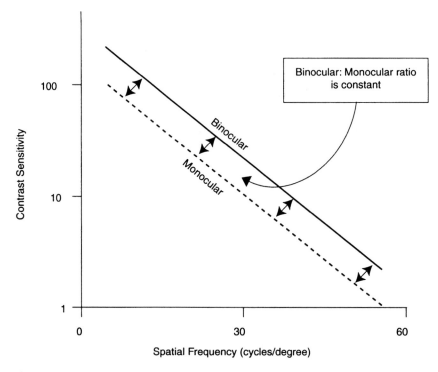

**Figure 6-4** By transforming the contrast sensitivity plot of Fig. 6-3 to a linear rather than a logarithmic scale on the x-axis, it can be shown that the improvement of binocular over monocular contrast sensitivity is constant across a broad range of spatial frequencies. The factor of improvement is 1.4.

performance is consistently about *1.4* times higher than the monocular performance, regardless of the spatial frequency measured (Campbell and Green, 1965).

---

### 🔑 Key Point

*For many experiments of binocular summation, we see an improvement of sensitivity under binocular viewing conditions of 1.4 times that of monocular viewing, or a 40% improvement.*

---

The above experiments show that binocular summation occurs. However, they do not explain how summation is achieved. There are two possible mechanisms of visual system binocular summation: probability summation and neural summation.

# PROBABILITY SUMMATION

The **independence theory** of binocular summation predicts that just because a person has two eyes, even if they were to work *totally independently*, lower thresholds would be expected under binocular conditions than with one eye alone (Pirenne, 1943). In other words, on a light detection task, for example, simply using two eyes instead of one eye would increase your chances of detecting a dim light, because the visual system could involve twice as many photoreceptors in the light collection process when both eyes were open. Stated another way, using two detectors produces better performance than does one detector. The inputs from the two eyes are not combined and are processed independently. A central decision-making process has access to both monocular inputs.

Let us look at a concrete example. Assume that the left eye alone detects a near-threshold target 60% of the time. The right eye can also detect it 60% of the time when it views the target by itself. How visible would the target be when viewed by both eyes? Statistically, the probability of seeing the target with both eyes open equals the sum of the probabilities of detecting it with either eye alone minus the probability of both eyes detecting it at the same time. In statistical terms,

$$p_{OU} = (p_{OD} + p_{OS}) - ((p_{OD})(p_{OS}))$$

where $p_{OD}$ is the probability of detecting the target with the right eye alone, $p_{OS}$ is the probability of detecting the target with the left eye alone, and $p_{OU}$ is the probability of detecting the target with both eyes together:

$$\begin{aligned} p_{OU} &= (p_{OD} + p_{OS}) - ((p_{OD})(p_{OS})) \\ &= (.60 + .60) - ((.60)(.60)) \\ &= 0.84 \end{aligned}$$

If we solve this equation for the case of monocular detection of 60% (0.6), we find that the binocular detection rate is 0.84 or 84%. When we compare the binocular detection rate to the monocular detection rate, we get a factor of $0.84/0.60 = 1.4$, or a 40% improvement. In other words, even if neurons in the two eyes act totally independently and the neurons from each eye did not converge onto a common binocular neuron in visual cortex, the binocular performance would be expected to improve by 40% because now you have "two shots" at seeing the stimulus instead of just one. This is called **probability summation**. Probability summation is the degree of improvement expected by using two eyes even without binocular combination of information.

In the experiments dealing with detection of targets mentioned above, thresholds were found to be lower (or sensitivity higher) with two eyes by a factor of 1.4, suggesting that probability summation is the only reason we see better with two eyes. However, can this degree of improvement be attributed to probability summation alone, or is it caused by **neural summation** as well? Does true binocular summation result from the convergence of monocular information in the visual system into binocular pathways? The equation described above for the probability of detection under binocular conditions depends on one particular model of probability summation. However, other statistical models exist as well, with differing predictions of the degree of improvement in detection thresholds under binocular conditions. There is, therefore, no way to predict with statistical modeling alone whether the 40% improvement in binocular thresholds over monocular thresholds is entirely attributable to probability summation or is in fact a result of a combination of probability summation and neural summation. Fortunately, there is an easy way to *directly* test for the existence of true *neural* summation. All that is needed is to display the target to both eyes under conditions where binocular fusion is not possible and compare the thresholds obtained to those measured when fusion is allowed. If you stimulate the two eyes, yet present the target to widely separated noncorresponding points, you would not expect binocular neural combination to occur. Similarly, presenting the two stimuli one after the other with a long temporal delay between them (a nonsimultaneous presentation) would prevent binocular neural combination yet allow probability summation. This is because probability summation does not require spatial or temporal synchrony between the two exposures of the target in both eyes (that is, stimuli presented at the same time and at corresponding points in each eye); it only requires that more than one exposure to the stimulus does occur. Conversely, presenting the target simultaneously to corresponding points in both eyes would allow true neural combination to occur if it does indeed exist. Therefore, the true test for neural binocular summation is to stimulate both eyes when fusion is allowed and also when it is prohibited. If the thresholds improve when fusion is allowed, neural summation must exist.

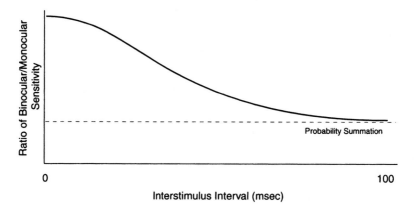

**Figure 6-5**   Matin measured absolute light detection thresholds under monocular and binocular conditions while varying the interstimulus interval (ISI) between the left and right eye presentations between 0 and 100 ms. At short interstimulus intervals, binocular sensitivity was higher than monocular, indicating neural summation. As the asynchrony of presentation to the two eyes was increased, the degree of improvement dropped, until the limits of the binocular integration period were reached at an asynchrony of 100 ms.

Matin (1962) was the first to use this technique to study binocular summation (Fig. 6-5). They measured absolute light detection thresholds under monocular and binocular conditions. The interstimulus interval (ISI) between the left and right eye presentations was varied between zero and 100 ms. When both eyes viewed the target at the same time (ISI = 0), the binocular thresholds were 80% lower than monocular thresholds, indicating neural summation. As the asynchrony of presentation to the two eyes was increased, the degree of improvement dropped, until at an asynchrony of 100 ms, only probability summation was observed. This experiment proves conclusively that neural summation does occur, but only if you stimulate both eyes within a **binocular integration period** of 100 ms. If such an experiment is repeated using widely noncorresponding points that fall outside of Panum's fusional area, no neural summation is seen (Harwerth et al., 1980) because these points would not converge onto a single binocular cortical neuron.

In summary, if you are careful to stimulate *corresponding* points in each eye at the same time, you *do* get evidence of **neural summation**—true binocular summation (for example, see Westendorf and Fox, 1977). Binocular summation has been shown to occur for both light flashes and grating stimuli.

This supports the competing theory to independence theory, called **interaction theory**. Interaction theory states that the increase in sensitivity from the use of two eyes is greater than that predicted by probability summation alone. This is not really that surprising because if you stimulate widely separated noncorresponding points, you would expect them to act independently because they are not directly neurologically connected. This is when simple statistical probability summation occurs: you have two shots at seeing the stimulus, so you are more likely to detect it. However, if you stimulate corresponding points, the inputs from each eye summate together onto a single binocular cell in visual cortex, and the cell responds better. The result is *even more* summation than probability summation alone.

---

### Key Point

*For neural binocular summation to occur, stimuli that are synchronous in both space and time must be presented to both eyes, imaged on corresponding points or on points within Panum's area, and be detected by each eye with an interocular delay of no more than 100 ms. Conditions that prevent the synchronous presentation of stimuli to both eyes, for example, strabismus, anisometropia, or amblyopia, will disrupt fusion and binocular summation.*

---

For binocular summation to occur, the stimuli presented to each eye must also be similar. If grating stimuli are presented to each eye, binocular summation occurs maximally for gratings of identical spatial frequency in each eye and falls off in strength as the spatial frequencies of each grating differ more and more. In other words, the binocular visual pathways are more adept at combining similar information from each eye. As we have seen in Chapter 5, as the stimuli presented to each eye differ more and more, the result is a loss of fusion (and summation) until there is, instead, a percept of binocular rivalry or suppression.

**CLINICAL APPLICATION**  Likewise, if a patient demonstrates a lack of binocular summation over a wide range of stimulus conditions, we can expect that other binocular vision problems resulting from a loss of fusion also exist. We can use evoked potential measurements to evaluate binocular summation even in very young infants. We will return to this point in Chapter 8.

**CLINICAL APPLICATION**  Because a loss of binocular summation results from binocular visual disorders, it is imperative to test for such losses in infants before the compromise of binocular vision becomes permanent.

Campbell and Green (1965) proposed that the improvement in sensitivity by using two eyes together would be 1.4 times the monocular sensitivity because sensitivity is proportional the *square root of the number of detectors*. With regard to vision, the number of detectors is two (i.e., we have two eyes), so the improvement using two eyes together would be by a factor of $\sqrt{2}$ or approximately 1.41. With two detectors whose neural activities are added together somewhere in the visual system to yield a binocular neural response, the activity in response to the stimulus (i.e., the "signal") will be added together or doubled. However, internal neural "noise" associated with a weak threshold neural response will also be added together from the two eyes. The signal improves, as does the noise. If the noise from the two eyes is random and uncorrelated, the noise from each eye will partially cancel when combined. The combined uncorrelated noise is $\sqrt{2}$ times each individual source's noise. When the neural signal and noise are combined in this fashion, the resultant binocular sensitivity will be $\sqrt{2}$ greater than monocular sensitivity. In other words, the **signal-to-noise ratio** is improved only by a factor of $\sqrt{2}$. The net result, as argued by Campbell and Green, is that a performance improvement by a factor of $\sqrt{2}$, as measured empirically, can be explained by neural combination of the activity from the two eyes rather than probability summation alone. Although the assumptions underlying their model may not be entirely true (for example, the noise added together from the two eyes may not be totally uncorrelated), the model does predict threshold binocular summation quite well.

## *BINOCULAR BRIGHTNESS AVERAGING*

In our examination of binocular summation, we have concentrated on *threshold* tasks. However, under normal everyday viewing conditions, we are dealing with *suprathreshold*, that is, easily seen stimuli. Is there any advantage of using two eyes in suprathreshold tasks? Do the eyes need to add together when targets are easily seen, or can they just work independently?

In experiments investigating binocular summation using suprathreshold stimuli, for example, increment threshold tasks or orientation discrimination tasks, it has been found that once stimuli are easily visible, there is less advantage to viewing with two eyes as opposed to one (Legge, 1984). Harwerth and coworkers (1980) measured reaction times to the presentation of grating stimuli to one eye alone and to both eyes. For any given grating contrast level, reaction times were shorter under binocular viewing conditions. In addition, the contrast needed to reach a criterion reaction time is lower with binocular viewing. There are binocular interactions for suprathreshold stimuli, although there is more variability in the degree of summation than noted for threshold stimuli; some subjects may even show binocular facilitation for suprathreshold stimuli.

Another way to answer this question is to compare the brightness of a target seen with two eyes versus one eye. This is a suprathreshold measure of the additivity of the two eyes in the binocular visual percept.

If you look at a pencil with one eye, then with two eyes, the pencil does not look twice as bright with two eyes, even though both eyes together will pick up twice as much light reflected off the pencil as does either eye alone. In this particular suprathreshold task, your performance is relatively unaffected by the use of one versus two eyes. If you cover one eye as you view the pencil, it does not appear to change in brightness at all.

Let us take this one step further and compare the brightness of a target when the individual eyes' inputs are not equal. If you place a neutral density filter over the left eye and view a light monocularly, the filtered left eye receives less light and sees the light as dim. The unfiltered right eye, when viewing monocularly, receives a lot of light, and sees the light as bright. What might you expect to see when you view with both eyes together? You see the light as *less bright* than when you shut the filtered left eye and use only the right eye. This is called **Fechner's paradox** (Fig. 6-6). It is a paradox because under binocular conditions, in which you actually receive more total light, you see the target as dimmer than when viewing with the unfiltered eye alone.

Two possible explanations were originally proposed for this percept. The **independence hypothesis** stated that the two eyes operate totally independently. However, this hypothesis would lead one to predict that if the left eye sees the target as dim, and the right eye as bright, closing the left eye would not change the percept because the right eye still receives a bright image under both conditions. In other words, there would be no difference in brightness perception under binocular versus monocular conditions. However, this conflicts with what we know occurs in Fechner's paradox, and so it cannot be correct.

The **summation hypothesis** predicted instead that the binocular brightness is the sum of the two monocular brightnesses. However, this hypothesis makes two incorrect predictions. First, it predicts that a binocular percept will be brighter than either monocular percept, which does not occur. Second, it predicts that closing the eye with a filtered, dimmer image will result in a perceived dimming. This is the exact opposite of what happens in Fechner's paradox.

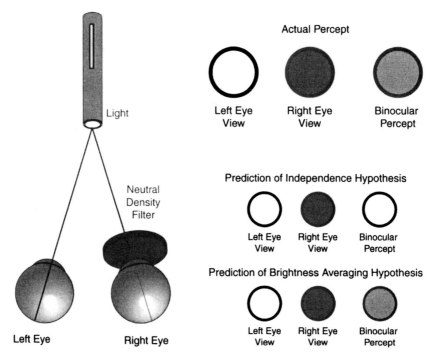

**Figure 6-6**    Fechner's paradox is demonstrated when a neutral density filter is placed before one eye. The binocular percept of a light viewed binocularly under such conditions is less bright than that seen with the unfiltered eye alone. If the two eyes were processed independently by the visual system, the binocular percept would be that of the unfiltered eye. Because this is not what we see, a brightness-averaging mechanism using information from both eyes is suggested.

Clearly, a third hypothesis is needed. This third hypothesis is the **averaging hypothesis** (Levelt, 1965). It states that the visual system simply averages the perceived brightnesses of each eye to arrive at a binocular brightness percept. In the case of unequal brightnesses in the two eyes, the binocular percept would be midway between the perceived brightness of each eye alone. This hypothesis correctly predicts that shutting the filtered eye would result in a perceived brightening of the target light.

If the two eyes really did not add together at all, it would be expected that you would just pay attention to the eye with the brighter light hitting its retina. This does not occur. If just probability summation were occurring, you would "add up" all the photons hitting each eye and see things as a little brighter with both eyes. This also does not happen.

What does happen is that you *average out the brightness* seen by each eye to get a binocular brightness percept. This process is called **binocular brightness averaging**, and it is further evidence that we do add together the information in each eye via neural summation. However, the binocular percept is not a precise average of the monocular brightnesses. The dominant eye's brightness is weighted more in the averaging. Just as the dominant eye is weighted more in the determination of binocular visual direction, the dominant eye is also weighted more in the determination of brightness, as the dominant eye's image is perceived to be relatively brighter even in normal observers (Corcoran and Roth, 1983). The physiological basis for the greater weighting of the dominant eye has been determined in recent studies using functional magnetic resonance imaging (fMRI) scans, which have demonstrated that the dominant eye activates a larger portion of striate cortex, driving more striate cortical neurons, than does the nondominant eye (Roumbouts et al., 1996). Not surprisingly, the dominant eye's stronger signal is also processed slightly faster (Coren and Porac, 1982).

## *INTEROCULAR TRANSFER OF AFTEREFFECTS*

Aftereffects are visual illusions that result from the fatiguing of tuned visual neurons so that the percept of a subsequently viewed target is biased. For example, one **motion aftereffect**, the waterfall illusion, is elicited by viewing an adapting stimulus, in this case unidirectional motion, for a sufficient period of time to fatigue neurons tuned to the direction of motion of the waterfall. Subsequent viewing of a stationary test stimulus will result in a percept that the test object stimulus is moving in a direction opposite to that of the adapting stimulus. This illusion of motion is the aftereffect. Similar aftereffects can be demonstrated for orientation (**tilt aftereffect**) and spatial frequency (**size aftereffect**).

Because many aftereffects are cortically mediated, one might expect them to occur under binocular conditions as well. If an adapting stimulus is presented to one eye, and the test stimulus to the fellow eye, and an aftereffect is still perceived, that is, there is **interocular transfer** of the aftereffect, the neurons mediating the aftereffect must have inputs from binocular neurons.

Interocular transfer can be demonstrated for the **tilt aftereffect**. When a tilted grating is viewed with one eye for a prolonged period of time, then a vertical grating subsequently viewed with the fellow eye will appear to tilt in the opposite direction as the adapting stimulus (Fig. 6-7). The magnitude of the apparent tilt is typically not as strong as that perceived in the monocular tilt aftereffect (Campbell and Maffei, 1971), yet it does occur. Not surprisingly, if the adapting stimulus is presented to the dominant eye, a stronger interocular transfer occurs than when it is presented to the nondominant eye. More recently, Paradiso and coworkers (1989) found that the tilt aftereffect transfers more strongly when **subjective contours** are used rather than real tilted contours. This occurs because visual **area V2** contains neurons that respond to subjective contours while V1 neurons respond to real tilted contours only. Because more binocularly driven cells exist in area V2 than in V1, it is expected that subjective contours would elicit stronger interocular transfer.

A. Monocular Tilt Aftereffect

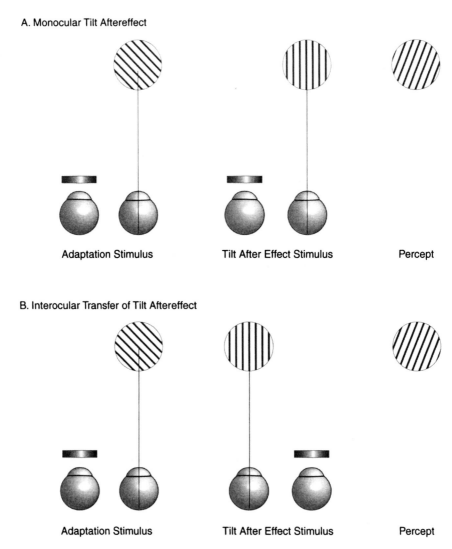

B. Interocular Transfer of Tilt Aftereffect

**Figure 6-7**    **A:** The monocular tilt aftereffect is evoked when one eye views an obliquely oriented adapting grating for an extended period of time and then views a vertical test grating. The percept of the vertical test grating is that it is tilted in the opposite direction from the adapting grating. **B:** The tilt aftereffect transfers interocularly, as shown when the adapting grating is presented to one eye and the test grating is subsequently shown to the fellow eye. Here, too, the percept is that of a grating tilted in a direction opposite to that of the adapting grating.

The **motion aftereffect** as well exhibits interocular transfer, with the magnitude of the aftereffect being weaker for interocular transfer than that of the monocular aftereffect (Lehmkuhle and Fox, 1976). Similarly to the tilt aftereffect, there is a dependence on the cortical area stimulated by the stimuli in question, and it occurs as in the tilt aftereffect. **Random-dot motion displays** (see Steinman and Nawrot, 1992) exhibit even more interocular transfer than do moving grating stimuli (Raymond, 1993). This may be explained by the fact that cortical **area MT**, which is instrumental in the computation of motion coherence, also contains a high concentration of binocularly driven cells.

## DICHOPTIC MASKING

Visual masking is the degradation of the percept of a test stimulus by a second, masking stimulus presented either before, simultaneously with, or subsequent to the test stimulus. **Dichoptic visual masking** occurs when such interference is produced when the mask stimulus is presented to one eye and the test stimulus to the fellow eye (Blakemore and Campbell, 1969; Legge, 1979). Dichoptic masking is strongest when the mask is presented to the dominant eye. In one form of simultaneous masking, the **crowding effect**, the presence of flanking contours near a target reduces the ability of the visual system to see that target. This effect is common in hyperacuity tasks such as vernier acuity. Lines parallel to the vernier target and in close proximity cause vernier thresholds to increase. This is true if the flanking lines are presented to the same eye or to the fellow eye. Similarly, **metacontrast masking**, the reduction in visibility of a target by a subsequently presented adjacent mask, may be demonstrated under dichoptic conditions. However, the most striking evidence for the existence of binocular interactions in masking comes from studies showing disparity-contingent masking effects in cyclopean stimuli (Lehmkuhle and Fox, 1980). Cyclopean stimuli, as we will see in Chapter 7, are perceived only by the binocular visual system and cannot be seen under monocular viewing conditions.

## BINOCULAR INTERACTIONS IN ABNORMAL BINOCULAR VISION

In patients with loss of binocularity because of strabismus, high anisometropia/aniseikonia, or amblyopia, one would expect binocular interactions to be abnormal. In stereoblind strabismic individuals, no binocular summation beyond that predicted by probability summation is seen (Lema and Blake, 1977; Levi et al., 1980). When flicker thresholds are measured under monocular and binocular conditions, (Cavonius, 1979, as noted above) in stereoblind subjects, there is no difference in sensitivity to in-phase and out-of-phase flicker (Levi et al., 1982). In addition, no **subthreshold summation** is noted in stereoblind strabismic amblyopes (Levi et al., 1979, 1980). However, anisometropic amblyopes exhibit less impairment of binocular summation than do strabismic amblyopes, failing to exhibit binocular summation and stereopsis only at high spatial frequencies (Holopigian et al., 1986).

**CLINICAL PROCEDURE** | As we discuss in Chapter 8, binocular "beat" VEPs are a means of testing for binocular summation in infants. Stereoblind individuals fail to perceive the binocular "beats" that arise from summation and exhibit no summation effects in their evoked potential recordings (Baitch and Levi, 1988).

Interocular transfer of aftereffects is also reduced or absent in subjects with early-onset strabismus (Movshon et al., 1972). However, this is mostly true for high-spatial-frequency stimuli. The tilt (or orientation) aftereffect can demonstrate some interocular transfer in strabismics when low-spatial-frequency stimuli are used, although the degree of transfer is still weaker than that of normal subjects. In these cases, the aftereffect is transferred more from the dominant to the nondominant eye. Similarly, motion aftereffects show no interocular transfer in early-onset strabismics (Mitchell et al., 1975), but only if the stimuli are restricted in area such that they are restricted to the central retina, where a suppression scotoma is likely to exist. Stimuli large enough to stimulate the normal peripheral retina of strabismics may demonstrate interocular transfer of aftereffects.

Interocular transfer of contrast threshold elevation is absent centrally *and* peripherally in patients with anisometropic amblyopia but confined to the central visual field in strabismic amblyopia. The lack of threshold elevation in the peripheral visual field of anisometropic amblyopes is thought to be attributed to the disruption of binocular summation processes created by optical aniseikonia.

Levi and coworkers (1979) demonstrated that dichoptic masking can still occur to a great degree in amblyopic individuals when the stimuli are of suprathreshold contrast, even though the same subjects exhibit no subthreshold binocular summation. This has led Levi and coworkers to propose that amblyopia has a differential effect on **excitatory and inhibitory binocular interactions** (Levi et al., 1979, 1980). That is, amblyopia eliminates excitatory binocular interactions such as subthreshold binocular summation, yet preserves inhibitory binocular interactions such as dichoptic masking and interocular suppression.

In the next chapter, we discuss more than just adding together the images in the two eyes. We will look at **stereopsis** — using differences in the two eyes' images to see *three-dimensional depth*.

## SUMMARY AND KEY POINTS

- **Binocular summation** is an additivity of the information from each eye to yield binocular visual performance. Information from the two eyes might be combined in any of the following ways: **binocular facilitation**, complete binocular summation, partial binocular summation, no binocular summation, or **binocular inhibition**.

- Under binocular viewing conditions, there is a slight improvement in critical flicker fusion frequency (CFF). At lower rates of flicker the binocular improvement in sensitivity to flicker is even greater than at the CFF.

- For spatial contrast sensitivity, we are more sensitive binocularly than monocularly by a factor of 1.41 (about 40%) regardless of the spatial frequency measured. This factor of 1.41 holds true for most visual functions measured binocularly over monocularly. This increase may result from statistical or neural factors.

- The **independence theory (probability summation)** states that we see better with two eyes than with one eye because of the laws of probability. There are several statistical theories with different predictions of how much better we should see binocularly. One theory assumes that the probability of either eye seeing the stimulus is 0.60 and increases by a factor of 1.4 with binocular viewing; this conclusion results from computing the probability of either of the two eyes seeing the stimulus minus the probability of both eyes seeing the stimulus.

- **Interaction theory (summation theory)** states that the increase in sensitivity from the use of two eyes is greater than that predicted by probability summation alone. **Neural summation**, a convergence of monocular information in the visual system into binocular pathways, improves detection thresholds under binocular conditions. Neural summation does occur, but only for similar stimuli imaged on corresponding points within a **binocular integration period** of 100 ms. The factor of 1.4 is the square root of the number of receptors (in our case two eyes) and represents the summation of the signal from the eyes minus neural noise.

- Binocular interactions occur for suprathreshold stimuli, but the degree of summation is more variable than for subthreshold stimuli, and binocular facilitation is possible.

- When one eye views a bright light and the other views the same light through a neutral density filter to dim the image, **Fechner's paradox** is seen. The binocular percept is of the light being *less bright* binocularly than with only the unfiltered eye. Neither of the above mentioned theories of binocular summation can explain this percept. Independence theory predicts no difference in brightness perception under binocular versus monocular conditions, whereas summation theory predicts that a binocular percept will be brighter than either monocular percept.

- **Binocular brightness averaging** is a suprathreshold measure of the additivity of the two eyes in the binocular visual percept. The binocular brightness-**averaging hypothesis** explains Fechner's paradox by stating that the visual system averages the perceived brightness of each eye to arrive at a binocular brightness percept midway between the perceived brightness of each eye alone. In addition, input from the dominant eye is weighted more than input from the nondominant eye.

- **Interocular transfer of aftereffects** occurs when tuned visual neurons in one eye are fatigued and this biases the percept of a target in the fellow eye. Such interocular aftereffects occur for motion and for tilt. These aftereffects are stronger for subjective contours and random dot motion because the cortical areas stimulated by these stimuli contain a higher percentage of binocular cells.

- **Dichoptic masking** occurs when a mask stimulus is presented to one eye and the test stimulus to the fellow eye. Dichoptic masking is strongest when the mask is presented to the dominant eye.

- Binocular interactions are abnormal in patients with loss of binocularity. **Stereoblind** individuals exhibit no binocular summation beyond that predicted by probability summation and exhibit no summation effects in binocular beat-evoked potential recordings. Subjects with **early-onset strabismus** have reduced or absent interocular transfer of aftereffects or motion aftereffects for stimuli lying within their suppression scotomas.

- Amblyopia eliminates excitatory binocular interactions such as binocular summation and subthreshold summation yet preserves inhibitory binocular interactions such as dichoptic masking and interocular suppression.

## QUESTIONS

1. The luminosity of an object viewed by the left eye alone is 70 mL, and when viewed by the right eye alone behind a neutral density filter it is 40 mL. What is the perceived luminosity when it is viewed by both eyes simultaneously?

2. Explain the two major theories that account for the factor of 1.41 increase in binocular sensitivity relative to monocular sensitivity. What are the major differences between them?

3. Would you expect interocular transfer of the motion aftereffect to occur in a patient with adult-onset strabismus?

4. Under what conditions would combining two monocular images make a visual stimulus more difficult to see than viewing either monocular stimulus alone in a normal subject?

## BIBLIOGRAPHY

BAITCH LW *and* LEVI DM (1988). *Evidence for nonlinear binocular interactions in human visual cortex.* Vis. Res. 28:1139–1143.

BLAKEMORE C *and* CAMPBELL FW (1969). *On the existence of neurones in the human visual system selectively sensitive to the orientation and size of retinal images.* J. Physiol. 203:237–260.

CAMPBELL FW *and* GREEN DG (1965). *Monocular versus binocular visual acuity.* Nature 208:191–192.

CAMPBELL FW *and* MAFFEI L (1971). *The tilt aftereffect: a fresh look.* Vis. Res. 11:833–840.

CAVONIUS CR (1979). *Binocular interactions in flicker.* Q. J. Exp. Psych. 31:273–280.

CORCORAN RA *and* ROTH N (1983). *Comparative monocular brightness contributions in normal binocular observers.* Am. J. Optom. Physiol. Optics 60:813–816.

COREN S *and* PORAC C (1982). *Monocular asymmetries in visual latency as a function of sighting dominance.* Am. J. Optom. Physiol. Optics 59:987–990.

HARWERTH RS, SMITH EL *and* LEVI DM (1980). *Suprathreshold binocular interactions for grating patterns.* Percept. Psychophys. 27:43–50.

HOLOPIGIAN K, BLAKE R *and* GREENWALD M (1986). *Selective losses in binocular vision in anisometropic amblyopia.* Vis. Res. 26:621–627.

LEGGE GE (1979). *Spatial frequency masking in human vision: binocular interactions.* J. Opt. Soc. Am. 69:838–847.

LEGGE GE (1984). *Binocular contrast summation. I. Detection and discrimination.* Vis. Res. 24:373–383.

LEHMKUHLE SW *and* FOX R (1976). *On measuring interocular transfer.* Vis. Res. 16:428–430.

LEHMKUHLE SW *and* FOX R (1980). *Effect of depth separation on metacontrast masking.* J. Exp. Psych. 6:605–621.

LEMA S *and* BLAKE R (1977). *Binocular summation in normal and stereoblind humans.* Vis. Res. 17:691–695.

LEVELT WJM (1965). *Binocular brightness averaging and contour information.* Br. J. Psych. 56:1–13.

LEVI DM, HARWERTH RS *and* SMITH EL (1979). *Humans deprived of normal binocular vision have binocular interactions tuned to size and orientation.* Science 206:852–853.

LEVI DM, HARWERTH RS *and* SMITH EL (1980). *Binocular interactions in normal and anomalous binocular vision.* Doc. Ophth. 49:303–324.

LEVI DM, PASS AF *and* MANNY RE (1982). *Binocular interactions in normal and anomalous binocular vision: effects of flicker.* Br. J. Ophthalmol. 66:57–63.

MATIN L (1962). *Binocular summation at the absolute threshold for peripheral vision.* J. Opt. Soc. 52:1276–1286.

MITCHELL DE, REARDON J *and* MUIR DW (1975). *Interocular transfer of the motion aftereffect in normal and stereoblind observers.* Exp. Brain Res. 22:163–175.

MOVSHON JA, CHAMBERS BEI *and* BLAKEMORE C (1972). *Interocular transfer in normal humans, and those who lack stereopsis.* Perception 1:483–490.

PARADISO MA, SHIMOJO S *and* NAKAYAMA K (1989). *Subjective contours, tilt aftereffects, and visual cortical organization.* Vis. Res. 29:1205–1213.

PIRENNE MH (1943). *Binocular and uniocular threshold of vision.* Nature 152:698–699.

RAYMOND JE (1993). *Complete interocular transfer of motion adaptation effects on motion coherence thresholds.* Vis. Res. 33:1865–1870.

ROUMBOUTS SARB, BARKHOT F, SPRENGER M, VALK J *and* SCHELTENS P (1996). *The functional basis of ocular dominance: functional MRI (fMRI) findings.* Neurosci. Lett. 221:1–4.

SHEEDY JE, BAILEY IL, BURI M *and* BASS E (1986). *Binocular vs. monocular performance.* Am. J. Optom. Physiol. Optics 63:839–846.

SHERRINGTON CS (1909). *On binocular flicker and the correlation of activity of "corresponding" retinal points.* Br. J. Psych. 1:26–60.

STEINMAN SB *and* NAWROT M (1992). *Software for the generation and display of random-dot cinematograms on the Macintosh computer.* Behav. Res. Meth. Instr. Comp. 24:573–574.

WESTENDORF O *and* FOX R (1977). *Binocular detection of disparate light flashes.* Vis. Res. 17:697–702.

# Stereopsis

**7**

## MONOCULAR CUES TO DEPTH

At the beginning of this book, it was stated that the existence of two eyes allows for **stereoscopic vision** as a means of estimating depth or distance. However, stereopsis is not the only means of obtaining depth information from a visual scene. Even after closing one eye, we are still able to determine the relative positions of objects around ourselves and our relationship to them. The cues that permit the interpretation of depth with one eye alone are called **monocular** or **empirical cues to depth**. Unlike binocular depth cues, these cues are not "hard-wired" into our visual systems; rather, they are learned *inferences* that the visual system has to make.

Empirical cues to depth include **pictorial cues** such as the size of the retinal image, linear perspective, texture gradients, aerial perspective, imposition and shading, as well as **nonpictorial cues** such as accommodation, motion parallax, and structure from motion. This material is generally covered in courses of monocular sensory processing and may be familiar to some readers. However, as these cues are also relevant to the binocular percept of depth, a brief review of monocular depth cues is provided here.

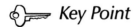 *Key Point*

*Pictorial cues can be remembered by thinking of them as cues to depth that can be seen in a picture or photograph.*

The **retinal image size** of any object is larger when an object is near, and smaller when it is more distant from the viewer. The use of retinal image size as a cue to determine depth is most obvious when all other cues to depth in the visual

173

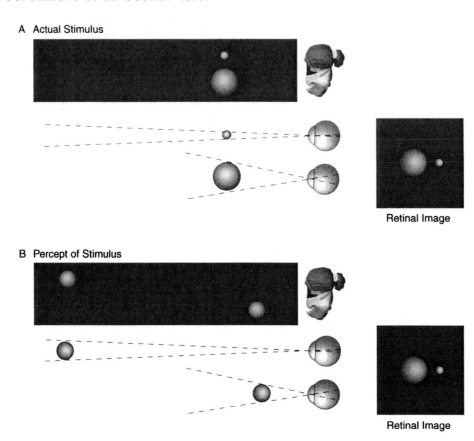

**Figure 7-1** **A:** An observer views two equally distant illuminated spheres of different sizes in a darkened hallway so that the only depth cue is retinal image size. The small sphere makes a small retinal image, and the large sphere makes a large retinal image. **B:** Because of the difference in retinal image sizes, the observer perceives both spheres to be the same size with the large sphere being closer and the small sphere being farther away.

scene are removed. This can be observed in a controlled environment, by viewing two equidistant illuminated objects, one large and one small, in a completely dark room in which no other visual stimuli can be seen (Fig. 7-1). When size is the only distance cue available, the larger object will appear to be closer because its retinal image is larger. Under natural viewing conditions, unfamiliar shapes seen for the first time that produce a large retinal image size may be interpreted by the visual system as being physically close.

The interaction of size and distance is not always straightforward. Just as the visual system makes judgments about the distance of an object based on its retinal image size, it also makes judgments about the size of an object based on the object's perceived distance. This effect can be observed by creating a localized

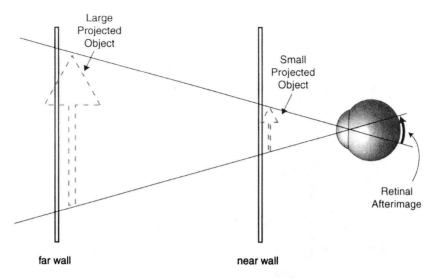

Large
Projected
Object

Small
Projected
Object

Retinal
Afterimage

far wall                                    near wall

**Figure 7-2**    A retinal afterimage is seen as being small when the visual system be-lieves the object to be close and large when it is perceived as far away.

afterimage on the retina with a brief exposure to a bright light, such as a camera flash. The light flash bleaches a portion of the retina, producing a fixed-size retinal image. Because this retinal image does not correspond to any real object in space, the visual system then will attempt to interpret an object based on the available evidence. If the observer looks at a wall, the afterimage of the flash will be seen "projected" onto the wall. If the wall is close to the observer, the afterimage will seem small. However, if the observer focuses on a more distant wall, the afterim-age seen on the wall will appear to be much larger (Fig. 7-2). In other words, the perceived size of the object producing a retinal image of a given fixed size is proportional to its perceived distance (**Emmert's law**). Another example of the application of Emmert's law is the **moon illusion**, in which the moon appears to be larger near the horizon than at the azimuth (apex) of the night sky. It has been demonstrated that this illusion occurs because the horizon is interpreted as being more distant than the azimuth.

It is also possible for two physical objects that produce retinal images of different sizes to be perceived as being the same physical size if these objects are judged to be at different distances. For example, an automobile 10 feet away from you is not interpreted as being twice as tall as an automobile that is 20 feet away from you. However, the retinal image size of the near automobile is twice that of the distant one (Fig. 7-3). This phenomenon, called **size constancy**, is main-tained by a perceptual "scaling" of the perceived size of an object according to its estimated distance.

In most natural scenes, numerous clues to distance are usually present. We make judgments of distance only after our visual systems consider all of the avail-able evidence. In the example (Fig. 7-1) of the two illuminated equidistant objects

A.

B.

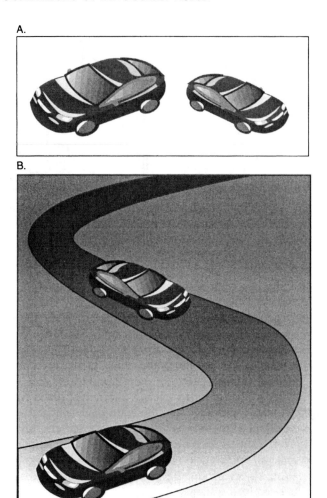

**Figure 7-3** Size constancy. **A:** Two objects with unequal retinal image sizes, in this case automobiles, can be interpreted as being objects of the same size if they are perceived to be at different distances. Here the smaller car seems to be the same size as the larger car, but farther away. **B:** If the perceived distance of the small automobile is twice as far as that of the large automobile, both autos will appear to be the same size.   (Source: Images © www. arttoday.com)

in the dark, our percept of the larger object being closer would correct itself immediately if we simply were to turn on the lights. This would allow us to avail ourselves of the other visual cues in the surrounding room when making our depth judgment. In other words, the visual system uses many cues to determine the distance of an object.

Holway and Boring (1941) demonstrated this by asking observers to match the size of a circular test stimulus at a 10-foot distance to that of a standard stimulus. The standard stimulus was placed at various distances from 10 to 120 feet from the observer, with its size scaled so that regardless of its distance, it always subtended the same 1° visual angle. Under deprived viewing conditions in which most depth cues were eliminated, subjects consistently adjusted the size of the test stimulus so that its retinal image size matched that of the standard stimulus at each test distance.

However, once the experimenters allowed other depth cues to be visible, subjects no longer judged the distance of the standard stimulus solely from retinal image size. Their visual systems now took advantage of available distance cues and used the information from the perceived distance to invoke size constancy. As the standard stimulus size increased at greater distances, so did the size of their matching test stimuli, matching the true linear size of the standard stimulus rather than its angular retinal image size.

**Figure 7-4** Our experience tells us that taxis are larger than people, so the visual system assumes that the taxi is farther away than the woman.   (Source: Images © www. arttoday.com)

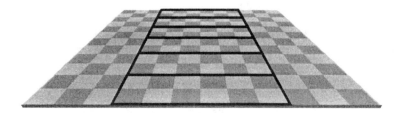

**Figure 7-5**    Linear perspective is the percept of lines converging toward a vanishing point on the horizon.

Another factor we consider in judging depth is our own experience. In natural settings containing familiar objects, we can readily interpret the relative sizes of the familiar objects from our own past experience and use this learned information to help us to estimate the distance of the objects from us. In Fig. 7-4 we see a lady hailing a taxi. The image of the lady is quite a bit larger than that of the taxi. If we were to interpret both images as being the same distance from us, we would perceive a giant lady attempting to hail a miniature taxi. Instead, because we know the relative sizes of a lady and a taxi, we rely on our experience and tend to perceive the taxi as being farther away from us. Even if we remove all other depth cues, we can use familiar size to judge distance (Schiffman, 1967).

**Linear perspective** is a percept of parallel lines or edges converging toward a distant vanishing point at the horizon. Such effects are seen in railroad tracks receding into the distance; the more distant tracks are seen as converging toward one another, and the ties between the tracks are seen as narrower (Fig. 7-5). Distant objects are seen not only as smaller but also as more densely packed than are near objects, a cue known as a **texture gradient** (Fig. 7-6). If you view a distant object, scattering of light by the atmosphere, as well as by smoke, fog, or air pollution, provides an **aerial perspective** cue; that is, the distant object will appear less sharp than a near object. In fact, simply reducing the contrast of an object makes it appear as if it is farther away (O'Shea et al., 1993). **Interposition**

**Figure 7-6**    A texture gradient is the reduction in size and spacing of distant objects or features as compared to near objects.

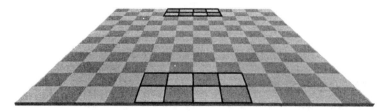

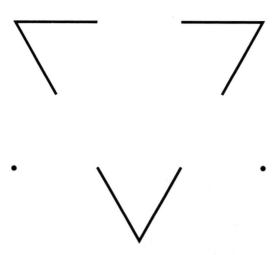

**Figure 7-7**   Interposition is a cue to relative
depth or distance in which a nearer object occludes
a portion of the view of the rearmost object. An
illusory interposition may also serve as a depth cue,
as demonstrated in the Kanisza triangle figure. The
illusory triangle is perceived as occluding a second
triangle, and therefore is perceived as floating
"above" the occluded background triangle.

is the obstruction of the view of a distant object by a closer object. Distant objects
cannot occlude the view of near objects. Therefore, we learn to interpret an
occluded object as being farther away. Subjective contours can mimic the effects
of a real interposition, with the phantom form being perceived as closer than the
remainder of the figure (see Fig. 7-7). Finally, the direction of lighting and **shading** of an object can tell us about the object's depth. The shading is interpreted as
the shadows formed from illuminated convex or concave shapes (Fig. 7-8).

　　Nonpictorial monocular cues can also be utilized in judging distance. For
example, we increase the degree of **accommodation** of the crystalline lens to
keep near objects in focus as they move closer to us. It has been suggested that
the level of innervation for accommodation could therefore provide distance
information, much like the mechanism of an autofocus camera. Surprisingly, studies have shown that accommodation is not utilized much in judging distance. It is
only a weakly effective cue at best, with considerable individual variance in its
effectiveness (Fisher and Ciuffreda, 1988).

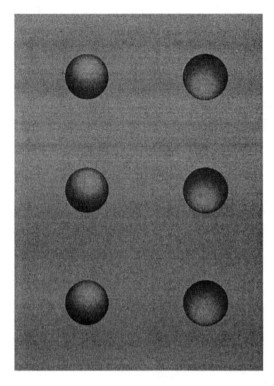

**Figure 7-8**    Shape from shading is a subtle use of lighting information to determine the three-dimensional curvature of an object.

Another nonpictorial cue that provides valuable information for calculating the location of objects in three-dimensional space is **motion parallax** (Fig. 7-9). An object at the same distance as an observer's fixation point will appear to be stationary while the observer (or just the observer's head) is in motion. However, objects that are either in front of or behind the fixation point will appear to move laterally relative to the fixation point if the observer moves. The direction of the motion is determined by whether the object is closer or farther than the fixation point. A nearer object will appear to move in a direction opposite to that of the observer ("against" motion), while farther objects will appear to move in the same direction as the observer ("with" motion). The relative distance of the object from the fixation point can be judged by the velocity of the motion. The velocity is proportional to the separation of the object from the fixation point. Motion parallax helps animals with limited binocular visual fields to see depth. An example is the head-bobbing movements of pigeons. However, motion parallax is still useful as a depth cue in species with well-developed stereopsis. Depth judgments based on motion parallax are almost as accurate as those based on binocular disparity; that

Stimulus Setup

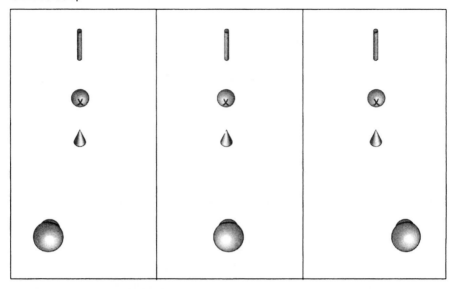

View of Stimulus

**Figure 7-9** Motion parallax as our bodies move can provide a cue to the three-dimensional arrangement of objects. As our eyes (or heads) move from side to side relative to an object, motion parallax can tell us if other objects are closer or farther away than the fixated object. Here fixation is maintained on the sphere. As the eye moves from side to side, the retinal images of the rod and cone shift position relative to that of the sphere. The rod is farther away from the eye than the sphere, and moving the eye causes the rod to seem to move in the same direction as the eye (with motion). Conversely, the cone is closer to the eye and moves in the opposite direction as the eye (against motion).

is, motion parallax thresholds are nearly as accurate as binocular stereoacuity thresholds (discussed later in this chapter). This is not surprising because motion parallax produces image displacements on the retina that are equivalent to those produced by disparity.

**CLINICAL**
**APPLICATION** | Motion parallax can be used during **direct ophthalmoscopy** to localize the position of opacities in the ocular media. For example, if you observe an opacity in the ocular media, you can determine if the opacity is in the anterior or posterior chamber of the eye by fixating and focusing the ophthalmoscope on the iris and then moving slightly from side to side. An opacity in the anterior chamber will exhibit "against" motion, while one in the posterior chamber will have "with" motion.

Related to motion parallax is a phenomenon known as **shape from motion**, in which a flat moving display gives rise to the percept of a three-dimensional object rotating in depth. A common demonstration of shape from motion is the **kinetic depth effect** (Fig. 7-10). If a wire is bent into an irregular three-dimensional shape and held in front of a light source, its shadow projected onto a screen will necessarily be two-dimensional and will be interpreted that way by an observer. However, if the wire is then rotated, the differential motion of the

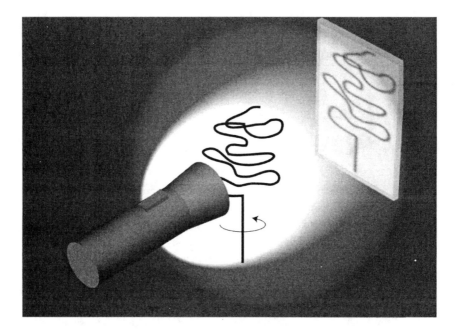

**Figure 7-10**    Similarly to motion parallax, the motion of parts of an object can reveal their relative positions in three-dimensional space, and therefore the shape of the object. The Kinetic depth effect is an example of the use of this depth information. A wire is bent into a three-dimensional shape, and its shadow projected onto a screen. The static shadow will appear to be arising from a flat object, but if the wire is rotated, the changes in the shadow over time will be interpreted as arising from rotation of a three-dimensional object.

various parts of the shadow allow the visual system to interpret the changes in the shadow over time as arising from a three-dimensional shape rotated in depth.

## THE CASE AGAINST BINOCULAR VISION

As discussed above, there are many ways to determine depth monocularly. In fact, it is quite possible to navigate around the world with only one eye. There are several reasons why having two eyes could be detrimental. First, two eyes require more neural machinery for the input of visual information than would one eye, so it could be argued that binocular vision is a duplication of resources. Furthermore, in order for binocular vision to be accurate, the visual system must ensure that the two eyes work together. This requires optimal binocular eye movement coordination, binocular fusion, equal visual acuity in the two eyes, an absence of binocular suppression, and a lack of anisometropia or aniseikonia, among other things. This means that coordinating the two eyes' inputs for a binocular vision system demands a much more precisely controlled visual system than a monocular visual system would require. The complexity of the binocular visual system creates the risk of numerous abnormalities (such as motor misalignments) that would not be present in monocular visual systems. Such abnormalities, if they occur, could make the presence of two eyes a liability rather than an advantage. Given these arguments, and knowing that we have at our disposal so many ways of seeing depth with one eye alone, it is reasonable to ask the question "why do we need binocular vision at all?"

## BINOCULAR VISION

The major advantage of a binocular vision system over a monocular system is that we are *much* more accurate at perceiving depth when we use two eyes than when we use only one eye. This is because with two eyes we can achieve **stereopsis**. Stereopsis greatly enhances our ability to judge depth. It allows us to be much better at **figure-ground segregation** (e.g., picking out camouflaged objects from their surrounds), **avoiding collisions** with looming objects, and accurately **navigating through our environment** than we would be with one eye alone. An important advantage of stereopsis in primates is that it allows for extremely accurate hand-eye coordination during manual manipulation of objects. This is especially obvious when one does fine motor tasks such as removing corneal foreign bodies.

Stereopsis is the combining of information from both eyes to achieve a three-dimensional percept of the world. Whereas monocular cues to depth are *inferences* that the visual system has to make, stereopsis is the visual system's only *direct* means of seeing depth, and it is mediated by special mechanisms built into the visual system.

Stereopsis is thought to be our sole *robust* binocular cue to depth. However, other binocular depth cues do exist. For example, if the visual system could take note of the level of innervation for **convergence** of the two eyes required to achieve motor and sensory binocular fusion on an object and could determine that object's distance from us. The closer the object, the greater the degree of innervation required for convergence. However, as we will see shortly, the visual system is able to use the neural signal for convergence as sole indicator of distance only to a limited extent. This is not to say that convergence is wholly ineffective as a depth cue. Under certain viewing conditions, convergence can *modify* our judgments of perceived distance and, therefore, perceived size. This can be observed by having a subject fixate a target at a fixed distance through base-out prisms. As increasingly strong base-out prisms are introduced, the subject will be forced to increase his convergence to keep the target single; and the target will be perceived as getting smaller and closer to the observer. Similarly, increasing the divergence produces a percept of the target becoming larger and moving farther away.

**CLINICAL PROCEDURE** | Such a change in perceived size and distance is frequently noted during vision examinations during testing of a patient's ranges of convergence and divergence. Clinically, it is called the **SILO** effect, which stands for "Smaller In, Larger Out." It results from a change in convergence level, and therefore perceived distance, with a fixed retinal image size. In other words, it is a natural consequence of size constancy. On rare occasions, however, an observer will have the opposite response. This is known as **SOLI** ("Smaller Out, Larger In"), and may be explained by an expectation on the part of the subject, based on their experience, that nearer objects should look bigger.

Changes in tonic vergence with prolonged viewing through prisms can also affect distance estimates and produce distance aftereffects when the prisms are removed (Fisher and Ciuffreda, 1990). For example, a subject can adjust to wearing a pair of prism spectacles for a sufficiently long period of time until he or she can correctly judge distances through them. If the subject then removes the prism spectacles, he or she will not instantly be able to correctly judge depth. Instead, the subject must gradually readjust to judging distances without the prism spectacles.

**CLINICAL APPLICATION** | A patient's spectacle lenses often introduce prism, resulting in SILO effects, during adjustment to a new prescription. An unexpected change in depth perception can be very disturbing, so it is a good idea to warn patients what to expect in advance, using SILO as a rule of thumb.

## *STEREOPSIS*

Stereopsis is thought to be our sole *robust* binocular cue to depth. It occurs most accurately when images in each eye are formed on noncorresponding retinal points that are *close together*, that is, within Panum's fusional area. Let us say that we have two objects that we are viewing, one slightly closer to us than the other; in

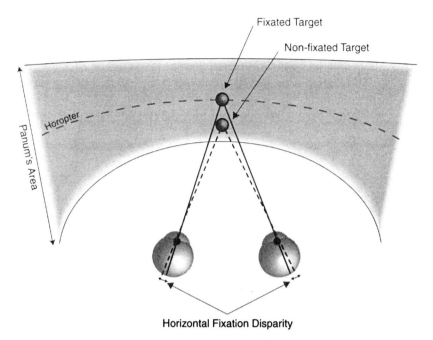

Fixated Target

Non-fixated Target

Horopter

Panum's Area

Horizontal Fixation Disparity

**Figure 7-11**    When a subject is fixating on the distant object, the near object falls within Panum's area. The monocular images of the fixated distant object fall on corresponding retinal points. The monocular images of the near object will not fall on corresponding points but will have a small disparity, which results in the near object being seen in three-dimensional depth.

other words, there is a difference in *distance* between the two objects (Fig. 7-11). We will select one object to fixate and use fusional eye movements to align the two monocular images of that fixated object. This places the fixated object's images on *corresponding retinal points*, and the object will be seen as single. The second object, however, will now produce images that *are not exactly* in the same relative positions in each eye; they are formed on *noncorresponding retinal points*. The two images will still be fused because they lie within Panum's area. However, rather than being perceived as lying on the horopter, the visual system assigns the object a perceived depth relative to the horopter. It is the difference in the lateral separation between the half-views of the fixated and non-fixated objects (**horizontal binocular disparity**) that allows the visual system to estimate to what degree the object is displaced from the horopter.

Stereopsis is achieved **preattentively** (Nakayama and Silverman, 1986; Steinman, 1987), meaning that it is achieved automatically without conscious effort. If you look at an array of targets on a page, in which only one target has stereoscopic disparity, that target will quickly "pop out" from all of the others. The target with stereoscopic disparity will appear to be in a closer or farther plane relative to the remaining targets on the page and may have a distinctly different three-dimensional form. It has been suggested that stereopsis is a basic "feature" or "building block" that the visual system detects to piece together our percept of objects and the world around us.

The direction or sign of the depth is determined by the direction of relative displacement of the images in the two eyes (Fig. 7-12). If the object is in front of the fixation point, the object produces retinal images that are formed on each

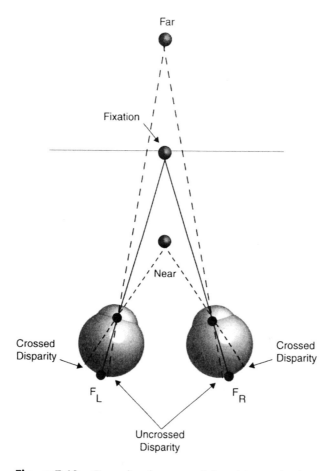

**Figure 7-12**  Crossed and uncrossed disparities result when objects produce images that are formed on closely separated retinal points within Panum's fusional area. The images will be fused into a single percept but will be seen at a different distance or three-dimensional depth than the fixation point. Crossed disparity produces a percept of an object closer than the fixation point, whereas uncrossed disparity produces a percept of an object farther away than the fixation point.

eye's temporal retina; this is called **crossed disparity**. Conversely, if the object is farther away than the fixation point, it will produce retinal images on the nasal retina of each eye, producing **uncrossed disparity**. An object that is precisely bifoveally fixated will have **zero disparity**. As we will see in the next chapter, the visual cortex contains specialized neurons that can directly determine the sign and magnitude of disparity.

It is important to distinguish between *absolute* and *relative* depth. **Absolute depth** is the distance of a given single object from the egocenter of the observer. It is determined by **absolute disparity**, the difference in the external longitudinal angles subtended by a single object at each eye. Absolute disparity simply serves as an aid to guide vergence eye movements (Pobuda and Erkelens, 1993). This is because convergence, like accommodation, is only a weak cue to depth, more effective at distances under twenty feet (Liebowitz and Moore, 1966). In addition, the relationship between depth and disparity is not completely linear, resulting in imprecision in our judgments of absolute distance. Although angular binocular disparity geometrically always varies inversely with the square of the fixation distance, the binocular visual system does not judge distances strictly by angular disparity. It also factors in **depth constancy**, a scaling of an object's perceived disparity based on the fixation distance. This means that the visual system could view an object with a particular angular disparity but judge it to be at different distances depending on the visual system's interpretation of its fixation distance. Therefore, stereopsis is poorly suited for determining the absolute distance of an object. The empirical monocular cues are more useful for determining absolute distance. Although we cannot judge distance accurately via absolute disparity and stereopsis, we can use the degree of convergence to do so to a limited extent (Erkelens and Regan, 1986).

**CLINICAL APPLICATION** | Prism-induced changes in vergence can cause **micropsia** or **macropsia** through changes in perceived distance. Long-term adaptation to prism will eventually reduce this effect, but then a postadaptational change in perceived distance will occur when the prism is removed.

Vergence is a necessary contributor to our ability to process large absolute disparities (Fisher and Ciuffreda, 1990) but is less useful for distinguishing small disparities. For small disparities, we can use stereopsis. **Relative depth** is a *comparison* of the distance between two objects, not precisely how far each object alone is from us, but which is relatively closer and which is farther away. This is what we typically think of when we refer to three-dimensional or "solid" vision. Once vergence eye movements are used to bifoveally fixate one object, relative depth between that object and its neighbors is encoded by **relative disparity**, the *difference* between the absolute disparities of two objects. Stereopsis is therefore a *relative* measurement in which the perceived depth is relative to the fixation distance. Stereopsis is less useful for determining the *absolute* distances of objects. In other words, motor fusion and the appreciation of perceived depth are two responses to disparity. Fusional eye movements are made to reduce absolute or relative disparity, but stereopsis is in response to relative disparity alone.

Because stereopsis is a relative measure, the lack of a reference for comparison of depth will degrade our ability to see depth. For example, if *all* targets in the visual field are given identical nonzero disparities, no object(s) will be seen to stand out in depth. Rather, all objects will be seen at the same distance. This is important because fixational drifts and tremors can result in disparity changes of up to 7′ to 8′ arc, well above disparity threshold. Because these disparities are added uniformly to all targets in the visual field, the disparity introduced does not introduce spurious changes in our depth perception (Fender and Julesz, 1967; St. Cyr and Fender, 1969). In order to see depth, we must compare differences in disparity at different spatial locations.

---

### 🔑 Key Point

*The binocular visual system processes* **relative disparity,** *not absolute disparity. Binocular disparity tells us an object's* relative *position in space, if it is closer to us or farther away from us compared to other objects. However, binocular disparity does not tell us the absolute position of any particular object.*

---

Nonetheless, relative disparity gives us more information than just estimates of relative distance. Spatial changes in disparity (**disparity gradients**) tell us about orientation (slant) of objects in three-dimensional space, and changes in the rate of change of disparity (**disparity curvature**) tell us about three-dimensional curvature of surfaces (Lappin and Craft, 1997). Relative disparity also makes it easier for the visual system to match corresponding features in the two retinal images, as we will see shortly.

It should be noted that depth information from disparity can be overridden because some processing of depth is cognitive in nature. A mask of a face, when viewed from behind, does not appear to be concave as it truly is. Instead, we see it as convex, as if we were viewing its front surface. Our expectation that a face should be convex overrides the correct interpretation of the depth of the mask as determined by binocular disparity, even though the direction of shading is also inappropriate. Depth constancy fails under artificial viewing conditions such as viewing stereograms in a stereoscope (see below), where the perceived disparity is inversely proportional to the target distance, not distance squared as predicted by the geometric relationship between disparity, reference distance, and PD. We tend to overscale the disparity in stereograms and see more depth than we should. As you move closer to the stereogram, the perceived depth increases.

Our eyes are separated horizontally, and it is generally accepted that horizontal disparities yield a percept of depth. However, the role of **vertical disparities** in depth perception has been more difficult to determine. Vertical disparities can arise under several conditions. The most obvious is the induced effect in aniseikonia, where the unequal image magnification between the two eyes along the vertical meridian produces vertical disparity. An astigmatic lens prescribed for one eye alone can also have such an effect. Vertical fixation disparity, head tilt, or strabismus can also produce vertical disparity. In addition, when viewing a target that lies very far in the periphery, the two eyes' images may be of different vertical lengths. However, in spite of the presence of available binocular disparity information, the binocular visual system seems unable to use this information to produce a percept of depth. Even when subjects were provided with feedback about the presence or absence of a vertical disparity, they could not learn to take advantage of this information. In fact, most studies have concluded that vertical disparity is not a robust cue to depth. One possible exception may be in the peripheral retina, where vertical disparities may give rise to a weak percept of depth (Rogers and Bradshaw, 1995). In addition, it has recently been proposed that the degree of three-dimensional tilt is determined by comparing the vertical and horizontal disparity of an object over a wide area of its surface (Kaneko and Howard, 1997).

**CLINICAL APPLICATION** | It is therefore important for the clinician to evaluate and potentially correct any significant vertical ocular imbalances.

Surprisingly, physical separation in three-dimensional space is not the only stimulus that can lead to a percept of depth. There exist a class of stimuli, some of which *do not* have any physical depth per se, that yet produce a robust percept of depth. One such stimulus is **orientation disparity**, in which differences in the orientation of targets presented to each eye might yield a percept of tilt in depth (Blakemore, Fiorentini and Maffei, 1972). However, it can be argued that the perception of depth is not related to orientation per se but to a gradually changing degree of *horizontal* disparity between the two targets resulting from the differing orientations.

Surprisingly, some monocular cues to depth are in fact quite similar to stereopsis. Shape from motion shares some underlying mechanisms with disparity-based depth perception because adapting to a given binocular disparity can bias or distort one's percept of shape from motion, and vice versa. Furthermore, the percepts arising from shape, motion, and disparity can be additive. However, they are not wholly processed by the same neurological mechanisms because stereodeficient patients can still perceive structure from motion.

Although motion parallax is a dynamic monocular cue, motion parallax and stereopsis are not altogether different. Motion parallax and stereopsis are both produced by slight shifts of position in the retinal image, suggesting possible shared physiological mechanisms. In experiments in which subjects viewed monocular dot patterns in which dot movement was introduced based on the amount and speed of head movement, motion parallax was artificially created, and subjects could rate the degree of depth seen (Rogers and Graham, 1979). If binocular disparity was then introduced instead, it became possible to equate the degree of head motion needed to produce a dot displacement that yields the same percept of depth as a particular amount of disparity (Rogers and Graham, 1982). From these experiments, it was found that motion parallax shares many of the properties of stereopsis. However, we are only half as sensitive to motion parallax as we are to stereopsis. In addition, only a weak correlation was found for thresholds

  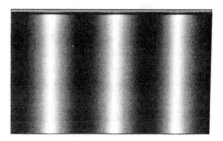

Left Eye View                    Right Eye View

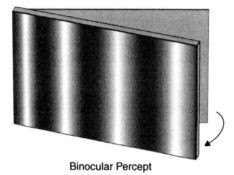

Binocular Percept

**Figure 7-13**    A percept of stereoscopic tilt is created by fusing two sine-wave gratings of differing spatial frequency, a phenomenon called "diffrequency." This percept is similar to that of aniseikonia, such as that produced by an axis 90 size lens before one eye.

obtained for both in a number of subjects, suggesting that despite their similarities, motion parallax and stereopsis reflect different underlying mechanisms.

Another way to produce a percept of depth where no depth really exists is to present to each eye vertical sine-wave grating stimuli of slightly different spatial frequencies (Fig. 7-13). The differing spatial frequencies create horizontal binocular disparities between corresponding bars of the two gratings ("**diffrequency**") (Blakemore, 1970; Schor and Wood, 1983). The result is an apparent tilting of the frontoparallel plane of the grating (Fig. 7-13). Although some investigators have argued that spatial frequency differences alone can yield this percept, this is unlikely because spatially filtered random-dot stereoscopic targets do not yield the robust depth percept that would be predicted by diffrequency (Halpern et al., 1996). The simpler explanation is that the difference in grating spatial frequency is similar to the geometric effect noted in aniseikonia because one grating is "magnified" or "minified" with respect to the other.

If a pendulum, consisting of a weight suspended on a string, is swung back and forth in a plane parallel to your eyes, you will correctly perceive the pendulum swinging in a frontoparallel plane. However, if a neutral density filter is placed in front of one eye, the pendulum will now appear as if it is moving in an *elliptical* path, toward you and away from you in depth. This percept is called the **Pulfrich phenomenon** (Fig. 7-14). The Pulfrich phenomenon occurs because the binocular visual system responds well to luminance contrast and processes information more slowly at lower luminance levels when the changes in luminance contrast are not so great. The neutral density filter therefore introduces a **temporal disparity** between the processing speed of the left eye and the right eye. This disparity is interpreted by the visual system as an equivalent spatial binocular disparity (Burr and Ross, 1979), and therefore an illusory depth is seen (for example, see Brauner and Lit, 1976). As a rule, if the filter is in front of the right eye, a counterclockwise elliptical path will be seen; conversely, if the filter is in front of left eye, a clockwise motion will be perceived. The darker the neutral density filter, the greater is the depth that will be seen. Increases in the pendulum motion velocity or horizontal width of the path traveled will also increase the apparent depth of the elliptical path.

Let us look at what happens to the retinal images of the two eyes when one experiences the Pulfrich effect. The neutral density filter darkens the image in one eye, in turn slowing the processing of that eye's image. If the pendulum moves, it will produce an image at the same locus on each eye's retina. The image falling on the unfiltered eye's retina will be processed and transmitted to the visual cortex quickly. However, the filtered eye's image will take a longer time to reach cortex. By the time the pendulum has moved from point A to point B, the unfiltered eye will see the pendulum at point B, but the filtered eye will still be seeing the pendulum at point A. The cortical image of the pendulum is now at different, noncorresponding retinal points in each eye, creating a percept that the pendulum has changed position in *depth*. The Pulfrich phenomenon can be observed whether the eyes remain stationary or track the pendulum, but the effect is more pronounced when the eyes are kept stationary.

**CLINICAL APPLICATION**

Although normal individuals require a neutral density filter to experience the Pulfrich effect, any condition that causes a visual processing delay in one eye will produce it. For example, patients with **optic neuritis** will sometimes have axonal conduction velocity delays in the affected optic nerve. They will see a Pulfrich effect even without a neutral density filter in place. Similarly, **anisocoria**, unequal pupil sizes, can create differences in retinal illumination. Anisocoria can be induced by trauma or by pharmaceutical agents that affect pupil size. This is one part of the reason why it is so irritating to a patient to have only one pupil dilated during an eye exam. **Monocular cataracts** and **corneal scars** can also limit the light entering one eye. In addition, end-stage diseases or glaucoma that reduces the responsiveness of one eye may cause a Pulfrich phenomenon, so long as the patients have not yet adapted to the reduced luminance in the affected eye. The same disorders that can produce Marcus Gunn afferent pupillary defect will also elicit a Pulfrich phenomenon.

We can take advantage of the Pulfrich phenomenon to grade the degree of a patient's **conduction velocity delay**. Progressively denser neutral density filters can be placed in front of the better eye until the Pulfrich effect is

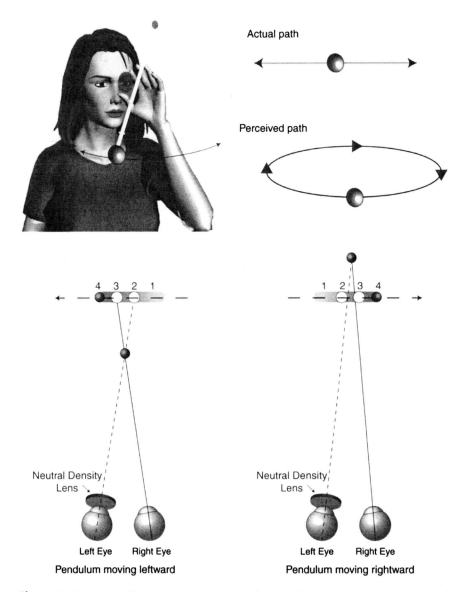

Actual path

Perceived path

4  3  2  1

Neutral Density
Lens

Left Eye    Right Eye

Pendulum moving leftward

1  2  3  4

Neutral Density
Lens

Left Eye    Right Eye

Pendulum moving rightward

**Figure 7-14**    The Pulfrich phenomenon is an illusion of depth arising from a temporal binocular disparity. A delay of visual processing in one eye produces a relative displacement of that eye's image with respect to that of the other eye. If a pendulum swinging in a frontoparallel plane is viewed in the presence of such a processing delay, such as that induced by viewing through a neutral density filter, the pendulum will be perceived as swinging in an elliptical path in three-dimensional space.

neutralized. The stronger the neutral density filter required to cancel out the effect, the more severe the delay in optic nerve conductivity.

An interesting variant of the Pulfrich effect can be seen by tuning a television set to a nonexistent channel so that only "snow," randomly changing dots on the screen, is received. If a neutral density filter is placed before one eye, the television screen will be perceived as moving dots that also move in depth. The screen will look like a cottony three-dimensional "cloud" of moving dots (Tyler, 1974).

The Pulfrich phenomenon also demonstrates that the binocular visual system responds well to luminance changes. In addition, although we can see depth well with targets created by contrast, we cannot see depth well under isoluminant conditions (Lu and Fender, 1972). Therefore, stereopsis is primarily a function of the achromatic channels of the magno and parvo (i.e., interblob) pathways.

Color can also deceive the visual system into seeing stereopsis. Because blue light has a shorter wavelength, dispersion of light by the eye's crystalline lens causes blue light to be refracted more than red light, an effect called **longitudinal chromatic aberration**. In addition, the lines of sight are decentered slightly nasally from the optical axes of the eyes, producing differential prismatic effects for red and blue light. Red and blue lights viewed at the same fixation distance will not be focused at the same lateral position on the retina; the image of red objects will be displaced temporally relative to blue objects (**transverse chromatic aberration**). Blue objects will therefore have less crossed disparity and will be seen as farther away than red objects at the same distance. That is, red and blue objects will have a relative disparity introduced by the differential refraction by the lens, causing the red object to appear closer to you than the blue object. This is known as **chromostereopsis**. Chromostereopsis is very noticeable if you look at red and blue lights in the same neon sign at night, a red object on a blue background, or red and blue text on a black background on a Web page. Because chromostereopsis is a purely optical effect, even color-blind patients can exhibit chromostereopsis.

It should be noted that the cues to depth are most informative when they each provide complementary information. Depth perception suffers when depth cues are in conflict. The information provided by each is additive, and no single source of depth information completely predominates our percept.

## STEREOACUITY

The human visual system is very sensitive to differences in depth. **Stereoacuity** is defined as the smallest depth difference we can see, that is, a **depth discrimination threshold**. Stereoacuity is typically measured in the laboratory using the method of constant stimuli or a staircase procedure. Humans are capable of detecting a shift of one eye's image (that is, a binocular disparity) of only 4″ to 5″ arc (Andersen and Weymouth, 1923). Stereoacuity can be thought of as the "resolving capacity" of stereopsis, much as visual acuity is the resolution limit of spatial vision. However, stereothresholds are actually closer in magnitude to the thresholds of vernier acuity than of resolution acuity. In other words, stereoacuity, like vernier acuity, is a form of **hyperacuity**.

Stereoscopic disparity is correctly calculated with respect to the Vieth-Müller circle (i.e., geometric, rather than functional, disparities measured relative to the horopter; see Chapter 4). However, we usually discuss stereoscopic disparities of near targets, and the horopter is very close to Vieth-Müller circle at near fixation distances, so the discrepancy between them is very small. Therefore, it is appropriate to use the horopter to measure stereoscopic disparity.

Although stereoacuity is one indicator of the intactness of stereopsis, it cannot be assumed that better stereoacuity necessarily translates to better stereopsis. Everyday stereopsis usually entails processing larger disparities. This is much like visual acuity, which represents the limits of spatial vision but does not reflect every aspect of spatial vision. One can demonstrate good stereoacuity, yet when tested on a **depth matching task**, still have poor depth perception because of a **depth perception bias** (constant error), which affects **stereoscopic accuracy** by an overestimation or underestimation of the depth of an object. In addition, some people may exhibit an inability to process certain disparity ranges, seeing crossed or uncrossed disparities less accurately.

**CLINICAL APPLICATION** | Clinically, stereoacuity is measured simply to see if the patient is capable of stereopsis when presented with a binocular disparity.

One instrument used to measure stereoacuity thresholds is the **Howard-Dolman apparatus** or two-rod test (Fig. 7-15A). The subject views two rods; one is at a fixed location, and the other is movable. The subject's task is to move the adjustable rod until a difference in depth between the rods is first noticed. The magnitude of displacement needed to see depth, that is, the difference threshold for depth, is the stereoacuity. However, one can also use the Howard-Dolman apparatus to determine the point of subjective equality by moving the test rod until it lies on the horopter with the fixation rod. Because the method of adjustment has traditionally been used to measure the stereoscopic threshold, published stereoacuity thresholds obtained with the Howard-Dolman apparatus are somewhat inaccurate and variable. However, one can also use the more accurate method of constant stimuli.

It should be noted that monocular cues are available to the observer in the Howard-Dolman apparatus. As the test rod is moved closer or farther away, its retinal image size, and therefore its apparent size, changes. However, the size difference threshold for these rods is over a log unit higher than the stereoscopic threshold, leaving the measured stereoscopic thresholds free of contamination from monocular cues.

Angular disparity is calculated from the amount of displacement of the test rod as follows (see Fig. 7-15B):

$$n = \frac{2a\Delta d}{d^2}$$

A

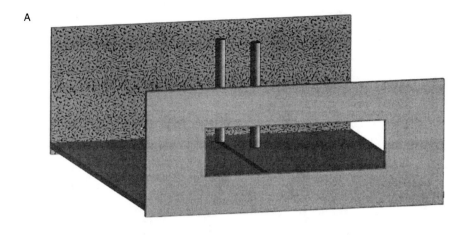

B

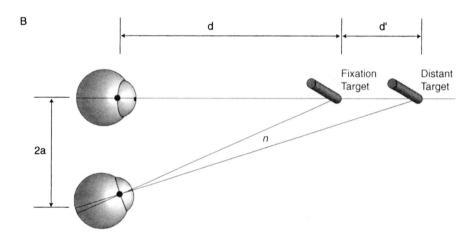

**Figure 7-15**    **A:** Stereoacuity may be measured with the Howard-Dolman apparatus, an instrument containing a reference rod at a fixed viewing distance and a test rod on a track whose distance may be varied. The subject's task is to align the rods at the same perceived distance (point of subjective equality) and determine the minimum displacement needed to perceive a difference in distance (stereoacuity threshold). **B:** The angular disparity of the test rod relative to the fixed rod is determined by the reference distance, the test rod displacement, and the interpupillary distance of the observer.

Where $n$ is the **angular stereoscopic disparity** in radians (to convert to seconds of arc, multiply by 206,256), $2a$ is the interpupillary distance (PD), $d$ is the fixation distance, that is, the distance of the fixed reference rod, and $\Delta d$ is the depth interval, i.e., the linear difference in distance between the fixation and test rods.

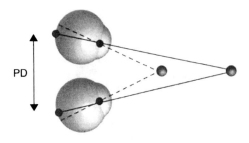

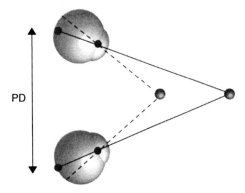

**Figure 7-16**   With two targets of a fixed separation in three-dimensional space, a patient with a larger interpupillary distance (PD) will perceive a larger binocular disparity and therefore more depth. The interpupillary distance must therefore be taken into account in measuring stereoacuity thresholds.

A few facts about stereoacuity become evident when this equation is studied. First, stereoacuity depends on the **interpupillary distance (PD)**. The larger the PD, the larger the disparity seen with a given test rod displacement (Fig. 7-16). Stereoacuity thresholds are therefore typically smaller in subjects with larger interpupillary distances because a given disparity will be more evident to them. Conversely, if two people exhibit the same minimum rod displacement, the person with the smaller PD will actually have the better stereoacuity.

Second, **viewing distance** also matters (Fig. 7-17). Disparity is inversely proportional to the square of the viewing distance (Schor and Flom, 1969). As you change viewing distance from 1 foot to 100 feet, the disparity will change by a factor of 10,000. That is, the same object displacement needed to see a depth difference at 1 foot must be increased by 10,000 times to be seen at 100 feet. You

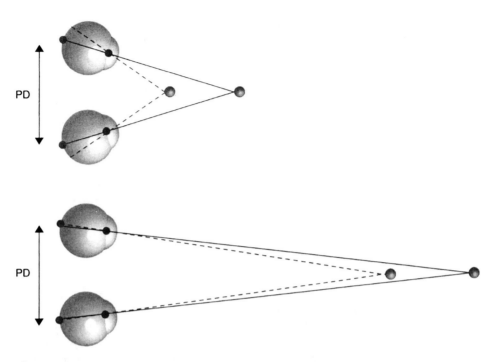

**Figure 7-17**   At a near fixation distance, a small difference in the distance between two targets yields a large, easily seen difference in the retinal positions of their images (binocular disparity). At a far distance, even a very large distance between the targets yields a small, possibly subthreshold, binocular disparity. At distances past 800 m to –1,300 m, stereopsis can no longer be appreciated.

are therefore much more accurate at using disparity at close distances than at long distances. The largest possible **geometric limit for disparity** occurs when $\Delta d = d$ (i.e., the depth interval equals the viewing distance) because you can not have a disparity greater than your viewing distance. For an average interpupillary distance, geometric limit can be calculated to occur when the fixation distance equals 1,320 m or 0.8 mile. Therefore, you cannot see depth for objects more than 0.8 mile away—objects beyond this limit all appear to be at the same distance. This is why your depth perception for objects on the ground disappears when you are in an airplane. You are forced to rely entirely on monocular cues.

Stereoacuity thresholds are typically less than 10″ arc and, under optimal testing conditions, can reach 2″ to 6″ arc in man and monkeys (Harwerth and Boltz, 1979). Binocular thresholds via disparity are better than the monocular threshold (i.e., using only monocular cues to depth) by a factor of 20 times; therefore, monocular cues do not aid one's detection of near-threshold disparities. Surprisingly, if you distribute the disparity offsets equally in each eye, the minimal offsets needed for stereopsis are even smaller than those needed for vernier threshold, which are typically thought to be the minimum monocular visible displacement.

**CLINICAL** | If we are so sensitive to disparity, why do most clinical tests of stereopsis use
**PROCEDURE** | a 40″ arc disparity? We use a 40″ arc disparity in clinical tests because 95%
| of the population (two standard deviations from the norm) has 40″ arc or
| better stereopsis. The clinical tests are used to *screen* for poor stereopsis and
| binocular problems, but they are not used to quantify a stereoacuity
| threshold.

Stereoacuity thresholds tend to improve with **practice (learning)** (Fendick and Westheimer, 1983). In addition, the ability to perceive depth in more complicated stereoscopic figures such as random-dot stereograms also improves with practice (Julesz, 1960). The exact reason for this is not yet known. Although it has been suggested that practice effects for stereopsis probably result from a combination of shortening latencies for vergence eye movements, several lines of evidence suggest instead that practice effects involve factors other than eye movements (Frisby and Clatworthy, 1975), such as changes in the subject's criterion for detecting depth.

Several factors influence how well we can detect disparity: one such factor is **luminance**. This is similar to the effect that luminance and **adaptation state** have on monocular visual acuity. The dimmer the background luminance, the less our sensitivity to depth, and our percept of depth degrades (Berry et al., 1950). This can be very noticeable under scotopic conditions.

The **color** of a stereoscopic stimulus can also affect our stereoacuity. Stereoacuity for targets that isolate blue cone function is poorer than for targets that stimulate the red and green cone systems (Pennington, 1970). This may be explained by both the lower resolution and lower contrast sensitivity of the blue cone system (Grinberg and Williams, 1985). As we will see shortly, both contrast and size affect the ability to detect small disparities.

Another factor is how long we are allowed to view the target, that is, the **exposure duration**. Although we can see depth at very short intervals, the stereothresholds are elevated (Ogle and Weil, 1958). We are much more sensitive to depth if are allowed to view the target for a longer time. We achieve our best stereoacuity with exposure times of about 1 second; that is, fine disparities take longer to detect than coarse disparities (Tyler, 1991). Certain types of stereoscopic targets, such as **random-dot stereograms** (to be discussed shortly) take even longer to process than simpler line stereograms (Harwerth and Rawlings, 1977), but subjects with poor binocularity take even longer to see them.

In addition to duration of target exposure, timing plays another important role in stereoacuity. If the right eye and left eye targets are presented with a temporal asynchrony, stereopsis is not impaired unless the asynchrony is over about 100 ms in duration (Ross and Hogben, 1974). This is to be expected because binocular fusion is disrupted with asynchronies over 100 ms. However, such interocular delays may be tolerated if the stimuli are presented repetitively. This aspect of stereopsis is utilized in liquid crystal stereoscopic goggles used to view three-dimensional scenes on computers, which is discussed later in this chapter (see Fig. 7-26). The computer will display alternate left- and right-eye views with a duration of less than

100 ms, and the goggles are synchronized to the computer so each eye can view only the appropriate display. The observer will not notice the changes in the display or the goggles but perceives a steady three-dimensional scene.

Perceiving depth is dependent on determining how far apart two monocular images are. This means that the resolution of the visual system is an important factor in detecting small disparities. This is why **retinal eccentricity** is important in depth perception. Our smallest receptive fields, the ones that have the finest resolution, are located at the fovea, and therefore our finest stereoacuity is noted at the fovea (Harris et al., 1997). The retinal periphery cannot detect fine differences in position, so our ability to see small disparities is hampered in the periphery. We are less sensitive to binocular disparity in the peripheral visual field (Rawlings and Shipley, 1969). Similarly, when we are forced to use the chromatic channels of the parvo pathway to see depth, our stereothresholds are much worse for blue targets, because blue cones have larger receptive fields than red or green cones.

Stereothresholds are elevated at contrast threshold so that it is difficult to see stereopsis at very low contrast. However, increasing the stimulus contrast even a little will greatly improve one's ability to see depth, as stereothresholds decrease by a factor of the square root of the stimulus (Cormack et al., 1991). Although we cannot judge the amount of depth accurately for targets at contrast threshold, we can still detect the sign of the depth (front vs. back) as soon as the images in each eye are of sufficient contrast to be seen (Simmons, 1998).

However, if the two eyes receive images of unequal contrast, stereoacuity will be degraded to an even greater degree (Westheimer and McKee, 1980; Halpern and Blake, 1988). Optical disorders such as unilateral cataracts can reduce image contrast unilaterally. In addition, unilateral neural disorders can affect the effective "neural" contrast of images processed by that eye. It is therefore not surprising that a recent study demonstrated stereoacuity losses in glaucoma (Bassi and Galanis, 1991). Glaucoma usually affects one eye first, leading to a unilateral contrast sensitivity loss and, therefore, impaired stereopsis. Similarly, **blur** or **defocus** may be a detrimental factor for depth perception, but stereoacuity is more robust to binocular blur than is spatial resolution. Blur has a much greater effect on stereoacuity when it is a monocular blur (Lit, 1968) because of binocular inhibition of the blurred eye, which has a lower contrast image, by the unblurred eye, whose image is of higher contrast (Legge, 1979). In addition, stereopsis is most pronounced when the images in each eye are of similar spatial frequency content (Schor et al, 1984). Monocular blur will remove the high-spatial-frequency components of the image in that eye alone.

**CLINICAL APPLICATION** | The deleterious effect of monocular blur on stereopsis is one reason why it is so important to correct anisometropia properly and why we should be aware of the consequences of inducing anisometropia, for example, in a monovision contact lens fit.

Surprisingly, our ability to see small differences in the depth of a disparate target does not deteriorate if the target moves laterally to the left or right (Fig. 7-18).

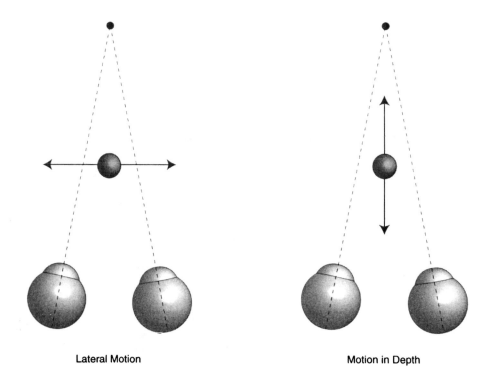

Lateral Motion                                    Motion in Depth

**Figure 7-18** Lateral motion of a target at a fixed disparity plane does not degrade our sensitivity to the depth of that target. Conversely, stereomotion, that is, motion of a target toward or away from the observer, is very detrimental to our sensitivity to depth.

In fact, we can see depth even when the target moves at relatively high velocities. A target can move up to 2° to 3° per second without degrading stereoacuity (Westheimer and McKee, 1978). This is very much different from what happens with resolution acuity (such as Snellen acuity), which is degraded seriously by motion. However, stereoacuity is a hyperacuity, and other hyperacuities such as vernier acuity are also not adversely affected by image motion. In fact, stereothresholds are better when a subject can make eye movements than when fixation must be maintained at one point. The microsaccades and drifting eye movements that occur during fixation also do not degrade stereoacuity, as shown by experiments in which the effects of these eye movements were eliminated by optically stabilizing the target's image on the retina. Under these conditions stereoacuity is the same as when both eyes are fixated on one point.

**CLINICAL APPLICATION** | One additional consequence of the robustness of stereoacuity to image motion is that patients with **nystagmus**, unless the nystagmus is unyoked in the two eyes, will have stereopsis that is less degraded than is their visual acuity.

Although we are sensitive to depth when a target moves horizontally, we are *not* very sensitive to depth with motion toward and away from us (**stereomotion**, or **motion in depth**). We are sensitive to lateral motion of the image of a line moving in the same direction in each eye. However it is more difficult to detect opposing horizontal motion of dichoptic lines changing in relative lateral separation that leads to a percept of a line moving in depth, a phenomenon called **stereomovement suppression** (Tyler, 1971). The sole stereomotion that we can see even moderately well occurs when an object moves toward us, directed toward our nose (**looming**). Motion in depth can also degrade stereoacuity, even though lateral motion has little effect on stereoacuity. Oscillating a target *in depth* degrades **dynamic stereoacuity** thresholds if the oscillations are slower than 1 Hz (Schor et al., 1983). It has been reported that there is poor correlation between dynamic stereoacuity and static stereoacuity (Zinn and Solomon, 1985).

|   |   |
|---|---|
| **CLINICAL APPLICATION** | Generally, in a vision examination, only measurements of **static stereoacuity** are made. Therefore, in patients who rely heavily on dynamic stereopsis, such as athletes who must catch moving balls, it is a good idea to specifically test **dynamic stereoacuity. Sports vision** practitioners may work with athletes to improve their dynamic stereopsis. |

It should be noted that the **sign of the disparity** can affect stereothresholds. Stereoacuity is two to three times worse for uncrossed disparity than for crossed disparity for most people. Most clinical tests of stereopsis measure only sensitivity to crossed disparities.

Stereoacuity exhibits a **"crowding effect"** like that noted for visual acuity. If the reference and test targets are laterally spaced 15' to − 50' arc apart, stereoacuity thresholds are low. However, if the targets are too widely separated (> 50' arc), it becomes difficult to compare them for a relative difference in depth, and stereoacuity suffers (Westheimer and McKee, 1979). If the targets are too close together (< 15' arc), stereoacuity is also degraded, and the impression of a depth difference between the two stimuli suffers. This is a purely spatial effect; flanking lines introduced in the same plane as and adjacent to the reference line also increase stereo thresholds.

Our best stereoacuity is achieved when we compare the test target to a reference target with zero disparity. In other words, our best stereoacuity is for displacements in depth just off the horopter. When we try to see depth relative to a second target that already has a disparity (**standing disparity**), a depth *discrimination* task, our sensitivity suffers (Ogle, 1953; Badcock and Schor, 1985). Stereothresholds increase exponentially with the size of the standing disparity.

## UPPER LIMIT OF STEREOPSIS

Stereoacuity represents the lower disparity limit of the visual system, that is, the smallest disparity that we can see. We can also ask what the **upper disparity limit** is. One might assume that the upper disparity limit is the extent of Panum's fusional area because objects are seen as diplopic if their disparity exceeds the fusional limit. However, this is not true. Outside of Panum's fusional area, we do

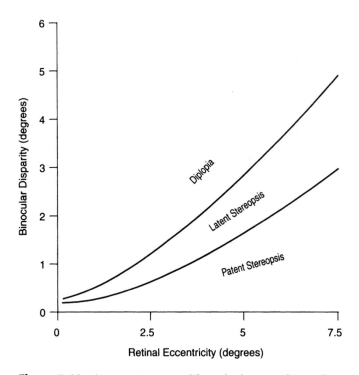

**Figure 7-19** For targets removed from the horopter by small disparities, patent (quantitative) stereopsis is appreciated, in which relative differences in depth can be seen and the percept of depth is robust. The limits of patent stereopsis coincide to the limits of Panum's fusional area. Outside of this region, images are diplopic. Within a range of disparities beyond patent stereopsis is a zone of latent (qualitative) stereopsis, in which diplopia provides some depth information. However, the depth percept is vague; although the observer can determine that a target is either closer than or farther than fixation, but all objects within this range appear to be at the same distance from fixation. Beyond the range of qualitative stereopsis, diplopia cannot be used to determine depth.

perceive diplopia, but this does not mean that we cannot judge depth at all (Ogle, 1952).

Within Panum's fusional area, we are able to distinguish relative changes in depth (**quantitative stereopsis** or **patent stereopsis**) with a robust percept of that depth (Fig. 7-19). In the region of quantitative stereopsis, the degree of depth perceived is directly proportional to the magnitude of binocular disparity. Outside of Panum's fusional area (from ± 10′ arc up to ± 1°, depending on the retinal eccentricity), diplopia is noted, and we cannot distinguish changes in distance (relative depth) accurately. However, we can still tell if an object is closer than or farther than the fixation point by taking advantage of the type of diplopia (**qualitative stereopsis** or **latent stereopsis**) (Westheimer and Tanzman, 1956). In other words, we can appreciate stereopsis without fusion, a clear violation of Worth's fusion hierarchy. Crossed diplopia signals that the object is closer than the fixation point, and uncrossed diplopia signals a farther distance. In experiments using a depth-matching paradigm (Richards, 1971) or a magnitude estimation of the amount of depth seen (Richards and Kaye, 1974), it was shown that outside of Panum's area the linear relationship between the magnitude of depth perception and magnitude of disparity breaks down. Beyond the limits of Panum's area, the perceived depth of diplopic images at first increases with increasing disparity and reaches a peak depth percept; that is, the maximum depth percept occurs not within Panum's area but for diplopic targets outside of Panum's area. However, beyond this peak value, the depth percept gradually diminishes with increasing disparity until an **upper disparity limit** is reached at 1,000′ arc disparity. At the upper disparity limit, disparity no longer evokes a percept of depth. However, it should be noted that the disparity values listed here represent the average limits noted by experimenters; the upper range of stereopsis is dependent on some of the same factors as stereoacuity, namely, contrast and exposure duration.

## METHODS OF DISPLAYING STEREOSCOPIC IMAGES

Stereopsis is studied by presenting stereoscopic half-views (collectively called **stereo pairs**) to each eye independently. The complete figures, as viewed binocularly, are called **stereograms**. Each image in the stereogram pair is of an object or scene viewed from either a left eye or a right eye vantage point that mimics the effect of having two eyes separated by an interpupillary distance.

Stereoscopic images have been in existence since 1838, when Sir Charles Wheatstone invented the **stereoscope**. Stereoscopes are instruments that alter the relationship between distance and disparity by means of mirrors, lenses or prisms so that independent images can be presented to each eye. The **Wheatstone mirror stereoscope** (Fig. 7-20) uses two mirrors to place the two separate images into each eye. One advantage of the mirror stereoscope is it does not have a fixed working distance. Targets can be placed at very distant positions so that the disparities in the images are small, allowing the measurement of stereoacuity.

**CLINICAL PROCEDURE** | A similar device that is used in vision therapy for examining and treating strabismics is called the **synoptophore** or **amblyoscope**.

A modern variant of the mirror stereoscope is the **electronic stereoscope** developed by Westheimer. Two oscilloscopes are used to present the half-views (Fig. 7-21), which are superimposed by a thin-film pellicle beam-splitter (see Steinman and Levi, 1992). Stereoacuity may be measured on such a device.

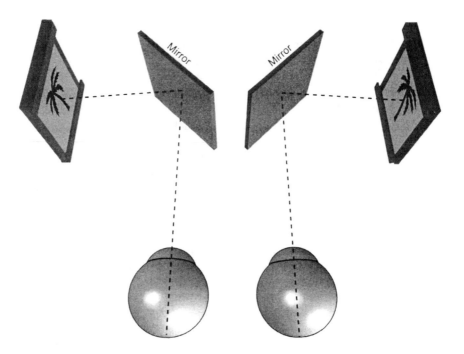

**Figure 7-20**    The Wheatstone mirror stereoscope uses two mirrors to present distinct images to each eye. The images may be dissimilar, producing binocular rivalry, or similar, producing binocular fusion. If disparities exist between the two images, stereopsis is appreciated.

In 1849, Sir David Brewster created another type of stereoscope using lenses instead of mirrors (actually, Wheatstone invented this form of stereoscope as well several years earlier but was not credited for its invention). The **Brewster refracting stereoscope** (Fig. 7-22) uses + 5.0D lenses to place the far point of accommodation at a fixation distance of 20 cm. The plus lenses are decentered outward to produce a *base-out* prismatic effect. The optical centers are placed at the temporalmost position of the eyepiece. When the stereogram is placed at the far point setting (20 cm), the separation between similar points in the two half-views of the stereogram equals the distance between optical centers of the lenses, and there is no standing disparity. Decreasing the separation by 2 mm induces one prism diopter of uncrossed disparity (convergence demand), whereas an increase in separation induces uncrossed disparity. The advantage of this type of stereoscope is that the stereogram can be viewed with different convergence and accommodation demands by independently changing the separation of the stereoscopic images and the viewing distance, respectively. However, measuring stereoacuity requires carefully printed stereograms, as a 10″ arc disparity needs a 0.1-mm lateral image displacement at the standard 20-cm viewing distance. Refracting stereoscopes are therefore better for viewing larger disparities. In fact,

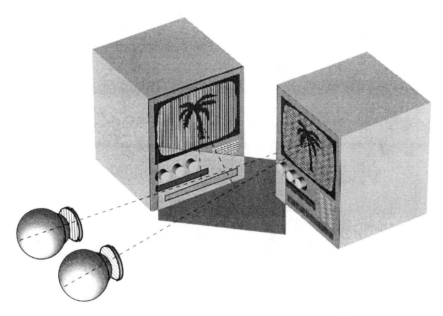

**Figure 7-21** The electronic stereoscope is a modern variant of the mirror stereoscope that uses a thin-film beam-splitter or half-silvered mirror to superimpose the half-views presented on two oscilloscopes. Such systems may present disparities in the stereoacuity range.

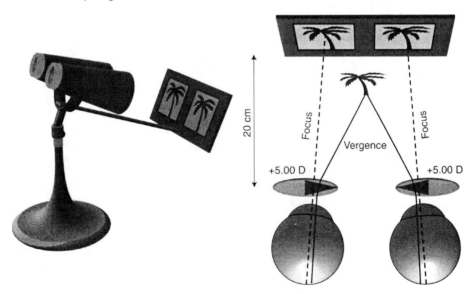

**Figure 7-22** The Brewster refracting stereoscope uses + 5D lenses to place a stereo pair viewed at a 20-cm working distance at optical infinity, displacing the lenses to introduce base-out prism. At this working distance, the separation of the eyepieces equals the separation of the stereo pair's half-images.

**Figure 7-23**    Stereophotographs are photographs that were taken at different vantage points to simulate the effect of the interpupillary distance when
viewed in a refracting stereoscope. Although stereopsis is seen in these photographs, the percept is not like that of viewing a natural scene, as the figures
in the stereophotographs tend to appear like flat cardboard cutouts placed
at different depth planes; that is, no disparity-based object curvature is appreciated. *(Source: "Barnacle Bill," a rock on the surface of the planet Mars, as
photographed by the Pathfinder Lander on June 2, 1998, National Aeronautics
and Space Administration.)*

refracting stereoscopes are well suited for viewing **stereophotographs** (Fig. 7-23),
photographs taken with special stereoscopic cameras. These cameras produce
two photographs of the scene, as "seen" by two laterally displaced lenses and film
planes. Stereophotography was an extremely popular form of entertainment in
the late 1800s to early 1900s, and experienced a revival in the 1950s to 1960s with
the **ViewMaster**™ stereo viewer. Stereophotography clubs still exist throughout
the world.

**CLINICAL**    In addition, the **Keystone Telebinocular** used in binocular vision testing and
**PROCEDURE**    vision therapy is a form of Brewster stereoscope. The Telebinocular comes
with a large assortment of stereograms of different photographic scenes and
containing a wide range of disparities as well as targets that are meant to test
for other aspects of binocular vision, mainly suppression.

Stereograms need not be viewed in instruments at all. One can view a pair of
pictures or photographs side by side and fuse them with vergence eye movements, a process called **free fusion**, achieved by converging in front of or diverging beyond the plane of the stereogram. The observer views a target, e.g., a finger,
as it is moved from the stereogram toward the nose along the midline, so that
uncrossed diplopia of the stereogram is produced, that is, four half-views are now
seen. At the appropriate distance, the middle two of the four perceived views are
then fused together into a single stereoscopic image. Similarly, an observer can

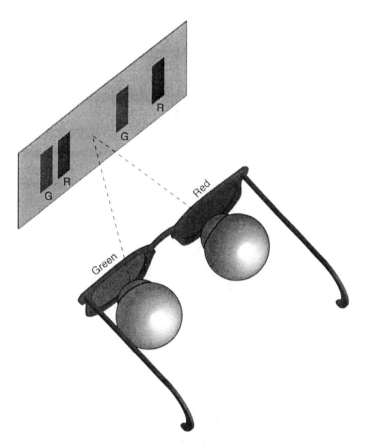

**Figure 7-24**  Anaglyphs are a means of separating stereo pairs so that each eye views only one half-image. One half-view is colored red, and the other is colored green. The patient wears a red filter over the right eye and a green one over the left eye. Free fusion may be used to fuse the two images.

use divergence to achieve the same effect, although the disparities in the stereogram will be reversed. Here, the observer tries to "look past" the stereogram until diplopia is achieved, diverging the eyes enough to fuse the middle two half-views.

A simpler means of separating the views of the two eyes without an instrument is the **anaglyph** method (Fig. 7-24). Here, the two half-views are printed in red ink for one eye's view and green (or blue) ink for the other. These images may actually be superimposed when printed into a single target. The observer wears red/green-filtered glasses so that the red-filtered eye sees only the green image and the green-filtered eye sees only the red image. In other words, color is used to distinguish between each eye's haplopic view. Fusional eye movements will bring the images into alignment, and a stereoscopic view will be perceived. Anaglyphic stereograms are very popular in comic books and magazines. For example, in 1998, National Geographic magazine published an issue filled with anaglyphic photographs of the surface of Mars.

**CLINICAL APPLICATION** | Anaglyphs are also used extensively clinically for measuring and expanding fusion ranges and **antisuppression therapy**.

The half-views of a stereogram may also be separated without an instrument by means of Polaroid filters, in what is called a **vectographic** presentation, or a **vectogram**. Vectograms (Fig. 7-25) use polarizing filters to separate out each eye's

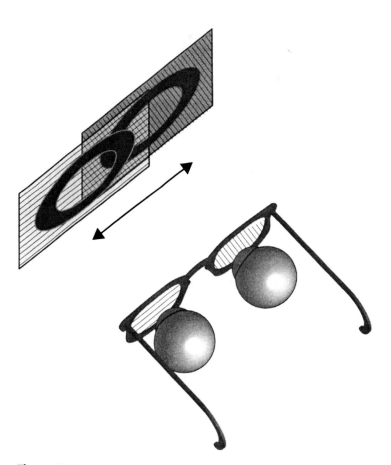

**Figure 7-25**   Vectographs employ Polaroid filters to isolate each eye's image. Polaroid filters of orthogonal orientations are placed over each half-image, and the viewer wears glasses with orthogonally-oriented Polaroid filters over each eye.

monocular view of the target. The filters before each half-view of the stereogram are polarized at right angles. The subject then wears spectacles with polarized filters before each eye, also at right angles, so that each eye can see only its own half-view of the target. The plastic sheets that create the target are overlapped and may be decentered relative to each other to introduce a stimulus for vergence eye movements.

**CLINICAL PROCEDURE** | Vectograms are commonly used for clinical tests. For example, the **Titmus Stereo Test** (Stereo Optical Co.) consists of three types of stereograms. The first is the **Stereo Fly**, a stereoscopic photograph of a housefly in which the fly is perceived as "popping out" of the page. The **Titmus Circles** are diamond-shaped areas containing four circles each, three of which have no disparity and one with crossed disparity that, if detected by the patient, will "pop out" toward the patient. The subject's task is to detect which target pops out, a four-alternative forced-choice method. The magnitude of the disparity of the Titmus Circles decreases through nine levels to a minimum of 40″ arc at the 40-cm working distance. A cruder test is the **Titmus Animals**, which presents disparities of 100″ to 300″ arc. Incorrect administration of vectographic targets can result in significant errors. Tilting the head will change the orientation of the Polaroid filters in the glasses with respect to the Polaroid filters overlying the stereogram. This removes the segregation of the images to each eye. In addition, significant monocular cues may be present in vectograms because of the obvious lateral displacement of the disparate contours in each monocular view with coarser disparities. Therefore, some subjects can use monocular cues to pass the Titmus Stereo Test even when they lack binocularity (Cooper and Warshowsky, 1977). Finally, as with the anaglyph method, the Polaroid filters decrease the image contrast significantly, which may make the disparities less visible.

The advent of computers has also made possible the generation of stereoscopic images on computer screens. Any of the above techniques may be used to generate stereoscopic images on the computer, so long as the computer displays stereo pairs side by side. In addition, computers offer a new means of separating the images presented to the two eyes. **Liquid crystal shutter stereogoggles** (Fig. 7-26) are goggles containing clear elements in their eyepieces that may be darkened until opaque by the application of an electrical current. One eye's eyepiece, then the other, is occluded alternately, such that one eye's view of the computer screen, then the other, is revealed. The screen image is alternated to display each eye's stereo half-image in synchrony with the exposure of its corresponding eye. If performed at a rapid rate, such as a 15-Hz or higher alternation rate between the two eyes, the percept is that of a single fused image in stereoscopic depth. Such displays have been used in industry for simulations and in video games.

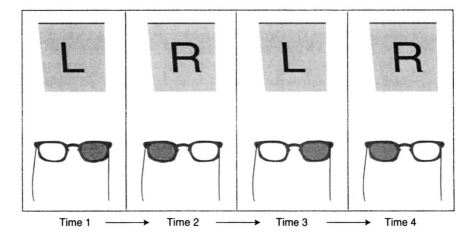

Time 1 ——→ Time 2 ——→ Time 3 ——→ Time 4

**Figure 7-26**    Liquid crystal shutter stereogoggles enable computers to alternately display images to the two eyes individually. The stereo half-images are alternated on the screen at the same rate that the liquid crystal shutters alternately expose each eye to its view. When this is done at a rapid rate, the half-views are fused into a single percept, allowing full-screen full-color stereograms and stereoscopic movies to be presented.

Recent experiments with lasers have created three-dimensional holographic displays in free space that do not require special viewing goggles, in which the observer can walk around the display and observe the virtual images from any viewing angle. Advances in this technology may eventually yield visually "solid" three-dimensional photographic-quality moving images for simulations.

## CLASSES OF STEREOSCOPIC TARGETS

The simplest type of stereoscopic target is what is called a **line stereogram**. As the name implies, line stereograms are pairs of simple line targets (one line of the pair viewed by each eye) with a disparity introduced into one or more of the pairs (Fig. 7-27). Line stereograms are typically used when carefully controlled stimulus conditions are needed, as in research projects. Because stereoscopic disparities smaller than the resolution limit of the eye can be seen, line stereograms can be used to measure stereoacuity. This is particularly useful because when such sub-threshold disparities are used, the relative displacement of the two line images cannot be seen. However, there is a crucial problem with using line stereograms at suprathreshold disparities. Here, the relative displacement of the images that provide the disparity is blatantly obvious, even under monocular conditions. What this means is that stereoblind patients may still report seeing depth just by noting whether or not the images are displaced. Therefore, line stereograms are best used for measurement of subthreshold disparities.

Left Eye View                    Right Eye View

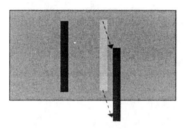

Stereoscopic Binocular Percept

**Figure 7-27**  Line stereograms are simple line drawings in which the individual lines are displaced in each half-image to yield stereoscopic disparity. Such stereograms are used in vision therapy or in industry to display stereoscopic wire-frame models of three-dimensional objects.

Line stereograms or stereophotographs have individual elements such as lines, edges, or contours that we can use to match up in each eye's half-view (**local stereopsis**). These features are visible monocularly as well as binocularly. Clearly, a way of removing these monocular cues to the presence of the displacements that create the binocular disparities in stereograms is critical when we wish to be certain we are measuring stereopsis. The solution to this problem is a special type of stereogram called a **random-dot stereogram**. Random-dot stereograms are made up of a dense array of dots randomly filled with either black or white. Some of the dots are displaced laterally in one half-view to produce a disparity (Fig. 7-28). However, monocularly, both views of the stereograms just look like random dots; there are no monocular contours to match in a random-dot stereogram (see Fig. 7-28). When fused binocularly, the disparate part of the stereogram appears in depth, and a figure made up from the disparate dots "pops out" in a different depth plane. The figure or form appears only in the *binocular* image but in *neither* of the two monocular images (Fig. 7-29). This has been termed **cyclopean depth perception**. Because the form is seen only under binocular

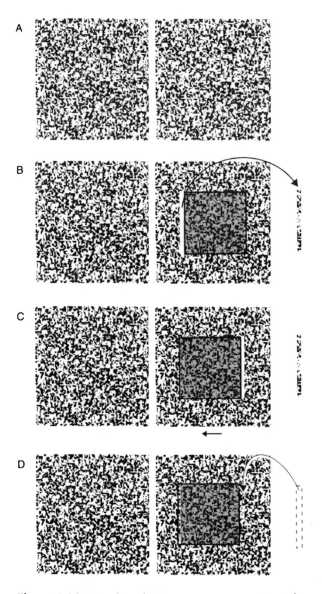

**Figure 7-28**    Random-dot stereograms are constructed by first generating a pattern of identical dots in each half-image, in which a given individual dot has a 50% chance of being black or white. To create a figure that will be presented in stereoscopic depth, in this case a square, the dots comprising the square are displaced in one eye's half-image by an amount determined by the magnitude of binocular disparity desired. The dots that were occluded by the displaced square are moved to the now-empty space vacated by the square.

**Figure 7-29**    The figure shown is the random-dot stereogram produced by the process depicted in Fig. 7-28. With free fusion, a central
square should be perceived in a different depth plane than the background dots of the figure.

conditions, patients cannot take advantage of monocular cues on this test. In
addition, we know that form perception on random-dot stereograms involves
only *cortical binocular processes* because, as we will see in Chapter 8, all binocular vision takes place in the visual cortex.

When combining the two monocular images together, the visual system must
find matching portions (matching contours) in each image, guide vergence eye
movements to bring these contours into alignment, and then determine the relative depth of the contours. A similar problem occurs in stereopsis, known as the
**stereo correspondence problem**. The visual system must determine what portion of one eye's image corresponds to a given portion of the other eye's image.
Such matching of contours is a problematic calculation for the visual system.

Difficulty in feature matching is not restricted to the binocular visual system and
can be demonstrated even in monocular images. For example, in perceiving apparent motion between successive frames of dot stimuli, the visual system must match
corresponding dots in each frame to determine the motion of the dot over time.

Although combining the two monocular images is simple for uncomplicated
figures such as line stereograms, an unambiguous solution to the correspondence
problem is more involved for more complex random-dot stereograms. The dense
packing of the individual random dots of a random-dot stereogram results in a
high degree of depth ambiguity. In other words, there is no obvious, indisputable
solution as to which dot each eye should fixate when attempting to fuse the two
half-views. If both eyes were to fixate the exact same dot in each view, no depth
would be seen. However, if each eye fixates a different dot, the resulting percept
will be of a single dot in a different depth plane than the rest of the stereogram.
The more dots, the more possible pairings of dots between the two eyes, and the
more possible depth planes we could see. This can be shown with a **Keplerian**

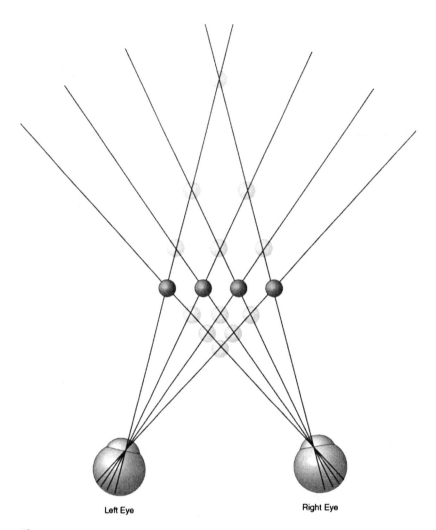

Left Eye                                      Right Eye

**Figure 7-30**   For each possible point that may be matched between the two eyes, there exist false "ghost images" at different disparity planes that may also be matched between the two eyes, as shown in this Keplerian projection. Because the false matches are distributed symmetrically in front of and behind the true depth plane of the image, a depth-averaging process in the visual system may remove the false matches and hone in on the true stereoscopic match.

projection (Fig. 7-30). The Keplerian projection demonstrates that when there is more than one similar object in each eye's field, there will be the possibility of "ghost images" resulting from particular improper (nonmatching) binocular image matches (Marr and Poggio, 1979). These ghost images do not exist in the actual physical targets. Mathematically speaking, the number of possible ghost images is $n^2$, where $n$ is the number of physical locations to be matched. For line stimuli, the features to be matched are sparse; $n$ is low, and therefore, so is $n^2$, so the likelihood of matching inappropriate targets together and getting ghost images is low. In natural scenes, we can use empirical cues to depth to help rule out the incorrect image matches. However, in random-dot stereograms, which can contain thousands of dots, $n$ is high, and $n^2$ is astronomical. Because random-dot stereograms have no monocular cues, we are forced to make the best binocular feature match we can with the information we have.

Many schemes have been postulated for the elimination of ghost matches in the Keplerian projection by the visual system. One such scheme is the **unique-matching rule,** which states that because an object can only occupy one place in space at a time, a single point in one eye's image may only match a single point in the other eye's image. If this one-to-one correspondence were true, it could be used to suppress any additional ghost images. However, the role of this rule in the human visual system is not yet certain. A more likely scheme is the **matching of similar features** in each eye's image. Because a single object in space should give rise to similar images in each eye; vastly different features in each eye's image would be more likely to arise from different objects. Therefore, those portions of each eye's image with the most similar features are matched. A third suggested scheme is that we match the two images in such a way as to **minimize disparity gradients** or to **match the sign of contrast** at corresponding retinal points of the two retinal images or to prevent discontinuities in the depth of surfaces (**surface smoothness constraint**). Computer neural networks can "learn" to use such constraints to perform correspondence matches in stereoscopic image pairs (Khotanzad and Lee, 1991).

One simple, possible image-matching method that is plausible in the human visual system is **depth averaging (disparity pooling)** (Foley and Richards, 1978). Depth averaging and the encoding of relative disparities helps to prevent a change in perceptual depth from fluctuations in either the vergence angle or neural noise in the visual system by averaging or "smoothing out" these fluctuations (Tyler and Julesz, 1980). This creates ghost matches that are located symmetrically in front of or behind the correct matches, so that the overall ghost image will average out to the same disparity plane as the correct matches. The downside of depth averaging is that it can also lead to erroneous depth percepts if applied under inappropriate circumstances. For example, surfaces that are slanted in depth may be erroneously perceived as less slanted than they truly are because depth averaging would cause the disparities of the slanted surface to be normalized more toward the mean disparity.

Surprisingly, random-dot stereograms do not exhibit depth ambiguity in practice. We do not see multiple "ghost" depth planes when two disparities are presented in the random-dot pattern. We see a clear-cut figure and a background at two distinct depth planes; the figure looks solid with sharp borders. Bela Julesz, the inventor of the computer-generated random-dot stereogram (Julesz, 1960), has suggested that the visual system seeks out the image-matching solution that yields the most unambiguous depth, that is, the depth plane having the most solid appearance and sharpest edges. The visual system does not perform an element-by-element (dot-by-dot) matching but rather forms a global perception over a larger spatial scale, pooling together information from the entire stereogram to create a global interpretation of depth and form. This process, called **global stereopsis**, performs a pattern-matching or cross-correlation between large groups of dots with similar disparities to yield a figure–ground segregation of a form in a different depth plane than the background. Edges of regions differing in depth are delineated, and the responses to isolated local matches or "ghost" matches are suppressed (Nelson, 1975). Random-dot stereograms demonstrate that the visual system does not need to perform monocular form recognition before processing binocular disparity; form perception can be carried out after binocular combination of visual information (Julesz, 1960).

This global matching process is aided in natural images by several constraints on disparities in real objects. First, natural images produce similar features (but displaced) in the image of each eye. Second, natural objects tend to have smoothly changing disparities along them; that is, their surfaces are smooth and not discontinuous in depth. Discontinuities in depth tend to occur at the edges of objects, which can also be detected monocularly. Third, because real objects can exist in only one place in three-dimensional space, one of the potential stereo matches between points on the objects surface must be accepted and all other alternative matches (ghost planes) rejected. Once a global match is made, the visual system can encode the relative disparity of each point in the binocular image. Just as encoding relative luminance (contrast) helps remove the influence of fluctuations of overall lighting on object perception, encoding relative disparity helps reduce the effects of fluctuations in vergence on depth perception.

In summary, there are two processes involved in seeing stereopsis in random-dot stereograms. First, the brain must match together similar dots in the two patterned monocular views and assign each locus a disparity. This is called local stereopsis. Next, the brain matches large areas of the binocular view of the stereogram, finding patches with similar disparity and combining them to see an overall shape in depth. This is called global stereopsis. In a simple line stereogram, only local stereopsis is required because there are no large areas of the binocular view to be matched. However, seeing shapes in random-dot stereograms is a more complex process than seeing simpler line targets in depth, requiring both local and global stereopsis. Because of this, random-dot stereograms do not seem to contain different depths immediately. It can sometimes take a *longer* time to see the depth in a random-dot stereogram. The percept of depth in random-dot stereograms is typically slow to develop, with the figure gradually appearing over a period of 500–1,000 ms. However, with practice (learning), the time needed decreases somewhat.

**CLINICAL APPLICATION** | Part of the delay in processing random-dot stereograms may result from **contour interactions (crowding effects)** between adjacent dots actually impairing your ability to process the figure. The high dot density promotes spatial crowding effects, similar to those that cause difficulty for amblyopes when reading eye charts. In fact, crowding effects may cause amblyopes who have residual stereopsis to fail random-dot stereogram tests. Some scientists have advocated the use of stereograms with fewer and larger dots to minimize crowding effects when testing amblyopic subjects.

We are probably performing both local and global stereoscopic matches in everyday life all of the time, but it is difficult to demonstrate the global process unless the more obvious local matches are minimized by using random-dot stereograms. Local and global stereopsis reflect distinct binocular processes. This is reflected by lesion studies, in which lesions of the inferotemporal cortex produce selective losses of global stereopsis (Cowey and Porter, 1979). It is also possible to utilize psychophysical means to disrupt one function and not the other. For example, we can wear prismatic devices to interchange the left and right eye views. This will switch the sign of disparity at each location in the visual field, completely disrupting local stereopsis (as revealed by line stereograms). However, global stereopsis will be unperturbed (Shimojo and Nakayama, 1981).

**CLINICAL APPLICATION** | When measuring stereopsis clinically, some patients are found who have the ability to see line stereograms, but not random-dot stereograms. This is because global stereopsis is a higher-order form of stereopsis, and is more easily disrupted than local stereopsis in patients with binocular visual disorders. However, at least some of the loss in global stereopsis may also be accounted for by the increased difficulty in fusing random-dot stereogram targets.

It is not possible to precisely measure stereoacuity with random-dot stereograms, since each dot is typically one min arc in size at the testing distance. This means that the smallest disparity you can then present in a random-dot stereogram is one dot's width, or one min arc. However, there is a way to predict a subject's stereoacuity using this method. You can take advantage of the fact that stereo thresholds improve linearly as a function of the viewing duration. By measuring stereo thresholds with random-dot stereograms exposed for different durations, then plotting the results, you can interpolate to predict the most acute stereoacuity (at infinite viewing duration).

**CLINICAL PROCEDURE** | Random-dot stereograms are used clinically to diagnose binocular visual disorders. The **Random-Dot E test** (Stereo Optical Co.) is a commonly-used random-dot stereogram in which the target seen in depth is a large Snellen letter "E" whose disparity varies with viewing distance (Reinecke and Simons, 1974). It is designed so that by varying the test distance until the patient can no longer sees the E, you can find their disparity threshold. At a 50-cm test distance, the disparity is four min arc. The problem is that an extremely long exam room is needed to present disparities near the stereoacuity threshold. The disparity in the E at 6 m (20 feet) is still only about 40 seconds. The

**Figure 7-31**    Autostereograms are stereographic figures that take advantage of repeating features so that with free fusion the observer may fuse any one of the repetitive features together. These stereograms take advantage of the wallpaper phenomenon, a percept of multiple disparity planes first noted when viewing repetitive patterns in wallpaper. This autostereogram displays a stereographic sine-wave grating in which the peaks and valleys of the sine wave are undulations in depth.

threshold of normal patients lies in the range of 2 to 38 seconds, so this test is generally used as a screening test for abnormal stereopsis in amblyopia and strabismus. The Random-Dot E test only is meant to display crossed dispari- ties, but by rotating the plates upside-down, it can also be used to test uncrossed disparities. The **TNO Test** employs red/green anaglyphic random- dot stereograms with "Pac-Man" targets similar to the Titmus Stereo Test. However, this test does not contain the monocular cues that hamper the Titmus test.

A relatively recent development in stereograms is the **autostereogram** (invented by Tyler and Clarke in 1979, but detailed in their paper of 1990). These are repetitive stereograms so that it does not matter which particular targets you match together with vergence eye movements (Fig. 7-31). Both the eyes' monocular views are contained in the same figure as repeated patterns. If you match together any one of the right eye patterns with any one of the left eye patterns, you will see depth in the figure. The autostereogram is based on the wallpaper illusion, in which repetitive patterns on wallpaper could be seen as lying in different depth planes. The degree of depth seen depends on the convergence of the observer and which particular patterns in the repetitious pattern are fused together. The popular "Magic Eye" posters in stores and in newspapers are examples of cyclopean random dot autostereograms.

Random-dot stereograms enable the measurement of the spatial and temporal properties of stereopsis purely in the cyclopean domain. Rogers and Graham (1982) created a random-dot stereogram in which each row of the stereogram contained a different spatial disparity, with the disparity changing gradually from row to row in a sinusoidal fashion (Fig. 7-32). The result was a corrugated sine-wave "depth grating" that is visible only under binocular conditions (Fig. 7-33). This was a disparity-based correlate of a luminance-defined sine-wave grating. It was therefore possible to manipulate (a) the "contrast" (the depth difference between peak and valley of grating, i.e., the **disparity gradient**) and (b) the "spatial frequency" (the distance between the peaks of the grating, i.e., the **depth spatial frequency**). By measuring stereoacuity (i.e., the smallest disparity gradient visible) at each depth spatial frequency, they were able to generate a stereo "contrast sensitivity function." The result was that subjects were most sensitive to fluctuations in depth at 0.3 cycles per degree (cpd) and less sensitive at other frequencies; in other words, stereopsis has a broad spatial tuning function (Tyler, 1973). The shape is similar to that of the spatial contrast sensitivity function. The lower sensitivity to low-depth spatial frequency suggests lateral inhibitory interactions between disparity channels just as similar interactions cause the low spatial frequency roll off in the spatial contrast sensitivity function. It has been proposed that the binocular visual system possesses **disparity receptive fields**. The center of these receptive fields would have an excitatory response to disparity, and the surround would have an inhibitory response. Such a model would account for the receptive fields being selective for differences in depth.

Cyclopean vision represents perceptions available only to the binocular visual system, as there are no monocular cues available. For example, we can see **cyclopean contours** in a random-dot stereogram that exists only from the disparity between the two eyes; the edge of such contours is formed by a *depth change* rather than a luminance or color change. The form perception mechanisms responsible for detecting such edges exist within visual cortex and are located after the site of binocular combination of information. Determination of the shape or structure of an object based solely on cyclopean information has been called **hypercyclopean perception**. For example, the corrugation spatial frequency tun-

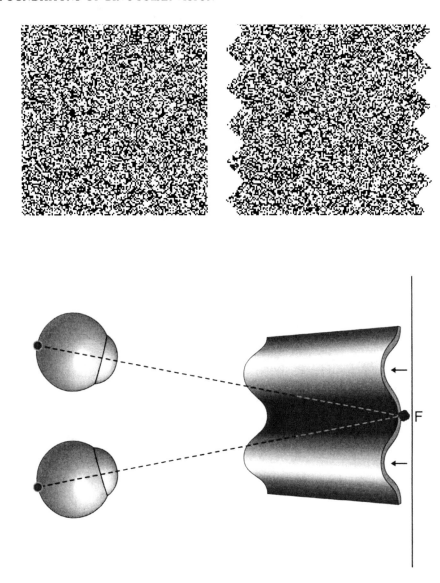

**Figure 7-32**    A three-dimensional sine-wave grating may be generated in a random-dot stereogram by displacing each row of dots in one eye's half-view by increasing then decreasing lateral displacement.

ing for cyclopean gratings may be considered to be a hypercyclopean perception. Many of the phenomena found in monocular shape perception, such as spatial frequency aftereffects, orientation aftereffects, object constancy, and visual illusions, are also manifested in the hypercyclopean domain using random-dot stereograms. This suggests some shared mechanisms for luminance-based, motion-based, and

**Figure 7-33** The stereogram produced by the process shown in Fig. 7-32. The percept is of an undulating surface in three-dimensional space.

disparity-based form perception. However, these mechanisms are not entirely shared because some visual illusions that occur in the luminance domain cannot be demonstrated to occur in the cyclopean domain, such as the Müller-Lyer illusion and the Hering grid.

In addition, it was mentioned earlier that the human visual system is less sensitive to stereomotion than it is to lateral monocular motion. By using random-dot stereogram stimuli, it can be shown that we are completely insensitive to cyclopean depth motion when no edges are present in the stimulus.

## PROCESSING OF STEREOPSIS

Richards (1971) was the first to postulate the existence of three broadly tuned **disparity channels** that are selective for either (a) zero disparity (i.e., is an object on the horopter or not), (b) crossed disparity, or (c) uncrossed disparity. By measuring subjects' ability to discriminate depth, he discovered that some observers demonstrated an unusual form of depth perception anomaly in which they had difficulty in seeing *specific kinds* of depth. Some were **stereoblind** for crossed or uncrossed disparities alone, and a third group performed as if they were missing the zero-disparity reference; that is, they could detect disparity but could not distinguish crossed from uncrossed disparity. Richards' findings agree well with what we know from single-unit recordings (see Chapter 8). Richards estimated that 30% of the population have a stereoanomaly of this type, although it is now known that the prevalence measured varies depending on the precise test used for the diagnosis of the stereoanomaly.

These stereoanomalies may exist even without evident sensory or motor disruption of fusion (Jones, 1977). It is not known whether these problems are caused by a past strabismus or if they could instead be a possible causative factor for strabismus. That is, if you cannot see depth in one direction, you will not be able to control your vergence in that direction.

**CLINICAL PROCEDURE** | Because some patients can see crossed disparity but not uncrossed disparity, it is important to invert the Stereo Fly and Titmus Circle targets to determine if the patient can perceive uncrossed disparity, especially if you suspect difficulties with divergence.

Just as in monocular stimuli, in which a nearby feature can bias your percept (e.g., the simultaneous contrast and simultaneous color effects), nearby features in another depth plane can cause depth "attraction" and "repulsion" effects (Stevenson et al., 1991). When disparate stimuli are closely spaced laterally, depth attraction (or depth averaging) occurs, whereas at larger lateral separations, depth repulsion occurs. Similarly, there are successive contrast-like effects in depth perception; depth aftereffects can be induced following prolonged exposure to a given disparity (Blakemore and Julesz, 1971; Mitchell and Baker, 1973). These effects can be explained by adaptation or "fatigue" of disparity-processing channels (for example, see Schumer and Ganz, 1979). Adaptation to a specific disparity produces distortions in depth perception in a manner similar to the monocular orientation and spatial frequency aftereffects. By determining which disparities can be adapted by a specific adapting disparity, a tuning curve can be measured for a disparity-tuned channel. Such experiments have demonstrated that disparity channels are very broadly tuned and are small in number (Rogers and Graham, 1985). For example, the crossed disparity channel has a maximum at 6' arc disparity, but its half-height bandwidth is 10' arc. This is quite broad when you consider that stereothresholds are on the order of only 10" arc. Recent experiments suggest that more than three channels may exist, but the precise number of disparity-tuned channels is not yet known.

There is a correlation between the size of the receptive field of a disparity detector and that neuron's preferred disparity (Smallman and MacLeod, 1994). This **size–disparity correlation** allows the visual system to process different ranges of disparity by pooling information over different size scales of the image (Ohzawa et al., 1996). This is similar to spatial frequency processing. Small disparities are processed by small receptive fields (high spatial frequency), and coarse disparities by large (low-spatial-frequency) receptive fields. Stereothresholds decrease as a function of increasing spatial frequency. The smallest disparity mechanisms, present at the foveas, integrate disparity information over a region as small as 4' to 6' arc (Harris et al., 1997). In addition, the upper limits of stereoscopic vision decrease with increasing spatial frequency. However, stereoacuity and the upper limits of stereoscopic vision do not decrease at the same rate, producing a narrower range of stereoscopic vision with increasing spatial frequency (Schor and Wood, 1983) until, at around 2.4 cpd, both the upper and lower limits asymptote.

In spatial vision, low spatial frequencies are processed before high spatial frequencies. It has been proposed that coarse disparities are likewise processed before fine disparities. In other words, disparity is also processed in a coarse-to-fine direction. Measurements of stereothreshold as a function of exposure duration bear this out. At short durations, only large disparities can be seen. In addition, coarse disparities are seen best with temporal modulations of depth (oscillations in depth), whereas fine disparities are seen best with static stimuli. This agrees with what we know about the transient/sustained or M/P parallel pathways of the visual system (see Chapter 8). In fact, studies introducing lesions into the lateral geniculate nucleus of monkeys suggest that fine stereopsis is mediated by the parvocellular (P) system and coarse stereopsis by the magnocellular (M) system.

The size–disparity correlation allows the clinician to distinguish between central and peripheral stereopsis. **Central stereopsis** operates over a narrow $\pm 0.5°$ range at the fovea; that is, it is specialized to detect small disparities (minutes of arc) at the fixation point. Central stereopsis is very specific for matching similar patterns in each eye, in other words, the local pattern-matching process. **Peripheral stereopsis**, on the other hand, operates over a range of up to $\pm 7°$ to $10°$. It is selective for large disparities, and the monocular images need not match precisely.

**CLINICAL APPLICATION** This distinction is important because central and peripheral stereopsis can be affected differentially. For example, one patient with anisometropia and a central macular scar in one eye had been prescribed a balance lens in the eye with the diminished acuity. Central stereopsis, as measured by a standard test of stereopsis, was poor. Years later, when the anisometropia was fully corrected, she noticed that the world no longer seemed to tilt, and she could walk with more confidence. Although her central stereopsis was lost as a result of the macular scarring, her peripheral stereopsis had been intact, and the uncorrected anisometropia still adversely affected her space perception. It is important to realize that correcting disorders of peripheral stereopsis can also make a big difference to patients.

# ABNORMAL STEREOPSIS

Sinusoidal modulation of a line's shape can provide information on the spatial tuning of stereopsis, and changes in this shape over time can probe the temporal tuning. Patients with elevated stereothresholds from strabismus exhibit decreased spatial resolution for stereopsis (that is, more stereo "crowding") (Schor et al., 1983). However, their upper stereoscopic limit remains intact. Similarly, higher temporal frequencies of depth modulation (i.e., 5 Hz) that are visible to normal subjects cannot be seen by strabismics. This loss of stereomotion perception is worse for higher-spatial-frequency (crowded) targets.

CLINICAL | Despite losses in stereopsis, strabismic patients may continue to demonstrate
APPLICATION | spared, albeit abnormal and coarse, sensory and motor fusion (Schor and Tyler, 1981), particularly if the angle of strabismus is relatively small and anomalous correspondence is present. The problem can be limited to perceiving small disparities rather than large disparities. The converse, however, is not true; patients without sensory fusion will not retain stereopsis.

Global stereopsis is much more sensitive than local stereopsis to the presence of abnormal binocular vision. Some patients may have lost global stereoscopic perception while maintaining some level of local stereoscopic discrimination. Typically, losses in local stereopsis also yield losses in global stereopsis, but the converse is not true (Reinecke and Simons, 1974).

Although binocular disorders such as strabismus and amblyopia cause problems with stereopsis, there can also exist some *subtler* anomalies in the absence of obvious strabismus or amblyopia. **Stereoperimetry** has revealed that even normal subjects can have localized **stereoscopic scotomas** for crossed or uncrossed disparity in the peripheral visual field (Richards, 1971). Similarly, normal subjects may have a **stereomotion scotoma**, a specific loss of stereomotion sensitivity, in specific portions of the visual field even when ability to see static depth at those locations is intact (Richards and Regan, 1973; Regan et al., 1986); this loss may be directional, affecting only looming motion or only motion away from the subject. Vergence eye movements in these regions are also decreased in gain.

CLINICAL | Strabismic patients, on the other hand, exhibit static and/or dynamic stereo-
APPLICATION | scopic losses in the central visual field as well as the peripheral field, but the peripheral field is less affected (Sireteneau and Fronius, 1981). Even **small-angle strabismus** can result in such central losses of stereoscopic perception, but the losses are more likely with **early-onset strabismus**. Suppression, such as that produced by significant aniseikonia, also produces reductions in stereopsis.

## SUMMARY AND KEY POINTS

- Monocular or empirical cues to depth are learned *inferences* that the visual system may use to infer the position of objects in three-dimensional space under monocular or binocular viewing conditions. They include **pictorial cues** such as **retinal image size, linear perspective, texture gradients, aerial** perspective, **imposition,** and **shading**. Other, nonpictorial, cues include **motion parallax** and **structure from motion**.

- **Accommodation** and **convergence** have been proven at best to be weak cues to depth.

- **Emmert's law** states that the perceived size of the object producing a retinal image of a given fixed size is proportional to its perceived distance. Afterimages appear to be larger when viewed against a more distant wall than when viewed on a near wall. Similarly, in the **moon illusion**, the moon appears to be bigger at the horizon, when it is perceived to be closer. When no distance cues are available, such as in a dark room, we judge distance from the size of the retinal image alone. Larger images will be interpreted as arising from nearer objects. In natural scenes containing familiar objects, learned information about object size can aid in the interpretation of distance. **Size constancy** is a perceptual "scaling" of the perceived size of an object according to its estimated distance. When distance cues are not available, the visual system defaults to using retinal image size as the main cue to stimulus size.

- **Motion parallax**, although derived by retinal image displacements on the order of those producing binocular disparity and therefore stereopsis, may yield thresholds that are not always correlated with stereothresholds in the same subjects. Stereopsis therefore cannot be explained by the same mechanisms as motion parallax. A related phenomenon, **shape from motion** also shares some underlying mechanisms with stereopsis, as shown by the ability of stereopsis to adapt or distort shape from motion, and vice versa. Here, too, shape from motion cannot fully be processed by the same mechanisms as stereopsis because stereodeficient patients can still perceive structure from motion.

- Although we can perceive depth with monocular cues, our depth perception is more accurate under binocular conditions. **Stereopsis** greatly enhances depth perception, an important basis for **figure-ground segregation, avoidance of collisions** with objects, and **navigation through our environment**. Stereopsis also improves performance on near visual tasks.

- **Stereopsis** is the visual system's only direct, innate means of seeing. Stereopsis is automatic or **preattentive**, suggesting that it is a basic "feature" or "building block" (**texton**) of visual perception.

- Stereopsis results from images in each eye being formed on closely spaced noncorresponding retinal points within Panum's fusional area. It is the difference in the lateral separation between the half-views of the fixated and nonfixated objects (**horizontal binocular disparity**) that allows the visual system estimate to what degree the object is removed from the horopter.

- Disparity is better suited for determining **relative distance** rather than absolute distance. If *all* targets in the visual field are given identical non-zero disparities, no overall change in depth will be perceived, since there will be no relative differences in distance. The empirical monocular cues may be used to determine absolute distance. The degree of convergence can also influence perceived distance and size. However, under certain viewing conditions, convergence can modify our judgements of perceived distance and size, as demonstrated by **SILO** (smaller in, larger out) or **SOLI** (smaller out, larger in) with changes in vergence level in retinal images of a fixed size when viewing targets in a stereoscope. Changes in convergence with prism can also produce **micropsia** and **macropsia**. In addition, cognitive processing may override the information derived from either disparity or monocular cues.

- The direction of relative depth from the horopter is determined by the direction of displacement of the images in the two eyes. If the object is in front of the fixation point, the object produces retinal images that are formed on each eye's temporal retina; this is called **crossed disparity**. Conversely, if the object is farther away than the fixation point, it will produce retinal images on the nasal retina of each eye, producing **uncrossed disparity**.

- The role of **vertical disparities** has been difficult to determine, but they may aid in the percept of surface slant. **Orientation disparity**, in which the fusion of contours of different orientation yields a stereoscopic percept, can be explained by different horizontal disparities along the fused contours.

- Changes in disparity (**disparity gradients**) tell us about orientation (slant) of objects in three-dimensional space, and changes in the rate of change of disparity (**disparity curvature**) tell us about three-dimensional curvature of surfaces.

- **"Diffrequency"** is the percept of an apparent tilting of a surface created vertical sinewave grating stimuli are presented to each eye of slightly different spatial frequencies. The differing spatial frequencies create horizontal binocular disparities between corresponding bars of the gratings, akin to the geometric effect noted in aniseikonia.

- A reduction in the retinal illumination of one eye by a neutral density filter, media opacity, or anisocoria (as well as a reduction in the effectiveness of one eye as in optic nerve disease) will yield the **Pulfrich phenomenon**, in which motion in a frontoparallel plane will appear as motion in an *elliptical* path. A **temporal disparity** is interpreted by the visual system as an equivalent spatial disparity. The Pulfrich phenomenon also demonstrates that the binocular visual system responds well to luminance changes, that is, stereopsis is a function of the achromatic channels of the visual system.

- **Chromostereopsis** is a perception of relative depth between colored lights as a result of horizontal disparity caused by dispersion and chromatic aberration by the crystalline lens of the eye.

- **Stereoacuity** is the smallest depth difference we can detect, or the "resolving capability" of stereopsis. Stereoacuity involves binocular disparities of 4″ to 5″ arc, thresholds in the **hyperacuity** range. Stereoacuity, although useful as a clinical measure of the intactness of binocular vision, does not necessarily guarantee proper stereoscopic perception when viewing large disparities.

- Stereoacuity thresholds can be measured with the **Howard-Dolman apparatus** or two-rod test, but these measures can be somewhat inaccurate and variable. Stereoacuity is better measured with clinical instruments such as a mirror stereoscope.

- Angular binocular disparity is defined as:

$$n = \frac{2a\Delta d}{d^2}$$

where $n$ is the angular disparity in radians (to convert to seconds of arc, multiply by 206,256), $2a$ equals the **interpupillary distance (PD)**, $d$ is the fixation distance, and $\Delta d$ is the linear difference in distance between the fixation point and test target. The larger the PD, the larger the disparity perceived with a given displacement. The larger viewing distance, the smaller the disparity. The **geometric limit for disparity** occurs a distance of 1,320 m.

- Stereothresholds are dependent on a number of factors, including practice (learning), luminance (adaptation state), exposure duration, retinal eccentricity, defocus, "crowding" effects, and motion in depth. Lateral motion does not degrade stereopsis greatly.

- **Monocular blur** is more detrimental to stereoacuity than is binocular blur.

- Stereoacuity is worse for uncrossed disparity than it is for crossed disparity.

- Stereothresholds increase with the presence of a **standing disparity**. A **fixation disparity** can introduce such a standing disparity and degrade stereoacuity.

- Within Panum's fusional area, we are able to distinguish relative changes in depth (**quantitative stereopsis** or **patent stereopsis**) with a robust percept of that depth. Outside of Panum's fusional area, diplopia is noted. At first, it was thought that we cannot see relative depth outside of Panum's area but only detect if an object is closer than or farther than the fixation point (hence the term **qualitative stereopsis** or **latent stereopsis**). However, it has been shown that perceived depth continues to increase even within the zone of "qualitative" stereopsis. Beyond an **upper disparity limit**, however, the perceived depth diminishes with increased distance.

- Stereoscopic images are viewed by presenting differing half-views to each eye. Several methods are available to do so, including the **Wheatstone mirror stereoscope** (used in vision therapy as the **synoptophore** or **amblyoscope**), the **electronic stereoscope**, the **Brewster refracting stereoscope** (used in vision therapy as the **Keystone telebinocular**), and computer **liquid crystal shutter goggles**.

- Stereoscopic pairs may be printed side by side, as in **stereophotographs** or **random dot stereograms**, and fused with **free fusion** or printed in a single image, as in **anaglyphs** or **autostereograms**. The half-views may also be printed on transparent plastic sheets that can be laterally displaced to vary the degree of disparity, as in **vectograms**. Many clinical tests of stereopsis employ these techniques.

- The simplest type of stereoscopic target is the **line stereogram**, which can be used to measure stereoacuity. Line stereograms are fused by matching lines, edges, or contours in each half-view (**local stereopsis**). However, this provides monocular cues that stereoblind patients may use to report depth.

- **Random-dot stereograms** are made of dense arrays of black and white dots so that there are no monocular contours to match. When fused binocularly, the disparate part of the stereogram appears in depth, and a figure made up from the disparate dots "pops out" in a different depth plane. The figure or form appears only in the *binocular* percept but in *neither* of the two monocular images (**cyclopean depth perception**).

- When combining monocular images, the visual system must find matching contours or features in each image, guide vergence eye movements to bring these contours into alignment, then determine the relative depth of the contours. Such matching of contours is a problematic calculation for the visual system (**stereo correspondence problem**). In this case, the visual system must determine what portion of one eye's image corresponds to a given portion of the other eye's image. The more points to match, the more possible pairings of the points between the eyes ("ghost images"), and the more possible depth planes we could see, as shown in the **Keplerian projection**. One simple possible method for removing ghost images is via **depth averaging**.

- In random-dot stereograms, the visual system forms a global perception over a larger spatial scale, pooling together information across the entire stereogram to create a global interpretation of depth and form (**global stereopsis**). Groups of dots with similar disparities are clumped together to yield a figure–ground segregation of a form in a different depth plane than the background. Global stereopsis demonstrates that form perception can be carried out after binocular combination of visual information. The global matching process is aided in natural images by several constraints on disparities in real objects, one of which is **depth averaging (disparity pooling)**. Global stereopsis is a more complex process than local stereopsis, and so it can sometimes take longer to see depth in random-dot stereograms.

- Local and global stereopsis reflect distinct binocular processes, as reflected by lesion studies of inferotemporal cortex, which produce selective losses of global stereopsis.

- **Random-dot sinusoidal stereograms** (corrugations in depth) enable the study of the spatial and temporal properties of stereopsis. Stereopsis has a broad spatial tuning function with a roll-off in sensitivity to low spatial frequency suggesting lateral inhibitory interactions between disparity channels.

- **Cyclopean vision** represents perceptions available only to the binocular visual system, as there are no monocular cues available. Determination of the shape or structure of an object based solely on cyclopean information has been called **hypercyclopean perception**.

- The binocular visual system contains at least three broadly tuned **disparity channels**, selective for zero disparity (i.e., is an object on the horopter or not), crossed disparity, and uncrossed disparity. **Depth aftereffects** can be induced following prolonged exposure to a given disparity, and can be explained by **adaptation** or "fatigue" of disparity-processing channels.

- The **size–disparity correlation** means that the visual system processes different ranges of disparity with different-sized receptive fields. Small disparities are processed by small (high-spatial-frequency) receptive fields and coarse disparities by large (low-spatial-frequency) receptive fields. The smallest disparity mechanisms are therefore present at the foveas. Because low spatial frequencies are processed by the visual system before high spatial frequencies, disparity is processed in a coarse-to-fine direction. At short durations, only large disparities can be seen, and fine disparities are seen best with static stimuli. Fine stereopsis is mediated by the parvocellular (P) system, and coarse stereopsis by the magnocellular (M) system.

- **Central stereopsis** operates over a narrow $\pm 0.5°$ range at the fovea and is specialized to detect small disparities (minutes of arc) and perform local pattern matching near the fixation point. **Peripheral stereopsis** operates over a range of up to $\pm 7°$ to $10°$. It is selective for large disparities, and the monocular images need not match precisely.

- Despite losses in stereopsis, strabismic patients may have normal Panum's fusional ranges; that is, sensory fusion may be spared. The problem seems to be limited to perceiving small disparities rather than large disparities. The converse, however, is not true; patients without sensory fusion will not retain stereopsis.

- Typically, losses in local stereopsis also yield losses in global stereopsis, but here too the converse is not true. Losses in global stereopsis alone are most often secondary to motor fusional instabilities.

- **Stereoperimetry** may reveal localized **stereoscopic scotomas** for crossed or uncrossed disparity in the peripheral visual field as well as **stereomotion scotomas**, a specific loss of stereomotion sensitivity. Patients may exhibit perceptual losses for *specific kinds* of depth, that is, *crossed* disparities only or *uncrossed* disparities only.

## QUESTIONS

1. A fixation target on the midline is viewed at a 1-m distance by a patient with an interpupillary distance of 50 mm. The patient is able to perceive a second target as being closer when it is 1 cm closer than the fixation target. What is the patient's stereoacuity in seconds of arc?

2. For the patient in question 1, what offset must the targets in a stereogram have to generate the same disparity at a viewing distance of 40 cm?

3. When a pendulum is swung back in forth before a patient's eyes, she perceives it to be moving in a counterclockwise elliptical path. This may be explained by a media opacity in which eye?

4. Two objects are imaged on the retina. One retinal image is large, and the other is small. Under what conditions will the two objects appear to be the same size? Under what conditions will they appear to be different sizes?

5. Compared to normal binocular visual function, what advantages and disadvantages would the monocular visual system of a Cyclops have? What visual tasks would you expect them to do well, and with which would you expect them to have difficulty?

## BIBLIOGRAPHY

ANDERSEN EE *and* WEYMOUTH FW (1923). *Visual perception and the retinal mosaic. I. Retinal mean local sign: an explanation of the fineness of binocular perception of distance.* Am. J. Physiol. 64:561–594.

BADCOCK DR *and* SCHOR CM (1985). *Depth-increment detection for individual spatial channels.* J. Opt. Soc. Am. 2A:1211–1215.

BASSI CJ *and* GALANIS JC (1991). *Binocular visual impairment in glaucoma.* Ophthalmology 98:1406–1411.

BERRY RN, RIGGS LA *and* DUNCAN CP (1950). *The relation of vernier and depth discriminations to field brightness.* J. Exp. Psych. 40:349–354.

BLAKEMORE C (1970). *A new type of stereoscopic vision.* Vis. Res. 10:1181–1199.

BLAKEMORE C *and* JULESZ B (1971). *Stereoscopic depth aftereffect produced without monocular cues.* Science 171:286–288.

BLAKEMORE C, FIORENTINI A *and* MAFFEI L (1972). *A second neural mechanism of binocular depth discrimination.* J. Physiol. 226:725–749.

BRAUNER JD *and* LIT A (1976). *The Pulfrich effect, simple reaction time, and intensity of stimulation.* Am. J. Psych. 89:105–114.

BURR DC *and* ROSS J (1979). *How does binocular delay give information about depth?* Vis. Res. 19:523–532.

COOPER J *and* Warshowsky J (1977). *Lateral displacement as a response cue in the Titmus Stereo Test.* Am. J. Physiol. Optics 54:537–541.

CORMACK LK, STEVENSON SB *and* SCHOR CM (1991). *Interocular correlation, luminance contrast and cyclopean processing.* Vis. Res. 31:2195–2207.

COWEY A *and* PORTER J (1979) *Brain damage and global stereopsis.* Proc. R. Soc. Ser. B 204:399–407.

ERKELENS CJ *and* REGAN D (1986). *Human ocular vergence movements induced by changing size and disparity.* J. Physiol. 279:145–169.

FENDER DH *and* JULESZ B (1967). *Extension of Panum's fusional area in binocular stabilized vision.* J. Opt. Soc. Am. 57:819–830.

FENDICK M *and* WESTHEIMER G (1983). *Effects of practice and the separation of test targets on foveal and peripheral stereoacuity.* Vis. Res. 23:145–150.

FISHER SK *and* CIUFFREDA KJ (1988). *Accommodation and apparent distance*. Perception 17:609–621.

FISHER SK *and* CIUFFREDA KJ (1990). *Adaptation to optically-increased interocular separation under naturalistic viewing conditions*. Perception 19:171–180.

FOLEY JM *and* RICHARDS W (1978). *Binocular depth mixture with non-symmetric disparities*. Vis. Res. 18:251–256.

FRISBY JP *and* CLATWORTHY JL (1975). *Learning to see complex random-dot stereograms*. Perception 4:173–178.

GIBSON (1950). The Perception of the Visual World. *Houghton Mifflin, Boston*.

GRINBERG DL *and* WILLIAMS DR *(1985)*. *Stereopsis with chromatic signals from the blue-sensitive mechanism*. Vis. Res. 25:531–537.

HALPERN DL *and* BLAKE R (1988). *How contrast affects stereoacuity*. Perception 17:483–495.

HALPERN DL, WILSON HR *and* BLAKE R (1996). *Stereopsis from interocular spatial frequency differences is not robust*. Vis. Res. 36:2263–2270.

HARRIS JM, MCKEE SP *and* SMALLMAN HS (1997). *Fine-scale processing in human binocular stereopsis*. J. Opt. Soc. Am. A14:1673–1683.

HARWERTH RS *and* BOLTZ RL (1979). *Stereopsis in monkeys using random dot stereograms: the effect of viewing duration*. Vis. Res. 19:985–991.

HARWERTH RS *and* RAWLINGS SC (1977). *Viewing time and stereoscopic threshold with random-dot stereograms*. Am. J. Optom. Physiol. Optics 54:452–457.

HOLWAY AH *and* BORING EG (1941). *Determinants of apparent size with distance variant*. Am. J. Psych. 54:21–37.

JONES R (1977). *Anomalies of disparity detection in the human visual system*. J. Physiol. 264:621–640.

JULESZ B (1960). *Binocular depth perception of computer generated patterns*. Bell Syst. Tech. J. 39:1125–1162.

KANEKO H *and* HOWARD IP (1997). *Spatial limitation of vertical-size disparity processing*. Vis. Res. 37:2871–2878.

KHOTANZAD A *and* LEE Y-W (1991). *Stereopsis by a neural network which learns the constraints*. *In:* Neural Information Processing Systems 3, *RP Lippmann, JE Moody and DS Touretzky, eds.*, Morgan Kaufmann, San Mateo, CA.

LAPPIN JS *and* CRAFT WD (1997). *Definition and detection of binocular disparity*. Vis. Res. 37:2953–2974.

LEGGE GE (1979). *Spatial frequency masking in human vision: binocular interactions*. J. Opt. Soc. Am. 69:838–874.

LIEBOWITZ HW *and* MOORE D (1966). *Role of changes in accommodation and convergence in the perception of size*. J. Opt. Soc. Am. 56:1120–1122.

LIT A (1968). *Presentation of experimental data*. J. Am. Optom. Assoc. 39:1098–1099.

LU C *and* FENDER DH (1972). *The interaction of color and luminance in stereoscopic vision*. Invest. Ophthalmol. 11:482–490.

MARR D *and* POGGIO T (1979). *A computational theory of human stereo vision*. Proc. R. Soc. Lond. 204:301–328.

MITCHELL DE *and* BAKER AG (1973). *Stereoscopic aftereffects: evidence for disparity-specific neurones in the human visual system*. Vis. Res. 13:2273–2288.

NAKAYAMA K *and* SILVERMAN GH (1986). *Serial and parallel processing of visual feature conjunctions*. Nature 320:264–265.

NELSON JI (1975). *Globality and stereoscopic fusion in binocular vision*. J. Theor. Biol. 49:1–88.

OGLE KN (1952). *On the limits of stereoscopic vision*. J. Exp. Psych. 44:253–259.

OGLE KN (1953). *Precision and validity of stereoscopic depth perception from double images.* J. Opt. Soc. Am. 43:906–913.

OGLE KN and WEIL MP (1958). *Stereoscopic vision and the duration of the stimulus.* AMA Arch. Ophthalmol. 59:4–17.

OHZAWA I, DEANGELIS GC and FREEMAN RD (1996). *Encoding of binocular disparity by complex cells in the cat's visual cortex.* J. Neurophysiol. 75:1779–1805.

PENNINGTON J (1970). *The effect of wavelength on stereoacuity.* Am. J. Optom. 47:288–294.

POBUDA M and ERKELENS CJ (1993). *The relationship between absolute disparity and ocular vergence.* Biol. Cybernet. 221–228.

PULFRICH C (1922). *Die stereoskopie im dienste der isochromen und heterochromen photometrie.* Naturwissenschaften 25:553–564.

RAWLINGS SC and SHIPLEY T (1969). *Stereoscopic acuity and horizontal angular distance from fixation.* J. Opt. Soc. Am. 59:991–993.

REGAN D, ERKELENS CJ and COLLEWIJN H (1986). *Visual field defects for vergence eye movements and for stereo motion perception.* Invest. Ophthalmol. Vis. Sci. 27:806–819.

REINECKE RD and SIMONS K (1974). *A new stereoscopic test for amblyopia screening.* Am. J. Ophthalmol. 78:714-721.

RICHARDS W (1971). *Anomalous stereoscopic depth perception.* J. Opt. Soc. Am. 61:410–414.

RICHARDS W and KAYE MG (1974). *Local versus global stereopsis: two mechanisms?* Vis. Res. 14:1345–1347.

RICHARDS W and REGAN D (1973). *A stereo field map with implications for disparity processing.* Invest. Ophthalmol. 12:904–909.

ROGERS BJ and BRADSHAW MF (1995). *Disparity scaling and the perception of fronto-parallel surfaces.* Perception 24:155–179.

ROGERS BJ and GRAHAM ME (1979). *Motion parallax as an independent cue for depth perception.* Perception 8:125–134.

ROGERS BJ and GRAHAM ME (1982). *Similarities between motion parallax and stereopsis in human depth perception.* Vis. Res. 22:216–270.

ROGERS BJ and GRAHAM ME (1985). *Motion parallax and the perception of three-dimensional surfaces. In:* Brain Mechanisms and Spatial Vision, D Ingle, M Jeannerod and D Lee, eds., Martinus Nijhoff, The Hague.

ROSS J and HOGBEN JH (1974). *Short-term memory in stereopsis.* Vis. Res. 14:1195–2201.

ST. CYR GJ and FENDER DH (1969). *The interplay of drifts and flicks in binocular fixation.* Vis. Res. 9:245–265.

SCHIFFMAN HR (1967). *Size estimation of familiar objects under informative and reduced conditions of viewing.* Am. J. Psych. 80:229–235.

SCHOR CM, BRIDGEMAN B and TYLER CW (1983). *Spatial characteristics of static and dynamic stereoacuity in strabismus.* Invest. Ophthalmol. Vis. Sci. 24:1572–1579.

SCHOR CM and FLOM MC (1969). *The relative value of stereopsis as a function of viewing distance.* Am. J. Optom. 96:805–809.

SCHOR CM and TYLER CW (1981). *Spatio-temporal properties of Panum's fusional area.* Vis. Res. 21:683–692.

SCHOR CM and WOOD I (1983). *Disparity range for local stereopsis as a function of luminance spatial frequency.* Vis. Res. 23:1649–1654.

SCHOR CM, WOOD I and OGAWA J (1984). *Binocular sensory fusion is limited by spatial resolution.* Vis. Res. 24:661–665.

SCHUMER RA and GANZ L (1979). *Independent stereoscopic channels for different extents of spatial pooling.* Vis. Res. 19:1303–1314.

SHIMOJO S *and* NAKAJIMA Y (1981). *Adaptation to the reversal of binocular depth cues: effects of wearing left–right reversing spectacles on stereoscopic depth perception.* Perception 10:391–402.

SIMMONS DR (1998). *The minimum contrast requirements for stereopsis.* Perception 27:1333–1343.

SIRETENEAU R *and* FRONIUS M (1981). *Naso-temporal asymmetries in human amblyopia: consequence of long-term interocular suppression.* Vis. Res. 21:1055–1063.

SMALLMAN HS *and* MACLEOD DIA (1994). *Paradoxical effects of adapting to large disparities: constraining population code models of disparity.* Invest. Ophthalmol. Vis. Sci. 35:1917.

STEINMAN SB (1987) *Serial and parallel search in pattern vision?* Perception 16:389–398.

STEINMAN SB *and* LEVI DM (1992). *Topography of the evoked potential to spatial localization cues.* Vis. Neurosci. 8:281–294.

STEVENSON SB, CORMACK LK *and* SCHOR CM (1991). *Depth attraction and repulsion in random dot stereograms.* Vis. Res. 31:805–813.

TYLER CW (1971). *Stereoscopic depth movement: two eyes less sensitive than one.* Science 174:958–961.

TYLER CW (1973). *Stereoscopic vision: cortical limitations and a disparity scaling effect.* Science 181:276–278.

TYLER CW (1974). *Stereopsis in dynamic visual noise.* Nature 250:781–782.

TYLER CW (1991). *Cyclopean vision. In:* Vision and Visual Dysfunction, *D Regan, ed.,* Macmillan, London.

TYLER CW *and* CLARKE MB (1990). *The autostereogram.* Proc. Int. Soc. Opt. Eng. 1256:182–197.

TYLER CW *and* JULESZ B (1980). *On the depth of the cyclopean retina.* Exp. Brain Res. 40:196–202.

WESTHEIMER G *and* MCKEE SP (1978). *Stereoscopic acuity for rmoving retinal images.* J. Opt. Soc. Am. 68:450–455.

WESTHEIMER G *and* MCKEE SP (1979). *What prior uniocular processing is necessary for stereopsis?* Invest. Ophthalmol. Vis. Sci. 18:614–621.

WESTHEIMER G *and* MCKEE SP (1980). *Stereoscopic acuity with defocused and spatially filtered retinal images.* J. Opt. Soc. Am. 70:772–778.

WESTHEIMER G *and* TANZMAN IJ (1956). *Qualitative depth localization with diplopic images.* J. Opt. Soc. Am. 46:116–117.

ZINN WJ *and* SOLOMON H (1985). *A comparison of stsaic and dynamic stereoacuity.* J. Am. Optom. Assoc. 56:712–715.

# Neuroanatomy and Neurophysiology of Binocular Vision

Now that we know something about what we see with two eyes, we are still left with a fundamental question: how is the visual system organized to use and interpret binocular information to produce a percept of depth? To answer this question, we must examine the anatomy and neurophysiology of the visual system. Understanding visual neurophysiology will also help us to understand many clinical aspects of binocularity. For example, the neurophysiology of the visual cortex is an essential factor in the development of binocular vision in babies. Development of binocular function in the cortex can be disrupted by a variety of factors during infancy, for example, strabismus, leading to permanent changes of binocular neurophysiology. In addition, exploring the activity of binocular neurons in the visual cortex will allow us to understand clinical tests for the early detection of abnormal binocular vision during infancy so that the effect of these abnormalities can be halted or, better yet, reversed.

## CORRESPONDING POINTS AND THE OPTIC CHIASM

As we noted in the chapter on visual direction, the **fovea** is used as the **primary visual direction** of each eye and, as such, acts as a reference point for aiming the eye. This is especially true for normal binocular viewing, in which the foveas of both eyes are aimed at the same locus in space. The two foveas are represented by corresponding retinal points in the visual cortex. All other locations in three-dimensional space, including the horopter, are calculated by the visual system relative to the bifoveal fixation point. The bifoveal fixation point can be thought of as the "fovea" of the cyclopean eye.

Once the two eyes are pointing at the same location, the information from both eyes must be combined into a single unified percept. The first structure in the visual system that contributes to binocular combination of information is the **optic chiasm**. When the ganglion cell axons, that is, the optic nerve fibers, exit the eye via the optic nerve, they reach the optic chiasm, and their information is **rearranged**, as shown in Fig. 8-1.

The nerve fibers from the **temporal retina** of each eye progress without crossing at the optic chiasm, terminating at the ***ipsilateral*** lateral geniculate **nucleus** (the LGN on the *same* side of the brain as the eye of origin). The fibers from the **nasal retina cross over at the chiasm, projecting *contralaterally*** to the LGN on the *opposite* side of the brain. Only the *nasal* optic nerve fibers make this crossing, so it is called a **hemidecussation** or *partial* decussation; **53% to 57% of the optic nerve fibers make the crossing**.

Why does this happen? In some lower animals, such as frogs, *all* of the optic nerve fibers from each eye cross at the chiasm (see Fig. 8-2). In what way are

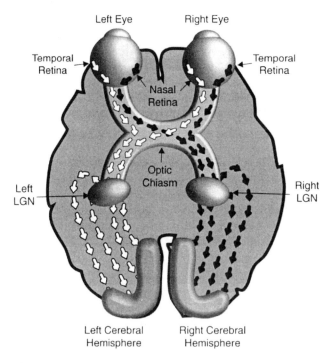

**Figure 8-1**   At the partial decussation of the optic chiasm, nasal optic nerve fibers cross to the contralateral LGN, and temporal fibers pass through to the ipsilateral LGN.

**Figure 8-2**  In animals lacking stereopsis, there is a full decussation at the optic chiasm, with no reorganization of the information from each eye.

these animals different from us? These animals have *laterally* placed eyes on the sides of their heads that do not point in the same direction, with little or no overlap of the monocular visual fields, and these animals lack significant stereoscopic binocular vision. Their two eyes serve simply to increase the total extent of their visual fields.

In animals with *frontal* eyes and stereoscopic vision, the partial decussation at the chiasm serves to reshuffle the nerve fibers so that **neurons containing information from corresponding points in the visual fields of the two eyes project to the same place in visual cortex**. The proportion of optic nerve fibers that cross at the chiasm is directly proportional to the size of the binocular visual field (Walls, 1963).

---

## ⌾═ *Key Point*

*Although the degree of binocularity is correlated with the degree of decussation at the optic chiasm, this relationship is not causal. Some lower animals have some degree of binocular vision even without a partial decussation at the chiasm. It is therefore possible that the partial decussation is more important for the accurate coordination of binocular eye movements, in which the two eyes must move as a team to keep corresponding points in alignment.*

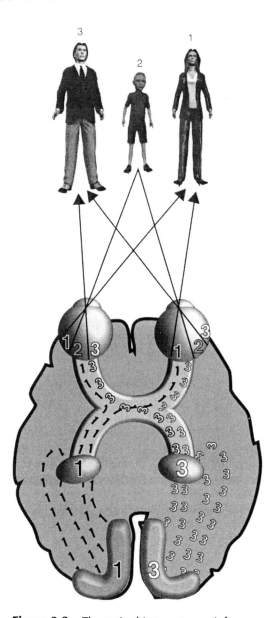

**Figure 8-3**   The optic chiasm regroups information from the two retinas so that optic nerve fibers from the right hemiretinas (left hemifields) project to the right LGN and right cerebral hemisphere, while fibers from the left hemiretina project to the left side of the brain.

Let us illustrate hemidecussation with an example, shown in Fig. 8-3. Let us say you are observing a man, a woman, and a baby while fixating on the baby. The image of the woman, on the *right* side of your visual field, will be formed on the left half of each retina. This image will be processed in the *left* LGN and in the *left* hemisphere of the brain. The image of the man, on the left side of your visual field, will be processed in the *right* LGN and in the *right* hemisphere of the brain. The two sides of the visual field therefore go to *opposite* sides of the brain—things seen to your left go to the right hemisphere, and vice versa.

---

 *Key Point*

*The optic chiasm reorganizes the visual information of each eye so that points to the left of the fixation point progress to the right cerebral hemisphere, and vice versa. This brings optic nerve axons from corresponding points in each eye into close proximity.*

---

**CLINICAL APPLICATION** | The rearrangement of visual information at the optic chiasm makes it easy to distinguish prechiasmal lesions from postchiasmal lesions with visual field testing. **Prechiasmal visual field defects** are seen in one eye or the other, **chiasmal lesions** produce binasal visual field defects, and **postchiasmal lesions** show up as a loss in a quadrant or half of the visual field at roughly corresponding field locations in both eyes.

**CLINICAL APPLICATION** | In **ocular albinism**, the degree of crossing over at the optic chiasm is abnormal. Many optic nerve fibers from the temporal hemiretinas are misrouted across the chiasm to the contralateral LGN. This disrupts the normal pattern of segregation of inputs into monocular layers in the LGN, at least for cells receiving abnormal contralateral input. As these fibers progress to visual cortex, the misrouted fibers wind up in the wrong cerebral hemisphere, thus mapping a part of the ipsilateral rather than the contralateral visual field. This greatly disturbs the possibility for binocular combination and vergence control and eliminates mechanisms for disparity processing. Patients with ocular albinism therefore typically have little or no stereopsis and manifest strabismus.

## THE DORSAL LATERAL GENICULATE NUCLEUS

The **dorsal lateral geniculate nucleus** (dLGN or simply LGN for short) is a **multilayered** structure. In primates, the LGN has **six layers**, with narrow **interlaminar regions** separating each layer. Layers 1 and 2, the most ventral layers, are comprised of the larger **magnocellular (M) neurons**, which are most sensitive to visual stimuli with low spatial frequencies, high temporal frequencies, and faster velocities of motion. They also have high sensitivity to contrast and rapid axonal conduction velocities but are essentially achromatic. The remaining layers, 4 through 6, contain the smaller **parvocellular (P)** neurons (Perry et al., 1984). The P cells are more responsive to high spatial frequencies, stationary or slowly modulated, slowly moving stimuli, or chromatic stimuli. Their conduction velocity is slower than that of M cells. These two sets of neurons form the basis for two **parallel visual streams or pathways** that are well suited for processing motion and pattern, respectively. Some scientists have described the M and P streams as being the "where" and "what" pathways, respectively, of the visual system. The M pathway tells us *where* objects are in relation to ourselves (and where we are in relation to our environment), while the P stream *identifies* what the objects are. We return to the role of the parallel visual streams in stereoscopic visual processing later in this chapter.

The organization of the LGN is **retinotopic**. In other words, visual space and positions along the retinal image are mapped directly onto the LGN in a logical sequence. Neighboring LGN cells have neighboring receptive fields serving neighboring areas of the visual field. This map is organized so that **as you move from the medial part of the LGN to the lateral part, the receptive fields represent first the foveal region of the visual field and then progress toward the periphery. As you move from anterior LGN to posterior LGN, the receptive fields progress from the lower visual field to the upper visual field**. In other words, the entire visual field is mapped out on a point-by-point basis as you move across the LGN in the medial–lateral or anterior–posterior directions.

---

### ⌨═ Key Point

*The* **retinotopic mapping** of the visual system from the optic nerve through the LGN and into visual cortex has profound implications on visual processing and abnormalities of vision. It is the retinotopic organization at each stage of the visual system that produces predictable visual field defects with lesions at each stage. More importantly, retinotopic mapping is the basis for monocular **visual localization** relative to the fovea, **corresponding retinal points**, and the remapping of the visual field that occurs in **anomalous correspondence**.

---

We are left with only one more direction you can move through the LGN: from the ventral side to the dorsal side. This *cuts across* **the layers of the LGN, with layer 1 the most ventral and layer 6 the most dorsal. As you move from ventral LGN to dorsal, what changes is not the placement**

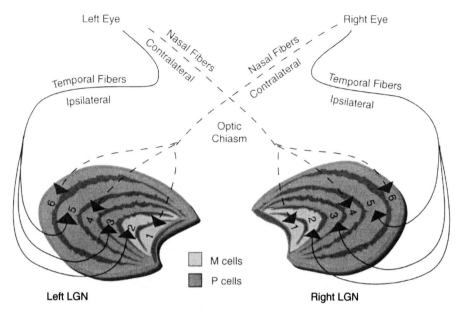

**Figure 8-4**   The dorsal lateral geniculate nucleus (dLGN) within the thalamus contains six layers of cells, the two ventral layers containing M cells and the remainder P cells. Optic nerve fibers from the ipsilateral eye synapse in layers 2, 3, and 5. Optic nerve fibers from the contralateral eye synapse in layers 1, 4, and 6.

in the visual field, but *which eye feeds into that layer*. As you can see in Fig. 8-4, each layer of the LGN gets input from *only one eye*, with each eye projecting to three of the six layers. **The ipsilateral eye (*uncrossed* fibers at the optic chiasm) projects to layers 2, 3, and 5. The contralateral eye (*crossed* fibers at the optic chiasm) projects to layers 1, 4, and 6.**

---

### ⚷ *Key Point*

*A handy mnemonic for remembering the inputs to the LGN is as follows: Remember the chemical symbol for the radioactive isotope of uranium used in atom bombs, $U^{235}$. The U stands for uncrossed, and the 235 stands for layers 2, 3, and 5. Therefore, layers 2, 3, and 5 of the LGN receive uncrossed fibers from the ipsilateral eye. (The remaining layers receive fibers from the contralateral eye.)*

---

Although the information from each eye is rearranged to be brought closer together in the LGN, it is still kept in *separate* LGN layers. The information from the two eyes *does not really mix*. Each layer of the LGN contains cells that are for

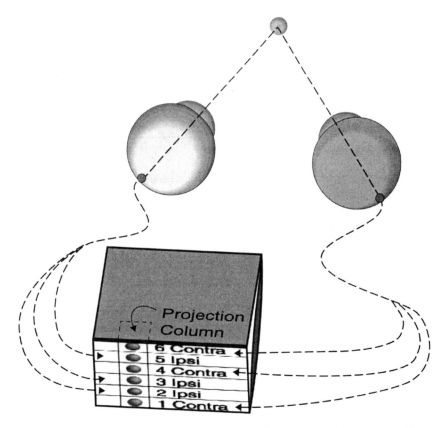

**Figure 8-5**  As an electrode is passed perpendicularly through all six layers of the LGN within a projection column, it encounters cells representing the same direction in visual space from each eye, that is, corresponding retinal points.

the most part **monocular**. Their receptive fields respond to stimuli presented in the visual field of *one* eye only. If you were to drive an electrode down *perpendicularly* into the LGN in a straight path passing through layers 1 to 6 (dorsally to ventrally), as seen in Fig. 8-5 (this path is called a **projection column**), you would record from receptive fields from one location in space as seen by one eye, then a receptive field that covers the **corresponding retinal point** in the other eye. The corresponding points are the *same position out in space as imaged on each eye's retina*.

The net result is that the partial decussation at the chiasm has brought the neurons whose receptive fields cover **corresponding points** in the visual field into close proximity in the LGN. The chiasm *organizes* the LGN in terms of corresponding retinal points, so that neurons from corresponding points in each eye are all lined up across the layers of the LGN.

This proximity organizes the fibers exiting the LGN that go to visual cortex in such a way that neurons "seeing" the same point in visual space (the same visual

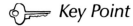 *Key Point*

*Corresponding retinal points are lined up across layers of the LGN in projection columns.*

direction) in each eye travel together within the optic radiations. Information from the two eyes is combined at a fairly early stage in the visual cortex, so that more complicated computations can be carried out on the binocular information later in higher visual cortical areas. Therefore, bringing inputs representing corresponding points in the monocular fields of each eye to neighboring locations in the LGN first, *before* they reach the visual cortex, makes it easier for the visual cortex to combine these monocular inputs early and derive *binocular* visual information for that location in space.

## BINOCULAR INTERACTIONS IN THE LGN

So far, it seems as if the LGN plays little role in binocular vision other than to bring information from the two eyes into close proximity. However, this isn't the entire story. Researchers have found that near the *border* between the layers of the LGN, some cells responded differently when both eyes were stimulated than when just one eye was stimulated. In other words, *some binocular interactions* could be found in these cells. The bulk of current evidence suggests that these binocular interactions are mostly *inhibitory* interactions between corresponding points in the two eyes; that is, one eye provides a primary excitatory input to the LGN cell in question, and stimulation of the corresponding location in the fellow eye *inhibits* the response of that neuron (Sanderson et al., 1969). These interactions are highlighted in Fig. 8-6. It has been suggested that these interactions involve cells within the *interlaminar* regions that interconnect cells with corresponding receptive fields in neighboring monocular layers of the LGN; that is, lateral inhibitory connections across LGN layers. However, it is also possible that these connections could be corticofugal *feedback* connections from visual cortex back to the geniculate, but the role of corticofugal connections to the geniculate nucleus in binocular vision is not fully understood at present; some studies suggest that corticofugal inputs to the LGN play a significant role in binocular interactions (Varela and Singer, 1987), but others have found that corticofugal inputs have little influence (Tumosa et al., 1989). Generally, at present the precise types and roles of binocular interactions in the LGN are still somewhat disputed, but although they may not explain excitatory binocular interactions as in binocular summation or stereopsis, it has been suggested that they could possibly play some role in inhibitory binocular phenomena such as binocular suppression or binocular rivalry (Varela and Singer, 1987).

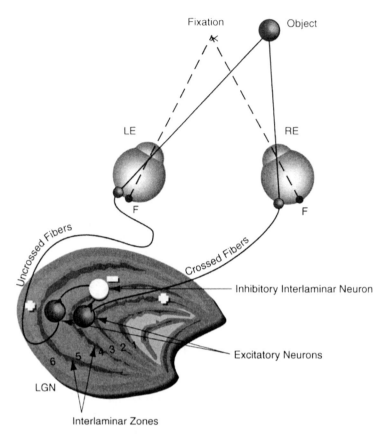

**Figure 8-6**    Although the LGN is predominantly a monocular structure, with neurons receiving input from each eye remaining segregated in different layers, some weak inhibitory interactions may be present there because of interlaminar cells that bridge these layers.

---

🗝 *Key Point*

*Although the LGN is primarily a monocular structure, some weak binocular interactions, probably of an inhibitory type, may occur there.*

# THE ROLE OF THE CORPUS CALLOSUM IN BINOCULARITY

You may have noticed that there is a problem with the scheme outlined above for bringing information from corresponding retinal points to the same locations in striate cortex. Think about what happens *at the fovea*, at the midline of the visual field. For objects on the midline, the *left* half of each fovea would send its optic nerve fibers to the LGN on the left side of the head, then to the occipital lobe in the left cortical hemisphere. The right half of each fovea would send its optic nerve fibers to the right side's LGN and cortex. These two cortical locations are widely separated from each other. How do the two halves of our visual fields interact to form one unified visual field when they are processed on opposite sides of the head? More importantly, how do we get stereopsis right at the midline of the visual field like this, remembering that stereopsis is particularly good at the fovea?

In the monkey, there is a 1°- to 3°-wide vertical patch of retina corresponding to cortical receptive fields that respond to the ipsilateral eye as well as those that respond to the contralateral eye (Stone, 1966); that is, there is a bilateral projection from the midline region of each retina resulting in overlapping of receptive fields from each eye.

**CLINICAL APPLICATION** | The clinical phenomenon of **macular sparing** is an exemplification of this bilateral projection. Unilateral occipital lesions are associated with homonymous (same-side) visual field defects that do not bisect the fovea as expected if there were a strict and complete partitioning of the nasal and temporal hemiretinas.

There is also a second pathway in addition to partial decussation that is specially designed to bring binocular information together along the vertical midline. That pathway is through the **corpus callosum**, a bundle of nerve fibers (white matter) that *interconnects* the two cerebral hemispheres (Hubel and Wiesel, 1967).

How do we know this system contributes to binocular vision? There has been the report of a patient whose optic chiasm was completely severed as the result of a bicycle accident. Not surprisingly, vision was completely lost in the temporal halves of each eye's visual field because the nasal optic nerve fibers, normally crossing over at the chiasm, now could no longer reach the LGN or cortex. What this also meant was that *uncrossed* disparity could not be detected in the direction of gaze, that is, depth in the direction of but farther away than the fixation point. However, what about the ability to see *crossed* disparity (depth *closer* than the fixation point)? The temporal retinas were both normal in this patient, but the temporal retinas each project to their respective *ipsilateral* hemispheres; they should not interact. Surprisingly, right in the region near the midline, this patient *still could still see crossed disparities* at the fovea, with very fine stereoacuity.

How could this be? This is because at the midline, and *only* at the midline, there is an *additional* crossing over of information from one side of the brain to the other through the corpus callosum, allowing inputs from corresponding points in each eye to come together in one place in each hemisphere. In summary, the callosal pathway is responsible for midline binocular integration supporting *coarse stereopsis* (see Bishop and Henry, 1971) as well as vergence eye movements for stimuli along the vertical midline (Westheimer and Mitchell, 1969). Fine stereopsis, on the other hand, is dependent on the overlap of receptive fields from bilateral projections along the midline.

**CLINICAL APPLICATION** | For many years, a mode of treatment for epileptic seizures was to section the corpus callosum, preventing the spread of uncontrolled electrical activity from one cerebral hemisphere to the other, keeping the seizure somewhat circumscribed and under control. What might be expected to happen when the corpus callosum is severed? A side effect of callosal sectioning surgery is that stereopsis is lost along the midline, and *only* along the midline. This is consistent with the anatomy of the corpus callosum—a loss of stereopsis at the vertical midline of the visual field.

 *Key Point*

*The* **corpus callosum** is vital for stereopsis, especially for crossed disparities, along the vertical midline of the visual field.

## BINOCULARITY IN VISUAL CORTEX

Now that we know how the information from corresponding points of the two eyes is brought to the same place in the cortex, let us look at how the information is combined and used. The traditional method for doing this is **single-unit recording**—measurements of electrical responses from single neurons in the visual system. Here an animal, usually a cat or monkey, is anesthetized and immobilized, then positioned in front of a rear-projection screen on which visual stimuli are presented. When you place an electrode into a single visual neuron, there will be a place in visual space (that is, on the screen) in which a projected light, contrast, or motion will trigger the cell. This location in space is that cell's **receptive field** (Hartline, 1938). The receptive field is a representation of where in space that individual neuron in the visual system responds. What you are looking for when studying binocular vision are cells or brain areas that respond differently to *binocular* stimuli than they do to *monocular* stimuli. Of course, we should note that a cell's responses are also dependent on the activity and interconnections of the neurons that feed into it. The single-unit method is like sticking a voltmeter inside a computer and contacting one wire, and trying to figure out what the whole computer does. It is not perfect because the activity of a given single neuron does not always reflect the behavior of large populations of neurons acting as a unit, but nevertheless, this method has contributed a considerable amount to our understanding of visual processing.

More recent experimental methods, including **voltage-sensitive dyes** that indicate active brain regions or **PET and fMRI scans**, which show how regions of the visual system respond and interact in living alert human beings, may tell us how entire brain *systems* rather than individual neurons respond.

Where are the first truly binocular cells in the visual system found? Obviously, because the two eyes are independent structures, the earliest binocular cells that could possibly exist would be at the LGN. However, the two eyes' neurons are located in *separate anatomic layers* within the LGN—the LGN is for the most part a *monocular* structure. Although there are some binocular interactions in the LGN, they are weak at best.

Most important for explaining binocular vision is the *striate cortex*. The LGN neuron inputs from each eye terminate in layer 4 of striate cortex (Hubel and Wiesel, 1977). However, even here, the first cells that LGN neurons synapse on, the nonoriented cells of layer 4, are totally *monocular* and are segregated according to eye of origin. At the next synapse after this, neurons from each eye both converge to synapse on a single neuron in the layers above and below layer 4. The result is the first true **binocular cells** in the visual system (Hubel and Wiesel, 1959) (Fig. 8-7). These binocular neurons are striate cortical simple cells and complex cells. About 50% of simple and complex cells exhibit binocular responses.

A binocular cell will increase its firing from a baseline rate when an appropriate stimulus (with that neuron's preferred orientation, contrast polarity, direction of motion, and so on) is within the receptive field of only one eye. The same cell will similarly increase its firing rate when the same stimulus is within the corresponding receptive field of the other eye. This demonstrates that information from each eye is converging onto this cell. But more importantly, binocular cells respond *even more vigorously* when corresponding receptive fields of *both* eyes are stimulated simultaneously (Fig. 8-8) (Hubel and Wiesel, 1962). This is true neural **binocular summation**; in fact, the binocular response can sometimes be *greater than twice* either eye's response—**binocular facilitation**.

This binocular response occurs, however, only under strict conditions. The orientations of the stimuli presented to each eye must be identical, and similar regions of each receptive field must be stimulated (e.g., both must be *on* regions). Therefore, although binocular cells respond to stimuli presented to both eyes, *the stimuli presented to each eye must match* in many of their properties (Hubel and Wiesel, 1962). We return to this point shortly. These cells, the first truly binocular cells in the visual system, are the first step in our brain's representation of depth. Without binocular summation, you cannot have stereopsis.

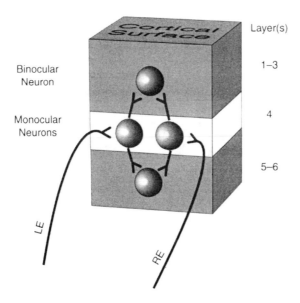

**Figure 8-7**   The first neurons that receive geniculate inputs in striate cortex are purely monocular. These synapse and converge on neurons outside of layer 4 that are true binocular cells.

One way to test clinically for the presence of binocular vision is to determine if even low-level binocular functions such as binocular summation are intact. In verbal children and adults, we can see if binocular summation is present by measuring visual acuity or contrast sensitivity under monocular and binocular viewing conditions. A patient's visual acuity or contrast sensitivity should be greater with binocular viewing than with either the left eye or the right eye individually.

**CLINICAL APPLICATION**

The **visual-evoked potential (VEP)** can give us objective information about binocular processing in visual cortex. The VEP is a gross electrical response from visual cortex as recorded from an electrode placed on the scalp in the occipital region. The VEP is more of a *mass response of groups of neurons* than a recording of *individual* neurons as in single-unit recordings. The VEP responses tend to be larger for binocularly viewed checkerboard or grating stimuli than for monocular ones because of the influence of binocular summation (Harter et al., 1973; Amigo et al., 1978). If fusion is disrupted, there is less binocular activity from visual cortex, and the binocular VEP no longer exhibits summation. This binocular VEP response has therefore been used as a clinical test of binocularity.

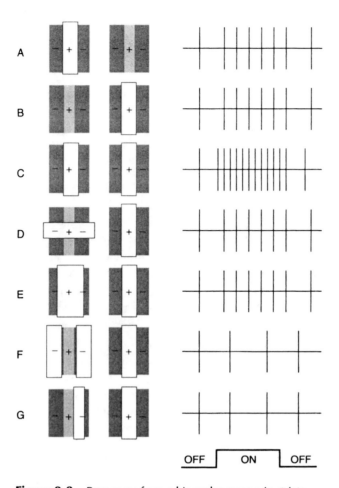

**Figure 8-8** Responses from a binocular neuron in striate cortex. **A,B:** Stimulation of the excitatory center region of either eye's receptive field alone increases the firing rate above the baseline level. **C:** Stimulation of both receptive field excitatory regions together with optimal stimuli (correct orientation, width, and so on) produces a larger response, that is, binocular summation. If one eye's stimulus is nonoptimal because of improper orientation (**D**), width (**E**), or location (**F,G**), less summation or even binocular inhibition may result.

There is one small problem with this. Apkarian et al. (1981) found that the degree of summation differed with different spatial frequency stimuli and with different temporal presentation rates, even in normal subjects. Depending on the precise combination of spatial and temporal frequency used, sometimes even normal binocular subjects showed no summation in the VEP response at all. This means that the binocular VEP is limited in its usefulness, but even so, it is still frequently used by both clinicians and scientists.

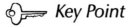 **Key Point**

*Always question the results obtained for the presence or absence of summation in binocular checkerboard or grating VEP recordings as a measure of binocularity.*

**CLINICAL PROCEDURE**

Fortunately, there is a better clinical test of binocularity using the **binocular "beat" VEP**. This evoked potential response, developed by Baitch and Levi (Baitch et al., 1988), uses uniform field unpatterned stimuli presented to each eye. Each eye's stimulus is flickered sinusoidally, but *at a slightly different rate in each eye*, for example, at 18 Hz (cycles per second) in one eye and 20 Hz in the other. When the VEP is recorded, it undergoes a Fourier frequency analysis. As expected, the response contains Fourier components at the two frequencies of stimulation, 18 and 20 Hz. However, this by itself doesn't indicate binocular summation, only that populations of cells in the visual cortex respond to either one eye or the other eye; that is, it could arise from either monocular or binocular cells in striate cortex. In individuals with binocular summation, additional responses are seen. A nonlinear combination of the inputs from each eye during binocular summation produces distortions in the VEP seen as two *modulation frequencies or "beats."* These additional beat frequencies occur at the sum and difference of the two original frequencies, that is, at (20 + 18) and (20 − 18) Hz, respectively, or 38 and 2 Hz in this case. *Beat frequencies occur only when true binocular summation is present* (Fig. 8-9), and, in addition, the amplitude of these components is proportional to the degree of binocular summation present. Binocular beat VEPs may be recorded even in infants to determine the presence of binocular anomalies or to monitor the efficacy of the treatment of infantile strabismus.

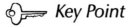 **Key Point**

*Binocular vision disorders that can lead to amblyopia most commonly develop during infancy. It is therefore imperative to measure binocularity with tools such as the binocular beat VEP in infants at risk of developing amblyopia or strabismus.*

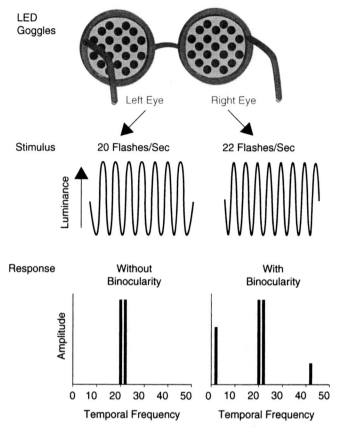

**Figure 8-9** The binocular beat VEP uses LED goggles to present uniform-field sinusoidal flicker, where the temporal frequency of the flicker differs slightly in each eye (in this case, 20 and 22 Hz). When no binocularity exists, the VEP response will contain the two input frequencies alone (20 and 22 Hz). When binocularity is present, extra sum (20 + 22 = 44 Hz) and difference (22 − 20 = 2 Hz) frequencies are introduced by visual cortex.

## OCULAR DOMINANCE COLUMNS

Visual cortex, like the LGN, is retinotopically mapped. Neurons encoding nearby locations in visual space are grouped together. Similarly, cortical cells with similar orientation preferences are grouped together. In what other ways are similar groups of cortical cells located together? In layer 4, simple cells are still mostly *monocular*—they get input more from one eye or the other. This is called **ocular dominance**. It so happens that cells whose inputs are dominated by a

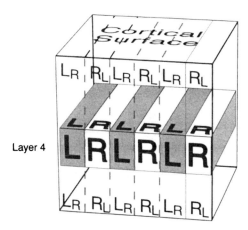

**Figure 8-10**   The inputs into layer 4 are segregated by eye of origin. Although this strict segregation diminishes as monocular inputs converge onto binocular cells outside of layer 4, there still exists a dominant influence of one eye's inputs over the other's in vertical slabs called ocular dominance columns. For example, the first ocular dominance column on the left in the figure contains monocular inputs from the left eye in layer 4. In the upper and lower layers of the striate cortex, binocular cells are stimulated by both the left and right eyes, but the left eye's input is predominant.

given eye are grouped together. If you insert an electrode into striate cortex and record a cell's responses at different depths into the cortex, you find that they are all dominated by the same eye. If you move a little sideways on the cortex and do it again, the cells will be dominated by the other eye's input. Cortical cells are grouped in slabs or columns running perpendicular to the cortical surface called **ocular dominance columns** (Fig. 8-10) (Wiesel et al., 1974). The width of an ocular dominance column is $1/4$ to $1/2$ mm. Visual cortex also contains orientation columns containing neurons that are selective for a particular orientation of target. A **hypercolumn** is a cortical unit that contains a full complement of ocular dominance and orientation columns representing one location in the visual field.

   If you stick the electrode obliquely through the striate cortex, the dominant eye for the cells you reach will flip back and forth as you intersect first one, then another, ocular dominance column. The cells in layer 4 are more monocular, and the columns show up strongly there, but as you move *outside* of layer 4, where more cells are *binocularly* driven, the eye-specific segregation of the ocular dominance columns, although still present, is not as pronounced. It is interesting to note that although the brain segregates the eye of origin of its inputs, this information is not available to our conscious perception—when both eyes are open, we cannot tell which of our two eyes received a given stimulation (Ono and Barbeito, 1985).

Another way to demonstrate these ocular dominance columns is with radioactive isotopes. If you inject **radioactive amino acids** into the vitreous humor of one eye of an animal, it will be transported along the axons of visual neurons up to the cortex. The animal is then sacrificed, and the brain is sliced into serial sections. If one section of cortex from layer 4 is placed against an x-ray plate, the regions containing the radioactive amino acids from the injected eye will react with the film, and you can see directly where the cortical cells are that serve that eye (Fig. 8-11). What you see are alternating bands of light and dark (radioactive and nonradioactive cells) corresponding to one eye, then the other. It is analogous to zebra stripes. This appearance will change in such disorders as **amblyopia**, in which binocular processing is disrupted. If one eye of an amblyope is injected with radioactive tracers, you find that the stripes corresponding to the amblyopic eye are much narrower than those of the nonamblyopic eye, indicating less effective driving of cortical cells by the amblyopic eye. People with amblyopia will have reduced or absent binocular summation and poor stereoscopic depth perception. Amblyopia is discussed in greater length in Chapter 9.

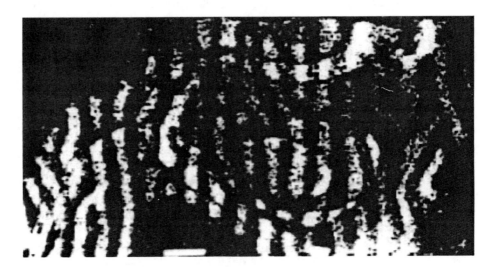

**Figure 8-11** This radioactively labeled section of striate cortex sliced along layer 4 shows the ocular dominance columns. Radioactive dye injected into the vitreous of one eye is transmitted through axoplasmic transport to the striate cortex. When a photographic plate is exposed to the radioactivity, it labels black all cells that receive input from that eye only; the plate remains white at the location of the fellow eye's cells. (Photograph from Hubel et al., 1976. Used by permission of the authors.)

## DETECTION OF DISPARITY

The existence of binocular summation in visual cortex is, in itself, exciting. Nevertheless, binocular neurons in the striate cortex can do much more than this: they can also detect *disparity*. That is, binocular neurons also serve as **disparity detectors** (Barlow et al., 1967; Pettigrew et al., 1968). About half of the binocular simple and complex cells in V1 also serve as disparity detectors.

How does a neuron "see" disparity? Figure 8-12A shows the response from one binocular cell whose **preferred disparity** is zero disparity. When two stimuli are presented to the same location relative to the fixation locus of each eye, that is, zero disparity, on corresponding points in each eye, this cell fires a lot. However, either crossed or uncrossed *disparity* can be introduced with prisms, so that the stimulated locations within each monocular receptive field are spaced closer together or farther apart. In Fig. 8-12B we are displacing one eye's image with a prism so that the image is formed farther and farther off the center of the receptive field. The binocular cell fires less and less until finally, at some particular prism strength, its firing rate reaches a minimum, then increases slightly again until the binocular response is the same as for each eye's individual response alone. That is, this cell undergoes *summation* at one particular preferred disparity (zero disparity in this case), then less and less summation with disparities increasingly deviating from the preferred disparity until *binocular inhibition* is achieved. Finally, with extremely large differences from the preferred disparity, the prism-displaced stimulus will no longer lie inside the monocular receptive field of that eye, and *no binocular interactions* at all (zero summation) will occur (which would be expected if the subject were diplopic). In sum, this binocular cell is exhibiting a response that is *tuned* for a specific *binocular disparity*. In Fig. 8-12C, the response for a cell tuned to a crossed disparity is shown, and Fig. 8-12D depicts the response from an uncrossed disparity detector.

However, although these cells can respond to binocular disparity, it does not necessarily follow that these cells are specialized to serve only as disparity processors. Recent studies have shown that disparity detectors in V1 can also respond to **anticorrelation**, or the matching of random dot stereo pairs in which the dots in one eye are of *opposite contrast* to those in the fellow eye (Cumming and Parker, 1997). Such patterns do not give rise to a percept of stereoscopic depth but instead indicate inappropriate matches in an attempt to solve the correspondence problem. Therefore, disparity-sensitive single neurons in V1 cannot explain depth perception on their own; pooling the outputs of many such cells would be necessary to solve the correspondence problem.

An important point to remember is that you have to *simultaneously stimulate the excitatory centers of both eyes' receptive fields* (that is, the two receptive fields must be *in register* or precisely superimposed) to get an increased response, or binocular summation. The receptive fields for each eye have to be a critical distance apart to get the best binocular summation—at their preferred disparity. Too close together or too far apart, and summation will not be maximum, or binocular inhibition can even occur because changing the disparity relative to the perfectly

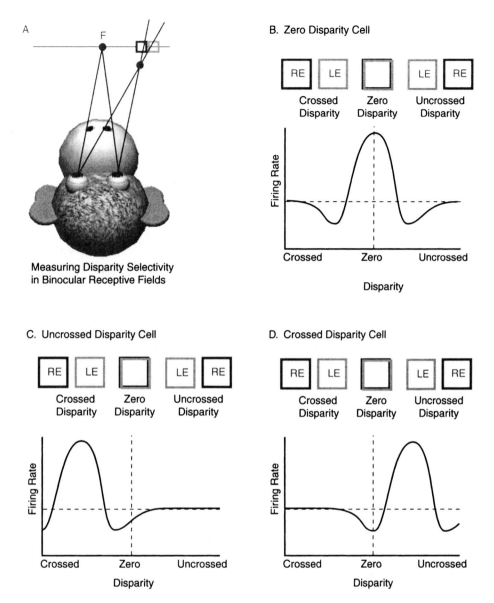

**Figure 8-12** **A:** Responses of a binocular neuron may be recorded to different disparities in monkey cortex by presenting half-images of a stimulus to each eye on a projector screen. Changing the separations of each half-image from the fixation point introduces different disparities. **B:** Cells that respond most when the two monocular receptive fields overlap completely are zero-disparity-tuned neurons. **C:** Crossed-disparity detectors respond optimally when the right eye receptive field is to the left of that of the right eye by a given displacement determined by the specific magnitude of disparity to which the cell is tuned. **D:** Uncrossed disparity-tuned neurons respond best to displacements of the two monocular receptive fields where the left eye receptive field is to the left of the right eye receptive field by a given displacement.

in-register condition can result in stimulating one monocular receptive field's center and the other's surround. Presenting even more disparity will eventually get you beyond the disparity range for binocular interaction.

Barlow and coworkers (1967) first provided evidence that differences in the *positions* of the monocular receptive fields of neurons feeding into a given binocular cell, that is, monocular receptive fields not precisely on corresponding retinal points, could yield a binocular cell that is tuned to a given amount of binocular disparity (Fig. 8-13A). Recently, however, it has been found that although position-based binocular encoding occurs, it is not the predominant way in which binocular neurons respond to disparity. Position-based disparity encoding may be used only for detecting disparity in high-spatial-frequency stimuli. What about low- and middle-spatial-frequency stimuli? Binocular disparity can also be represented by small differences in the *phase* between the monocular receptive fields (Anzai *et al.*, 1997). In other words, the entire receptive fields are not

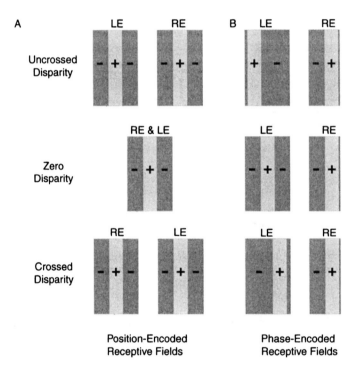

**Figure 8-13**    Two different mechanisms exist for detecting binocular disparity in binocular cells. **A:** Position encoding. The relative positions of the entire receptive fields of each eye may shift to produce different disparity tunings. **B:** Phase encoding. The positions of the receptive fields may remain the same, but the relative phase of the centers of the receptive fields may change to produce sensitivity to different disparity ranges.

displaced relative to one another; instead, the receptive field profiles of the two monocular input neurons differ in their internal *shape* so that only the *excitatory regions* of each lie at nonexactly corresponding locations (Fig. 8-13B).

For each receptive field in one eye, there are many receptive fields in the other eye that will interact with it; this is like a neurophysiological version of Panum's area. If you plot the number of cells at a given location that respond to each disparity, you get a normal distribution in which the most cells are tuned to zero disparity, with fewer cells tuned to crossed or uncrossed disparities of greater magnitude. This relates well to our sensory thresholds for disparity (stereoacuity). We are most sensitive to disparity near *zero* disparity, the location of the horopter, and least sensitive to disparities off the horopter, until we reach the edges of Panum's area. In fact, one working definition of the horopter mentioned earlier was the locus in three-dimensional space with maximal stereoacuity.

If we repeat single-cell recordings of binocular cells at various lateral separations from the cell corresponding to the fixation point, we can produce a neurophysiologically based *horopter* (Fig. 8-14). At larger lateral eccentricities from the fixation point, we get larger and larger populations of monocular cells feeding into each disparity-detecting neuron, mirroring the increased size of Panum's area as we move into the retinal periphery. You also find that the mean displacement between each eye's monocular receptive fields gets smaller as you move eccentrically from fixation. This corresponds to curvature of the horopter closer toward you as you measure the horopter laterally off the fovea.

You can also find out some things about these pools of cortical disparity detectors through psychophysical experiments. A subject shown a sine-wave grating for a long exposure duration *adapts* to that particular spatial frequency. Adaptation makes the visual system less sensitive to gratings of that spatial frequency and to similar frequencies but does not affect sensitivity to much different spatial frequencies. This is because of the presence of many sets of spatial-frequency-tuned cells in visual cortex, each set tuned to a different range of frequencies. Adaptation occurs in one of these sets, so that it responds less well.

The same type of adaptation occurs for *disparity*. You can adapt to a particular disparity and not others (Long and Over, 1974). This is really a binocular phenomenon because viewing the target with either eye alone produces no disparity adaptation. This confirms that we have sets of disparity-tuned cortical neurons in striate cortex.

Binocular cells do not necessarily have to be narrowly tuned to respond to *one* particular disparity alone. It was first proposed by Richards (1971) that cortical disparity detectors are, in fact, not finely tuned. By *comparing* the responses between *pools* of these cells, each tuned to a different specific disparity range, we could still compute the depth of an object. In fact, Richards' hypothesis was proven when four major types of disparity cells were discovered by Poggio and Fischer (1977), based on their **disparity-tuning curves** (Fig. 8-15). These cells are true **binocular disparity processors** in visual cortex.

1. **Tuned excitatory cells**. We discussed this type of cell a few pages ago. These are cells tuned for locations *precisely* on the horopter (zero disparity).

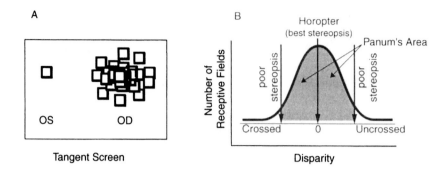

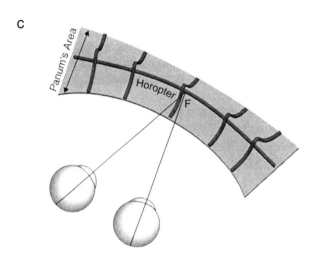

**Figure 8-14**    **A:** In the neurophysiological analog of Panum's fusional area, a single receptive field in one eye may correspond to a distribution of many receptive fields in the fellow eye, each with a differing binocular disparity. **B:** By measuring the number of receptive fields in the fellow eye that correspond to that single receptive field at each disparity, a plot is obtained that relates to the sensitivity of stereopsis at each disparity. The greatest density of disparity detectors will be at the zero-disparity location, and the range of the distribution will correspond to the extent of Panum's fusional area. **C:** When this process is repeated for several lateral target positions, a neurophysiological horopter is mapped.

They do not respond well to crossed or uncrossed disparities, and their responses drop to baseline by as little as 10' arc disparity. They therefore tell you if an object is *the same distance* as the point you are fixating.

2. **Tuned inhibitory cells**. These cells respond at the horopter too, but in an *inhibitory* fashion. If both monocular receptive fields' centers are stimulated, the binocular cell fires less. These cells are *not* inhibited by either crossed or

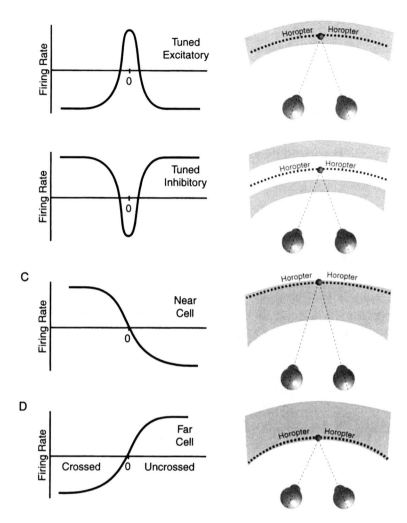

**Figure 8-15** Four classes of disparity-tuned cortical neurons exist.
**A:** Tuned excitatory cells fire more when a stimulus lies on the horopter.
**B:** Tuned inhibitory cells fire most when a stimulus is moved off the
horopter in either direction and are inhibited by stimuli lying on the
horopter. **C:** Near cells increase their firing rate when presented targets
closer than the horopter (crossed disparity). **D:** Far cells respond to
uncrossed disparities, that is, targets farther than the fixation point.

uncrossed disparity. These cells would be good for telling you that an object is *off*
the horopter—that is, it has a depth relative to the fixation point. It is thought
that these neurons help to maintain fusion, as they would respond if vergence
drifted off the horopter.

3. **Near cells**. These cells are untuned; that is, they do not respond to one single particular disparity. They simply tell you if a stimulus is *anywhere* closer to you than the fixation point.

4. **Far cells**. These are the same as near cells in concept, but they tell you if a stimulus is *more distant* than the fixation point. Near and far cells are thought to be responsible for coarse stereopsis, that is, qualitative stereopsis.

These cells therefore form the basis of both coarse and fine stereopsis. When a stimulus falls within the receptive fields of a *combination* of these cells, the pattern of responses of the ensemble of cells will tell you if the stimulus is on or off the horopter (fine stereopsis) or, if the disparity is large (coarse stereopsis), in what direction relative to the horopter the stimulus lies, that is, closer or farther away.

Although the remarkable abilities of striate cortical binocular cells make it seem as if all binocular processing is accomplished within striate cortex alone, other visual processing areas outside of area V1 are also involved in depth processing. **Area V2**, located laterally to area V1 on the surface of the occipital lobe, is organized very similarly to striate cortex in that it is retinotopically mapped. The cells in V2 are similar in many respects to striate cortical cells, except that their receptive fields tend to be larger. Area V2 also contains cells with binocular response properties. In fact, it contains even more binocular cells than striate cortex—up to 70% of the cells in V2 respond to disparity (Poggio, 1984).

Structures within area V1 can been identified by staining with a metabolic marker called cytochrome oxidase. V2 can be also stained with cytochrome oxidase, but instead of showing structures like blobs and interblobs found in area V1, area V2 shows **cytochrome oxidase *stripes*** (Fig. 8-16). There are three sets of regions in V2 based upon cytochrome oxidase staining: thick stripes, thin stripes, and interstripes, which do not stain. The thin stripes and interstripes receive their inputs from the striate cortical blobs and interblob regions, respectively. These inputs are therefore predominantly parvocellular in origin, and the cells contained within them therefore prefer high-spatial-frequency, low-temporal-frequency, and chromatic stimuli. The **thick stripes contain many cells selective for binocular disparity and motion.** The thick stripes receive their inputs from the layers of V1 containing **complex cells**, which are predominantly **magnocellular** in origin. Such cells prefer low spatial frequencies, high temporal frequencies, or *motion* and are achromatic. Therefore, in area V2, we start to see an association between stereoscopic vision and motion processing.

However, there is one thing missing from this information. The complex cells of V1, like magnocellular-driven cells in general, favor large, low-spatial-frequency stimuli. If the only cells capable of processing disparity in V2 fell within the thick stripes, we would only be capable of processing *coarse* stereopsis. Clearly, other cells within V2 must also be capable of processing disparity, and this is precisely what has been found. There are cells in the **interstripes** that receive parvocellular input via simple cells in V1 and can also respond to disparity stimuli. These cells have smaller receptive fields that can retrieve disparity information at high spatial frequencies and therefore are capable of *fine* stereopsis.

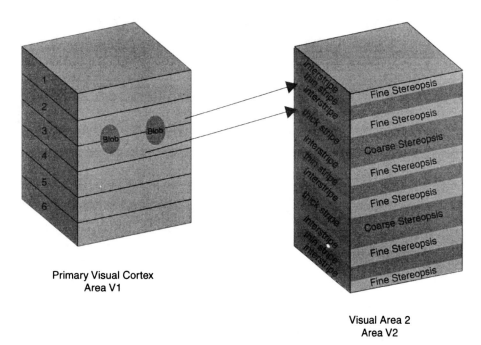

Primary Visual Cortex
Area V1

Visual Area 2
Area V2

**Figure 8-16**   Cytochrome oxidase staining of area V2 reveals thick and thin stripes plus interstripe regions. The thick stripes, receiving inputs from M-driven complex cells in striate cortex, are selective for coarse disparities. The interstripes contain P-driven cells capable of fine stereopsis.

What this means is that unlike orientation selectivity or color selectivity, **disparity processing requires both the M and P processing streams**. This has been borne out by experiments by Schiller and coworkers (1990). After lesioning of the parvocellular layers of the LGN of a monkey, thereby inactivating the cortical cells that receive predominant P-stream inputs, the monkey had deficits in fine stereopsis. Similarly, lesions in the magnocellular layers of the LGN produced deficits in coarse stereopsis.

Area V3 contains cells that can respond to orientation, motion, or disparity. About half of the cells in V3 are disparity selective. PET scans reveal that area V3 responds to static stereopsis but not to motion in depth (Nagahama et al., 1996). Even so, the major function of area V3 has yet to be determined. Perhaps the precise role of area V3 in vision is still unknown because the proper stimulus to test V3 neuron selectivity has not been found.

The **middle temporal (or MT) cortex**, also known as **area V5,** is a higher visual cortical area in which most cells are responsive to motion, but there are also some cells that are responsive to disparity (Maunsell and van Essen, 1983). The MT cortex appears to be the cortical area where motion and depth information are combined to yield sensitivity to **motion in depth**—objects approaching you or receding from you (Nagahama et al., 1996). It is also possible that MT is the area that provides depth perception from *monocular* motion cues, such as **motion parallax**. We have already seen that motion parallax or differences in motion speed can make a two-dimensional pattern of moving random dots appear to lie on the surface of a *three-dimensional* shape (**structure from motion**).

The MT cortex projects to the adjacent **middle superior temporal (or MST) cortex**, which processes complicated patterns of motion resulting from movement through the environment. These patterns of expanding or contracting motion are called **optic flow**. Once again, motion information provides a means of assessing position in three-dimensional space, in this case our own position relative to objects around us, as we move about in our environment. Some neurons in MST are also sensitive to object rotation in three-dimensional space (Saito et al., 1986).

Finally, the **parietal cortex** has some usefulness for **orienting in space**, in other words, in finding spatial relationships between objects and between ourselves and those objects. This is very important for motion perception and for guiding eye movements as well.

**CLINICAL APPLICATION** | Lesions of the posterior parietal lobe result in an impaired ability to determine the spatial relationships between objects, impaired spatial memory, disturbances of spatial attention, and reduced stereopsis.

As we will see when we discuss the development of binocular vision, single-unit recordings have also helped to explain anomalies of binocular vision. Recently, scientists recorded from cells in higher visual cortical areas that have retinotopic mapping, as does area V1. These higher visual areas' orderly arrangement of receptive fields are "remapped" in animals with artificially induced ARC—that is, over time, points in visual space are "relocated" (for example, see Sireteneau and Best, 1992). Why is this remapping found in higher cortical areas but not in striate cortex? It may be simply because receptive fields are much bigger outside of striate cortex, as anomalous correspondence is demonstrated more frequently in the peripheral retina, where receptive fields are larger than in the central retina (Sireteneau and Fronius, 1989). It is therefore easier for two widely separated points in each eye (such as the fovea in one eye and the anomalous point in the other) to be encompassed within these larger receptive fields outside of V1. Exactly how this remapping is accomplished is still unknown.

# *EVOKED-POTENTIAL CORRELATES WITH BINOCULAR VISION*

The early waves of the visual-evoked potentials, or VEP, provide insight into neuronal activity within areas V1 and V2 of visual cortex. An important point to remember, however, is that the VEP is a *mass response of groups of neurons*; it does not indicate what *individual* neurons are doing. What it does tell us, however, is how ensembles of cells combine to process visual stimuli. When binocular stimuli are presented, the VEP can tell us about how the visual cortex responds to binocular information.

Earlier in this chapter, we saw that visual-evoked potentials can provide a means of demonstrating binocular summation in visual cortex. The visual-evoked potential can also give us evidence for cortical processing of other aspects of binocular information.

One thing you can do is record the VEP to a vertical grating in one eye, then a horizontal grating to the other eye, then both together—a *rivalrous* stimulus. What happens? When the left eye is dominant during rivalry, the responses resemble those recorded from the left eye alone, and when the right eye is dominant during rivalry, it looks like a right-eye-only response (Cobb, Morton and Ettlinger, 1967). In addition, during the rivalrous percept, no binocular summation is seen in the VEP.

What about **stereoscopic** responses in the VEP? One process involved in perceiving depth is matching corresponding features of the images in each eye to form a single percept, in other words, a correlation of corresponding points. This process was examined via VEP recordings to **random-dot correlograms**, random-dot sequences in which the haplopic images either exactly correlate or match or are precisely unmatched (black dots in one eye's stimulus are white in the other, and vice versa). These are true cyclopean stimuli because the monocular images are just groups of dots as in a random-dot stereogram; the matching occurs only when the monocular images are combined by binocular cells. A binocular VEP response is produced by creating or disrupting the binocular correspondence of the images between the two eyes (Julesz and Tyler, 1976).

More importantly, VEP responses can be recorded to depth changes in **random-dot stereograms**. Stereograms in which groups of dots with disparity-produced checkerboards alternating in depth generated even larger VEP responses than did correlograms and responses of different waveform (Julesz et al., 1980). Although disparity is produced by breaking exact correlation of the images between the two eyes, the correlation process by itself cannot account for the entire response to the random-dot stereogram. The larger stereoscopic VEP response is caused by the additional *percept of depth* arising from the disparity.

Random-dot stereograms alternated in depth produce an evoked potential response that differs from those to monocular stimuli. With stereoscopic stimuli, the VEP responses have a very long latency (200 to 250 ms) as compared to nonstereoscopic grating or checkerboard stimuli (100 ms). Although the smaller element size of the random-dot stimuli as compared to checkerboard squares or grating bars could delay the VEP, it is the stereoscopic disparity that creates the greater latency effects. Dot hyperacuity stimuli show a much longer VEP latency for stereoscopic dots than for oriented or vernier-offset dots (Steinman and Levi, 1992).

Changes in VEP amplitude in response to disparity can be demonstrated by presenting grating stimuli of the same orientation in each eye and changing the spatial frequency of one grating; you get a situation similar to **meridional magnification**—an apparent tilting of the grating occurs as disparity is introduced. The VEP recordings become larger as this disparity is increased, and the surface appears to be increasingly tilted (Fiorentini and Maffei, 1970). In addition, binocular summation in the VEP is disrupted once the induced aniseikonia exceeded 5% (Katsumi et al., 1986).

## SUMMARY AND KEY POINTS

- **Single-unit recordings** and **evoked-potential studies** show us that for just about any aspect of binocular perception, there is a recordable neurophysiological analog. Similarly, single-unit recordings and the anatomic layout of the visual pathways help show how these responses come to be. This amplifies the basic tenet of vision research that we can only truly discover how the visual system performs its duties by combining evidence from anatomic, physiological, and psychophysical research.

- The structure of the visual system from the **optic chiasm** through the LGN to area V1 is specialized to reorganize each eye's monocular information so that it can be more easily combined into a binocular percept.

- Nerve fibers from the nasal retina cross over at the optic chiasm, projecting to the contralateral LGN, while fibers from the temporal retina project to the ipsilateral LGN; this is known as a **partial decussation**. Information seen to the left of the fixation point progresses to the right cerebral hemisphere, and vice versa.

- The **dorsal lateral geniculate nucleus (dLGN)** has six layers, with narrow interlaminar regions separating each. Layers 1 and 2 are comprised of the **magnocellular** (M) neurons, and the remaining layers contain **parvocellular** (P) neurons. The LGN is organized so that moving from medial to lateral within LGN, cells are encountered the represent the fovea progressing to the retinal periphery, and moving from anterior to posterior, the representation moves from lower visual field to the upper. **Retinotopic mapping** is therefore the basis for monocular visual localization (**local sign**) relative to the fovea and **corresponding points**.

- As you move from ventrally to dorsally across layers of the LGN, what changes is the eye represented. The ipsilateral eye projects to layers 2, 3, and 5, and the contralateral eye to layers 1, 4, and 6. The end result is that corresponding retinal points are lined up across layers of the LGN in **projection columns** so that binocular combination can occur early once these fibers continue to area V1.

- Fibers from the fovea experience only a partial decussation at the optic chiasm, so that visual information from the midline region is forwarded as a bilateral projection. This results in the clinical phenomenon of **macular sparing**. **Fine stereopsis** is dependent on these bilateral projections along the midline.

- The **corpus callosum** (callosal pathway) interconnects the two cerebral hemispheres and serves as a second mechanism that brings binocular information together along the vertical midline. That pathway is responsible for midline binocular integration supporting **coarse stereopsis**.

- Striate cortical cells in layer 4 of **striate cortex** are monocular, but outside of layer 4, these inputs converge onto the first true **binocular cells** that increase their firing rate when an appropriate stimulus lies within corresponding receptive fields in both eyes (**binocular summation**) relative to their response to either eye alone. This response can be greater than the sum of the response for each individual receptive field (**binocular facilitation**). Binocular summation can be measured clinically with **VEPs** in nonverbal patients.

- The simple cells of layer 4 are monocular. Cells whose inputs are dominated by a given eye are grouped together in **ocular dominance columns** running perpendicular to the cortical surface. *Outside* of layer 4, where more cells are *binocularly* driven, the strict eye-specific segregation of the ocular dominance columns begins to vanish. In **amblyopia**, in which binocular processing is disrupted, the stripes corresponding to the amblyopic eye are much narrower than those of the nonamblyopic eye, indicating less effective driving of cortical cells by the amblyopic eye.

- Binocular neuronal responses throughout visual cortex become more complex and specialized to first detect binocular correlation, binocular disparity, three-dimensional shape, interactions of depth and motion, and finally three-dimensional motion of our bodies in space.

- Binocular neurons in the striate cortex are tuned to detect specific **binocular disparities**. Less and less summation occurs as disparities increasingly deviate from the preferred disparity until, eventually, binocular inhibition is achieved.

- For each receptive field in one eye, there are many receptive fields in the other eye that will interact with it, the neural analog of **Panum's fusional area**. We are most sensitive to disparity near zero disparity, the location of the **horopter**, and least sensitive to disparities off the horopter. At larger lateral eccentricities from the fixation point, larger and larger populations of monocular cells feed into each disparity-detecting neuron, enlarging Panum's area.

- Four major types of disparity-tuned cortical neurons exist in striate cortex, which form the basis of both coarse and fine stereopsis: (a) **tuned excitatory cells**, cells tuned for locations precisely on the horopter (zero disparity); (b) **tuned inhibitory cells** that fire only if an object is off the horopter; (c) **near cells**, which fire if a stimulus is *anywhere* closer than the fixation point; and (d) **far cells** that respond if a stimulus is more *distant* than the fixation point.

- The **thick stripes of area V2** contain cells selective for binocular disparity and motion, which receive inputs from M-driven complex cells in area V1. The **thin stripes** contain P-driven cells with smaller receptive fields that can retrieve disparity information at high spatial frequencies and therefore are capable of *fine* stereopsis. Unlike orientation selectivity or color selectivity, **disparity processing requires both the M and P processing streams**.

- The **middle temporal (MT) cortex** is a higher visual cortical area in which most cells are responsive to motion, but there are also some cells that are responsive to disparity. This area is thought to yield information about **motion in depth** and **structure from motion** or **motion parallax.**

- The adjacent **middle superior temporal (or MST) cortex** and the **parietal cortex** process complicated patterns of optic flow that help determine our **orientation in space**.

- The retinotopic mapping of higher visual areas' receptive fields is not fixed but can be "remapped" with artificially induced **anomalous correspondence**.

- The **visual-evoked potential (VEP)** also provides evidence for cortical processing of binocular information. The VEP response to a rivalrous stimulus shows recordings only from the eye that is dominant at the time. With stereoscopic stimuli, the VEP responses have a very **long latency**.

The complexity and power of binocular vision come with a price: with disruption of the binocular visual pathways, depth perception and other binocular functions may be adversely affected. In the next chapter, we explore the influence of development on normal and abnormal binocular vision.

## QUESTIONS

1. As we discussed in Chapter 7, stereoacuity thresholds may in fact be lower than monocular acuity thresholds. Given what you have learned in the present chapter, how could the visual system extract such fine-grained information?

2. A patient has a pituitary tumor that compresses the center of the optic chiasm. How might this affect the patient's depth perception?

3. How do the responses of binocular cells differ from those of monocular cells? What is the optimal stimulus for a binocular cell?

4. How can binocular summation be measured in nonverbal patients? If an infant shows little or no binocular summation, what other signs and symptoms might you expect?

## BIBLIOGRAPHY

AMIGO G, FIORENTINI A, PIRCHIO M *and* SPINELLI D (1978). *Binocular vision tested with visual-evoked potentials in children and infants.* Invest. Ophthlamol. Vis. Sci. 17:910–915.

ANZAI A, OHZAWA I *and* FREEMAN RD (1997). *Neural mechanisms underlying binocular fusion and stereopsis: position vs. phase.* Proc. Natl. Acad. Sci. U.S.A. 94:5348–5443.

APKARIAN PA, VAN VEENENDAAL W *and* SPEKREIJSE H (1986). *Albinism: an anomaly of maturation of the visual pathway.* Doc. Ophthalmol. 45:271–284

BAITCH LW *and* LEVI DM (1988). *Evidence for nonlinear binocular interactions in human visual cortex.* Vis. Res. 28:1139–1143.

BARLOW HB, BLAKEMORE C *and* PETTIGREW JD (1967). *The neural mechanisms of binocular depth discrimination.* J. Neurosci. 193:327–342.

BISHOP PO *and* HENRY GH (1971). *Spatial vision.* Annu. Rev. Psychol. 22:119–160.

COBB WA, MORTON HB *and* ETTLINGER G (1967). *Cortical potentials evoked by pattern reversal and their suppression in visual rivalry.* Nature 216:1123–1126.

CUMMING BG *and* PARKER AJ (1997). *Responses of primary visual cortical neurons to binocular disparity without depth perception.* Nature 389:280–283.

FIORENTINI A *and* MAFFEI L (1970). *Electrophysiological evidence for disparity detectors in human visual system.* Science 169:208–209.

HARTER MR, SEIPLE WH *and* SALMON L (1973). *Binocular summation of visually evoked responses to pattern stimuli in humans.* Vis. Res. 13:1433–1446.

HARTLINE HK (1938). *The responses of single optic nerve fibres of the vertebrate eye.* Am. J. Physiol. 121:400–415.

HUBEL DH *and* WIESEL TN (1959). *Receptive fields of single neurons in the cat's visual cortex.* J. Physiol. 148:574–591.

HUBEL DH *and* WIESEL TN (1962). Receptive fields, binocular interaction and functional architecture in the cat's visual cortex. J. Physiol. 160:106–154.

HUBEL DH *and* WIESEL TN (1967). *Cortical and callosal connections concerned with the vertical midline in the cat.* J. Neurophysiol. 30:1561–1573.

HUBEL DH *and* WIESEL TN (1977). *Functional architecture of the macaque monkey visual cortex.* Proc. R. Soc. Lond. B198:1–59.

JULESZ B *and* TYLER CW (1976). *Neurontropy, an entropy-like measure of neural correlation in binocular fusion and rivalry.* Biol. Cybernet. 22:107–119.

JULESZ B, KROPFL W *and* PETRIG B (1980). *Large evoked potentials to dynamic random-dot correlograms permit quick determination of stereopsis.* Proc. Natl. Acad. Sci. U.S.A. 77:2348–2351.

KATSUMI O, TSUYOSHI T *and* HIROSE T (1986). *Effect of aniseikonia on binocular function.* Invest. Ophthalmol. Vis. Sci. 27:601–604.

LONG N *and* OVER R (1974). *Stereospatial masking and aftereffect with normal and transformed random-dot patterns.* Percept. Psychophys. 15:243–248.

MAUNSELL JHR *and* VAN ESSEN DC (1983). *Functional properties of neurons in middle temporal visual area of the macaque monkey. II. Binocular interactions and sensitivity to binocular disparity.* J. Neurophysiol. 49:1148–1167.

NAGAHAMA Y, TAKAYAMA Y, FUKUYAMA H, YAMAUCHI H, MATSUZAKI S, MAGATA Y, SHIBASAKI H *and* KIMURA J (1996). *Functional anatomy on perception of position and motion in depth.* Neuroreport 7:1717–1721.

ONO H *and* BARBEITO R (1985). *Utrocular discrimination is not sufficient for utrocular identification.* Vis. Res. 25:289–299.

PERRY VH, OEHLER R *and* COWEY A (1984). *Retinal ganglion cells that project to the dorsal lateral geniculate nucleus in the macaque monkey.* Neuroscience 12:1101–1123.

PETTIGREW JD, NIKARA T *and* BISHOP PO (1968). *Binocular interaction on single units in cat striate cortex: simultaneous stimulation by single moving slit with receptive fields in correspondence.* Exp. Brain Res. 6:391–410.

POGGIO (1984). *The analysis of stereopsis.* Annu. Rev. Neurosci. 7:379–412.

POGGIO GF *and* FISCHER B (1977). *Binocular interaction and depth sensitivity in striate and prestriate cortex of behaving rhesus monkey.* J. Neurophysiol. 40:1392–1405.

RICHARDS W (1971). *Anomalous stereoscopic depth perception.* J. Opt. Soc. Am. 61:410–414.

SAITO H, YUKIE M, TANAKA K, HIKOSAKA K, FUKADA Y *and* IWAI E (1986). *Integration of direction signals of image motion in the superior temporal sulcus of the macaque monkey.* J. Neurosci. 6:45–57.

SANDERSON KJ, DARLAN-SMITH I and BISHOP PO (1969). *Binocular corresponding receptive fields of single units in the cat dorsal lateral geniculate nucleus.* Vis. Res. 9:1297–1303.

SCHILLER PH, LOGOTHETIS NK and CHARLES ER (1990). *Role of the color-opponent and broadband channels in vision.* Vis. Neurosci. 5:321–346.

SIRETENEAU R and BEST J (1992). *Squint-induced modification of visual receptive fields in the lateral suprasylvian cortex of the cat: binocular interaction, vertical effect and anomalous correspondence.* Eur. J. Neurosci. 4:235–242.

SIRETENEAU R and FRONIUS M (1989). *Differences in the pattern of correspondence in the central and peripheral visual field of strabismic observers.* Invest. Ophthalmol. Vis. Sci. 30:2023–2033.

STEINMAN SB and LEVI DM (1992). *Topography of the evoked potential to spatial localization cues.* Vis. Neurosci. 8:281–294.

STONE J (1966). *The nasotemporal division of the cat's retina.* J. Comp. Neurol. 126:585–600.

TUMOSA N, MCCALL MA, GUIDO W and SPEAR PD (1989). *Responses of lateral geniculate neurons that survive long-term cortical damage in kittens and adult cats.* J. Neurosci. 9:280–298.

VARELA FJ and SINGER W (1987). *Neuronal dynamics in the visual corticothalamic pathway revealed through binocular rivalry.* Exp. Brain Res. 66:10–20.

WALLS GL (1963). *The Vertebrate Eye and Its Adaptive Radiations.* Hafner, New York.

WESTHEIMER G and MITCHELL AM (1969). *The sensory stimulus for disjunctive eye movements.* Vis. Res. 9:749–755.

WIESEL TN, HUBEL DH and LAM DMK (1974). *Autoradiographic demonstration of ocular-dominance columns in the monkey striate cortex by means of transneuronal transport.* Brain Res. 79:273–279.

# Development of Binocular Vision

Visual development is a very important topic for eye care in two respects. First, eye doctors are asked to assess the vision of infants and small toddlers in their practices. Second, knowing how the visual system develops normally helps in understanding what happens when something goes *wrong*; that is, the causes, effects, and treatment of visual disorders that arise in infancy and childhood.

## *THE ROLE OF EXPERIENCE IN DEVELOPMENT*

Like everything else in the study of perception, binocular vision has gone through the "nature or nurture" battle. If newborns do not see the same way that adults do, then the challenge is to determine how much of the visual system's development is dictated by the expression of inborn, genetic factors versus guided by environmental factors or learning as the result of visual experience during infancy. In the case of binocular vision, the question is whether binocularity and stereopsis are an inborn "hard-wired" visual capabilities that are present at birth or whether we must *learn* to see binocularly and three-dimensionally.

We now know that most, if not all, aspects of vision exhibit some degree of development after birth. When does this development start, and is there some age when we stop developing? Do visual experiences always have the same effect no matter when in our lifetime they occur?

Logically the starting age at which visual development is influenced by experience would be at birth because the retinas cannot receive patterned visual images before then. However, we can also reason that there must be *upper bounds* to when visual experience can affect visual development. For example, if a toddler has a cataract for 2 years from the ages of 1 to 3, that toddler will never see well out of that eye after the cataract is removed. By degrading the visual input, the cataract affects the eye's visual development (we will discuss this condition,

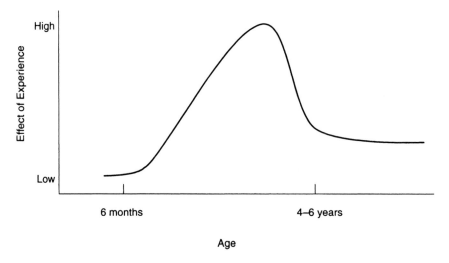

**Figure 9-1**    The critical period of development begins shortly after birth and is most pronounced during infancy and early childhood. Although the critical period is essentially over by age 6 to 7 years in humans, experience still may have an effect on the function of the visual system, even in adulthood.

**amblyopia**, shortly). On the other hand, if a 50-year-old adult has a cataract for 2 years, he or she will see well out of that eye once the cataract is surgically removed. A degraded image has no lasting effect on adult visual systems.

This demonstrates that there has to be some upper age limit to when experience can affect the development of the visual system's capabilities, but when exactly is this cutoff age? What we know now is that there is a **critical period of development**, a range of ages during which experience has a very powerful effect on the structure and function of the visual system (Fig. 9-1). Outside of this age range, experience has a much smaller effect.

In general, visual experience has its greatest effects at about 6 months of age, with markedly diminishing effects until about 4 to 6 years of age *(but never tapering off completely)*. However, this is a bit of an oversimplification. Different aspects of vision—color vision, form perception, motion perception, on so on—each have their own, slightly different critical period (Harwerth et al., 1986). One visual function may develop at a different rate than another (Fig. 9-2).

 *Key Point*

*Different visual functions have different critical periods. Visual experience affects the development of each of these visual functions at different times during infancy.*

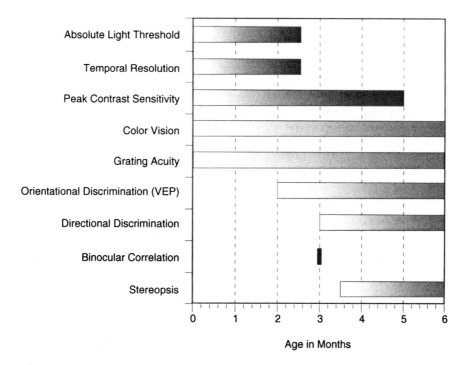

**Figure 9-2**  Although we tend to think of a single critical period of development, there are in fact multiple critical periods for different visual functions. Here, the time span of the critical period is shown from onset (light) tp offset (dark). Note that some critical periods last beyond the 6-month time period shown here. In general, functions whose processing is dependent mostly on retinal neurons are developed at an earlier age than cortically based functions. In addition, spatial vision and binocular vision take the longest time to develop, leaving them the most susceptible to the effects of abnormal visual inputs.

For example, the absolute threshold for detection of light when dark-adapted is mostly developed by approximately the first month after birth. Although absolute light thresholds under dark-adapted conditions are elevated in 1- to 3-month-old infants relative to adults (Hansen et al., 1986), the scotopic luminosity curve is adult-like in shape even at age 1 month, with a peak near 500 nm (Dobson, 1976). This indicates that the rhodopsin photopigment in the rods is already developed at this age. The scotopic sensitivity of an infant is lower than that of an adult simply because the photoreceptors are not yet shaped correctly and capture less light. The *photopic* luminosity curve of a 1-month-old infant, on the other hand, is adult-like in the middle- and long-wavelength portion, with elevated thresholds only in the short-wavelength portion of the curve. The entire photopic luminosity function matures by age 2 to 3 months.

Temporal resolution also develops rapidly. The critical flicker fusion frequency (CFF) of a 1-month-old infant is about 40 Hz. At 2 months of age, it increases to 50 Hz, and by 3 months, it is at approximately adult level of 60 Hz.

By age 2 months, infants can start to make some color discriminations based on wavelength, but these discriminations are not quite adult-like (Teller and Bornstein, 1987), as the short-wavelength (blue) color system is slower to develop (Adams et al., 1991). It is not until 6 months of age that infants exhibit trichromatic behavior.

Motion sensitivity develops rapidly as well. If you measure the responses to changes in direction of moving dots with a VEP method, infants can detect changes in direction as young as 10 to 12 weeks of age (Wattam-Bell, 1991). In summary, light, color, and motion perception have developed fairly early in infancy.

## THE DEVELOPMENT OF SPATIAL VISION

Most research on visual development has concentrated on the development of visual acuity and spatial contrast sensitivity. Estimates of visual acuity in young infants can be obtained rapidly with **sweep visual-evoked potentials (VEP)**, which present gratings of higher and higher spatial frequency in sequence (Norcia and Tyler, 1985). The highest spatial frequency that yields a recordable VEP is taken as the acuity limit. This is an *indirect* measurement because it tells us only that the infant's striate cortex has received a signal regarding the stimulus; that is, that the retina and striate cortex have functioning receptive fields small enough to resolve the test target. It does *not* mean that the rest of the infant's visual system can decode and *interpret* that information properly; therefore, we cannot know from VEP recordings if the infant really "sees" the stimulus, only that his or her brain has "received" it.

**CLINICAL APPLICATION** This distinction has important implications for the clinical presentation of cortical blindness. Children with congenital or acquired brain injury respond poorly or not at all to most visual stimuli and are considered "blind." However, VEP testing may record normal occipital lobe activity. In this case, the occipital area is disconnected from damaged extrastriate cortical areas, which then cannot act on the information provided.

**CLINICAL PROCEDURE** Behavioral measurements of acuity can be obtained with the **forced preferential looking** technique (Dobson and Teller, 1978). This test is based on the assumption that infants actively seek out contours to look at. Two stimulus fields are presented to an infant typically seated on a parent's lap. One field has a grating stimulus, and the other a homogeneous gray area of the same mean luminance as the grating field, indistinguishable from the background. With normal visual development, infants will look at the more interesting contours of the grating rather than the blank gray field. Centered between the two fields is a small peephole through which an observer views the infant. The observer watches the infant and judges which side the grating is on based on where the infant fixates. If the gratings are of low enough spatial frequency and above the infant's spatial resolution threshold, the infants will clearly prefer to look at the grating. At higher unresolvable spatial frequencies, the infant's direction of gaze will not show a preference for the grating but will be equally distributed between it and the blank gray field. A grating just beyond their resolution limit will look the same as a uniform gray field.

The commercially available **Teller Acuity Cards** are a clinical test of grating visual acuity in infants using the preferential looking technique.

Although both preferential looking and evoked-potential techniques tend to give slightly different acuity thresholds, they do show a common effect in that the rate of development of acuity measured with both tests is similar. Acuity tends to improve as a function of age in a semilogarithmic fashion; that is, initially for about every month of age, the infant's acuity doubles. Responses to stimuli as small as 1-minute arc (20/20) can be demonstrated with VEPs as early as 6 months of age (Norcia and Tyler, 1985). However, it usually requires 18 to 24 months to reach this level of acuity using behavioral methods such as the preferential looking technique.

During this same period, contrast sensitivity also develops. There is a change in the entire contrast sensitivity curve with age, in terms of both its shape and overall sensitivity level (Atkinson et al., 1977; Banks and Salapatek, 1978). At $2\frac{1}{2}$ months, contrast sensitivity is low at all spatial frequencies, and the contrast sensitivity function does not have a marked low-frequency rolloff as it does in adults; rather, it has a *low-pass* shape (Fig. 9-3). With age, the sensitivity increases, and a more dramatic low-frequency rolloff emerges; that is, the adult-like *bandpass* shape develops. The peak sensitivity shifts toward higher spatial frequencies, as does the high-spatial-frequency cutoff. What this means is that a very young infant does not see very well at all. An infant's view of the world is the equivalent of a diffused image, like looking through wax paper held over one's eyes.

 *Key Point*

*Light perception and color perception develop earlier than does spatial vision.*

Are there corresponding *anatomic* or *physiological* changes in the infant visual system? Anatomically, these changes have been studied in kittens, and it has been found that after about the first 3 to 4 weeks of life in kittens, the eye itself is nearly completely developed, but the visual cortex is still undergoing major changes, with the number and complexity of the interconnections between neurons steadily increasing. If the sensitivity of the neurons within the visual system is measured with physiological recordings, you see dramatic changes as the kitten ages. As the neurons mature, their center–surround antagonism becomes stronger, and the cells become more narrowly tuned to spatial frequency or size. Secondly, the receptive

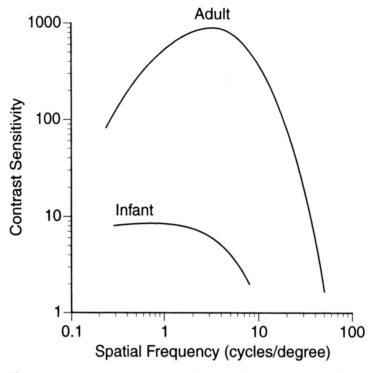

**Figure 9-3**    The contrast sensitivity function changes in shape and height with development. In infants, contrast sensitivity is low at all spatial frequencies, and the function is low pass in shape. In adults, the contrast sensitivity function reveals increased contrast sensitivity and a low-frequency rolloff, yielding a bandpass shape.

fields gradually become smaller with age, shifting the contrast sensitivity function to higher spatial frequencies. These changes correlate well with the development of visual acuity and contrast sensitivity during this same period.

## THE DEVELOPMENT OF BINOCULAR VISION

We have seen that different aspects of vision can develop at different times and at different rates, but how does binocular vision fit into this scheme? The basic pattern of retinal correspondence between the two eyes is determined before birth, so the newborn's visual system is somewhat ready to use the two eyes binocularly. However, at birth, muscular control of eye movements is not well developed, especially binocular coordination of the movements of the two eyes. The oculomotor system at first only loosely couples the movements of the two eyes; accurate binocular yoking of eye movements develops later and may possibly be partially learned (King and Zhou, 1998). This inaccuracy of binocular oculomotor coordination, though not pronounced enough to be noted by gross observation of an infant's eye movements in the clinic, still can result in intermittently diplopic images for the infant. If the critical period were to begin exactly at birth, the diplopia that the infant would experience from uncorrelated eye movements could have a strong detrimental influence on visual development, in particular the development of binocularity. This would almost certainly ensure that every infant would develop binocular visual problems. It would be advantageous for the visual system to wait, that is, to hold off the critical period for the development of binocularity until precise binocular extraocular muscular control could be exerted by the infant. This is, in fact, what happens. The critical period for binocular vision does not begin immediately at birth, and binocular vision takes months to begin to develop. For example, human infants do not develop amblyopia from the presence of cataracts or strabismus before 2 months of age.

**CLINICAL APPLICATION** | To prevent amblyopia, newborn infants should ideally be examined and treated for amblyogenic conditions during the first 2 months of life.

A major factor that delays the development of binocular vision is the development of the accommodative and vergence systems. In other words, if an infant is incapable of accommodating or converging accurately enough to get the left and right monocular retinal images of an object aligned onto corresponding points, then precise binocular vision is not possible or even necessary. The correspondence between points in each retina is programmed before birth so that the visual system is already capable at birth of registering the images in the two eyes to achieve sensory fusion; it is the oculomotor control needed for motor fusion that is the problem. Our question therefore has to be when can infants first accommodate and converge accurately enough so that the visual system is capable of taking advantage of two eyes together?

Even very young infants can demonstrate an avoidance response to a **looming target**, one that appears to be rapidly approaching the infant. For example, by about 8 weeks of age, infants consistently blink in response to a rapidly approaching ball. Curiously, if the infant is raised with a striped toy placed overhead above the crib, they develop this blinking reflex 3 weeks earlier than infants who do not. This has been explained by an accelerated development of the accommodative response evoked by the near toy.

Infants have been shown to have an accommodative response as early as 2 weeks old. However, although they can accommodate somewhat to a near target, this response is not at all accurate, in that their accommodative level does not match the accommodative demand of the object they are observing. This is not surprising, as the spatial resolution of the newborn infant's visual system is poor, and the depth of focus quite large; hence, changes in target clarity are not detectable (Banks, 1980). As the infant's spatial resolution develops further, the accuracy of accommodation improves until fairly accurate and consistent responses should be noted by 3 to 5 months of age.

Convergence, on the other hand, is not as well controlled by infants as is accommodation, although there is at least some association between accommodation and vergence in infants under 3 months of age. The eye movements of young infants are quite inaccurate. Some have even suggested that the two eyes' movements are not completely yoked in newborns (Guernsey, 1929), but this has been disputed (Schor, 1990). Even so, infants as young as 1 month of age can be shown to exhibit some vergence response in the proper direction (that is, a convergence rather than a divergence movement) to a near stimulus if you photograph and examine their corneal light reflexes (Aslin, 1977). At this age, the convergence responses are brief and are not closely matched to target speed. During the next 2 to 3 months of life, full convergence first occurs (Thorn et al., 1994). The ability to detect and make a consistent and accurate vergence response to the introduction of prism does not occur until about 6 months of age. In summary, vergence develops at the slowest rate of all eye movements.

The development of vergence responses is dependent on the development of fine oculomotor control, at least some relative depth judgments (to determine the direction of vergence movement to make), and spatially tuned receptive fields that can detect small ranges of disparities. Larger, spatially untuned receptive fields would yield larger Panum's areas that would tolerate larger vergence errors and would have poor stereoscopic discrimination (Birch et al., 1983). What this means is that we would expect infants to be poor at seeing stereoscopic depth until at least age 3 to 4 months, when eye muscle control and vergence have developed and receptive fields are beginning to become more finely tuned.

However, although this pattern of development is generally true, there is one surprising twist: Birch et al. (1983) have found that *fine* stereoacuity thresholds actually develop *before* infants can make extremely accurate vergence movements. That is, infants can have low stereothresholds even in the presence of relatively large vergence errors. This suggests that the development of stereoscopic vision is not held back completely by the rate of development of vergence, as we predicted; rather, its development is also limited by another factor. We return to this point shortly.

## PSYCHOPHYSICAL MEASURES OF THE DEVELOPMENT OF DEPTH PERCEPTION

If we are to measure the time course for the development of stereopsis in humans, we must first invent methods of determining if an infant can see depth or not. One commonly used method is by placing the infant on a **visual cliff** (Fig. 9-4), a specially constructed tabletop with a plexiglass cover on it (Gibson and Walk, 1960). On one side, there is a checkerboard pattern just beneath the glass, and on the other side there is a steep dropoff underneath the glass. The infant is placed at the border between these two sides, and the scientist observes if the infant crawls to the "shallow" side or to the "deep" side. If the infant in fact has depth perception, it will not crawl onto the potentially dangerous side (the side that

**Figure 9-4**  Depth perception in infants may be assessed using a visual cliff. Infants who avoid crossing the transparent cover onto the side with a large drop in depth are presumed to have some form of depth perception.

looks as if it might fall off). The problem with this technique is that there are also *monocular* cues to depth in the visual cliff. This experiment does not equivocally prove that an infant can necessarily detect *disparity*. Even so, research has shown that infants can use at least monocular cues to depth as early as 6 to 8 weeks of age, even before they can crawl about, by measuring the infant's heart rate when placed on the shallow or deep side of the plexiglass. The stress evoked from seeing a dropoff below it induces a faster heartbeat in the infant.

What about measurement of the ability to see disparity itself? Fox et al. (1976) presented a dynamic random-dot stereogram to infants in which a stereoscopic *contour* was present. The stereoscopic contour was made to move side to side, and the investigators watched if the infant's eyes tracked the movement of the contour. There were no monocular cues to the contour's motion; that is, the contour was cyclopean. By age $3\frac{1}{2}$ months, an infant could track a moving contour defined by 45- to 135-minute of disparity (Fox et al., 1980). What is fascinating about this is that the onset of binocular depth perception was *very abrupt*

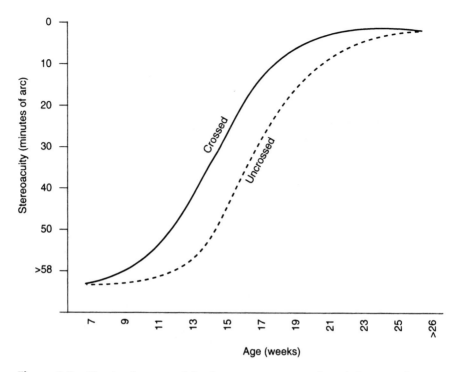

**Figure 9-5**    The development of depth perception occurs abruptly between the ages of 3 to 5 months of age. The ability to see crossed disparities develops slightly before the ability to see uncrossed disparities.

(Fig. 9-5). It was not present before age 3 months, and then suddenly the capability to see disparity appeared. In addition, the ability to see crossed disparities may develop a little earlier than does the ability to see uncrossed disparities (Birch et al., 1985). At the same time, infants become more accurate at reaching for objects in front of them. This makes sense in that it is more important for safety to detect an object moving toward oneself than one moving away.

After this initial development, the ability to see fine stereoscopic disparities develops very rapidly and reaches adult-like thresholds of under 1-minute arc a few weeks later (5 to 6 months of age). Surprisingly, although both stereoacuity and visual acuity depend on the development of finely tuned receptive fields, the ability to see stereoscopic disparity develops at a much faster pace than does form perception. Visual acuity does not reach adult levels that quickly. Stereoacuity is a **hyperacuity** (that is, it has thresholds of a few seconds of arc) like vernier acuity, and both stereoacuity and vernier acuity demonstrate a period of rapid development at about the same period in infancy (Held, 1988).

Other aspects of binocularity develop at about the same time as stereopsis. For example, infants do not exhibit adult-like binocular summation before stereopsis develops, but they do immediately afterward. Fusion and stereopsis develop in synchrony (Birch et al., 1985). In addition, once stereopsis develops, infants avoid rivalrous stimuli, finding them to be disconcerting; before then, infants may even prefer rivalrous stimuli (Shimojo et al., 1986). Stereopsis is first measurable in kittens at about the same age that the ocular dominance columns are fully segregated (LeVay et al., 1978), and it is likely that a similar correlation is found in human infants (Hickey and Peduzzi, 1987).

In summary, complete binocular vision is not present at birth. There is gross motor alignment but no convergence, fusion, or stereopsis. Over the first 3 to 5 months of life, binocularity develops, then stereopsis. Between $3\frac{1}{2}$ and 7 months, stereopsis can be demonstrated with random-dot stereograms.

# BINOCULAR DEVELOPMENT
# OF THE VISUAL SYSTEM

The development of spatial vision is accompanied by anatomic and physiological changes in the neurons of the visual system. The same is true for the development of binocularity. We review some of the animal data on the development of the visual system as it relates to binocular vision. Keep in mind, however, when we discuss the timetable of development, that different species develop at different rates. For example, monkeys develop at four times the rate of humans—1 month of monkey infant development equals 4 months of a human infant's development. Kittens develop even faster once their eyelids open, but their eyes remain fused shut after birth for several days. Although many early studies of binocular visual neuron development focused on kittens, scientists have found that the development of vision in cats differs in some important ways from that in primates. We therefore discuss studies using monkeys whenever possible because of the similarity of their visual systems to those of humans.

It was noted in the previous chapter that the anatomic structures of the optic chiasm, LGN, and layer 4C of striate cortex were designed to bring corresponding retinal points together for combination into binocular cells in striate cortex. These structures all essentially complete their anatomic development in the monkey prenatally or shortly after birth (for example, see Rakic, 1976). In monkeys, there are no clear-cut ocular dominance columns at birth; although ocular dominance columns start to develop prenatally, at first there is nearly total overlap of dendritic projections onto each eye's inputs into layer 4C (Fig. 9-6). The left eye and right eye inputs project equally onto the same cortical cells in layer 4C for at least 3 to 4 weeks after birth (Wiesel and Hubel, 1974; Rakic, 1976). This overlap of information from the two eyes within layer 4C prevents the existence of binocularity and stereopsis, as the cells outside of layer 4C destined to become binocular cells then receive two inputs *each with mixed information from both eyes,* rather than two inputs with distinct left- and right-eye information.

The dendritic trees of LGN cell axons then shrink (and their numerous axon terminals synapsing in layer 4C start to get pruned off), reducing the overlap of each eye's inputs into layer 4C. By age 4 to 6 weeks in the monkey, the left- and right-eye afferents to visual cortex have atrophied enough to completely segregate and synapse onto separate cells in independent ocular dominance columns

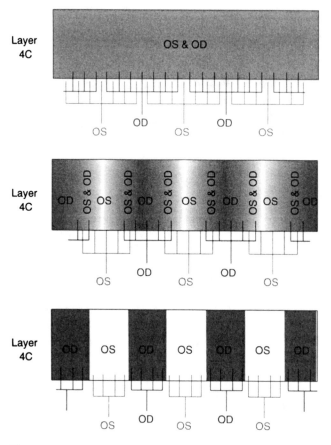

**Figure 9-6**   In normal animals, at first there is intermingling of the inputs to striate cortex from the right and left eyes. During development, the axon terminals of these inputs are pruned so that their overlap diminishes and is eventually eliminated, resulting in segregation of the monocular inputs into ocular dominance columns.

(LeVay et al., 1980). This roughly corresponds to the age at which stereopsis appears in infant monkeys, as well as the age at which binocular responses can be obtained by single-unit recordings of striate cortical cells outside of layer 4C. This has led scientists to suggest that the limiting factor on the development of stereopsis in infants is the development of clear-cut ocular dominance columns and functional binocular cells. Taking into account the overall slower rate of development in humans, human infants would develop ocular dominance columns and binocular cells by about 4 to 6 months, which, as we saw earlier, corresponds to the age range at which stereopsis does emerge in infants.

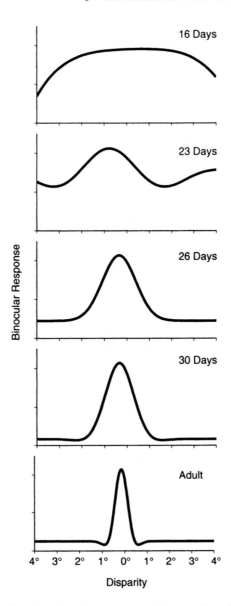

**Figure 9-7** In young kittens, disparity-selective neurons exist but are broadly tuned for disparity, that is, unselective for any given disparity. With age, the tuning bandwidth of the disparity detectors narrows until they are selective for a specific range of disparities. (Curves fitted to the data of Pettigrew, 1974.)

Although cortical cells can respond to binocular stimulation, this does not necessarily mean that they are tuned for binocular disparity. Although little data are available about this, it is known that in kittens, binocular disparity-detecting neurons are totally untuned at first. The neurons respond with the same level of activity to an extremely wide range of disparities. However, with time, the tuning of these neurons becomes increasingly specific for a given narrow set of disparities (Fig. 9-7) (Freeman and Ohzawa, 1992). This increasingly narrow disparity tuning allows an infant to discriminate finer and finer disparities.

# ABNORMALITIES OF BINOCULAR VISION

As we have seen, dramatic changes in the human visual system occur during the first few months after birth. During this critical period, the rapid rate of development provides a greater potential for abnormalities of visual development to occur compared to any other time in life. Infants are therefore extremely susceptible to severe visual disorders arising from inadequate visual experience during the critical period.

**CLINICAL PROCEDURE** | Amblyopia is caused by abnormal visual experience during the critical period of development in infancy. The **case history** for an amblyopic child should focus on the development of the child and the presence of **amblyogenic factors** during infancy.

How can we determine the influence of abnormal visual experience on human binocular visual development? We cannot perform the same experiments on humans that we can on animals, but we can take advantage of individuals who have had abnormal visual experience during various stages of life and study their vision to see the final outcome of abnormal development. One drawback to this approach, however, is that we cannot explore how the changes in the visual systems of these individuals occur *chronologically*.

What has been learned is that deprivation of visual input has a very powerful effect. Visual capabilities either are arrested in their development, deteriorate, or never develop (which exactly occurs is difficult to distinguish when one can examine only the outcome of the deprivation). Deprivation affects *many* aspects of vision.

---

## ⚷━ Key Point

*Just as normal visual experience helps the visual system develop properly during the critical period, abnormal visual experience during this same time can disrupt normal development and cause vision disorders.*

Remember again that *there are several critical periods*. The length of the critical period differs with the aspect of vision being examined. In monkeys, the critical period for spectral sensitivity (luminosity) functions is from 3 to 6 months of age, for spatial vision until age 25 months, and for binocular vision longer than 25 months. Therefore, each visual function is differentially susceptible to changes in the visual environment at different times during infancy. Deprivation is more likely to disrupt functions whose critical periods are long lasting, such as spatial vision or binocularity, rather than functions whose critical period is short and completed early in infancy, such as color vision. In addition, because the small, high-spatial-frequency-specific neurons responsible for visual acuity develop more slowly than the larger, low-spatial-frequency-tuned cells, they are more susceptible to the effects of deprivation, leading to reductions in spatial resolution.

**CLINICAL APPLICATION** | Abnormal visual experience is more likely to disrupt spatial vision and binocularity, which have longer critical periods. Therefore, as we will see, abnormal development leads to the classical clinical problems of **amblyopia** and **strabismus:** abnormal acuity and space perception and stereoblindness.

Abnormal visual development of spatial vision results in **amblyopia**, decreased visual acuity that can not be attributed to uncorrected refractive error or ocular pathology. Classically, amblyopia is defined as reduced acuity in one eye below $^{20}/_{40}$, with at least two lines difference in Snellen acuity between the two eyes. It is now known that this definition is not precisely accurate; we discuss this shortly. What is important for now is that amblyopia is a reduction in visual function caused by abnormal visual experience during development. Amblyopia represents direct evidence for the influence of environmental factors on the development of vision.

Amblyopia is not really a single disorder. There are several categories of amblyopia, each caused by a different amblyogenic factor (that is, a process that puts one at risk for amblyopia):

• Strabismic amblyopia
• Anisometropic amblyopia
• Refractive amblyopia
• Stimulus deprivation amblyopia
• Meridional amblyopia

The type of amblyopia is related to the history of the individual and is typically classified by the **etiology** of the abnormal visual development, although recent research suggests that amblyopia might be more correctly classified in terms of the visual and oculomotor disturbances noted (McKee et al., 1992). **Strabismic amblyopia** refers to amblyopia that is associated with the presence of strabismus, typically either esotropia or exotropia. The strabismus is unilateral and constant, so there is one "good" (nonamblyopic) eye and one "bad" (amblyopic) eye. In almost all cases, the strabismus can be traced back to infancy or early childhood. Old photographs can be quite helpful in determining the age of onset of the strabismus.

**CLINICAL APPLICATION** | Premature and low-birth-weight infants are at four to six times greater risk for development of strabismus and therefore strabismic amblyopia. At-risk infants should be tested for the presence of strabismus and amblyopia during infancy.

**CLINICAL APPLICATION** | How does age of onset of the strabismus affect the likelihood of developing a strabismic amblyopia? A strabismus that occurs after the critical period or in adulthood will not lead to amblyopia. The adult-onset strabismic patient will have constant **diplopia** because suppression of one eye is difficult at this age, but both eyes will retain good acuities. However, if a constant unilateral strabismus emerges between birth and 3 years of age and continues until 5 to 7 years of age, the strabismic eye will develop amblyopia. The strabismic eye also shows a pronounced, deep **constant suppression** of at least the central visual field. Patients with this condition have experienced abnormal form or pattern vision during the development of their visual systems as a result of the strabismus. Surgery and/or orthoptics (depending on the particular patient) might result in the patient maximizing whatever function remains, but it will not likely restore *all* lost function.

**Anisometropic amblyopia** is amblyopia caused by significant *unequal* refractive errors between the two eyes. One eye tends to be favored and takes up the role of controlling the degree of accommodation, while the other eye, because of consensual accommodation, has a constantly defocused retinal image. The blurred eye never receives a sharp patterned retinal image, resulting in abnormal development of visual acuity and spatial contrast sensitivity. Another related type of amblyopia is called **refractive or isoametropic amblyopia**. Here, the two eyes may have equal refractive errors, but they are either extremely myopic (more than $-6$ D to $-9$ D) or hyperopic (more than $+4$ D). In this case, neither eye receives a good focused image, and the result is acuity loss in each eye, a *bilateral* amblyopia. This is the exception to the original definition given for amblyopia in which only one eye has an acuity loss, but because it is bilateral, there is usually less acuity loss than in other types of amblyopia.

**CLINICAL APPLICATION** | Because high hyperopia can also induce an **accommodative esotropia**, it is important to determine the refractive error of infants and correct any significant hyperopia. However, the correction of high refractive errors, whether uniocular (anisometropia) or biocular (isoametropia), is not straightforward, as there are two somewhat conflicting constraints on refractive correction in infants. The infant must be provided a sharp retinal image to prevent further form deprivation as well as to start reversing the effects of the deprivation and equalizing the function of the two eyes. However, during the critical period infants undergo the process of **emmetropization**, which will tend to reduce or remove the refractive error. Recent studies suggest that fully correcting a high refractive error during this period may disrupt the emmetropization process by removing the image blur that serves as a feedback mechanism for eye growth (McBrien et al., 1999). This leaves the infant with a permanent high refractive error roughly equal in power to the corrective lens used; that is, emmetropization compensates for the corrective lens power rather than the refractive error already present. Partial correction of hyperopia in infants may not impede emmetropization (Atkinson et al., 1996).

The contrast sensitivity function of a strabismic or anisometropic amblyopic eye reflects the severity of the amblyopia (Hess and Howell, 1977). Less severe amblyopia results in contrast sensitivity losses only at high spatial frequencies. Deeper amblyopia results in losses in sensitivity across all frequencies but still more pronounced at higher spatial frequencies. This is the type of amblyopia seen in individuals with very early onset (and longer durations) of strabismus or anisometropia. In the most severe cases of amblyopia, the contrast-processing deficit is marked, and the patient can barely see contours at all with the amblyopic eye. This subgroup of amblyopes typically has had more serious visual abnormalities during infancy, as we discuss shortly.

Scientists investigating amblyopia have concluded that strabismic and anisometropic amblyopia are fundamentally different disorders. One early argument given for this difference was that contrast sensitivity and hyperacuity are affected to different degrees in strabismic and anisometropic amblyopes. Strabismic amblyopes tend to exhibit severe **spatial distortions** and misperceptions not seen in anisometropic amblyopes (Bedell and Flom, 1981). Objects, including visual acuity letter targets, look "scrambled" with the amblyopic eye. In other words, strabismic amblyopes do not just have problems resolving high spatial frequencies and detecting low contrast, as do anisometropic amblyopes. Strabismic amblyopes also have confusion of their representation of visual space, resulting in perceived distortions similar to metamorphopsia. This disrupts hyperacuity and Snellen acuity more than grating acuity (Levi and Klein, 1983). In fact, grating acuity may not be degraded at all in some mild strabismic amblyopes, even though Snellen acuity is reduced. Grating acuity is affected to a lesser degree than Snellen acuity because as a homogeneous, repetitive stimulus pattern, the grating remains detectable despite the distortions that make Snellen letters indistinguishable (Levi and Klein, 1982; Levi et al., 1994). In anisometropes, Snellen and grating acuity are degraded to the same degree.

Another difference between strabismic and anisometropic amblyopes is the extent of the visual field over which their spatial vision is degraded. In strabismic amblyopia, the reduction in contrast sensitivity is limited to the central visual field, the region at which their **suppression scotoma** exists. In anisometropic amblyopia, the contrast-processing deficit persists throughout the entire visual field, even in the retinal periphery (Hess and Pointer, 1985).

The cause of the spatial distortions is a hot topic of debate among scientists. There is some evidence that they may be caused by a **disorganization of retinotopic mapping** as a result of uncertainty about the position of each receptive field (Hess and Field, 1994). However, the neurophysiological basis for such a positional uncertainty has not been clearly stated. A compelling argument posed by the research of Levi et al. (1987) is that **spatial undersampling** produces these distortions. If receptive fields are too coarsely spaced to adequately sample a high-spatial-frequency retinal image (that is, the image is undersampled by the receptive fields), false low frequencies are introduced into the representation of that image, a process called **spatial aliasing** that distorts the representation of that image. This occurs in the normal peripheral retina, where receptive fields are larger and farther apart than in the fovea. It also happens in amblyopia, in which small receptive fields are not functioning; the dropout of small receptive fields increases the spacing between neighboring receptive fields, leading to undersampling and aliasing.

Whatever the cause of these distortions, they cause the amblyopic eye to make erroneous judgments about the positions of objects in space (see Fig. 9-8) (Bedell and Flom, 1981). When spatial distortions are coupled with the typical erratic eye movements of amblyopes, strabismic amblyopes see the world with their amblyopic eye as a place where objects in particular parts of the visual field are constantly changing shape and position. The severity and field location of this spatial distortion can be mapped with a **bisection hyperacuity task** using lines or dots at various separations in different parts of the visual field.

 *Key Point*

*In anisometropic amblyopes, grating acuity, Snellen acuity, and hyperacuity are affected to the same degree. The common mechanism for these losses is a decrease in contrast sensitivity. Hyperacuity and Snellen acuity are affected to a greater degree than grating acuity in strabismic amblyopia because of the additional presence of spatial distortions, which may be attributable to either spatial undersampling or scrambling of strict retinotopic mapping.*

**CLINICAL APPLICATION**

Patients with strabismic amblyopia will also experience **crowding effects** in which neighboring contours interfere with the visibility of the target stimulus. This phenomenon is manifested clinically by the differences in visual acuity determined by single-letter, whole-line, and whole-chart presentations. A significantly better visual acuity can be obtained in many strabismic amblyopes with isolated letters or symbols as opposed to displays containing multiple letters or symbols. Although these effects can be induced in normal subjects with extremely fine contours, crowding effects are much more noticeable and troubling in amblyopes because of their lower acuity. In order to minimize crowding effects, acuity in amblyopes is also measured with isolated **single letters** on the Snellen chart.

**Figure 9-8**   Idealized views of the world as perceived by amblyopes. **A:** Actual image. **B:** The ani-sometropic amblyope perceives the world as blurred and of reduced contrast throughout the visual field be-cause of "neural blurring" or the inability to process high-spatial-frequency information. and reduced con-trast sensitivity. **C:** The strabismic amblyope in addition perceives the central visual field as "scrambled" as a result of spatial undersampling and distortions of retinotopic mapping.

In most cases, color vision, dark adaptation, the scotopic and photopic luminosity functions, glare recovery, and temporal vision will be unaffected by amblyopia. There are two reasons for this. First, problems with these aspects of vision are often tied to pathological conditions of the retina. Amblyopia is not retinal in origin. If such deficits occur, they can usually be attributed to a secondary abnormal process or to stimulus deprivation amblyopia, discussed below. Second, the critical periods for these functions occur extremely early and end early as well, making them less likely to be affected by disruption of the visual environment.

Surprisingly, unlike other aspects of temporal vision, motion perception has been shown to be abnormal in amblyopia (Steinman et al., 1988). However, this deficit occurs only with low-velocity stimuli. Because amblyopia preferentially affects high spatial frequencies, which are processed by small receptive fields, it should be expected that low velocities of motion, also encoded by small receptive fields, should be similarly affected by amblyopia. In fact, the deeper the amblyopia (the worse the visual acuity), the greater the range of velocities at which motion perception is disrupted.

**Stimulus deprivation amblyopia** occurs in patients with a constant obstruction in the image formation mechanism of the eye, such as congenital or traumatic cataracts, congenital ptosis, or congenital or traumatic corneal opacities that were left untreated for some time (Garzia and Nicholson, 1991). Even short periods of deprivation at an early age can cause severe visual loss. During the occlusion of vision, a clear patterned retinal image is never formed, creating **pattern deprivation**, which produces more profound effects on the visual acuity and contrast sensitivity than the milder image degradation produced by strabismus or anisometropia. Amblyopia with acuity worse than about $^{20}/_{200}$ is often traced to stimulus deprivation, and stimulus deprivation may also produce abnormalities of light sensitivity and color vision, functions that are typically spared in strabismic and anisometropic amblyopia. This suggests that deprivation amblyopia involves mechanisms in addition to those of milder forms of amblyopia. Furthermore, unilateral deprivation is much more devastating than the bilateral form. In this case, in addition to the detrimental effects of deprivation, there is an additional amblyogenic contribution from abnormal binocular interaction.

**CLINICAL APPLICATION**

Conventional wisdom is that it is not effective to treat an amblyope older than 7 years of age. This is not true. Even if you can not fully restore normal acuity to the amblyopic eye with lenses, occlusion, and vision therapy, you can still maximize whatever function that eye does have. Even if you can not "cure" a given amblyope, vision therapy can help stabilize their eye movements, improve their accommodative skills, and reduce spatial misperceptions, so that the patient can achieve the best possible acuity that the amblyopic eye can get. In summary, even when the amblyopia is not totally reversible, the clinician has a responsibility to help the patient to restore the highest possible function.

Another kind of amblyopia that is subtler is called **meridional amblyopia**, which is caused by pronounced astigmatic refractive errors. An infant with very high astigmatism has one meridian blurred while the orthogonal meridian is in focus. Even this *subtle* type of deprivation will produce an amblyopia *along the blurred astigmatic meridian only,* even with full astigmatic correction later in life. Astigmatism can lead to meridional amblyopia if it remains uncorrected after 2 years of age.

**CLINICAL APPLICATION**
A child with meridional amblyopia will show much lower acuities and contrast sensitivities for targets in that orientation as compared with other orientations. For example, a patient who had a large oblique astigmatism during infancy might read the Es on the Snellen chart more easily than the Vs or Ws, which contain obliquely-oriented lines, even after full astigmatic correction. Meridional amblyopia is not untreatable. The authors have seen a patient who had had uncorrected high-monocular astigmatism treated with a balance lens his entire life, with no depth perception. After the patient's astigmatism was finally corrected, he stood up, looked down at his feet and remarked, "I'd never noticed my feet being above the floor like that before."

Amblyopia, although defined clinically as decreased visual acuity caused by abnormal development, encompasses visual deficits beyond just a loss of acuity. We alluded to this when we discussed spatial distortion and aliasing, crowding effects, and motion perception deficits in amblyopia. Amblyopes may also use an eccentric retinal locus other than the fovea of the strabismic eye to fixate objects when the nonamblyopic eye is occluded. This condition is known as **eccentric fixation**. This eccentric point serves as their primary visual direction reference. These anomalies are *monocular* deficits resulting from the abnormal binocular experience leading to amblyopia.

However, distinctly binocular visual deficits exist in amblyopia as well. Amblyopes demonstrate abnormal stereopsis; they either lack stereoscopic vision (**stereoblindness**) or possess only residual stereopsis. Some of their loss of binocularity may be accounted for by the inequality of the image quality in the two eyes (that is, lowered binocular summation because of unequal stimulus strengths in each eye), but an additional degrading factor is also in play, an accentuated form of binocular suppression known as a **suppression scotoma**. The contribution of a given retinal locus in one eye to the combined binocular percept is actually *inhibited*; although this locus may be somewhat capable of processing visual information under monocular conditions, it is effectively "shut off" under binocular conditions. In some cases, local stereopsis at the fovea may be lost, with an accompanying loss of stereoacuity, but peripheral global stereopsis may still be retained.

**CLINICAL APPLICATION**
The monocular and binocular visual deficits seen in amblyopia are part of a *continuum* of binocular visual problems resulting from abnormal development during infancy. Amblyopia, in effect, represents the most severe deficit. However, it is possible for an infant to develop *strabismus without amblyopia,*

such as in an alternating strabismus. In this case, binocular anomalies may occur without accompanying monocular deficits in the strabismic eye. These patients may exhibit stereoscopic deficits such as stereoblindness or reduced stereopsis without a suppression scotoma or amblyopia. In milder cases, patients may only possess **stereoanomalies** such as a reduced ability to see crossed or uncrossed disparities alone or an inability to see stereomotion in one direction only; these anomalies may occur throughout the visual field or may be restricted to particular field locations.

Finally, one more phenomenon may indicate abnormal binocular development. During the development of binocular vision, there is a simultaneous development of correlated eye movements. The ability to see stereomotion in a direction toward or away from you develops concurrently with the ability to make balanced binasal and bitemporal optokinetic nystagmus (OKN) and pursuit eye movements; accurate binasal and bitemporal eye movements are needed to keep vergence alignment during stereomotion. In very young infants, monocular nasal and temporal OKN or pursuit does not develop at the same rate, resulting in a **nasotemporal OKN or pursuit asymmetry;** that is, nasal eye movements in each eye are of a higher gain than their temporal counterparts to equal velocities of stimulus motion. By the time stereopsis develops, this asymmetry disappears, and infants can make nasal and temporal eye movements equally accurately.

However, patients with anomalous binocular vision of childhood (strabismus) continue to exhibit this nasotemporal OKN asymmetry. The asymmetry occurs equally for nasotemporal stimulation of either eye.

 *Key Point*

*As normal binocular development of the visual cortex progresses during infancy, the deficit disappears. Conversely, when the normal development pattern of the visual system is interrupted, the asymmetry persists.*

The asymmetry was thought to arise from the loss or reduction of stimulation of the pretectum by afferent fibers from binocular cells in the visual cortex. However, recent research suggests that the nasotemporal OKN asymmetry is the result of abnormal oculomotor control and motion perception in strabismus rather than the disruption of binocularity (Fawcett et al., 1998).

**CLINICAL APPLICATION** | Although amblyopia is defined clinically by a loss of *acuity,* amblyopes actually tend to have other visual problems than just a loss of acuity, including eye movement anomalies, poor stereopsis or stereoblindness, inaccurate accommodation, distortions of spatial perception, and abnormal motion perception.

## ANIMAL RESEARCH ON VISUAL DEPRIVATION

Amblyopia is a **neural deficit**, not an optical problem. Even after spectacle correction has been provided for an amblyopic patient, the best corrected acuity is still subnormal. What is the neural abnormality that produces this? The anatomic and physiological mechanisms of the development of amblyopia after visual deprivation have been studied in animals by inducing amblyogenic factors artificially. For example, infant animals can be reared with **artificial strabismus**, induced either by optical prisms or by surgically sectioning the extraocular muscles, producing the same visual perception and oculomotor defects noted in human amblyopes. The same is true for anisometropic amblyopia, where the animal is raised wearing a high-power plus lens on one eye or with **atropine** applied to one eye to paralyze accommodation in that eye relative to the other. Aniseikonia can be induced with a **size lens**. Stimulus deprivation amblyopia is created by **suturing the eyelids** of kittens to produce an effect similar to a very dense cataract. Later, when the lids are parted, the kitten will have a very severe amblyopia. Similar deprivation effects are seen in monkeys, though less severe. The difference may be related to cats having dense lids as compared with the thinner lids of young monkeys; thus, more pattern stimulation reaches the retina of the monkey through the closed lids. Meridional amblyopia has been produced in animals by rearing them in **special environments**, such as in a drum with stripes of only one orientation, and keeping the animal from changing the orientation of its head relative to the stripes.

Producing the same types of amblyopia in animals that occurs in human patients provides an opportunity to do anatomic and physiological studies of amblyopia. We can directly answer the question of how abnormal visual experience perturbs the development of the visual system and determine the effect abnormal visual experience has at different ages to map out the duration of the critical period. Finally, we can attempt to treat the results of the deprivation and examine the efficacy of that treatment.

The effects of visual deprivation are most severe in the visual cortex, so our discussion will start there.

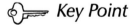 *Key Point*

*The neurophysiological and anatomic effects of amblyopia are most pronounced in striate cortex.*

Let us first consider **stimulus deprivation amblyopia**. Although stimulus deprivation amblyopia is a rare form of naturally occurring amblyopia, it is easy to produce artificially, and therefore many research studies were conducted with deprived animals. In most experiments, a kitten is reared with one or both eyelids

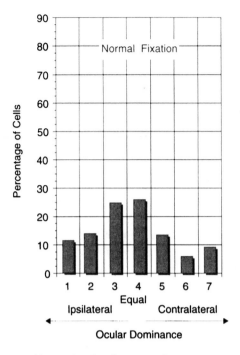

**Figure 9-9**    In animals with normal binocular development, the striate cortex contains mostly binocularly responsive visual neurons (ocular dominance categories 2 to 6), with few purely monocular neurons (1 and 7).

sutured shut from birth until 4 to 5 months of age. The lids are then parted, and responses of cortical cells of the animal are recorded.

Two properties of normal cortical cells are that they are sensitive to orientation and many of them are driven binocularly. For normal animals, we can plot an **ocular dominance histogram** for cortical cells that depicts the degree of response of cortical cells to stimulation of the left or right eyes (Fig. 9-9). The histogram, first used by Hubel and Wiesel (1962), is composed of seven categories, each reflecting a different degree of response to one eye or the other. Category 1 represents *monocular* cells that can only be driven by stimulation of the ipsilateral eye, while category seven contains cells driven only by the contralateral eye. Category 4 is marked by cells that respond equally to stimulation of each eye. The remaining categories also respond to both eyes, that is, contain *binocular* cells, but the response is greater for one eye than the other, that is, an *ocular dominance* is shown. In the monkey, 72% of striate cortical cells are binocular; that is, they fall into categories 2 through 6. This categorization has been found to be flawed in that category 1 and 7 cells are not really exclusively monocular; they can exhibit binocular subthreshold summation under some testing conditions, and so the proportion of cells in V1 that are binocular may be even higher. However, the

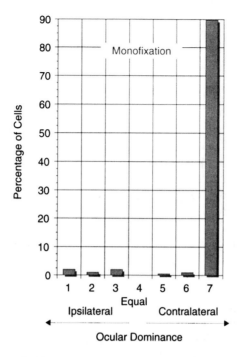

**Figure 9-10** Following monocular deprivation, most striate cortical neurons are monocularly driven by the nondeprived eye. There is an almost total loss of binocularly responsive neurons.

classification is still useful for determining the effects of abnormal visual experience on the binocularity of visual cortex.

The majority of the cells in a normal cat are binocular, driven by stimulation of either eye. If an animal is reared with the right eyelid sutured during early development (Fig. 9-10), the ocular dominance histogram reveals that very few cells are driven by the right (deprived) eye. By far, the majority of the cells are driven by the nondeprived (left) eye. Thus, **monocular deprivation** has had a very powerful effect on the binocularity of cortical cells. This is to be expected; the ocular dominance histogram is simply reflecting the reduced ability of the amblyopic eye to drive cortical cells. This is why contrast sensitivity and visual acuity are reduced in the amblyopic eye. The concurrent loss of binocularly driven cells leads to a loss of binocularity and stereopsis.

The key to the development of amblyopia following monocular deprivation is that disrupting the formation of simultaneous clear images to corresponding retinal locations in the two eyes leads to degradation of vision. Amblyopia will develop no matter how simultaneous clear images are disrupted, whether it is blurring one eye's image (anisometropia), diffusing or blocking one eye's image (stimulus deprivation), or placing confusing nonidentical stimuli on corresponding points (strabismus). Both eyes must receive identical, focused images to develop proper visual acuity and binocularity. The same shifts in ocular dominance that occur with monocular lid sutures in kittens can be demonstrated with artificially strabismic monkeys whose haploscopic views of the world have been dissociated by prisms (Baker et al., 1974) because the monkeys' developing binocular cells never receive simultaneous strong inputs from both eyes.

The effects of monocular deprivation may also be seen in the pattern of ocular dominance columns in layer 4C of striate cortex in both kittens and monkeys. In the normal animal, equal numbers of monocular cells in layer 4C receive input from the left eye and the right eye. The widths of the left eye and right eye ocular dominance columns are equal (Fig. 9-11) (Hubel and Wiesel, 1962). However, in animals that have experienced monocular deprivation, this is no longer true; in these animals, fewer inputs remain for the deprived eye. The visual cortex *reorganizes itself* in such a way that the width of the deprived eye's ocular dominance columns shrinks, with a corresponding increase in width of the nondeprived eye's columns (LeVay et al., 1980).

The mechanism for the reorganization of striate cortex following monocular deprivation is simply the same process of axonal growth and pruning that occurs in the normal development of ocular dominance columns (refer back to Fig. 9-6). Remember that, at first, the left and right eye inputs into layer 4C overlap totally, but with time these inputs are pruned back until there is no overlap. With monocular deprivation (Fig. 9-12), the neurons serving the deprived eye also show smaller and sparser dendritic branching, as their dendrites atrophy more than do those of the nondeprived eye during development of the ocular dominance columns. The result is a narrower zone of cells receiving input from the deprived eye, that is, narrower ocular dominance columns for the deprived eye. The nondeprived eye's inputs, which are not pruned back as much, remain plentiful, and the ocular dominance column of the nondeprived eye remains wide. Although the basic structure of the ocular dominance columns is innate, existing even before eye opening at age 3 weeks in kittens, proper binocular experience is needed for maintaining the equal representation of each eye and the responsiveness of cortical neurons to each eye (Crair et al., 1998).

What happens to the vision in the deprived eye? Because neurons from that eye now feed into striate cortex binocular cells to a lesser degree, the deprived eye is now less capable of stimulating binocular cells. This means that the deprived eye has relatively less function and has a weaker input relative to the good eye. Binocular vision is compromised as that eyes input is weakened. In other words, this eye has **amblyopia**.

What if we were to deprive *both* eyes, that is, perform **binocular deprivation**? After rearing of a kitten with both eyelids sutured, the result is a *normal* ocular dominance histogram (Fig. 9-13). Why would this happen? Would you expect that, if both eyes were deprived, no cortical cells would respond well to stimulation of either eye? After all, neither eye is receiving normal visual experience. It is therefore unexpected that depriving both eyes would produce less

A
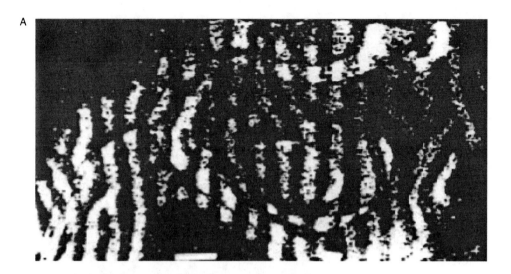

B
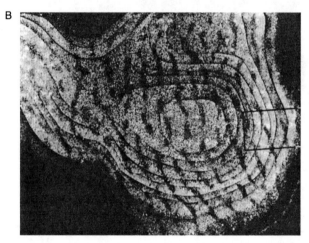

**Figure 9-11**   Ocular dominance columns may be visualized by injecting the vitreous of one eye with a radioactive protein that is transported through the visual pathways to the striate cortex. **A:** Slices through layer 4 of striate cortex in normal animals will show equally wide alternating zebra-like stripes of light and dark, indicating the monocular inputs from the injected and noninjected eyes. **B:** In monocularly deprived animals, the ocular dominance columns of the deprived eye are greatly narrowed, reflecting the reduced number of cortical cells responding to stimulation of that eye. Conversely, the ocular dominance columns of the nondeprived eye are now relatively wider. (Photographs from Hubel et al., 1976. Used by permission of the authors.)

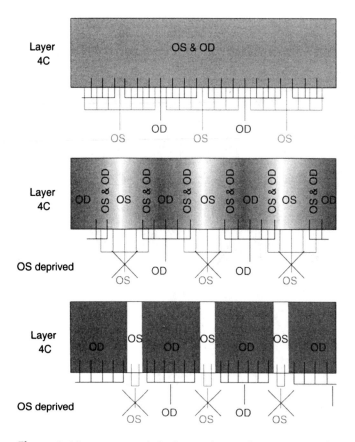

**Figure 9-12** In monocularly deprived animals, axon terminals of monocular inputs to striate cortex are pruned just as in normal animals. However, the axon terminals from the deprived eye are pruned to a greater degree, and those of the nondeprived eye to a lesser degree. The result is a narrowing of the ocular dominance columns of the deprived eye and a widening of those of the non-deprived eye.

effect on the ocular dominance histogram than depriving only one eye (Wiesel and Hubel, 1965).

However, there is another factor at play here. One way of interpreting this normal-looking ocular dominance distribution following binocular deprivation is by using the concept of **binocular competition**. A computer scientist named Hebb first postulated when dealing with mathematical models of neural networks that the development and retention of connections between neurons are determined by how much those connections are used; that is, a connection between neuron A and neuron B is determined by the strength of the signal from neuron A onto neuron B. If that signal is strong, the synapse is retained; if not, it deteriorates. In other words, "use it or lose it."

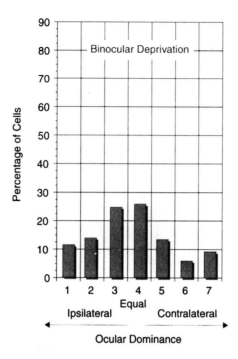

**Figure 9-13**    Binocular deprivation does not affect the overall ocular dominance distribution. However, the majority of visual neurons are relatively unresponsive or possess untuned spatial properties.

The idea behind binocular competition is that inputs from the two eyes *compete* for synapses or connectivity onto cortical binocular neurons. During development, the number and strength of the synaptic connections that form on a given binocular neuron depend on the strengths of the monocular inputs onto that cell. As an example, two monocular cells synapse onto one binocular cell (Fig. 9-14). If the activity from both input cells is high, both cells will retain strong synaptic connections with the binocular cell. The cell receiving inputs from the two eyes will be easily driven by stimulation of either eye; it will remain binocular. However, if only one input cell has high activity and the other does not, the cell with the stronger input to the binocular neuron will retain a strong synaptic connection. The weaker input cell will eventually lose its connection to the binocular cell, and the eye of origin of the weaker input cell will be less able to evoke responses in visual cortex later. The cell that should have developed to be a binocular cell now responds only to stimulation of a *single* eye; binocularity is lost.

This is the mechanism for the occurrence of amblyopia during development of the visual cortex. When both eyes receive normal visual experience, neither eye has a synaptic advantage over the other, and both end up having an equal ability to drive binocular cortical cells. However, if you place one eye at a **competitive disadvantage** (you have a stronger eye and a weaker eye in terms of visual experience) via monocular deprivation, the stronger eye will dominate the cortical cell responses. The correlation of activity in the inputs to a binocular neuron is essen-

dLGN Neuron
from Blurred Eye

dLGN Neuron
from Clear Eye

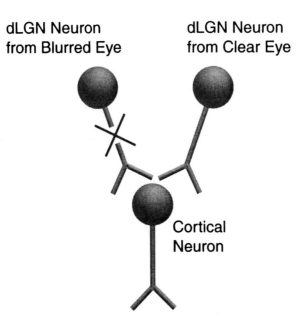

Cortical
Neuron

**Figure 9-14**   The Hebbian model states that binocular neural development is dependent on the receipt of simultaneous strong monocular inputs. If one monocular input is compromised through deprivation, the binocular cell fails to develop binocular responsiveness and is driven primarily by the nondeprived eye alone; that is, it becomes a monocularly driven cell.

tial for the development of disparity tuning in these neurons. If there is no correlation of the two eyes' images (i.e., clear, focused, and on corresponding locations simultaneously), only monocular cells will develop. With occasional interocular image correlation, only zero-disparity (tuned excitatory) cells will develop, but not the normal complement of cells tuned to different ranges of disparity.

In monocular deprivation, if you later focus the image in the formerly deprived eye or straighten it out, nothing much happens. The nondeprived eye, which had the competitive advantage during development, predominates and still tends to **suppress** the formerly deprived eye even when it is open. It has been suggested that the there is an *active* inhibition of the deprived eye by the nondeprived eye; however, enucleation of the nondeprived eye does not improve performance of the deprived eye (Harwerth et al., 1984).

The binocular competition model also explains the differing effects of monocular deprivation and binocular deprivation. If you deprive both eyes, there is *no imbalance* between the inputs from the two eyes, resulting in an unchanged normal ocular dominance histogram.

CLINICAL
APPLICATION

The critical period therefore has two consequences: (a) First of all, anything that can lead to poorer retinal image quality in one eye in an infant (so-called **amblyogenic factors**) must be diagnosed quickly before the infant loses binocular function. Low-birth-weight infants, primarily **premature infants**, are at *greater risk* for binocular vision problems. Premature infants have an even higher rate of strabismus than the general population. It may be related to the relatively immature stage of development of the premature infant's visual system at birth. (b) Treatment for losses of binocular function should be implemented early, while the infant is still within the critical period and its visual system is maximally modifiable or **plastic**.

How can we test for binocular visual abnormalities in infants during that period of development before it is too late to get the best results from therapy? Remember, we not only want to detect a developmental problem before it causes permanent loss of binocular function, but we also want to initiate treatment during that period while treatment can have its greatest effects. We must use special techniques to test the vision of infants. Among these techniques are photorefraction, forced-choice preferential looking (FPL), binocular beat VEPs, and motion-processing asymmetry.

## Photorefraction

A flash camera with a special lens is used to photograph the infant's eyes. The camera flash acts as a streak retinoscope, the camera photographing the image of the flash as it is refracted on entering and leaving the eye. Analyzing the image of the reflex allows for the detection of high refractive error or anisometropia, two of the risk factors for amblyopia. The light reflex also tells you if there is an opacity in the optical media of the eye, which could result in form vision deprivation. Finally, the position of the reflection of the flash off the corneal surface (corneal reflex), that is, the first Purkinje image typically observed in the **Hirschberg test**, tells you if there is a strabismus present. All in all, photorefraction can tell you if most of the risk factors for amblyopia are present or not in very young infants (Fig. 9-15), although it should not be substituted for retinoscopy.

## FPL with Stereo Gratings

Just as you can use the FPL technique to test acuity in infants, you can also use it to measure stereopsis if you use gratings with alternate stripes that have a binocular disparity (Fig. 9-16). In other words, you measure the infant's stereoacuity limit instead of a spatial resolution limit.

## Binocular Beat VEPs

Visual evoked potentials have the advantage of being objective tests of vision that require little cooperation from patients. This is useful when it comes to infants be-

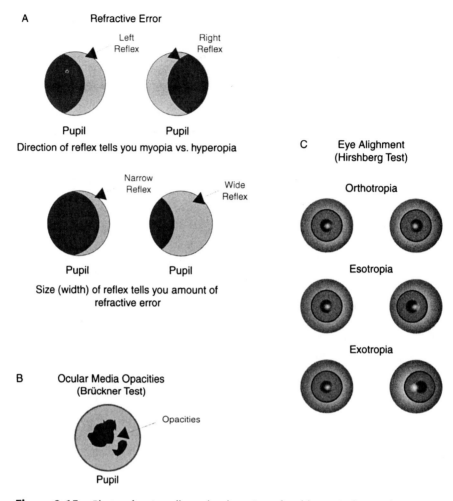

**Figure 9-15**  Photorefraction allows the detection of amblyogenic factors during infancy such as high refractive error, as evidenced by the narrowness and direction of the photorefractive reflex (**A**), opacities of the ocular media, seen as dark patches in the reflex (**B**), and strabismus, by the position of the first Purkinje image (Hirschberg test) (**C**).

cause sometimes even a little cooperation is still too much to ask from them. The binocular beat VEP technique developed by Baitch (Baitch et al., 1988) (see Fig, 8-9) requires so little cooperation to measure binocular summation that it can even be used on sleeping infants. Although the presence of binocular summation and fusion does not necessarily imply by itself that the infant will see stereoscopic depth, a lack of summation would definitely indicate a binocular vision problem that would preclude depth perception. Therefore, the beat VEP can tell you if an infant is at risk for loss of binocularity.

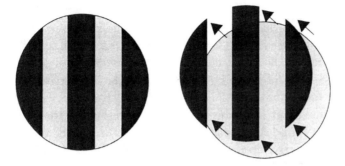

**Figure 9-16** Stereoscopic thresholds may be measured in infants with forced-choice preferential looking task using three-dimensional gratings of varying disparities.

### Motion-Processing Asymmetry

Earlier we noted that young infants exhibit a nasotemporal OKN or pursuit asymmetry that disappears by the time stereopsis develops. In infantile strabismics, however, the asymmetry persists even into adulthood. This asymmetry may be detected by oculomotor (OKN or pursuit) recordings (Atkinson and Braddick, 1991), psychophysical measures (motion detection) (Tychsen et al., 1996), or electrodiagnostic (motion VEP) recordings (Norcia et al., 1991). If such an asymmetry is detected in an infant over 6 months old, that child is considered to be at risk for the development of strabismus and amblyopia. However, it should be noted that recent studies of motion perception suggest that the motion-processing asymmetry can occur even when stereopsis is not impaired; the motion-processing asymmetry results not from a loss of binocularity but from the developmental oculomotor abnormality that underlies strabismus (Fawcett et al., 1998).

---

⚷ *Key Point*

*If one eye is deprived of proper form vision by either a blurred image, strabismus, or an obstruction of the ocular media, the visual cortex reorganizes itself in response to the unequal binocular competition and will predominantly respond to the nondeprived eye. The ocular dominance columns of the nondeprived eye widen at the expense of those of the deprived eye. Fewer cortical cells are driven by the deprived eye, and binocularity is lost.*

---

**CLINICAL PROCEDURE** | The concept of binocular competition also proves to be very important clinically in the use of **occlusion therapy** to treat amblyopia. After refractive correction, the amblyopic eye is provided with a clear image and then placed at a competitive *advantage* by patching the good eye, thereby giving the amblyopic eye a chance to reestablish connections and recover some of its ocular dominance column width by ensuring that only it supplies input to visual cortex. To be maximally effective in reversing the amblyopia, occlusion has to be done during the *critical period* for the development of binocular vision, when neural development is still taking place at a rapid rate. After the critical period, occlusion will have less direct effect. However, even after the critical period is essentially over, occlusion can still be of benefit. It may be too late to take full advantage of binocular competition mechanisms to reestablish normal connections from the amblyopic eye, but patching and vision therapy may still force the amblyopic visual system to learn to accommodate and move more efficiently, which is of benefit to the patient.

Although the ocular dominance histogram generated following binocular deprivation appears normal, do not assume that binocular deprivation has *no* effect on the animal at all. If you look more carefully at the response properties of cortical cells, you do see some effects of binocular deprivation. These are *subtle changes* in the response properties of the cortical cells. The orientation selectivity of the cortical cells is broader following binocular deprivation than in normal animals, and directional sensitivity is also degraded. These more subtle effects are caused by deprivation per se; they do not follow the binocular competition model.

Monocular deprivation has powerful effects on binocularity, but stimulus deprivation is also a severe condition, typically seen only in relatively rare cases of congenital cataracts or corneal opacities in children. Strabismic amblyopia has a less dramatic effect on vision than does deprivation, with less consistent effects on the ocular dominance histogram. Some strabismic animals will exhibit an ocular dominance histogram similar to that of monocular deprivation, where most cortical cells will be driven by the nonstrabismic or fixating eye (Fig. 9-17). However, other strabismic animals will develop an ocular dominance histogram in which monocularly driven cells are present that respond to *one eye or the other*, but no *binocularly* driven cells exist. This histogram differs from what we saw with either monocular or binocular deprivation.

**CLINICAL APPLICATION**  The difference between these two populations of strabismic animals lies in their fixation preferences. Those animals that develop *exotropia* are more likely to develop **alternating strabismus (alternating fixation)**, switching which eye is fixating and which is deviating, sometimes at will. Humans with alternating fixation do not tend to have an *acuity loss* because both foveas are used at one time or another, and therefore there is no amblyopia. However, this does not mean that they are normal; their lack of binocularly driven cells results in a loss of normal binocular vision and stereopsis.

In experiments with monkeys reared with 27 prism diopter base-in prisms, thereby inducing exotropia, the population of binocular neurons is reduced from

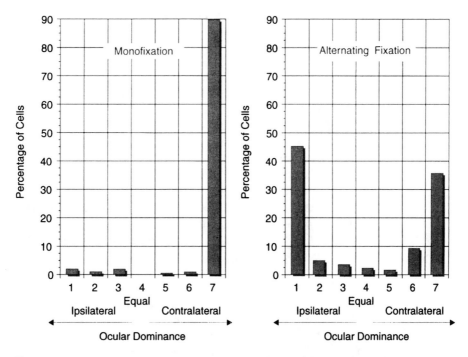

**Figure 9-17** The ocular dominance histograms obtained from strabismic kittens depend on the type of strabismus that is developed. **A:** Esotropes tend to develop monofixation; that is, they favor one eye for fixation and allow the other eye to turn, leading to the classic monocular deprivation histogram and to amblyopia **B:** Exotropes tend to alternate fixation from one eye to the other, so that neither eye receives an improper image all of the time. The result is an equal complement of monocular neurons responding to each eye, and amblyopia does not occur; however, because the visual system never receives a proper binocular input, there is a marked reduction in binocularly responsive cells.

81% of neurons in areas V1 and V2 to 22% of such neurons (Crawford et al., 1983b). These monkeys exhibit normal visual acuity but reduced binocular summation and stereopsis (Crawford et al., 1983a).

**CLINICAL APPLICATION** | Individuals with *esotropia* tend to fixate constantly with one eye and have a **unilateral strabismus** in the other eye. Their likelihood of developing amblyopia is very high. In this case, the patient or animal tends to **suppress** the esotropic eye. After a period of habitual suppression, amblyopia develops in the strabismic eye. This is part of the reason why treatment for amblyopia must involve occlusion or penalization of the nonamblyopic eye. Simply using both eyes together will not cure amblyopia because the amblyopic eye will continue to be suppressed by the good eye; the amblyopic eye is *not* at a competitive advantage with both eyes open (Mitchell et al., 1977).

What about **meridional amblyopia**, such as that traced to a prominent astigmatism? This effect can be produced and then studied by raising infant animals in an environment in which they receive exposure only to vertical stripes. Following this, most visual cortex cells develop an orientation selectivity (bias) for only that orientation; in this case, stimuli that have orientations that lie along the vertical axis. Cortical cells do not respond to the orientation defocused by the astigmatism; it is akin to pattern deprivation along the defocused meridian. Without the neural machinery to process those orientations, even if you optically correct the astigmatism later in life, the animal is left with an inability to perceive the formerly deprived orientations.

Let us now consider the lateral geniculate nucleus (LGN). Does amblyopia, the result of deprivation, *originate* in striate cortex, or do the cortical neuronal responses in amblyopic animals merely reflect abnormal responses from cells *earlier* in the visual system such as the LGN? This becomes important when attempting to find a cure for amblyopia; one must know where the problem arises before one can correct the problem.

The LGN is indeed affected by visual deprivation, but these effects are subtler than the deprivation effects within visual cortex. The size of the soma (cell body) of neurons in the LGN shrinks when binocularity is disrupted, that is, cells serving the deprived eye shrink (Hickey et al., 1977), and this reduction in cell size is thought to be secondary to their reduced metabolic demands following the loss of cortical binocular cells innervated by those cells (Tieman et al., 1984). The levels of cytochrome oxidase, a metabolic enzyme, in these cells is reduced (Wong-Riley, 1979).

If you monocularly suture the lids in one eye in the kitten, you can still drive cells from the deprived eye located in the appropriate layers of the LGN. This is vastly different from what we saw in the cortex, where only few neurons could be driven by the deprived eye. However, when you look closely at the response properties of deprived eye LGN cells, they have changed very dramatically.

There is in fact evidence of loss of a particular LGN cell type in amblyopia. P cells in the LGN are found in normal numbers in the deprived laminae of the LGN, but single-unit recordings reveal that they have a lower spatial resolution, that is, a loss of sensitivity at higher spatial frequencies. These LGN P cells are reflecting the loss of acuity in amblyopia. M cells, on the other hand, are relatively spared by most types of amblyopia. It is only under severe pattern deprivation conditions (e.g., lid suture) that loss of M cells may occur.

The effects of deprivation are not uniform throughout the LGN. The geniculate is topographically mapped so that, as you move from medial to lateral in the LGN, the region of the visual field subserved by LGN cells shifts from the primary visual direction at the fovea out to the periphery. At the very extreme of the lateral extent of the LGN are cells that lie in the **monocular temporal crescent** of visual space, the area of visual space that only one eye can see. The binocular competition model would predict that binocular competition would not be possible in an area of visual space that is represented only monocularly; these cells make connections to cortical cells driven by only one eye. Thus, by virtue of being in the monocular portion of space, these cells are exempt from the process

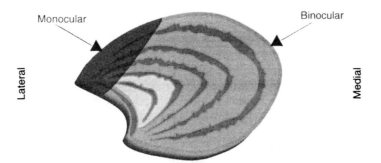

Monocular    Binocular

Lateral    Medial

**Figure 9-18**    When an animal is monocularly deprived, neurons from the deprived eye within the LGN are reduced in size, but only within the portion of the LGN that is within the binocular portion of the visual field. Neurons within the monocular crescent are spared, indicating that the effects of deprivation on the LGN are secondary to those of striate cortex and that binocular competition is required for these effects to occur. Because there is no binocular competition for neurons serving the monocular crescent, monocular deprivation has no effect on those neurons.

of binocular competition. If the pattern of loss of cells followed the binocular competition model, the observed loss of cells would necessarily be restricted to the *binocular* segment of the LGN cells, and the monocular crescent of the LGN would contain a normal complement of cells. This, in fact, is what vision scientists have found (Fig. 9-18); cell loss is restricted to the binocular segment of the LGN (Guillery, 1972). In fact, in anisometropic amblyopia, decreases in the soma size and metabolic rates of LGN cells occur only within the binocular region of the LGN and not in the monocular crescents. This is significant because the blur caused by anisometropia occurs across the entire retina, and yet cells in the monocular portions of the LGN are spared from the effects of the blur.

As there is no binocular competition between cells within the LGN itself, binocular competition occurs only at the site of the synapse between monocular and binocular cells in striate cortex, suggesting that the main site of the deficit in amblyopia is *cortical*. The changes in LGN cell size with amblyopia correlate with the changes in ocular dominance column width in striate cortex (Vital-Durand et al., 1978); the degradation of cells in the LGN therefore represents **retrograde degeneration**. This conclusion is strengthened by the fact that although the spatial resolution of cortical cells is reduced in amblyopia, that of LGN cells is affected to a lesser degree (Blakemore and Vital-Durand, 1986; Chino et al., 1994). Amblyopia begins and has its greatest effect in striate cortex.

One would then predict that the effects of deprivation would be even less in the retina. This is true. Ganglion cells seem to respond in the normal way in the deprived eye, and their numbers are normal. None of the geniculate effects seem to be manifested in the retinal ganglion cells. Amblyopia appears to be primarily a *cortical* disorder.

# NEUROPHYSIOLOGICAL STUDIES OF THE CRITICAL PERIOD

Experience has differing effects on the visual system at different ages. In cats, the general critical period lies between 3 weeks and 4 months of age, whereas in humans it is between 6 months and 5 to 7 years of age. The length of the critical period is known from neurophysiological experiments in which the visual system is disrupted during development. Although it is common to equate the time course for normal development of binocular vision and the time course over which binocular vision may be disrupted, there is no direct evidence to prove the precise correspondence between the two.

One of the two procedures to map out the time course of critical periods in cats is called **brief deprivation**. As the name suggests, animals are deprived of normal visual experience for *brief* periods in order to ascertain how short a period of deprivation is needed before observable neurophysiological and behavioral correlates of amblyopia emerge. Timney (1990) measured the ocular dominance histograms for kittens at 26 to 32 days of age that were either provided normal visual experience or monocularly deprived for periods up to 8 days in length. The normally reared kittens displayed the typical normal distribution with the majority

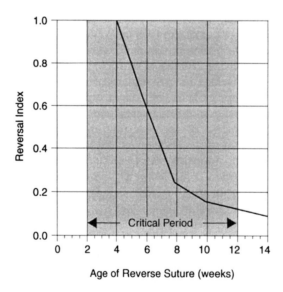

**Figure 9-19**    The effects of monocular deprivation may be reduced or eliminated by reverse suturing during the critical period. In reverse-sutured kittens, the reversal index, a measure of shifts in the ocular dominance histogram to favor the now open (previously deprived) eye, is highest before 8 weeks of age. The kitten's critical period, as measured by the reversibility of monocular deprivation, is over at about 12 weeks of age. (Modified from Blakemore and van Sluyters, 1974.)

of cells showing binocularity, whereas after monocular deprivation for only 8 days, cortical cells were totally driven by the nondeprived eye alone. What is interesting is that a slight shift or asymmetry in the ocular dominance histogram was evident after as little as *12 hours* of deprivation (Malach et al., 1984). Thus, even *very brief* periods of deprivation have marked effects on visual development.

The other procedure used to map the critical period is **reverse suturing**. The animal is reared with one eye deprived from birth until a certain age, at which the animal is *reverse* sutured; in other words, the eye that was previously sutured is opened, and the formerly nondeprived eye is now closed. The goal is to determine if the ocular dominance histogram *reverses* so that more cells are now driven by the previously deprived eye. This should be possible only if the reverse suturing is done *within* the critical period and not after the conclusion of the critical period. If kittens are monocularly deprived for a period from birth to 5 weeks of age, their ocular dominance histograms reveal, as expected, that most of the cells are driven by the nondeprived eye (Fig. 9-19). If reverse suturing is then initiated at age 5 weeks, effects on ocular dominance are noted by as little as *3 days* of reverse suturing. After 9 days of reverse suturing, the ocular dominance pattern has reversed itself so that most of the cells are now driven by the previously deprived eye. Thus, we conclude that during this timeframe, from 5 weeks of age until just over 6 weeks of age, the visual system of the kitten is still within the critical period. The visual system is still completely **plastic**, that is, very modifiable by changes in visual experience.

**CLINICAL PROCEDURE** | This reversibility of amblyopia with occlusion has important implications for the clinician. The lesson to be learned is that occlusion therapy should be used judiciously when treating amblyopia for fear of creating **occlusion amblyopia**. Overzealous use of occlusion during the critical period can reverse the eye with amblyopia; that is, although the formerly amblyopic eye has now improved, it is at the expense of the formerly good eye, which now has a deprivation amblyopia (Murphy and Mitchell, 1987). To guard against this, clinicians have adopted a useful formula, namely, 1 day of occlusion for each year of life. For example, a 3-year-old should be occluded full-time for no more than 3 consecutive days. The patch is then removed or switched on the fourth day.

We can use both of these techniques — brief deprivation and reverse suturing — to map the course of the critical period. In one case, we are seeing if plasticity is present to the extent that deprivation has a deleterious effect on visual development; in the other, we have already produced amblyopia and we are determining if the visual system is still plastic enough for the amblyopia to be overcome. It is during the critical period that each of these approaches has its greatest effects, and after the critical period these approaches produce little effect.

Figure 9-20 displays the data obtained from brief deprivation and reverse suturing experiments on kittens. The brief deprivation data are scored with an

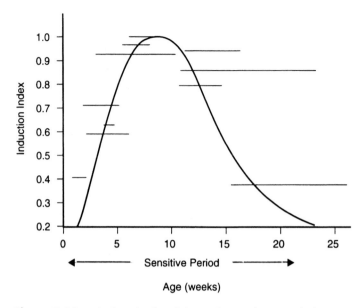

**Figure 9-20**    The length of each bar indicates the period of deprivation. Dramatic shifts of the ocular dominance histogram, as measured by the induction index, can occur after very brief periods of deprivation during the critical period. Once the critical period has tapered off, even very long periods of deprivation will have little effect.

*induction index* that represents the proportion of cortical cells dominated by the nondeprived eye; the higher the number, the more powerful the effect of the deprivation. The lengths of the data lines indicate the duration of the deprivation, and the height of the data lines indicates the degree of effect of the deprivation. Thus, deprivation for 1 day beginning at an age of 2 to 3 weeks will shift ocular dominance, but the effect is not as great as for the same period of deprivation starting at age $4\frac{1}{2}$ to 5 weeks. The effects of deprivation become less pronounced thereafter. For example, a 15-week deprivation beginning at age 15 weeks has less effect than a half-week of deprivation starting at age $4\frac{1}{2}$ to 5 weeks. These data suggest that the critical period does not start immediately at birth and does not commence suddenly, like turning on a switch; it begins with a rapid increase in plasticity soon after birth and ends with a more gradual decrease in plasticity.

Data from the reverse suturing experiments show similar results. Here the data are quantified with a *reversal index*, which is simply the proportion of cortical cells now driven by the previously deprived eye that is now open. Once again, the lengths of the data lines indicate the periods of reverse suturing (9 weeks in each eye); what varies is the age at which the reversal is initiated. If reverse suturing is started at age $4\frac{1}{2}$ to 5 weeks, reverse suturing has a very powerful effect, completely shifting the ocular dominance histogram so that the previously de-prived eye drives all cortical cells, but if reverse suturing is delayed until age 15 weeks, the effect on ocular dominance is much weaker.

What do the *human* critical period data look like? Although we do not know the precise duration of the critical period in humans, scientists have compared experimental data obtained from children with **congenital or infantile strabismus**, in whom strabismus was diagnosed by age 5 months, versus data from children with **late-onset strabismus**, who developed strabismus after age 1 year. One experimental procedure used is a psychophysical test called **interocular transfer (IOT)**. It employs aftereffects such as the orientation and motion aftereffects that are typically studied monocularly. In monocular aftereffects, an adapting stimulus is displayed to the eye for a period of time, fatiguing the neural mechanisms responsible for encoding that stimulus. The effects are then seen when viewing a test stimulus whose appearance is altered by the prior adaptation. For example, after viewing motion in a single direction for several minutes, a subsequently viewed stationary stimulus will appear to move in the opposite direction.

In the interocular transfer paradigm, one eye is displayed the adapting stimulus, while the other eye is tested to see whether the aftereffect can transfer between the two eyes. The assumption is that *binocular mechanisms* are fatigued by viewing the adaptation stimulus, and the effects would therefore be noted by either eye viewing the test stimulus. If binocularity is absent, such a transfer would be impossible. The higher the strength of the interocular transfer of the aftereffect, the larger would be the binocular cell population that was adapted. In Fig. 9-21, the interocular transfer of the tilt aftereffect is measured relative to the strength of the monocular percept of the aftereffect; that is, (strength of IOT)/(strength of monocular aftereffect), where a score of 100% means the IOT effect is as strong as the monocular aftereffect, and a score of 0% means that you have no transfer. Normal subjects tend to produce a score of about 60% interocular transfer. If a child was strabismic from birth until 4 years or more of age, the IOT score tends to be 0% or abnormally low, indicating virtually no binocularity. However, children who were strabismic for only portions of time between birth and age 4 years show degrees of binocularity that are intermediate between these two extremes, demonstrating that the duration period of strabismus is an important factor in developing amblyopia. The most powerful effect of strabismus is in children aged 1 to 3 years; strabismus occurring between birth and 1 year of age has less effect. Plotting these data and fitting a curve to them produces a relative measure of the effect of experience (in this case, the strabismus) on binocular visual function, in other words, an indirect measure of the critical period of development for binocularity. Notice that the critical period for binocularity does not begin at birth but initiates rapidly between 6 months and 1 year of age. The critical period peaks at 1 to 2 years of age and then gradually diminishes, although strabismus can affect interocular transfer of aftereffects until age 7 or 8 years. Similarly, reverse occlusion improves the acuity of 90% of amblyopes before age 7 years but is less effective (but still helpful) after that age (Rutstein and Fuhr, 1992).

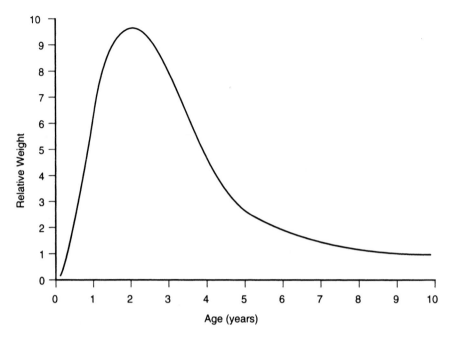

**Figure 9-21**    The human critical period as measured by the psychophysical inte-rocular transfer paradigm. The interocular transfer of the tilt aftereffect is measured relative to the strength of the monocular percept of the aftereffect in subjects with stra-bismus beginning at various ages. The less the interocular transfer, the greater the effect of the strabismus on binocularity, that is, the more plastic the visual system. By this method, it has been found that the critical period for binocularity initiates between 6 months and 1 year of age and gradually diminishes after a peak at 1 to 2 years of age.

**CLINICAL APPLICATION**    Surgical correction of large-angle strabismus is also more effective for the restoration of stereopsis earlier in life, although the timing of surgical cor-rection for congenital esotropia has been broadly debated. The question becomes at what age must ocular alignment be obtained for the best chance to establish (or reestablish) binocular vision? The consensus is that the best opportunity for surgical correction of strabismus occurs before 3 years of age (Banks et al., 1975), although even early strabismus surgery for infantile esotropia does not lead to a significant recovery of stereopsis (Birch et al., 1990; Atkinson et al., 1991); the surgery simply restores cosmetic alignment and, at times, some recovery from amblyopia. Crawford et al. (1996) demon-strate that early binocular experience is essential for the proper development of binocular vision; a short period of proper binocular stimulation can "protect" the visual system from permanent loss of stereopsis if a strabismus develops afterward. Therefore, the earlier strabismus can be detected and treated, so that proper binocular development can be restored, the better is the prognosis for binocular function. Ideally, special vision therapy tasks for infants should be prescribed in order to enhance binocular function.

In addition, it must be remembered that even later in life, surgery can bring corresponding points into closer alignment, restoring coarse stereopsis if not fine stereopsis (Kitaoji and Toyama, 1987). Vision therapy should then be employed to enhance the accuracy of fusional responses. Although the prognosis for developing normal levels of binocular vision (i.e., fine local stereopsis) is quite poor in these cases, an opportunity for fusion and gross stereopsis is present. These fusion responses are often based on anomalous retinal correspondence.

Note that the critical period does not ever completely end; the visual system is always somewhat susceptible to the effects of experience. The visual system can be demonstrated to be plastic to some degree even in adulthood (Ciuffreda, 1986; Levi and Polat, 1996; Chino, 1997). Even those functions that are developed early in infancy can still be modified later. For example, although retinal correspondence is organized prenatally, it must maintain some plasticity throughout development in childhood. As the head grows during childhood, the interocular distance grows, requiring continual adjustments in retinal correspondence so that our depth perception does not radically change. In addition, the existence of **anomalous correspondence** suggests that the mapping of corresponding points in each eye can be dramatically reset in response to binocular abnormalities.

It has also been demonstrated that different parts of the visual system mature at different rates, so that the critical period differs at distinct stages of the visual system. For example, layer 4C matures before the other layers of area V1. Similarly, the retina matures before the visual cortex, and so the retina and ganglion cells are not affected by monocular deprivation, as evidenced by normal flash and pattern electroretinograms in amblyopia. An important aspect of maturation rate is a difference in the timing of the critical period for the nasal and temporal retina; this may also help account for the increased susceptibility of esotropes for the development of amblyopia, as the esotropic eye's confusing image is formed on the nasal retina of the nondeviating eye, as opposed to the temporal retina for an exotropia.

**CLINICAL APPLICATION** | The data on the critical period stress the importance of not only detecting visual abnormalities early in infancy but also correcting these problems and treating amblyopia as early as possible, while the visual system is at its most plastic. Just as reverse suturing is used in animals to place the deprived eye at a competitive advantage, **occlusion therapy** is used to treat amblyopia in human children. Note that reverse suturing can totally *reverse* the ocular dominance histogram. **Constant occlusion** of the amblyopia eye, 24 hours a day, can do the same, leading to improved vision in the amblyopic eye at the expense of *decreasing* vision in the nondeprived eye. **Alternating occlusion** does not provide a solution to this problem, as it produces the same effects as does alternating fixation; acuity is improved in both eyes, but binocularity is still absent because the child never views with both eyes at once. To avoid these deleterious side effects, clinicians now use **part-time occlusion**. Here, the amblyopic eye is patched for prescribed times of the waking day, the patient is provided with vision therapy procedures to do during that period, and both eyes are left unpatched for the remainder of the day to allow a period of binocular viewing. Again, we would like to point out the importance of placing a clear image on the retina of the amblyopic eye first, before patching the good eye, and leaving the clear image there during those periods when the patient is using both eyes. This may seem obvious, but many clinicians do not get it.

Thus far, we have stated that the critical period began at a particular chronological age after birth, but how can this be if the critical period connotes an influence of experience? Would a fixed age period suggest instead a genetic, prewired influence on the critical period? Research suggests that the onset of the critical period is, in fact, not rigidly tied to the chronological age of the animal but is itself strongly influenced by the early experiences of the animal.

If a kitten is allowed normal visual experience for its first 4 months of life and then is monocularly deprived for an additional 3 months, there is little shift in the ocular dominance histogram. The critical period has essentially ended. But if a kitten is **dark-reared**, so that it has no visual experience or even light exposure for the first 4 months of its life, and is then brought into the light, what effect will monocular deprivation have at that point? Dark-rearing differs from binocular lid suturing, in that light can penetrate the eyelids; in dark-rearing no light can reach the retina. If the critical period were totally tied to chronological age, then the kitten, now aged 4 months, would be expected to be at the end of its critical period, and monocular deprivation at this point should have little effect. What is found instead is that monocularly patching the dark-reared animal provides a *dramatic shift* in the ocular dominance distribution so that it is strongly biased toward the nondeprived eye. It is as if the critical period has been *delayed* in that animal; monocular deprivation now has an effect.

These same results have been replicated for kittens dark-reared for as long as 1 year. Thus, the critical period begins for dark-reared animals when they are first brought into the light; their visual development is arrested while they are in the dark. Behaviorally, animals reared in the dark will, on entering the light, show a time course for the development of visual acuity that is identical to that seen in newborn kittens when both groups of kittens are equated in terms of *"visual age,"* that is, how many days of visual experience it has acquired, rather than chronological age. The development of visual acuity for newborn kittens and dark-reared kittens first exposed to light are very similar in the timing of their onset (30 days after exposure to light), the age for attainment of adult levels (at about 3 to 4 months), and the final spatial resolution threshold achieved (about 6 cycles/

degree). What this means is that visual stimulation is required as a signal to start the critical period of development; the critical period seems to be triggered by the retina's being exposed to light. The critical period is therefore not hard wired.

## DETERMINANTS OF PLASTICITY IN VISUAL CORTEX

The development of binocularity is accompanied by changes in neurotransmitter concentrations and neural dendritic receptor site activity in visual cortex.

The development of ocular dominance columns may depend on postsynaptic neuronal responses to the neurotransmitter **glutamate**. These responses are, in turn, mediated by postsynaptic receptors that use a messenger called *N*-methyl-D-aspartate, or **NMDA** for short. The density of NMDA-glutamate receptors changes in direct proportion to the degree of plasticity in visual cortex. Therefore, as the ocular dominance columns begin to segregate, the density of NMDA receptors increases within neurons in striate cortex. As the critical period comes to an end, the NMDA-glutamate receptor density diminishes (Fox et al., 1989).

The development of binocular neurons also depends upon NMDA activity. We have seen that synchronized inputs from neurons from the two eyes is required for proper development of binocular neurons. The inputs must also be strong enough to elicit NMDA release from the binocular neuron. This NMDA release strengthens the connection between the presynaptic monocular neuron and the postsynaptic binocular neuron. Inputs that are too weak to elicit NMDA release weaken over time and are lost. Therefore, NMDA may provide the neurochemical mediator for binocular competition, as predicted by the Hebbian model (Singer, 1990).

NMDA is not the only neurochemical involved in plasticity. **Nerve growth factor** and **norepinephrine** are also present in higher concentrations in the visual cortex during the critical period.

By manipulating neurotransmitter concentrations and receptor activity levels, the duration of the critical period and the effects of deprivation can be altered. For example, chemically inhibiting NMDA receptors in kittens prevents monocular deprivation from shifting the ocular dominance histogram; it is as if the critical period, and therefore plasticity, have been shut off, preventing the deleterious effects of the deprivation (Bear et al., 1990). Depletion of norepinephrine by injections of its inhibitor, **6-hydroxydopamine**, has the same effect (Kasamatsu and Pettigrew, 1979).

If the critical period and the plasticity of connections between visual neurons are determined by neurotransmitter concentrations, would it then be possible to *reinstate* the critical period, that is, restore maximum plasticity, in adults and modify the visual environment to correct an existing amblyopia?

Perfusion of norepinephrine directly onto the exposed striate cortex of kittens reestablishes plasticity past the critical period. It is thought that connections between neurons are most easily established when animals are in a state of arousal; norepinephrine release is associated with aroused states. Similarly, injections of nerve growth factor allow recovery of binocular cellular responses in monocularly deprived animals (Camignoto et al., 1993). Nerve growth factor is being explored as a treatment for other neurological disorders as well.

Finally, it should be noted that neuronal growth, formation of synaptic connections, and pruning of dendritic trees may be only one mechanism responsible for amblyopia and loss of binocularity. The deprived eye may also be actively *inhibited* neurochemically. **GABA** (g-aminobutyric acid) is an inhibitory neurotransmitter found in the retina and visual cortex. When GABA is antagonized by a chemical called **bicuculline**, cortical cells previously unresponsive to a deprived eye recover responsiveness (Sillito et al., 1981). Neurochemical research on amblyopia is still in its early stages. Perhaps in the near future, we will develop a pharmacological cure for amblyopia.

## BINOCULAR VISION AND AGING

Although not completely investigated, the maintenance of binocular vision appears to be relatively stable throughout one's lifetime. Once established in early childhood, and in the absence of direct challenge (e.g., brain injury or oculomotor nerve insult), binocular vision persists unchanged throughout the aging process. The same cannot be said for other well-established age-related anatomic or physiological changes in the visual system, for example, the amplitude of accommodation, clarity of the ocular media, contrast sensitivity, or smooth pursuit eye movements.

**CLINICAL APPLICATION**

Major losses of binocularity in adulthood do not occur naturally. Adult-onset acquired strabismus should always be viewed with caution, considered caused by some disease process, and managed accordingly. Two possible exceptions are the unilateral pseudophakia patient who may lose binocular vision because of induced aniseikonia and/or interocular visual acuity differences and the patient with asymmetric cataract development.

Having said this, however, more subtle changes in the nature of binocular vision do occur. Although most individuals do not experience gross loss of function or suffer from significant breakdowns, the age-related changes that do occur require astute clinicians to detect. Most of these changes occur in the vergence system.

There is little change in the level of tonic vergence as indicated by the distance heterophoria, which remains relatively stable throughout life. The nearpoint heterophoria, on average, shows a moderate increase in exophoria (4 to 6 prism diopters). There is a corresponding increase of exo fixation disparity. The increase

in exo imbalance at near is not as large as predicted from the loss of accommodative amplitude because it is thought that presbyopes retain the use of some
accommodative convergence. However, disparity vergence ranges remain unchanged, indicating that the vergence system increases in efficiency to compensate for the increase in exophoria. There is also a slight increase in the prevalence
of measurable vertical imbalance.

Stereopsis is relatively unchanged up to the age of 45 or 50 years. Beyond this
age, the evidence suggests that there is a small decline in stereoscopic discrimination. These changes may be the result of the decline in contrast sensitivity and
selective loss of the magnocellular pathway that is responsible for coarse stereopsis
(see Chapter 8).

**CLINICAL APPLICATION** | Meaningful changes also occur in the clinically measured near point of conver-
gence. The near point of convergence recedes by an average of approximately
2 cm from the fifth to the seventh decade of life (from 8 to 10 cm). This is
most likely related to a decrease in the amplitude of accommodation and the
resulting decreased available accommodative convergence. The prevalence
rate of the clinical diagnosis of convergence insufficiency using this test increases significantly with age.

It is therefore important for the clinician to review these convergence
functions carefully in the visual assessment of the elderly patient. Patients with
symptoms of visual discomfort, blurred vision, or diplopia should be investigated for subtle binocular dysfunctions as part of the standard primary care
workup. Vision therapy for the management of convergence insufficiency
remains an effective and viable option for these cases, regardless of age.

## SUMMARY AND KEY POINTS

- There is a **critical period of development** during which experience has a very
  powerful effect on the structure and function of the visual system. The critical
  period is different for different aspects of vision but on the average has its greatest
  effects at about 6 months of age. The critical period occurs soonest for detection
  of light, temporal resolution, and motion. Color vision, spatial vision, and binocular vision develop later.

- Development of the visual cortex lags behind development of the eye, with
  the number and complexity of the interconnections between neurons steadily
  increasing after the eye is nearly completely developed.

- At birth, retinal correspondence is already developed, but the oculomotor system
  is still immature, with uncorrelated eye movements that can produce intermittently diplopic images. The critical period for the development of binocularity
  does not begin until after the first 2 months of life, when the infant is able to

exercise precise control over the binocular extraocular muscles. This delay of the critical period gives clinicians a window of opportunity to correct binocular amblyogenic factors before amblyopia can develop.

- Infants are generally poor at seeing stereoscopic depth until at least age 3 to 4 months, when vergence control starts to develop and receptive fields become more finely tuned. Surprisingly, *fine* stereoacuity thresholds actually develop earlier, *before* infants can make very extremely accurate vergence movements. The ability of infants to detect binocular disparity appears abruptly between the ages of 3 and $3\frac{1}{2}$ months and can be measured using random-dot stereograms. Adult-like stereoscopic thresholds of less than 1-minute arc are reached at 5 to 6 months of age. The ability to see crossed disparities may develop earlier than the ability to see uncrossed disparities. Immediately after stereopsis develops, infants exhibit adult-like binocular summation.

- At birth, there is nearly total overlap of LGN inputs from both eyes into layer 4C, which prevents the existence of binocularity and stereopsis. The dendritic trees of the cells in 4C then are pruned, reducing the overlap of each eye's inputs into layer 4C until the input from each eye is completely segregated into independent ocular dominance columns. The time frame corresponds to that for the onset of stereopsis.

- With time, the tuning of binocular neurons becomes increasingly specific for a given narrow set of disparities, allowing an infant to discriminate finer and finer disparities.

- Abnormal visual experience during the critical time for binocular vision can *disrupt* normal development and cause amblyopia or strabismus. Visual deprivation is more likely to disrupt functions whose critical periods are prolonged such as spatial vision or binocularity, rather than functions whose critical period is short and completed early in infancy such as color vision.

- Amblyopia, a decreased visual acuity that can not be attributed to uncorrected refractive error or ocular pathology, is the result of abnormal visual development. There are several categories of amblyopia, each classified by the **etiology** of the abnormal visual development: strabismus, anisometropia, refractive error, stimulus deprivation, or meridional refractive differences.

- **Anisometropic amblyopes** experience a decrease in contrast sensitivity with spatial vision degradation across the extent of the visual field. Grating acuity, Snellen acuity, and hyperacuity are all affected to the same degree.

- In **strabismic amblyopes**, hyperacuity and Snellen acuity are affected to a greater degree than grating acuity, but the effect is limited to the central visual field. These amblyopes undergo both contrast sensitivity loss and spatial distortions. Patients with strabismic amblyopia will also experience pronounced **crowding effects** in which neighboring contours interfere with the visibility of a target stimulus.

- **Stimulus deprivation amblyopes** have more profound reductions in visual acuity and contrast sensitivity than the milder image degradation produced by strabismus or anisometropia. This is caused by severe **pattern deprivation**. Unilateral deprivation is much more devastating than the bilateral form because of an additional amblyogenic contribution from abnormal binocular interaction.

- **Meridional amblyopia** is caused by pronounced astigmatic refractive errors so that vision in one meridian is blurred while the orthogonal meridian is in focus. Amblyopia occurs only *along the blurred astigmatic meridian,* even with full astigmatic correction.

- Amblyopes also demonstrate binocular visual deficits such as abnormal stereopsis; they either lack stereoscopic vision (**stereoblindness**) or possess only residual stereopsis. Some experience an accentuated form of binocular suppression known as a **suppression scotoma** in which the contribution of a given retinal locus in one eye to the combined binocular percept is *inhibited*.

- **Ocular dominance histograms** are composed of seven categories, each reflecting a different degree of cortical cell stimulation by each eye. Category 1 represents *monocular* cells that can only be driven by stimulation of the contralateral eye, while category 7 is comprised of cells driven only by the ipsilateral eye. Category 4 contains cells that respond equally to stimulation of either eye. A normal ocular dominance histogram contains mostly binocularly responsive cells.

- In monocular deprivation, very few cortical cells are driven by the deprived eye; the majority are driven by the nondeprived eye. The dendrites of neurons serving the deprived eye atrophy more than do those of the nondeprived eye during development of the ocular dominance columns, resulting in narrower ocular dominance columns in layer 4C of striate cortex for the deprived eye and a corresponding increase in width of those of the nondeprived eye. The deprived eye is less capable of driving cortical cells, including binocular cells, than the nondeprived eye.

- The Hebbian model of **binocular competition** suggests that inputs from the two eyes *compete* for synaptic connectivity onto cortical binocular neurons. If the signal from a given eye is strong, the synapse is retained; if not, it deteriorates. If the activity from both eyes' inputs is high, both eyes will retain strong synaptic connections with the binocular cell. In binocular deprivation, neither eye has a competitive advantage, so the result is a normal ocular dominance histogram. In monocular deprivation, the nondeprived eye has the advantage during development and retains the most synapses.

- Prevention of amblyopia must be achieved by removing amblyogenic factors and implementing treatment for losses of binocular function early, while the infant is still within the critical period. Low-birth-weight infants, primarily **premature infants**, are at *greater risk* for binocular vision problems, as they have higher rates of strabismus than the general population.

- Several techniques are available for testing for binocular abnormalities in infants. In **photorefraction**, the infant's eyes are photographed using a special lens, and analysis of the image detects high refractive error, opacities, and strabismus. With regard to detecting strabismus, photorefraction is analogous to the **Hirschberg test**. **Forced-choice preferential looking (FPL) with stereo gratings** allows for measurement of the infant's stereoacuity limit. **Binocular beat VEPs** require little cooperation and can measure the presence of binocular summation, even in sleeping infants. The presence of a nasotemporal OKN or pursuit **motion processing asymmetry** indicates that stereopsis has not yet developed.

- In **occlusion therapy,** the amblyopic eye is provided with a clear image and the nonamblyopic eye is patched in order to place the amblyopic eye at a competitive advantage so it can reestablish synapses and recover its ocular dominance columns. Occlusion therapy is most beneficial during the critical period but is still helpful to some extent throughout life.

- In constant strabismus, most cortical cells will be driven by the nonstrabismic (fixating) eye. In alternating strabismus, monocularly driven cells are present that respond to one eye or the other, but no binocularly driven cells exist. Esotropes are more likely to have a constant strabismus with suppression of the esotropic eye. It is also possible to develop strabismus without amblyopia, as in an **alternating strabismus**. In this case, stereoscopic deficits may occur without accompanying monocular deficits in the strabismic eye. This is more common in exotropic strabismics.

- In **meridional amblyopia,** the majority of visual cortex cells develop an orientation selectivity (bias) for the orientation presented with a clear image. Cortical cells do not respond to the stimuli in other orientations.

- In the LGN, visual deprivation of one eye does not reduce the number of cells receiving inputs from that eye or eliminate their responses. However, the P cells receiving input from that eye will have lower spatial resolution, reflecting the loss of acuity in amblyopia. M cells, on the other hand, are spared by most types of amblyopia, with the exception of severe pattern deprivation amblyopia. Affected cells will have smaller somata and lower metabolic rates. The effects of amblyopia on the LGN are restricted to the binocular portion of the LGN; cells in the monocular temporal crescent are spared.

- Because amblyopia relies on binocular competition mechanisms not present in the LGN, the changes in LGN cell size with amblyopia represents **retrograde degeneration** from binocular cells in the striate cortex. The LGN changes correlate with the changes in ocular dominance column width in striate cortex.

- The critical period for binocularity initiates rapidly between 6 months and 1 year of age, peaks at 1 to 2 years of age, and then gradually diminishes. The duration of the period of strabismus is therefore an important factor in developing amblyopia.

- Even *very brief* periods of monocular deprivation during the critical period have marked effects on visual development.

- Reverse occlusion treatment improves the acuity of 90% of amblyopes before 7 years of age. Though less effective, reverse occlusion is still helpful after that age, as the critical period does not ever completely end; the visual system is always somewhat susceptible to the effects of experience, even in adulthood. **Reverse suturing** while still in the critical period can reverse the ocular dominance histogram so that more cells are now driven by the previously deprived eye. This reversibility of amblyopia can also occur in overzealous use of occlusion therapy, creating **occlusion amblyopia**.

- Surgical correction of a large-angle strabismus is also more effective for the restoration of stereopsis earlier in life; however, remember that even later in life, surgery can bring corresponding points into closer alignment, restoring coarse stereopsis if not fine stereopsis. The best opportunity for surgery occurs at 2 years of age. Although the prognosis for developing normal levels of binocular vision (i.e., fine local stereopsis) is quite poor in these cases, an opportunity for fusion and gross stereopsis is present. These fusion responses are often based on anomalous retinal correspondence. Ideally, customized vision therapy tasks for infants should be used in combination with surgery to foster not only binocular alignment but proper binocular processing.

- The onset of the critical period is not hard wired based on age. Visual stimulation is required as a signal to start the critical period of development; the critical period seems to be triggered by the retina's being exposed to light.

- The development of ocular dominance columns depends on the neurotransmitter **glutamate** and its postsynaptic messenger *N*-methyl-D-aspartate (**NMDA**). The density of NMDA glutamate receptors changes in direct proportion to the degree of plasticity in visual cortex. NMDA is probably also the neurochemical mediator for binocular competition as predicted by the Hebbian model, because only strong inputs from the presynaptic monocular neuron will elicit NMDA release from a postsynaptic binocular neuron, strengthening the bond between them.

- **Nerve growth factor** and **norepinephrine** are also present in higher concentrations in the visual cortex during the critical period.

- If NMDA is depleted, the visual system will respond as if the critical period, and therefore plasticity, has been shut off, preventing the deleterious effects of the deprivation. This is also true for norepinephrine depletion.

- The critical period can be extended, pointing to the possibility of a cure for amblyopia in the near future. Perfusion of the exposed striate cortex with norepinephrine reestablishes plasticity past the critical period, and injections of nerve growth factor allow recovery of binocular cellular responses in monocularly deprived animals. Removing the inhibitory effects of the neurochemical GABA with bicuculline can make cortical cells previously unresponsive to a deprived eye recover responsiveness.

- With advanced age, most measures of binocular vision are unchanged or only mildly affected in the absence of neurological damage to the visual pathways or oculomotor system.

## QUESTIONS

1. What is the best age at which to examine a child's vision for the first time? What conditions are most important to test for when examining the eyes of an infant? Why?

2. Explain the rationale for using patching therapy in amblyopia. What is the best age to use patching therapy? Is there any age at which patching should not be used?

3. Does a normal ocular dominance histogram demonstrate that a subject has normal binocular vision? Why or why not?

4. Define amblyopia. How is amblyopia caused? How does the etiology relate to the specific visual deficits found in each type of amblyopia? Which type of amblyopia is most severe?

## BIBLIOGRAPHY

ADAMS RJ, COURAGE ML and MERCER ME (1991). *Deficiencies in human neonates' color vision: photoreceptoral and neural explanations.* Behav. Brain Res. 43:109–114.

ASLIN RN (1977). *Development of binocular fixation in human infants.* J. Exp. Child Psych. 23:133–150.

ATKINSON J and BRADDICK O (1981). *Development of optokinetic nystagmus in infants: an indicator of cortical binocularity? In:* Developmental Neurobiology of Vision, RD Freeman, *ed.,* Plenum Press, New York.

ATKINSON J, BRADDICK O and MOAR K (1977). *Development of contrast sensitivity over the first three months of life in the human infant.* Vis. Res. 17:1037–1044.

ATKINSON J, SMITH J, ANKER S, WATTAM-BELL J, BRADDICK OJ and MOORE AT (1991). *Binocularity and amblyopia before and after early strabismus surgery.* Invest. Ophthalmol. Vis. Sci. 32:820.

ATKINSON J, BRADDICK O, BOBIER B, ANKER S, EHRLICH D, KING J, WATSON P *and* MOORE A (1996). *Two infant screening programmes: prediction and prevention of strabismus and amblyopia from photo- and videorefractive screening.* Eye 10:189–198.

BAITCH LW and LEVI DM (1988). *Evidence for nonlinear binocular interactions in human visual cortex.* Vis. Res. 28:1139–1143.

BAKER FH, GRIGG P *and* von NOORDEN GK (1974). *Effects of visual deprivation and strabismus on the response of neurons in the visual cortex of the monkey, including studies on the striate and prestriate cortex of the normal animal.* Brain Res. 66:185–208.

BANKS MS (1980). *The development of visual accommodation during early infancy.* Child Dev. 51:646–666.

BANKS MS and SALAPATEK P (1978). *Acuity and contrast sensitivity in 1, 2 and 3-month-old human infants.* Invest. Ophthalmol. Vis. Sci. 17:361–365.

BANKS MS, ASLIN RN *and* LETSON RD (1975). *Sensitive periods for the development of human binocular vision.* Science 190:675–677.

BEAR MF, KLEINSCHMIDT A, GU Q *and* SINGER W (1990). *Disruption of experience-dependent synaptic modification in striate cortex by infusion of an NMDA receptor antagonist.* J. Neurosci. 10:909–925.

BEDELL H *and* FLOM MC (1981). *Monocular spatial distortion in strabismic amblyopia.* Invest. Ophthalmol. Vis. Sci. 20:263–268.

BIRCH EE, GWIAZDA J *and* HELD R (1983). *The development of vergence does not account for the onset of stereopsis.* Perception 12:331–336.

BIRCH EE, SHIMOJO S *and* HELD R (1985). *Preferential-looking assessment of fusion and stereopsis in infants aged 1-6 month.* Invest. Ophthalmol. Vis. Sci. 26:366–370.

BIRCH EE, STAGER DR, BERRY P *and* EVERETT MP (1990). *Prospective assessment of acuity and stereopsis in amblyopic infantile esotropes following early surgery.* Invest. Ophthalmol. Vis. Sci. 31:758–765.

BLAKEMORE C *and* VITAL-DURAND F (1986). *Effects of visual deprivation on the development of the monkey's lateral geniculate nucleus.* J. Physiol. 380:493–511.

CARMIGNOTO G, CANELLA R, CANDEO P, COMELLI MC and MAFFEI L (1993). *Effects of nerve growth factor on neuronal plasticity of the kitten visual system.* J. Physiol. 464:343–360.

CHINO YM (1997). *Receptive-field plasticity in the adult visual cortex: dynamic signal rerouting or experience-dependent plasticity.* Semin. Neurosci. 9:34–46.

CHINO YM, CHENG H, SMITH EL, GARRAGHTY PE, ROE AW and SUR M (1994). *Early discordant binocular vision disrupts signal transfer in the lateral geniculate nucleus.* Proc. Natl. Acad. Sci. U.S.A. 91:6938–6942.

CIUFFREDA KJ (1986). *Visual system plasticity in human amblyopia. In:* Development of Order in the Visual System, SR Hilfer *and* JB Sheffield, *eds.,* Springer-Verlag, New York.

CRAIR MC, GILLESPIE DC *and* STRYKER MP (1998). *The role of visual experience in the development of columns in cat visual cortex.* Science 279:566–570.

CRAWFORD MLJ, von NOORDEN GK, MEHARG LS, RHODES JW, HARWERTH RS, SMITH EL III *and* MILLER DD (1983a). *Binocular neurons and binocular function in monkeys and children.* Invest. Ophthalmol. Vis. Sci. 24:491.

CRAWFORD MLJ, SMITH EL III, HARWERTH RS, *and* von NOORDEN GK (1983b). *Stereoblind monkeys have few binocular neurons.* Invest. Ophthalmol. Vis. Sci. 24:491.

CRAWFORD MLJ, HARWERTH RS, EL SMITH III *and* von NOORDEN GK (1996). *Loss of stereopsis in monkeys following prismatic binocular dissociation during infancy.* Behav. Brain Res. 79:207–218.

DOBSON V (1976). *Spectral sensitivity of the 2-month-old infant as measured by the visually evoked potential.* Vis. Res. 16:367–374.

DOBSON V *and* TELLER DY (1978). *Visual acuity in human infants: a review and comparison of behavioral and electrophysiological studies.* Vis. Res. 18:1469–1483.

FAWCETT S, RAYMOND JE, ASTLE WF *and* SKOV CMB (1998). *Anomalies of motion perception in infantile esotropia.* Invest. Ophthalmol. Vis. Sci. 39:724–735.

FOX R, ASLIN RN, SHEA SL *and* DUMAIS ST (1980). *Stereopsis in human infants.* Science 207:323–324.

FOX K, SATO H *and* DAW N (1989). *The location and function of NMDA receptors in cat and kitten visual cortex.* J. Neurosci. 9:2443–2254.

FREEMAN RD *and* OHZAWA I (1992). *Development of binocular vision in the kitten's striate cortex.* J. Neurosci. 12:4721–4736.

GARZIA RP *and* NICHOLSON SB (1991). *Deprivation amblyopia. In:* Problems in Optometry, R Rutstein, *ed.*, JB LIPPINCOTT, Philadelphia.

GIBSON E *and* WALK R (1960). *The "visual cliff."* Sci. Am. 202:64–71.

GUERNSEY M (1929). *A quantitative study of the eye reflexes in infants.* Psychol. Bull. 26:160.

GUILLERY RW (1972). *Binocular competition in the control of geniculate cell growth.* J. Comp. Neurol. 144:117–130.

HANSEN RM, FULTOM AB *and* HARRIS SJ (1986). *Background adaptation in human infants.* Vis. Res. 26:771–779.

HARWERTH RS, SMITH EL, CRAWFORD MLJ *and* von NOORDEN GK (1984). *Effects of enucleation of the nondeprived eye on stimulus deprivation amblyopia in monkeys.* Invest. Ophthalmol. Vis. Sci. 25:10–18.

HARWERTH RS, SMITH EL, DUNCAN GC, CRAWFORD MLJ *and* von NOORDEN GK (1986). *Multiple sensitive periods in the development of the primate visual system.* Science 232:235–238.

HELD R (1988). *Development of cortically mediated visual processes inhuman infants. In:* Neurobiology of Early Infant Behavior, C von Euler, H Forssberg *and* H Lagercrantz, *eds.,* Stockton Press, Stockholm.

HESS RF *and* FIELD DJ (1994). *Is the spatial deficit in strabismic amblyopia due to loss of cells or an uncalibrated disarray of cells.* Vis. Res. 34:3397–3406.

HESS RF *and* HOWELL ER (1977). *The threshold contrast sensitivity function in strabismic amblyopia: evidence for a two type classification.* Vis. Res. 17:1049–1055.

HESS RF *and* POINTER JS (1985). *Differences in the neural basis of human amblyopia: the distribution of the anomaly across the visual field.* Vis. Res. 25:1577–1594.

HICKEY JL *and* PEDUZZI JD (1987). *Structure and development of the visual system. In:* Handbook of Infant Perception, P Salapatek *and* L Cohen, *eds.,* Academic Press, Orlando, FL.

HICKEY TL, SPEAR PD *and* KRATZ AE (1977). *Quantitative studies of cell size in the cat's dorsal lateral geniculate nucleus following visual deprivation.* J. Comp. Neurol. 172:265–282.

HUBEL DH *and* WIESEL TN (1962). *Receptive fields, binocular interaction and functional architecture in the cat's visual cortex.* J. Physiol. 160:106–154.

KASAMATSU T *and* PETTIGREW JD (1979). *Preservation of binocularity after monocular deprivation in the striate cortex of kittens treated with 6-hydroxydopamine.* J. Comp. Neurol. 185:139–161.

KING WM *and* ZHOU W (1998). *Premotor commands encode monocular eye movements.* Nature 393:692–695.

KITAOJI H *and* TOYAMA K (1987). *Preservation of position and motion stereopsis in strabismic subjects.* Invest. Ophthalmol. Vis. Sci. 28:1260–1267.

LEVAY S, STRYKER MP *and* SCHATZ CJ (1978). *Ocular dominance columns and their development in layer IV of the cat's visual cortex: a quantitative study.* J .Comp. Neurol. 179:223–244.

LEVAY S, WIESEL TN *and* HUBEL DH (1980). *The development of ocular dominance columns in normal and visually deprived monkeys.* J. Comp. Neurol. 191:1–51.

LEVI DM *and* KLEIN SA (1982). *Differences in vernier discrimination for gratings between strabismic and anisometropic amblyopes.* Invest. Ophthalmol. Vis. Sci. 23:389–407.

LEVI DM *and* KLEIN SA (1983). *Spatial localization in normal and amblyopic vision.* Vis. Res. 23:1005–1017.

LEVI DM *and* POLAT U (1996). *Neural plasticity in adults with amblyopia.* Proc. Natl. Acad. Sci. U.S.A. 93:6830–6834.

LEVI DM, KLEIN SA *and* YAP YL (1987). *Positional uncertainty in peripheral and amblyopic vision.* Vis. Res. 27: 581–597.

LEVI DM, KLEIN SA *and* WANG H (1994). *Discrimination of position and contrast in amblyopic and peripheral vision.* Vis. Res. 34:3293–3313.

MALACH R, EBERT R *and* van SLUYTERS RC (1984). *Recovery from effects of brief monocular deprivation in the kitten.* J. Neurophysiol. 51:538–551.

MCBRIEN NA, GENTLE A *and* COTTRIALL C (1999). *Optical correction of induced axial myopia in the tree shrew: implications for emmetropization.* Optom. Vis. Sci. 76:419–427.

MCKEE SP, SCHOR CM, STEINMAN SB, WILSON N, KOCH GG, DAVIS SM, HSU-WINGES C, CHAN CL, MOVSHON JA, FLOM MC, LEVI DM *and* FLYNN JT (1992). *The classification of amblyopia on the basis of visual and oculomotor performance.* Trans. Ophthalmol. Soc. 90:123–148.

MITCHELL DE, CYNADER M *and* MOVSHON JA (1977). *Recovery from the effects of monocular deprivation.* J. Comp. Neurol. 176:53–63.

MURPHY KM *and* MITCHELL DE (1987). *Reduced visual acuity in both eyes of monocularly deprived kittens following a short period of reverse occlusion.* J. Neurosci. 7:1526–1536.

NORCIA AM *and* TYLER CW (1985). *Spatial frequency sweep VEP: visual acuity during the first year of life.* Vis. Res. 25:1399–1408.

NORCIA AM, GARCIA H, HUMPHREY R, HOLMES A, HAMER RD *and* OREL-BIXLER D (1991). *Anomalous motion VEPs in infants and in infantile esotropia.* Invest. Ophthalmol. Vis. Sci. 32:436–439.

RAKIC P (1976). *Prenatal genesis of connections subserving ocular dominance in the rhesus monkey.* Nature 261:467–471.

RUTSTEIN RP *and* FUHR PS (1992). EFFICACY *and stability of amblyopia therapy.* Optom. Vis. Sci. 69:747–754.

SCHOR CM (1990). *Visuomotor development. In:* Principles and Practice of Pediatric Optometry, AA Rosenbloom *and* MW Morgan, *eds.,* JB LIPPINCOTT, Philadelphia.

SHIMOJO S, BAUER J, O'CONNELL KM *and* HELD R (1986). *Prestereoptic binocular vision in infants.* Vis. Res. 26:501–510.

SILLITO AM, KEMP JA *and* BLAKEMORE C (1981). *The role of GABAergic inhibition in the cortical effects of monocular deprivation.* Nature 291:318–320.

SINGER W (1990). *The formation of cooperative cell assemblies in the visual cortex.* J. Exp. Biol. 153:177–197.

STEINMAN SB, LEVI DM *and* MCKEE SP (1988). *Temporal asynchrony and velocity discrimination in the amblyopic visual system.* Clin. Vis. Sci. 2:265–276.

TELLER DY *and* BORNSTEIN M (1979). *Infant color vision and color perception. In:* Handbook of Infant Perception, Vol. I, From Sensation to Perception, P Salapatek *and* L Cohen, *eds.,* Academic Press, Orlando, FL.

THORN F, GWIAZDA J, CRUZ AA, BAUER JA *and* HELD R (1994). *The development of eye alignment, convergence and sensory binocularity in young infants.* Invest. Ophthalmol. Vis. Sci. 35:544–553.

TIEMAN SB, NICKLA DL, GROSS K, HICKEY TL *and* TUMOSA N (1984). *Effects of unequal alternating monocular exposure on the sizes of cells in the cat's lateral geniculate nucleus.* J. Comp. Neurol. 225:119–128.

TIMNEY B (1990). *Effects of brief monocular deprivation on binocular depth perception in the cat: a sensitive period for the loss of stereopsis.* Vis. Neurosci. 5:273–280.

TYCHSEN L, RASTELLI A, STEINMAN SB *and* STEINMAN BA (1996). *Biases of motion perception revealed by reversing gratings in humans who had infantile-onset strabismus.* Dev. Med. Child Neurol. 38:408–422.

VITAL-DURAND F, GAREY LJ *and* BLAKEMORE C (1978). *Monocular and binocular deprivation in the monkey: morphological effects and reversibility.* Brain Res. 158:45–64.

WATTAM-BELL J (1991). *Development of motion-specific cortical responses in infancy.* Vis. Res. 31:287–297.

WIESEL TN *and* HUBEL DH (1965). *Comparison of the effects of unilateral and bilateral eye closure on cortical unit responses in kittens.* J. Neurophysiol. 28:1060–1072.

WIESEL TN *and* HUBEL DH (1974). *Ordered arrangement of orientation columns in monkeys lacking visual experience.* J. Comp. Neurol. 158:307–318.

WONG-RILEY M (1979). *Changes in the visual system of monocularly sutured or enucleated cats demonstrable with cytochrome oxidase histochemistry.* Brain Res. 171:11–28.

# Appendix A. Viewing the Stereograms in this Book

Stereograms, that is, three-dimensional drawings or photographs, do not require special instruments for viewing. One can view a pair of pictures or photographs side by side and fuse them with vergence eye movements, a process called **free fusion**.

There are two means of performing free fusion. Free fusion is most commonly achieved with **forced convergence**, or crossing of the eyes (Fig. A-1). The observer views a finger midway between his or her eyes at a distance of 2 to 3 inches from the nose, so that uncrossed diplopia of the stereogram is produced, that is, four half-views are now seen. By moving the finger progressively outward, the middle two of the four perceived views will move progressively closer to one another until they are fused together via fusional eye movements into a single stereoscopic image.

Similarly, an observer can use **"parallel viewing"** to achieve the same effect (Fig. A-2), although the disparities in the stereogram will be reversed relative to those obtained with forced convergent viewing, yielding a percept that is reversed in depth. In other words, features that would look closer than the surface of the page with forced convergent viewing will now appear to be farther away than the page, and vice versa. In parallel viewing, the observer tries to "look past" the page on which the stereogram is printed, much like viewing through a window, until diplopia is achieved, then converges the eyes just enough to fuse the middle two half-views.

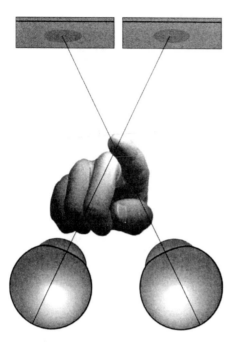

**Figure A-1**    Viewing a stereogram using free fusion via forced convergence.

**Figure A-2**    Viewing a stereogram using free fusion via parallel viewing or divergence.

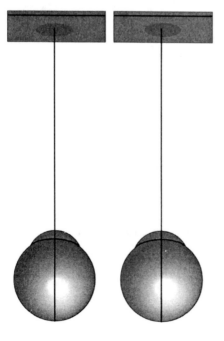

**Figure A-3** A makeshift stereoscope can be made by using cardboard tubes or rolled-up magazines to serve as a septum to separate the views of the two eyes.

If you have trouble with these two techniques, there is a third alternative: creating a makeshift septum to separate the views of the two eyes. By using two cardboard tubes or rolled-up magazines (Fig. A-3) whose diameter closely matches that of each half-view, each half-view can be fixated with one eye alone. Sensory fusion will allow the observer to combine the two pictures into one three-dimensional percept.

# Subject Index

# Subject Index